OXFORD EARLY CHRISTIAN STUDIES

General Editors

Gillian Clark   Andrew Louth

THE OXFORD EARLY CHRISTIAN STUDIES series includes scholarly volumes on the thought and history of the early Christian centuries. Covering a wide range of Greek, Latin, and Oriental sources, the books are of interest to theologians, ancient historians, and specialists in the classical and Jewish worlds.

Titles in the series include:

Marcellus of Ancyra and the Lost Years of the Arian Controversy 325–345
Sara Parvis (2006)

The Irrational Augustine
Catherine Conybeare (2006)

Clement of Alexandria and the Beginnings of Christian Apophaticism
Henny Fiskå Hägg (2006)

The Christology of Theodoret of Cyrus
Antiochene Christology from the Council of Ephesus (431) to the Council of Chalcedon (451)
Paul B. Clayton, Jr (2006)

Ethnicity and Argument in Eusebius' *Praeparatio Evangelica*
Aaron P. Johnson (2006)

Union and Distinction in the Thought of St Maximus the Confessor
Melchisedec Törönen (2007)

Contextualizing Cassian
Aristocrats, Asceticism, and Reformation in Fifth-Century Gaul
Richard J. Goodrich (2007)

Ambrosiaster's Political Theology
Sophie Lunn-Rockliffe (2007)

Coptic Christology in Practice
Incarnation and Divine Participation in Late Antique and Medieval Egypt
Stephen Davis (2008)

Possidius of Calama
A Study of the North African Episcopate in the Age of Augustine
Erica T. Hermanowicz (2008)

Justinian and the Making of the Syrian Orthodox Church
Volker L. Menze (2008)

The Christocentric Cosmology of St Maximus the Confessor
Torstein Theodor Tollefsen (2008)

Augustine's Text of John

Patristic Citations and Latin Gospel Manuscripts

H. A. G. HOUGHTON

OXFORD
UNIVERSITY PRESS

OXFORD
UNIVERSITY PRESS

Great Clarendon Street, Oxford OX2 6DP

Oxford University Press is a department of the University of Oxford.
It furthers the University's objective of excellence in research, scholarship,
and education by publishing worldwide in

Oxford New York

Auckland Cape Town Dar es Salaam Hong Kong Karachi
Kuala Lumpur Madrid Melbourne Mexico City Nairobi
New Delhi Shanghai Taipei Toronto

With offices in

Argentina Austria Brazil Chile Czech Republic France Greece
Guatemala Hungary Italy Japan Poland Portugal Singapore
South Korea Switzerland Thailand Turkey Ukraine Vietnam

Published in the United States
by Oxford University Press Inc., New York

First published 2008

British Library Cataloguing in Publication Data
Data available

Library of Congress Cataloging in Publication Data
Data available

Typeset by SPI Publisher Services, Pondicherry, India
Printed in Great Britain
on acid-free paper by
CPI Antony Rowe, Chippenham, Wiltshire

ISBN 978–0–19–954592–6

1 3 5 7 9 10 8 6 4 2

To my parents and my wife
with admiration, gratitude, and love

Preface

This book is part of the preparation for a new edition of the Old Latin versions of John, the *Vetus Latina Iohannes*. While my colleagues were transcribing the surviving manuscripts and fragments, I began to collect and analyse biblical citations in the Church Fathers which might be significant for the early history of the text. Augustine was an obvious place to start, being the most prolific author of this period, whose sermon-commentary on the Gospel held the field for several centuries. I therefore took him as a test case for wider questions concerning the use and transmission of the Bible: What is his attitude to the translation and circulation of Scripture? Does he comment on the treatment and availability of biblical codices? How does he reconcile the inevitable differences between copies? Are his own citations consistent, or does he provide evidence for a variety of versions? When does he quote from memory, and when does he refer to a manuscript? The latter leads on to a number of more technical questions about the use of patristic material in New Testament textual criticism, including: What variation is there in the text of biblical citations within the manuscript tradition of Augustine's own works? Is there any evidence of alteration by later copyists or editors? In the case of Augustine, I believe that we can be confident that his scriptural text has, for the most part, been transmitted accurately. Several of the arguments which support this can be extended to other Church Fathers, although each author's citation technique has to be studied individually in order to evaluate their significance for the text of the Bible.

A fairly full picture can be reconstructed of Augustine's attitude to different versions of the Gospels and the way in which he used manuscripts, and this is presented in Part I. The rest of the work offers analyses of Augustine's text of John in greater detail. Part II traces the development of his biblical text over time and in different works. Part III supplies a verse-by-verse commentary on the text of the Gospel. Although this will in due course serve as a companion to the citations of Augustine in the *Vetus Latina Iohannes*, it has been written to be read in conjunction with a copy of the Latin Vulgate, and does not require any specialist materials. Nonetheless, the first stage of the new edition, an electronic edition of the surviving Old Latin manuscripts of John, was published at the website www.iohannes.com in September 2007. Similarly, the collection of citations which underlies this study will be integrated into the database of patristic material and also be made available online in due course. As neither of these was complete at the time of writing, however, I have taken Old Latin manuscripts from the edition of Matzkow–Jülicher–Aland and citations of other Church Fathers from the Vetus Latina Database and earlier studies.

Since the inception of this project over five years ago, it has been a great pleasure to be based at what was initially the Centre for Editing Texts in Religion and is now the Institute for Textual Scholarship and Electronic Editing in the Graduate Institute for Theology and Religion at the University of Birmingham. David Parker, director of the Centre, and Philip Burton supervised the doctoral work which has been considerably revised and expanded in the present volume. I am much indebted to them for their initial guidance and encouragement, and continue to be grateful for their support and the many opportunities which they have generously made available to me. The Arts and Humanities Research Council funded both my initial research and the continuation of the *Vetus Latina Iohannes* project, and I am pleased to acknowledge their support. I owe a considerable debt of gratitude to several members of the International Greek New Testament Project committee, including Keith Elliott and Ulrich Schmid, who examined my thesis, and Roderic Mullen, who brought to my attention several articles on the early manuscripts of Augustine and gave details of citations in the Greek Fathers. Among my colleagues at Birmingham, I would like to mention Jon Balserak, Barbara Bordalejo, Mark Goodacre, Helen Ingram, Peter Robinson, Catherine Smith, and Andrew West. Thanks are also due to Professor David Wright, who lent me his microfilms of several *Tractatus in Iohannem* manuscripts, and to Verity Allan and Rowena Pailing for sharing information from their own research. Without the suggestion of Professor Colin Mayer, I would not have submitted my typescript to Oxford University Press. I am grateful to Gillian Clark, Andrew Louth, and the anonymous reader for their encouragement, and to Tom Perridge, Jenny Wagstaffe, Elizabeth Robottom, Alice Jacobs, and the others involved in the production of this book for their care and attention. Thanks, too, to Catherine Templier and the Scriptorial museum in Avranches, for permission to use on the cover the splendid image of Augustine with his codex from Mont St. Michel ms 72. Finally, words are insufficient to express my gratitude to my family: to my parents Guy and Jenny, who provided me with many of the skills needed to write this book, and my wife Josephine, who has encouraged me throughout its production and even read the whole work in draft, I offer its dedication.

Postscript

Continuing work on the *Vetus Latina Iohannes* means that, even in the short time it has taken to typeset this book, there have been new developments which affect some of the statements in the text.

A full transcription of *Codex Gatianus* (gat, 30), not included in Matzkow–Jülicher–Aland, reveals parallels for several of Augustine's readings. Of these, the most notable is *panibus meis* in John 6:26, not previously known outside Augustine. This occurs in *Tractatus* 25, whose unusual division of John 6:32–3 in its initial citation may be related to a comparable text in Codex Gatianus reading *uerum enim panis dei est.*

The manuscript to which Fischer gives the siglum **Bw** has now been recognised as an Old Latin text in two portions of John. This is set out in my article "A Newly-Identified Old Latin Gospel Manuscript: Würzburg Universitätsbibliothek M.p.th.f.67", forthcoming in the *Journal of Theological Studies.*

As I have already noted, this book is based on the published editions current at the time of writing. I have no doubt that as more evidence becomes available it will be necessary to make further qualifications. The reader is encouraged to check the electronic editions of John mentioned above for the latest information: I also hope to offer updates and material related to the present volume on the website www.iohannes.com/augustinus/.

Contents

Abbreviations for Editions of the Bible

Matzkow–Jülicher–Aland	Jülicher, Adolf, Matzkow, Walter, and Aland, Kurt (eds.). *Itala. Das Neue Testament in altlateinischer Überlieferung*. Berlin; W. de Gruyter. I. Matthäus-Evangelium. Zweite verbesserte Auflage. 1972; II. Marcus-Evangelium. Zweite verbesserte Auflage. 1970; III. Lucas-Evangelium. Zweite verbesserte Auflage. 1976; IV. Johannes-Evangelium. 1963.
Nestle–Aland	Nestle, E. and E., Aland, K. and B. *et al.* (eds.) *Novum Testamentum Graece. Editio vicesima septima revisa.* Stuttgart; Deutsche Bibelgesellschaft. 1993.
Tischendorf	Tischendorf, Constantin (ed.). *Novum Testamentum Graece. Editio octava critica maior.* Leipzig; Giesecke and Devrient. 1869.
Vetus Latina Eseias	Gryson, Roger (ed.). *Eseias. Vetus Latina—Die Reste der altlateinischen Bibel.* Band 12. Freiburg, Herder. 1987–94.
Weber–Gryson	Weber, R. and Gryson R. *et al.* (eds.). *Biblia Sacra iuxta Vulgatam versionem.* Fifth edition. Stuttgart; Deutsche Bibelgesellschaft. 2007.
Wordsworth–White	Wordsworth, J. and White, H. J. (eds.). *Novum Testamentum Domini Nostri Iesu Christi Latine secundum editionem Sancti Hieronymi. Pars Prior—Quattuor Evangelia.* Oxford; Clarendon Press. 1889–98.

Part I

Augustine and the Gospels

Introduction

The manuscript culture of the early Church was very different from today's world with its printed Bibles. This opening part relies on information from Augustine's writings to shed light on the nature and use of the Gospels in antiquity. Chapter 1 considers the history of the early Latin translations and Augustine's attitude to the variety of versions in circulation. In addition to the correction of errors of translation and copying, these texts were frequently revised more systematically in order to bring them into greater conformity with each other and with Greek exemplars. Comparatively few manuscripts of the Old Latin Gospels remain, so Augustine's observations on the history of these versions are of great interest in tracing their history. The form and function of biblical codices and other writings is treated in Chapter 2. Despite the laborious process of copying by hand, a wide variety of books seems to have been available in the Church in North Africa including, of course, the works of Augustine and other Church Fathers. The use of stenographers to transcribe sermons and public debates gives an insight into aspects of oral culture. These records also provide indications of how the copies of the Bible belonging to each congregation were used for teaching and liturgical purposes, as do Augustine's comments in his other works. Chapter 3 treats Augustine's exposition of the Bible and explores what the authority of Scripture meant for him both in theory and in practice. This leads in to an analysis of Augustine's citation technique, involving the manner in which he referred to the Bible, his engagement with the text, and the accuracy with which he quotes scriptural verses. Certain types of alteration are shown to be characteristic of citations which he makes from memory. Finally, Augustine is assessed as a witness to the text of the New Testament in Chapter 4. Several of his explicit statements concerning individual verses are quoted, while different types of citation of John are compared with biblical textual traditions. This demonstrates the affiliation of certain works with particular Old Latin Gospels or Vulgate witnesses, which is considered in greater detail in Part II. This chapter also identifies readings of particular value for the Greek text. A full commentary on his text of the Gospel according to John is given in Part III.

1

Augustine and the History of the Biblical Text

The defining moment for the Latin Bible occurred during the lifetime of Augustine of Hippo (354–430). In 384 Jerome's revised version of the Gospels appeared, followed over the next twenty years by new translations into Latin of many other books of Scripture. These texts were adopted throughout the Western world as the canonical form of the Bible, known from the sixteenth century as the 'Vulgate' (common edition), and constitute the basis for the official Latin text of the present day. The origins of the Latin versions which preceded Jerome are more obscure, and they are often quite different in character, as demonstrated by a few surviving manuscripts and the observations and biblical text of the Church Fathers. Among these, the lion's share of the evidence is to be found in the writings of Augustine, which also provide unique evidence for the processes through which Jerome's text came to be accepted as authoritative.

The recovery of these first Latin versions is of key significance for the study of the biblical text. The process of translation from the original Greek may have begun within a century of the composition of the Gospels. At any rate, by the middle of the third century different Latin traditions may be seen in the works of Cyprian and Novatian. Not only do these versions date from the same time as many of the oldest surviving fragments of the Bible in Greek, predating the great codices from the fourth and fifth centuries, but they also derive from witnesses which do not appear to have been preserved. Tracing the history of these early translations also sheds light on the spread of Christianity in the West, in terms of both geographical and social diversity, and gives some insight into the development of theology and worship within the early Church.[1]

Augustine imagines the practice of the earliest translators in his manual of Christian teaching, *De doctrina christiana*:

ut enim cuique primis fidei temporibus in manus uenit codex graecus et aliquantulum facultatis sibi utriusque linguae habere uidebatur, ausus est interpretari. (*De doctrina christiana* 2.11.16)

For, in the first days of the faith, whenever a Greek manuscript came into the possession of someone who believed himself to have a modicum of ability in both languages, he hazarded his own translation.

This disparaging judgment has too often been uncritically accepted. For a start, the reference of this passage to translations of the Old rather than the New Testament is frequently overlooked. The Hebrew Scriptures present a special case: despite working from Greek versions, Latin translators were sometimes nonplussed by the Semitic grammar and idioms which their forerunners had reproduced. Notwithstanding basic errors of identification and translation, their subsequent rendering of the Greek text often failed to elucidate its obscurities of meaning, compounded by being at two removes from the original language. It could also result in a confusing literalism which contravened acceptable Latin usage. In an age when a scholar had to verify the accuracy of the text in the manuscript in front of him before he could expound its meaning, textual emendation was a common practice:

talia quidem non obscura sed falsa sunt. quorum alia conditio est non enim intellegendos sed emendandos tales codices potius praecipiendum est.

(*De doctrina christiana* 2.12.18)

Such readings, indeed, are not mysterious but incorrect: in this second case, the instruction should be to emend, rather than understand, such manuscripts.

[1] On the attitude to translation among the first Christians, see Sawyer 1999. The claim that the Latin used by the Church was a special language, or *Sondersprache*, based on preconceived social theories and put forward by the Nijmegen school (especially Schrijnen and Mohrmann) is no longer widely accepted, although many of the related studies retain their interest. For current views of the relationship between Christian Latin and later Latin, see Coleman 1987 and Fredouille 1996.

Augustine's concern in these chapters is that the Greek version known as the Septuagint should be treated as the standard authority against which texts were emended. At the end of the discussion, he adds almost as an afterthought that recourse should also be made to Greek manuscripts to confirm queries concerning the New Testament:

libros autem Noui Testamenti, si quid in latinis uarietatibus titubat, graecis cedere oportere non dubium est, et maxime qui apud ecclesias doctiores et diligentiores repperiuntur. (*De doctrina christiana* 2.15.22)

As for the books of the New Testament, if the variety of Latin manuscripts leads to any uncertainty, there is no doubt that they should give way to Greek ones, especially those which are found in more learned and responsible churches.

The information that certain churches were reputed for the quality of their scriptural text is a further indication of the importance accorded to such textual scholarship.

Another feature of Augustine's treatment of different versions of Scripture in *De doctrina christiana* is the reference to the *Itala*:

in ipsis autem interpretationibus, Itala ceteris praeferatur; nam est uerborum tenacior cum perspicuitate sententiae. (*De doctrina christiana* 2.15.22)

As for the translations themselves, the *Itala* is preferable to the rest; for it keeps more closely to the words and gives the sense with clarity.

Various attempts have been made to explain this word.[2] The most satisfactory is that it indicates translations of Italian origin, perhaps specifically North Italy, such as Augustine would have encountered during his time in Milan. Augustine's identification of certain biblical manuscripts as African (e.g. *Retractationes* 1.21.3) is another argument in favour of *Itala* as a geographical description.[3] However, the term became generic, and *Itala* was used for a long time to refer to

[2] Schildenberger 1952 offers a convenient summary of earlier interpretations, several of which claim that the reading is corrupt; however, as Burkitt 1896:64–5 notes, Augustine also uses *Italus* at *De ordine* 2.5.15 and 2.17.45. (A shorter survey in English can be found at Metzger 1977:291–3.)

[3] Several scholars make the plausible assertion that Augustine returned from Milan with biblical books, most recently Bogaert (1998:43 and 2006:522), and Lancel (2002:176).

the earliest Latin versions of the Bible, regardless of origin. Indeed, the debate continues as to whether these translations were first made in Italy or Africa, although the current consensus favours the latter.[4]

Although it is plausible to imagine a growing need for translations of the Scriptures being met by similar independent developments at around the same time, in keeping with Augustine's description of the earliest translators, the Latin versions of the Gospels at least soon coalesced into two or three principal textual traditions. Of these, the oldest stratum is sometimes identified as the 'African' on the basis of translations of certain Greek words, including key theological terms, which seem to have persisted longer in Africa and are frequently found in the writings of African Fathers such as Tertullian and Cyprian. Versions which prefer an alternative rendering of these words, such as *parabola* rather than *similitudo*, or *uerbum* for *sermo*, are described as 'Italian' or 'European'. Whatever their origin, these translations were frequently revised on the basis of other manuscripts. The introduction of 'European' elements into 'African' texts is believed to have happened as early as the time of Cyprian, while there are also numerous examples of older, 'African' renderings finding their way back into later versions.[5]

Such was the situation in which Pope Damasus, who also oversaw the replacement of the Greek liturgy in Rome by Latin, commissioned a version from Jerome which would serve as a standard. Jerome began with the Gospels, for which he lightly revised an existing 'European' version already in circulation:

quae ne multum a lectionis latinae consuetudine discreparent, ita calamo imperauimus ut, his tantum quae sensum uidebantur mutare correctis, reliqua manere pateremur ut fuerant. (*Praefatio in Euangelio*)[6]

[4] e.g. Bogaert 1988:143 and 2006:514, and the summary at Elliott 1992:200–2. The Acts of the Scillitan Martyrs, composed in Africa in 180, is one of the earliest original Latin references to New Testament documents, but it does not specify the language of the *Libri, et epistulae Pauli uiri iusti.* Mohrmann 1949 cites technical Christian terms appearing in Latin documents of the second century as an argument for Roman origin.

[5] Burton 2000 is indispensable as a modern account of the history of the Old Latin gospel translations and analysis of their different text-types. On the early 'European' influence on 'African' gospel traditions, see Fischer 1972:34 and Frede 1972:464.

[6] Text in Weber–Gryson 1515–16. Note that a number of witnesses read *temperauimus* ('restrained') rather than *imperauimus* ('directed').

In order that there would not be great discrepancies from the customary Latin readings, I directed my pen only to correct errors which seemed to change the sense, and allowed the rest to remain as it had been.

It is worth observing that, like the majority of revisions of the early translations, Jerome's version often brings the Latin into closer verbal correspondence with the Greek. His alterations are more thoroughgoing in Matthew and Mark than Luke or John, suggesting that he lost interest half-way through. For example, there is a particularly notable shift in the middle of John, revealed by a change in the rendering of the word δόξα, which is translated by *gloria* in John 1–12 but *claritas* in later chapters.[7] Jerome's work on the Old Testament appears to have a similar history. He started by revising certain books based on the text of the Greek Septuagint found in Origen's *Hexapla*, but following his move to Bethlehem he began a new Latin translation of the canonical Hebrew Scriptures from the original language. The prophetic books came first, in 390, and the work was completed around 405.[8] In spite of its many departures from the text of the Septuagint, which provoked some resistance, this version gradually achieved recognition as the *interpretatio ex hebraica*. The completion of Damasus' project, comprising the other New Testament books, appears not to have been the work of Jerome as his own citations do not correspond to the revised text: Rufinus the Syrian, another translator working in Rome at the same time, has been proposed as a likely candidate for at least some of the work.[9]

[7] For more instances of Jerome's inconsistency between Gospels, see Burkitt 1920:38. Harrison 1986 likewise concludes that Jerome worked through the Gospels in a linear fashion, making contextual alterations which resulted in a more literal translation than the Old Latin versions: examples of this are presented at Burton 2000:192–9.

[8] Although Jerome claimed to have completed his Septuagint translation (cf. Jerome *Epistula* 134.2, also preserved among Augustine's letters as *Epistula* 172), he is only known to have translated the Psalms, Job, Chronicles, Proverbs, Ecclesiastes, and the Song of Songs. Similarly, despite the presentation of his version from Hebrew as a new work, it has been suggested that Jerome relied heavily on the literal Greek translations of Symmachus and Aquila, and probably also drew on existing Latin versions. For a good summary of Jerome's biblical translations, see Bogaert 1988:156–9; Elliott 1992:240–1 also gives a chronology of the translation of each book from the Hebrew.

[9] Jerome writes in *De uiris illustribus* 135 and *Epistula* 71.5 as if he had translated the entire New Testament: although this is taken at face value by Elliott 1992:221 and

For the sake of convenience, the term Vulgate will be used in this book to describe the version of the Latin Bible later known as such, consisting of the translation of the Hebrew Scriptures and revision of the Gospels by Jerome and the supplementary books from a different source in both Testaments. The earlier Latin translations are collectively called the Old Latin, or *Vetus Latina*: given the later predominance of the Vulgate, this description commonly indicates any non-Vulgate form of text which might conceivably derive from these early versions.[10] The Latin text of the New Testament is, however, better described as a continuum on which surviving manuscripts may be located. A number of manuscripts sometimes classified as Old Latin are actually 'mixed texts', a fusion of *Vetus Latina* and Vulgate forms, and the same is true of certain Vulgate witnesses, where contamination with Old Latin readings and further revision have resulted in a complicated textual history.[11] It should be noted that the term *Vulgata* was first used to distinguish the Old Latin translations of the Septuagint from Jerome's Hebrew versions: this is the sense in which it is used by Augustine (e.g. *De ciuitate dei* 16.10.2).

Augustine was aware of Jerome's translation projects from an early stage. In *Epistula* 28, written in 394/5, Augustine urged Jerome to return to the revision of the Latin version of the Septuagint, on the model of his translation of Job. This became a constant theme of their correspondence: Augustine also argues for the authority of the Septuagint in *Epistula* 71 from 403. In this letter he relates the story of the congregation of Oea which was scandalized by the rendering *hedera* ('ivy') rather than *cucurbita* ('gourd') when Jerome's new version of Jonah was used for the liturgical lection.[12] Augustine

Sutcliffe 1969:84, it is rejected by the majority of scholars, including Sparks 1970:519. Metzger 1979:187 notes some of the discrepancies between Jerome's preferred text and the Vulgate; see also Metzger 1977:356–9. For Rufinus, see Fischer 1972:49, 73 and Thiele 1972:117.

[10] For this definition of Old Latin as 'heute nur eine Abgrenzung gegenüber der Vulgata', see Fischer 1972:4. Sutcliffe 1948 treats the history of the term Vulgate.

[11] Berger 1893 remains the key account of the transmission of the Vulgate, supplemented by Fischer 1985 and 1986.

[12] *Epistula* 71.5; Jonah was among the first books Jerome translated from Hebrew, in 390. On this controversy, see also Jerome's response at *Epistula* 112 (*Epistula* 75 in Augustine's corpus) and further Augustine *Epistula* 82.35. Bouton-Toubolic 2006 presents the contrasting positions of Jerome and Augustine regarding the Septuagint as shown through their correspondence.

also points out that reliance on the Hebrew text would divide the Greek and Latin Churches and mean that Christians could be forced to rely on Jewish scholars to arbitrate in disagreements (*Epistula* 71.4). In *Epistula* 82, dated around 405, Augustine acknowledges the utility of Jerome's Hebrew research, but asks Jerome to send him a copy of a complete Septuagint translation:

deinde nobis mittas, obsecro, interpretationem tuam de septuaginta, quam te edidisse nesciebam. (*Epistula* 82.34)

Please, then, will you send us your translation of the Septuagint, which I did not know you had published.

Jerome's reply that he is unable to fulfil this request has led to doubts that this complete version ever existed.[13]

Augustine's continued adherence to the authority of the Septuagint has been interpreted as a rejection of Jerome's Hebrew translations. There are, however, a number of citations which indicate that Augustine had recourse to these, especially in his later works. For example, in the *Quaestiones in Heptateuchum* (419/420), La Bonnardière identifies eighteen comparisons of the Latin of the Septuagint with a rendering of the Hebrew which could only have come from Jerome.[14] In the second half of *De doctrina christiana* (written around 427), Augustine explicitly attributes a Hebrew form to Jerome:

sicut ex hebraeo in latinum eloquium presbytero Hieronymo utriusque linguae perito interpretante translata sunt. (*De doctrina christiana* 4.7.15)

As they have been rendered from Hebrew into the Latin tongue by Jerome, translator and priest, skilled in both languages.

A similar encomium is found at *De ciuitate dei* 18.43 in the context of a discussion upholding the inspiration of the Septuagint, while at *De ciuitate dei* 22.29.2 Augustine cites Jerome's version of 2 Kings (IV Regum) 5:26. References to Hebrew are more scarce in Augustine's

[13] Jerome *Epistula* 134.2; see note 8 above and the comments at White 1990:9 and Zarb 1938:125.

[14] La Bonnardière 1986:305 ff.: she also lists five contemporary examples from *De ciuitate dei*. It has been observed that the absence of references to Hebrew where it would have been germane to his argument in the first four books of *Quaestiones in Heptateuchum* imply that Augustine only acquired Jerome's version while composing this work (De Bruyne 1913:306–7, Deléani 1992:33).

earlier writings. *Epistula* 71 shows that Augustine was familiar with Jerome's later version of Job in 403, within a decade of its publication, although he did not have a manuscript of it to hand.[15] At *Ad Simplicianum* 2.1.6, however, written six or seven years earlier, the citations from 1 Samuel 16 correspond exactly to the Vulgate translation made in 392/3. The context strongly suggests that these were drawn directly from a codex, and the discussion includes an explicit mention of Hebrew versions.

The most remarkable evidence concerns the book of Isaiah, which Jerome translated from Hebrew in 393. Augustine always cites Isaiah 46:8 in a non-Septuagintal form which is identical to the Vulgate: the earliest instance is in *Enarratio* 101.s1.10, which may be as early as 395, and the reading is found in several works from 397.[16] In the discussion of good and bad translations in *De doctrina christiana* 2.12.17, Augustine compares different versions of two verses of Isaiah: in both cases, the first text corresponds to the Septuagint and the second to Jerome's translation from Hebrew. This is in the earlier part of the book, dating from 397, and seems to confirm that Augustine had access to Jerome's version at this time, although he makes no reference to his source.[17] In the conclusion to the *Vetus Latina* edition of Isaiah, Gryson identifies Augustine as one of the earliest witnesses to Jerome's Hebrew translation, while noting that he also acquired Jerome's hexaplaric version later. In addition, Augustine transmits an otherwise unknown Old Latin version in several lengthy citations (e.g. *Sermo* 374, *De ciuitate dei* 20.21, *De peccatorum meritis* 1.27.54).[18]

[15] *Sed mihi ad horam codex defuit qui ex Hebraeo est* (*Epistula* 71.3). Augustine cites the Vulgate text of Job at *De ciuitate dei* 22.29.4. He also mentions Jerome by name at *De doctrina christiana* 4.20.41 and *De peccatorum meritis* 3.6.12.

[16] A thorough discussion of Augustine's citations of this verse is found in Deléani 1992. She observes that, as Jerome did not write his commentary on Isaiah until 408, Augustine cannot have encountered the text by this intermediary, but there is no reason why he should not have possessed a copy of Jerome's translation.

[17] Although Augustine completed *De doctrina christiana* in 427, mentioning Jerome explicitly (see above), there is no evidence that he revised the earlier books: De Bruyne's attempt to identify interpolations in book two is not convincing (1913:308 ff.), and the hypothesis that the earliest surviving manuscript represents the first stage of the work (Green 1959) also tells against revision. For further discussion, see Bochet 1997:519–21.

[18] *Vetus Latina Eseias* 1667; see also Bogaert 2006:525. In fact, at *De ciuitate dei* 20.21.4, Augustine criticizes the Vulgate rendering *cadauera uirorum* in Isaiah 66:24.

Augustine's adoption of Jerome's Gospels is far less controversial. In the final paragraph of *Epistula* 71, Augustine praises Jerome's revision and notes that he has compared it with the Greek himself:

proinde non paruas deo gratias agimus de opere tuo, quod euangelium ex graeco interpretatus es, quia et paene in omnibus nulla offensio est, cum scripturam graecam contulerimus. unde, si quisquam ueteri falsitati contentiosus fauet, prolatis collatisque codicibus uel docetur facillime uel refellitur. et si quaedam rarissima merito mouent, quis tam durus est qui labori tam utili non facile ignoscat, cui uicem laudis referre non sufficit? (*Epistula* 71.6)

Accordingly, we give no small thanks to God for your work on translating the Gospel from Greek, because it is almost without fault when we compare it with a Greek Bible: when these manuscripts are brought out and compared, anyone argumentative who prefers an error of the old version will be either corrected most easily or refuted. Although very few things are truly inspirational, who is so set in their ways as not readily to justify such a useful task, to which it is insufficient to respond with praise?

It seems very likely that Augustine's analysis of Jerome's text provided the foundation for his study *De consensu euangelistarum.* This comparison of the four Gospels, composed in 403–4, is clearly based on a Vulgate text (see further pp. 157–62 below). Not only does it include readings not present in surviving Old Latin sources, but these distinctive forms are found in reminiscences of the Gospels which have been grammatically incorporated into the argument, and are therefore unlikely to have been altered by later copyists. As Augustine published comparatively little on the Gospels before *De consensu*, it is difficult to determine when he first became acquainted with Jerome's revision. In *De diuersis quaestionibus* 64, written some time between 388 and 395, he cites an extract from John 4 in an Old Latin version. As he makes no mention of the Gospels in his first letter to Jerome, *Epistula* 28, written in 394/5, but praises them with the enthusiasm of a new discovery in *Epistula* 71, we may assume that he was introduced to Jerome's version in the intervening period. After 403, Augustine does not switch exclusively to Jerome's text, but there is a gradual process of convergence between his citations and the Vulgate. Nonetheless, he reads from a Vulgate manuscript of Luke in his debate with Felix held in 404.

Further evidence for the influence of Jerome's version may be provided by Augustine's citations of John 1:23. See p. 196.

In addition to certain textual alterations, one of the principal changes which Jerome introduced in his revision was in the order of the Gospels. Most surviving Old Latin witnesses have the sequence Matthew, John, Luke, Mark.[19] By putting the Gospels in the order found in Greek manuscripts (Matthew, Mark, Luke, John), Jerome was able to add the Eusebian canon tables which identified parallel passages in different Evangelists. Indeed, this sort of apparatus would have facilitated Augustine's composition of *De consensu euangelistarum*, although he makes no mention of this either in the work itself or the letter to Jerome. The order of the Gospels given by Augustine may therefore be significant. In his enumeration of the canon in *De doctrina christiana* he gives the Vulgate order:

Noui autem quattuor libris euangelii: secundum Matthaeum, secundum Marcum, secundum Lucam, secundum Iohannem. (*De doctrina christiana* 2.8.13)

But of the New Testament, in four books of the Gospel: according to Matthew, according to Mark, according to Luke, according to John.

Although this may suggest that Augustine was aware of Jerome's innovative sequence in 397, it occurs within a complete list of books of the Bible which Augustine probably took from an episcopal council at which he was present. The only such surviving source, however, the *Breuiarium Hipponense*, does not name the individual evangelists.[20] In the first chapter of *De consensu euangelistarum*,

[19] This is supported by nine of the eleven extant Old Latin codices with more than one Gospel, as listed in Metzger 1977:297 and Elliott 1992:207. Note, however, that the Muratorian fragment puts Luke as the third Gospel and John as the fourth (see Grant 1970:300–1). Jerome is also held responsible for the ordering of the biblical text in sense-lines, *per cola et commata*, although he only mentions this in regard to his translations of Isaiah and Ezekiel: this was less of an innovation, as it was also known in classical antiquity (see McGurk 1994:13–14 and Petitmengin 1985:103–4).

[20] The *Breuiarium Hipponense* records the decrees of the Council of Carthage in 397, but its canonical list may go back to the Council of Hippo in 393: for the transmission of the councils and an account of the variants in the scriptural canon, see Munier 1972. It is printed at Munier 1974:43, and although its New Testament sequence also begins *Noui autem*, it differs from Augustine by placing the Acts of the Apostles after the Gospels (in *De doctrina christiana* 2.8.13 Acts is the penultimate book, preceding the Apocalypse). Further discussion of Augustine's list may be found in Bochet 1997:506 ff and La Bonnardière 1986:292–3. For a summary of Augustine's attitude to the biblical canon, see Polman 1961:63–6 and 177–82.

Augustine explains the principles behind each way of ordering the Gospels without reference to Jerome, which appears to imply that he was already familiar with both:

> *isti igitur quattuor euangelistae... hoc ordine scripsisse perhibentur: primus Matthaeus, deinde Marcus, tertio Lucas, ultimo Iohannes. unde alius eis fuit ordo cognoscendi atque praedicandi, alius autem scribendi. ad cognoscendum quippe atque praedicandum primi utique fuerunt qui secuti dominum in carne praesentem, dicentem audierunt facientemque uiderunt, atque ex eius ore ad euangelizandum missi sunt. sed in conscribendo euangelio, quod diuinitus ordinatum esse credendum est, ex numero eorum, quos ante passionem dominus elegit, primum atque ultimum locum duo tenuerunt, primum Matthaeus, ultimum Iohannes, ut reliqui duo, qui ex illo numero non erant, sed tamen Christum in illis loquentem secuti erant, tamquam filii amplectendi ac per hoc in loco medio constituti utroque ab eis latere munirentur.* (*De consensu euangelistarum* 1.2.3)

Therefore these four evangelists... are shown to have written in this order: first Matthew, then Mark, third Luke and finally John. So there was one order for their getting to know and preach the Gospel, and a different one for their writing, since the first to know and preach were those who followed the Lord in the flesh, heard him speaking and saw him acting, and were sent by his own mouth to preach the good news. But in the writing of the Gospel, which must be held to have been ordered by divine providence, two from the number of those whom the Lord chose before his Passion held the first and last place, first Matthew and last John, just as the other two, who were not of that number but followed Christ speaking in them, like sons to be embraced and set in the middle place for this reason, are contained by the others on either side.

If this work represents Augustine's first use of Jerome's revised (and re-ordered) Gospels, it may be that he felt it necessary to explain here the change from the traditional Old Latin order. It also seems that the sequence in which the Easter Gospels were read at Hippo was altered during Augustine's episcopate, a detail which has been connected with his adoption of the Vulgate.[21]

It has sometimes been suggested that Augustine was himself involved in revising the text of Scripture. The over-enthusiastic case

21 Thus Willis 1962:66–7, who dates the change to 400; Lambot and La Bonnardière place it later, around 418, based on their chronology of the sermons involved. *Sermones* 235, 236A, 239, and 247 support the older order Matthew, Luke, Mark, John, while *Sermo* 234 indicates that Mark followed Luke.

put forward by De Bruyne has been generally dismissed, because it relies on a far greater knowledge of Greek than is plausible for Augustine in his early period.[22] Nevertheless, in a public announcement made on 26 September 426, Augustine referred to a 'concern for the Scriptures' (*cura scripturarum*) which had been laid on him several years earlier by two episcopal councils, and to which he devoted himself for five days of each week.[23] It may be that, following Jerome's refusal to revise the Latin version of the Septuagint, Augustine had taken on this task himself. The appearance in 419 of the *Locutiones in Heptateuchum*, a list of peculiar words and turns of phrase in the first seven books of the Hebrew Scriptures with comments about variants in different translations, further supports this theory. It should, however, be observed that Augustine rarely, if ever, champions one reading over another, which casts doubt on the idea that he was producing his own version. It is more likely that he was engaged in the task of correcting a set of biblical manuscripts according to the principles which he had set out earlier in *De doctrina christiana.* This appears to be confirmed by Augustine's declaration in a letter to Audax, probably dating from 420, that he had been emending the Psalter:

> *Psalterium a sancto Hieronymo translatum ex hebraeo non habeo. nos autem non interpretati sumus, sed codicum latinorum nonnullas mendositates ex graecis exemplaribus emendauimus.* (*Epistula* 261.5)[24]

[22] De Bruyne 1931: details of subsequent scholarship disproving his claims can be found in Fischer 1972:20, Frede 1972:466, and Bogaert 2006:522. Most of Augustine's direct quotation of Greek only occurs in works composed after 415, and he appears to have spent the decade before this improving his knowledge of the language: see the summary provided by Bonner 1986:394–6.

[23] *Nostis ante aliquot annos quid facere uoluerim, et non permisistis. placuit mihi et uobis propter curam scripturarum, quam mihi fratres et patres mei, coepiscopi mei, duobus conciliis Numidiae et Carthaginensi inponere dignati sunt, ut per quinque dies nemo mihi molestus esset* (*Epistula* 213.5, a set of *Acta Ecclesiastica* from the basilica at Hippo). The Council of Numidia was probably held at Milevis in 416, while the Council of Carthage to which Augustine refers here took place in 419. The principal concern of this announcement is the appointment of Eraclius as Augustine's successor, who will fulfil some of his pastoral duties with immediate effect in order to give Augustine time to study.

[24] The reference to *sancto Hieronymo* is noteworthy: it may help to fix the date of this letter after Jerome's death in 420, although it should be noted that in *De doctrina christiana* 4.7.15 from 426, quoted above, Augustine only calls him a *presbyter.*

I do not have the Psalter rendered from the Hebrew by Saint Jerome. For our part, we did not translate it but corrected several faults in Latin codices from Greek exemplars.

Furthermore, Anne-Marie La Bonnardière observes several peculiarities in the biblical citations of *De gratia et libero arbitrio* (426) and suggests not only that Augustine was gradually working his way through the Old Testament, but more specifically that he was responsible for the text of Ecclesiasticus in this work.[25]

One of the principal drawbacks for theories of a systematic biblical revision is that Augustine never mentions this in the *Retractationes*, a catalogue and list of corrections to all his published works which he produced in 426–7. In this, he displays scrupulous attention to the biblical text, sometimes adducing evidence from the Greek and occasionally correcting biblical citations in his earlier works, for which he blamed the inadequacy of codices. For example, Augustine claims that his early commentary on the Epistle of James, now lost, was vitiated by a poor translation:

adiuuant ergo aliquid, nisi quod ipsam epistulam quam legebamus quando ista dictaui non diligenter ex Graeco habebamus interpretatam. (*Retractationes* 2.32)

They may, then, serve some purpose, except that when we dictated these observations, the copy of the Letter we possessed and from which we were reading was not carefully translated from the Greek.

He also refers to a codex which read 'two' rather than 'twelve' apostles in Matthew 20:17:

in primo ergo libro in eo quod positum est *dominus seorsum duobus discipulis suam retulisse passionem*, mendositas codicis nos fefellit; nam duodecim scriptum est non duobus. (*Retractationes* 2.12 on *Quaestiones euangeliorum* 1.27)

In the first book, therefore, where it is written *The Lord announced his Passion to two disciples separately*, the fault of the manuscript led us astray; twelve is written, not two.

Bogaert (2006:524) observes that Augustine had Jerome's hexaplaric Psalter from 415, and used it for the dictated *Enarrationes in Psalmos*.

[25] La Bonnardière 1963:84–5. Bogaert 2006:522–3 represents the current consensus on the likely extent of Augustine's emendation of biblical manuscripts.

In addition, Augustine took the opportunity to correct some of his own errors of memory:

et alio loco illud quae dixi: *sicut ait apostolus: omnis ordo a deo est*, non eisdem uerbis hoc dixit apostolus, quamuis eadem uideatur esse sententia. ait quippe ille: *quae autem sunt a deo ordinata sunt.* (*Retractationes* 1.13.8 on *De uera religione* 41)

In another place, my reference 'As the Apostle says: *Every institution is from God*' the Apostle did not say in these very words. Nonetheless, his meaning seems to be the same, since he does say: *But what exists is instituted by God.*

He proposes several emendations to his earlier biblical readings, such as *Retractationes* 1.10.3 where he says that his text of Genesis 2:5 should be changed to *faenum* ('hay'); his original citation is the only surviving example of *pabulum* ('food') in this verse.[26] All of this is consistent with an increasing familiarity with the text of Scripture and further study in later years.

Variation in the text of the different versions of the Bible which he encountered was, for Augustine, a practical rather than a theological problem. In *De ciuitate dei* he explains on several occasions that variety in Latin biblical manuscripts occurred because they had been translated from Greek (e.g. *De ciuitate dei* 13.24.1, 14.8.1; see also *De doctrina christiana* 2 on p. 7 above). Augustine saw nothing unusual in a multitude of different translations, the variety of which could be explained through historical causes. Furthermore, the correction of a copyist's errors by emendation was a necessary stage in reading any book in antiquity.[27] The emphasis he places on documents is a fundamental principle of textual criticism:

ut si uerbi causa Pauli epistolam, quae ad Romanos scripta est, corruptam esse contendis, aliam proferas incorruptam uel alium codicem potius, in quo eiusdem apostoli eadem epistola sincera et incorrupta conscripta sit. (*De moribus* 1.29.61)

If, for the sake of argument, you claim that the Epistle of Paul to the Romans has been corrupted, you should produce another, uncorrupted one, or rather another codex in which the same Epistle of the same apostle has been copied genuinely and accurately.

[26] For more examples, see *Retractationes* 1.7.2 (Psalm 43:33), 1.7.3 (Wisdom 8:7, Ecclesiastes 1:2), 1.19.4 (Matthew 5:22), 1.21.3 (Sirach 34:30), 2.24.2 (Galatians 3:19).

[27] The four elements of ancient textual study were: *lectio, emendatio, enarratio*, and *iudicium*: see Marrou 1938:20–5 and 424 ff., and Gamble 1995:126.

The Manichees frequently alleged that the text of the New Testament had been altered by 'Judaizers'. In one of his responses Augustine sets out a hierarchy of evidence, giving priority to older manuscripts and versions in other languages:

tamen cum ea de his codicibus proferretis quos dicitis infalsatos... quid facitis, dicite mihi, nisi clamaretis nullo modo uos potuisse falsare codices, qui iam in manibus essent omnium christianorum? quia mox ut facere coepissetis, uetustiorum exemplarium ueritate conuinceremini. qua igitur causa a uobis corrumpi non possent, hac causa a nemine potuerunt. quisquis enim hoc primitus ausus esset, multorum codicum uetustiorum conlatione confutaretur, maxime quia non una lingua, sed multis eadem scriptura contineretur. nam etiam nunc nonnullae codicum mendositates uel de antiquioribus uel de lingua praecedente emendantur. (*Contra Faustum* 32.16)

However, since you bring these proofs [concerning Mani] from manuscripts which you say have been falsified... tell me, what do you do but claim that you could not have falsified the manuscripts in any way as they are already in the hands of all Christians? Because if you had begun to do this, you would soon be shown up by the truth of the oldest exemplars. Therefore, for the same reason that they cannot be corrupted by you, they cannot be corrupted by anyone. For whoever first dared to do this would be refuted by comparison with many ancient manuscripts, especially because the same text is transmitted not in one language but in many. Even now, indeed, several faults in manuscripts are corrected against older ones or those in the source language.

Although Faustus claimed that certain verses were interpolations (e.g. John 5:46 at *Contra Faustum* 16.2), there is no evidence that the Manichees produced an abbreviated version of the New Testament. Instead, the above statement implies that they used similar exemplars of Scripture, which is also borne out by the textual character of Faustus' citations.[28] By the same token, Augustine's comment suggests that he was not familiar with the Manichaean use of the Diatessaron, a harmonized version of all four Gospels produced

[28] Augustine gives more information on the Manichaean attitude to the Bible at *De haeresibus* 46.15, *Confessiones* 5.11.21, and *Epistulae* 82.6 and 237.2. François Decret affirms in his seminal works on Augustine and his Manichaean opponents that both sides used the same type of biblical codices (1970:153, 164, 202; 1978:21–2). Augustine uses a similar argument against the corruption of the Old Testament in *De ciuitate dei* 15.13.1 and 18.46.

by Tatian. Although this is consistent with the origins of the sect in Syria, where the Diatessaron was prevalent, distinctive Tatianic readings are notoriously difficult to identify: some possibilities are considered on pp. 96–7 below, but most of these have parallels in manuscripts of the individual canonical Gospels.[29]

The same is true of Augustine's comments on the translations used by other sects. The biblical citations of his Donatist opponents often differ markedly from the versions preferred by Augustine and found in the extant Old Latin manuscripts, but he proclaims that they share the same Bible:

fratres sumus, unum deum inuocamus, in unum Christum credimus, unum euangelium audimus, unum psalmum cantamus, unum amen respondemus, unum alleluia resonamus, unum pascha celebramus: quid tu foris es, et ego intus sum? (*Enarratio in Psalmos* 54.16)

We are brothers, we call on one God, we believe in one Christ, we hear one Gospel, we sing one psalm, we respond with one Amen, we cry out one Alleluia, we celebrate one Easter: why are you outside and I inside?

His anti-Donatist works contain the greatest number of corrections made by Augustine to his opponents' scriptural text, yet in his surviving works he never suggests that the variants are deliberate alterations. The only occasion on which this happened was in the lost *Contra epistolam Donati*, when he claimed that Donatus had deliberately omitted a phrase from Sirach 34:30. Augustine admitted his mistake in the *Retractationes*:

nos autem, et antequam esset pars Donati, sic habuisse codices plurimos uerumtamen Afros, ut non esset in medio: *et iterum tangit illum*, postea didicimus. quod si iam scirem, non in istum tamquam in furem diuini eloquii uel uiolatorem tanta dixissem. (*Retractationes* 1.21.3)

However, we later learnt that, even before Donatus' faction existed, very many African manuscripts however had this text, so that the phrase *And touches him again* was not included. If I knew this now, I would not have inveighed against him as if he were a thief of divine words or a profaner.

[29] On the Diatessaron, see Petersen 1994 and 1995 (especially 1994:334–8, 344, 403, and 441 for Augustine and the Manichees). He admits that, despite the claims of Leloir 1962 and Quispel 1975, Augustine is unlikely to be a source of Diatessaronic readings. General problems with the hypothesis of an Old Latin gospel harmony are raised by Schmid 2003.

The correspondence between Donatist Bibles and African Old Latin texts is not surprising given that the sect was exclusive to Africa. In fact, the Donatists believed themselves to be the legitimate branch of the Catholic Church in Africa and were in communion with Christians outside the province. Despite the absence of any obvious ideological objection to the circulation of biblical manuscripts, their reverence for Cyprian may have contributed to their preference for the older version.[30]

In conclusion, Augustine is a source of information about a variety of versions of the Latin Bible. Although he is rarely thought of as a textual critic, he displays considerable interest in the history and transmission of Scripture. His correspondence with Jerome and traces of the latter's biblical translations in his writings are important evidence for their diffusion. Although Augustine continued to maintain the authority of the Septuagint against Jerome, he seems to have used his versions of certain Old Testament books from the Hebrew, notably Isaiah, soon after their publication. He also adopted Jerome's revised text of the Gospels some time around 403. Like any reader in antiquity, Augustine had to establish the accuracy of the manuscripts he used: this task of textual emendation appears to be a feature of his later ministry, when he had a particular responsibility laid on him by the other African bishops. It is an overstatement to speak of a systematic revision of the whole Bible by Augustine, but it is likely that he corrected Latin versions of the Septuagint. His comments on readings found in the earlier Old Latin traditions supplement what is preserved in surviving manuscripts: some of these come from his encounters with sectarian opponents who used slightly different versions. Without the testimony of Augustine, our knowledge of the history of the Bible in Latin would lack important evidence from a key period.

[30] On Donatism, see the summary in Lancel 2002:162–73 and the monographs of Frend 1952 and Tilley 1997. The movement began as a reaction against clergy who had surrendered copies of the Scriptures to Roman authorities and became a parallel Church, occupying buildings formerly belonging to the Catholics. Although they frequently destroyed the liturgical vessels as an act of purification, it is unclear what they did with biblical codices. Optatus 6.5 appears to suggest that the Donatists reclaimed copies of the Scriptures from the authorities, although he ridicules their inability to purify them. Bogaert (1988:286 and 2006:518) notes that the Donatist origin of certain biblical summaries and *capitula* lists implies that the Donatists produced their own biblical codices.

2

The Use of the Bible and the Production of Books in the Time of Augustine

The physical nature of the manuscripts of the Bible available to Augustine and his contemporaries has a bearing on the analysis of their text, as does the way in which they were used. Each codex, written in ink on parchment, had to be copied by hand. The production of books was a laborious and time-consuming task, but the expense involved was not as prohibitive as has sometimes been claimed. Several surviving Old Latin gospel manuscripts are deluxe editions written in gold and silver ink on parchment dyed purple. The majority of books from this time, however, consist simply of a plain text in black ink (very occasionally supplemented with red) with no decorations or pictures.[1] Although the earliest single-volume copies of Scripture in Greek date from around the time of Augustine, pandects of the whole Latin Bible are not attested until much later. Instead, books were bound in smaller collections, such as the Epistles or the Gospels, or circulated individually.

Each church had a set of scriptural books, which were the responsibility of the *lector*. Indeed, the public presentation of a codex was part of their commissioning rite.[2] Court records show that it was customary for the *lector* to keep the codices at home, as illustrated in

[1] Jerome refers somewhat critically to purple manuscripts in his *Prologus in Iob* (Weber–Gryson 732) and *Epistula* 22.32.1; on writing materials and practices in antiquity, see Bischoff 1990:7–45.

[2] This is recorded in the minutes of the Fourth Council of Carthage from 475 (Munier 1974:344). Paoli-Lafaye 1986 observes that lectors were well established in Africa, and they did not deliver sermons; many were children. A survey of their rôle can also be found at Gamble 1995:218–23.

the minutes of a confiscation of church property cited in the *Gesta apud Zenophilum* (Ziwsa 1893:187–8). After handing over the single large-format manuscript stored in the church, *codicem unum pernimium maiorem*, the subdeacon Catullinus says:

plus non habemus quia subdiacones sumus; sed lectores habent codices.

We have no more because we are subdeacons: the lectors have the codices.

A search around six of the lectors' houses results in the confiscation of a further thirty-two *codices* and four *quiniones* ('fascicles'). This does not seem to have been unusual, but corresponds to Optatus' description of fourth-century Africa:

bibliothecae refertae sunt libris; nihil deest ecclesiae; per loca singula diuinum sonat ubique praeconium; non silent ora lectorum; manus omnium codicibus plenae sunt; nihil deest populis doceri cupientibus. (Optatus 7.1)

The libraries are stuffed with books; the church lacks nothing; throughout each locality the sacred message resounds everywhere; the mouths of the lectors are not silent; the hands of all are full of manuscripts; nothing is lacking for the crowds who wish to be instructed.

Copies of the Christian Scriptures were also available on the open market, as two comments from sermons preached by Augustine in Carthage show:

cottidie codices dominici uenales sunt, legit lector; eme tibi et tu lege quando uacat, immo age ut uacet: melius enim ad hoc uacat quam ad nugas. (*Sermo* 114B.15 [*Dolbeau* 5])

The Lord's manuscripts are daily on sale, and readers read them; buy one for yourself and read it when you have time—in fact, make time for it: it is better to have time for this than for trifles.

arguat quisque, murmuret, si non per totum orbem haec scriptura recitatur atque cantatur; si cessat etiam uenalis ferri per publicum. (*Enarratio in Psalmos* 36.s1.2)

Let someone complain, let him grumble, if this Scripture is not proclaimed and chanted throughout the world, if it should even stop being available to buy in public.

At *Confessiones* 6.11.18, Augustine considers buying a copy of the Scriptures in Milan: he was already acquainted with biblical books (e.g. *Confessiones* 3.5.9), and a copy of Romans plays an important part in the conversion scene itself (*Confessiones* 8.12.29). Other Fathers also read the Bible before becoming Christians, and Augustine expected catechumens to be familiar with certain texts prior to their baptism.[3] In a remarkable apologetic statement he even invites the worshippers of Juno to purchase their own copies:

litterae nostrae prodant eis quod colimus sed non timemus. codices nostri publice uenales feruntur: lux non erubescit. emant, legant, credant; aut emant, legant, irrideant. nouit scriptura illa reos tenere qui legunt et non credunt. circumfertur uenalis codex sed ille qui praedicatur in codice non est uenalis.... eme tu codicem et lege, nos non erubescimus. (*Sermo* 198.20 [*Dolbeau* 26])

Our writings reveal our religion to them, but we are not afraid. Our manuscripts are put on sale in public: the daylight does not blush for shame. Let them buy them, read them and believe them; or let them buy them, read them and laugh at them. Scripture knows how to call to account those who read and do not believe. A manuscript is carried around for sale, but the one whom its pages proclaim is not for sale... Buy a manuscript and read it: we are not ashamed.

Even allowing for exaggeration in Christian polemic, biblical books appear to have enjoyed a wide readership in this period.

The Church had its own secretaries and copyists alongside the scribes employed by the imperial administration, private individuals, and the book trade. These early *scriptoria* were often associated with particular authors such as Origen or Jerome, and Augustine had such a team at Hippo.[4] Books were normally copied to order: the customary procedure was that a copyist would be sent to transcribe a manuscript *in situ*. For example, after listing his recent works in a letter to Evodius, Augustine says:

haec omnia si habere uolueris, aliquem mitte qui tibi cuncta describat. (*Epistula* 169.4.13)

If you wish to have all these, send someone to copy everything for you.

[3] Readers of the Bible included Cyprian (Fahey 1971:16), and Marius Victorinus (*Confessiones* 8.2.4). *Tractatus in Iohannem* 96.3 refers to catechumens, and Augustine discusses those with biblical knowledge in *De catechizandis rudibus* (see Duval 1985:20).

[4] For the *scriptoria* of Origen and Augustine, see Gamble 1995:120 and 168 respectively, and, on Jerome, Sutcliffe 1969:98. Petitmengin 2003 and Bischoff 1990:181–9 have more information about publication in antiquity, the former with particular reference to Augustine.

Similarly, a letter from Jerome to Aurelius of Carthage (preserved as *Epistula* 27* among Augustine's letters) invites him, like certain bishops from Gaul and Italy had already done, to send a scribe to Bethlehem for a year to copy scriptural commentaries for his church collection. Sometimes, there seems to have been an expectation that books would be produced locally, as demonstrated by Jerome's comment on the scarcity of Latin scribes in the area when refusing Augustine's request for a copy of his translation of the Septuagint.[5] Manuscripts could also be sent to a *scriptorium*: Paulinus of Nola dispatched a text of Eusebius to be copied in Carthage (see *Epistula* 24.3 among Augustine's letters) and it has been suggested that the earliest surviving manuscript of Augustine, dating from the fifth century, is also a product of this centre.[6] This codex may have been a presentation copy for Simplicianus in Milan: Augustine also actively promoted his own writings, and sent books throughout Italy and Africa. *Epistula* 25 records Paulinus of Nola's gratitude at receiving five of Augustine's anti-Manichaean works, while in *Epistula* 101 Augustine responds to a request from Memorius, Bishop of Capua, for a copy of *De musica*. He sent Count Darius not only the *Confessiones*, as asked, but five other works with *Epistula* 231.7, just as he included a selection of writings with his first letter to Jerome (*Epistula* 28.6). These examples show the constant traffic of books and ideas across the Mediterranean. In many cases, Augustine used Alypius or Romanianus as his agents to deliver manuscripts or co-ordinate the copying of books in return. Alypius had imperial scribes available to him, although Augustine says that he resisted the temptation to have books copied at cheap rates (*Confessiones* 6.10.16)!

The church library at Hippo not only served as the repository for copies of Augustine's works, but also included other patristic writings. Augustine's biographer Possidius notes the bishop's special concern for the collection:

[5] *Grandem latini sermonis in ista prouincia notariorum patimur penuriam, et idcirco praeceptis tuis parere non possumus* (Jerome, *Epistula* 134.2 = *Epistula* 172.2 in Augustine's letters; he makes a similar comment to Aurelius at *Epistula* 27*.3).

[6] Steinhauser 1995:40, who also proposes the connection with Simplicianus; for the dating of this manuscript, see Green 1959.

ecclesiae bibliothecam, omnesque codices diligenter posteris custodiendos semper iubebat. (Possidius *Vita Augustini* 31.6)

He always gave instructions that the library of the church and all its codices should be carefully preserved for future generations.

Further evidence of this is provided by the *Retractationes* and Possidius' later edition of the catalogue of Augustine's works, the *Indiculum*.[7] The extent of other authors in the library is more difficult to determine. Extensive research has been devoted to gleaning evidence from Augustine's requests for copies made in surviving letters and his verbatim quotations.[8] The majority of the works would have been in Latin, including translations of Greek texts, although Augustine also makes a few references to checking Greek witnesses himself, as in the following comment on John 20:2:

nonnulli codices etiam graeci habent *tulerunt dominum* ***meum*** quod uideri dictum potest propensiore caritatis uel famulatus affectu, sed hoc in pluribus codicibus quos in promptu habuimus non inuenimus. (*Tractatus in Iohannem* 120.6)

Several manuscripts, including Greek ones, have *They have taken* ***my*** *Lord*. This may seem to be said with greater affection or through a closer relationship, but we have not found this among the many manuscripts which we have to hand.

This exemplifies the practice he advocates in *De doctrina christiana* 2.14.21, and is particularly frequent in his scriptural commentaries.[9] In addition to biblical codices, there may also have been a handful of Greek patristic writings, such as the works to which he refers in *Contra Iulianum* and the text of Pseudo-Epiphanius which formed the basis of *De haeresibus*.[10]

[7] For the text and history of the *Indiculum*, see Wilmart 1931.

[8] For Augustine's use of classical Latin texts, see the works of Hagendahl along with O'Donnell 1980 and Müller 2003; Christian sources are considered by Altaner and Dulaey. Cipriani 2006, however, notes that a substantial proportion of his references may have come from *florilegia*, and warns against an over-zealous identification of Augustine's sources in modern editions.

[9] e.g. *sic enim habent uerba euangelica collata cum exemplaribus graecis* (*Tractatus in Iohannem* 3.8), and the discussion of John 16:13 at *Tractatus in Iohannem* 96.4 and 100.1. For other references to the Greek in order to clarify the Latin text, see *Tractatus in Iohannem* 38.11, 41.1, 101.4, and 115.4, and *Epistula* 149 *passim*. La Bonnardière 1965:121 lists fifty-five points at which Augustine compares Latin and Greek manuscripts in his thirty-two *Enarrationes* on Psalm 118.

[10] See Altaner 1952 and Cipriani 2006:543–4.

Like the Bible, texts by Church Fathers seem to have been generally available. When preaching in Carthage, Augustine alludes to the wide diffusion of Cyprian's works:

et quid plura dicam? multi usquequaque habent magnum corpus librorum eius. sed nos uberiores gratias domino agamus, quod habere meruimus sanctum corpus membrorum eius. (*Sermo* 313C.2)

What more shall I say? Many people all around have the great body of his writings. But let us give richer thanks to God, since we have been found worthy to have the holy body of his physical remains.

References to reading at home imply that a fair proportion of the congregation was literate.[11] Furthermore, the enthusiasm of the reading public did not just extend to published works. The story of the theft and premature circulation of the unfinished manuscript of Augustine's *De trinitate* is well known (see the Prologue to *De trinitate* and *Retractationes* 2.15.1). Possidius similarly writes of the transcription of his sermons even by his opponents:

et hos eius libros atque tractatus mirabili dei gratia procedentes ac profluentes, instructos rationis copia, atque auctoritate sanctarum scripturarum, ipsi quoque haeretici concurrentes cum catholicis ingenti ardore audiebant: et quisquis, ut uoluit, et potuit, notarios adhibentes, ea quae dicebantur excepta describentes. (Possidius *Vita Augustini* 7.3)

As these, his books and sermons, were brought out and flowed forth by the wondrous grace of God, founded on the riches of reason and the authority of the Holy Scriptures, the heretics themselves, too, would gather and listen with the catholics, matching their great zeal: whoever desired and could afford it engaged secretaries to take down a record of what was being said.

He notes later that many of these were Donatists, who would take the text to their bishops (*Vita Augustini* 9.1). This practice may underlie Augustine's comment at the beginning of the *Retractationes*:

quia multa scripsi, uel quia multa etiam quae dictata non sunt tamen a me dicta conscripta sunt. (*Retractationes* 1.prol.2)

[11] Compare Augustine's description of the *formica dei* at *Enarrationes in Psalmos* 66.3 (*ab omnibus uidentur procedere ad ecclesiam, redire de ecclesia, audire sermonem, audire lectionem, inuenire librum, aperire et legere*); see also *Tractatus in Iohannem* 10.4 and 12.11. Gamble 1995:231–2 mentions exhortations to congregational reading in early Greek Church Fathers: Hippolytus, Clement of Alexandria, Origen, and Chrysostom.

... because I have written much, or because much which was not even dictated was, however, recorded as I spoke it.

Epistula 4*.3 provides an example of Augustine comparing the exemplar kept in Hippo with a copy of his *De gestis Pelagii* which had been alleged to contain an interpolation. The doctrinal significance of patristic writings highlighted the importance of ensuring that copies were accurate.[12]

Official stenographers were also employed by the Church to record the minutes of councils and debates. The surviving text of the Conference of Carthage held in 411 offers an insight into the creation of these documents.[13] The opposing sides each brought a team of six secretaries (*notarii*), supervised by four bishops. The speeches were recorded in shorthand by stenographers (*exceptores*). When the scribes ran out of paper or the current team needed to be relieved, the debate was interrupted. After a full day's discussion, the proceedings were adjourned for a day while the shorthand was transcribed under supervision and the copies compared. To ensure authenticity, each speaker then signed his acceptance in the official copy next to each of his utterances with the word *recognoui*.[14]

Several of the debates transmitted within the works of Augustine were recorded in this fashion, although on a smaller scale. At the end of his public discussions with Felix (*Contra Felicem*) and Maximinus (*Collatio cum Maximino*), both parties signed the minutes as an accurate record. In the latter, a copyist has noted that each signature is in a different hand to the rest of the text (*alia manu*), and there is also the word *contuli*, possibly indicating a comparison with a second transcription.[15] At *Collatio cum Maximino* 10, when Augustine queries the exact words of his opponent, the stenographer notes that

[12] On these concerns in and immediately after the lifetime of Augustine, see Vessey 1996 and 1998.

[13] Text and French translation in Lancel 1972–5.

[14] Earlier scholarship distinguished between *notarii*, shorthand scribes employed by churches, *exceptores*, shorthand scribes employed by magistrates, and *librarii*, transcribers of shorthand into longhand (e.g. Deferrari 1922:106–7). For the difference between *exceptores* and *notarii* compare *Conf. Carth.* 1.3 and 1.16 with 1.132. The other details recorded in this paragraph are described at *Conf. Carth.* 1.10, 1.132, 2.38, 2.43, 2.53, and 3.279.

[15] Possidius refers to the role of the *notarii* in Augustine's debates: see *Vita* 6.6, 16.4, 17.2. On the detail *alia manu*, see Dekkers 1952:128–31.

Antonius the *notarius* read out part of the minutes. The accounts of the debates with Felix and Fortunatus record when the interlocutors take up a manuscript of the Bible:

et cum reddidisset codicem euangelii, accepit Actus Apostolorum... et recitauit. (*Contra Felicem* 1.3)

And when he had returned the codex of the Gospel, he took the Acts of the Apostles... and read from it.

Similarly, a codex of Paul is used at *Contra Felicem* 1.7–8 and *Contra Fortunatum* 16, 19. As shorthand technique is based on continuous transcription, the stenographic record of these citations has a particularly strong claim to represent the text of Scripture as it appeared in these manuscripts. This is supported by the text-types of the two citations in *Contra Felicem* 1.3: the passage from Luke accords with the Vulgate, but the Acts citation is completely Old Latin in character. As Burkitt says:

Unless this is mere literary fraud, the text of *Contra Felicem* must rest on mechanical reporting; if so, the probability is all the stronger that the words of the biblical text of Lc xxiv, and of Ac i and ii, were taken down as they were read out of the codices. (Burkitt 1896:70)

Furthermore, as the minutes of debates were checked by each party, it is unlikely that gaps would have been left for biblical passages to be filled in later or compared with an exemplar.

The transmitted text of Augustine's sermons also derives from a stenographic record. This is confirmed by his spontaneous observations on that day's weather or the size of the congregation.[16] Possidius notes that Augustine died before completing the revision of his sermons, although an earlier reference to *tantaque in ecclesia disputata, excepta atque emendata* suggests that certain spoken addresses were later edited and may have formed the basis of theological

[16] The more recently discovered sermons supplement the comments assembled in Deferrari 1922, who includes a reference to the cold weather at the opening of *Tractatus in Iohannem* 6 and Augustine's comments about talking in the congregation during his sermon (*Sermo* 23.8). In *Sermo* 114B (*Dolbeau* 5) Augustine asks the congregation if he can postpone his commentary on the psalm, and at the end of *Sermo* 272B* (*Dolbeau* 31) he reminds them to arrive early for the hymn singing the next morning!

works.[17] The stenographers themselves added explanatory comments, such as the indication *post sermonem* before an exhortation to pay attention to preachers at *Sermo* 20.5, or the heading of an additional section at the end of *Sermo* 163B.6, when Augustine complains about the demands of the congregation. The commotion when a girl who had recently been miraculously healed is brought into the apse is recorded in *Sermo* 323.3.4; Augustine seems to have cut short his sermon as a result (cf. *De ciuitate dei* 22.8.23). It has sometimes been suggested that variations in the manuscript tradition of Augustine's sermons can be traced to transcriptions of the same address by different scribes. Although it seems unlikely that more than one copy of each sermon would have been stored at Hippo and more plausible that divergences were introduced during later copying, Augustine would not have been able to control the circulation of his sermons, especially those preached elsewhere. Indeed, distinctive scribal characteristics have been identified in some of the sermons preached at Carthage.[18]

Augustine appears usually to have preached extempore, as he himself recommends in *De doctrina christiana*:

uersandum est quod agitur multimoda uarietate dicendi, quod in potestate non habent qui praeparata et ad uerbum memoriter retenta pronuntiant.

(*De doctrina christiana* 4.10.25)

[17] Possidius *Vita Augustini* 18.9 and 28.1–2. Commentators are divided on the extent to which Augustine may have revised his sermons. Verbraken (1976:197) maintains that he did revise some, although the collections were the work of later editors. The quotation of *Tractatus in Iohannem* 99 in *De trinitate* 15.27.48 is often adduced as an example of his re-use of material, although this was originally dictated rather than preached (see further Deferrari 1922:217–19 and Milewski 2002:74). For the conversion of sermons into longhand, compare Augustine's request to Aurelius: *ut iubeas singulos quos uolueris sermones eorum conscriptos et emendatos mitti nobis* (*Epistula* 41.2). The later abbreviation of Augustine's sermons some time before the seventh century, revealed by the discovery of the *Sermones Dolbeau*, is described at Dolbeau 1993:525–6.

[18] Paoli-Lafaye (1986:63) suggests that the greater number of references to the *lector* preserved in Augustine's sermons delivered in Carthage may be due to the stenographers. Dolbeau (1996:172) attributes differences between the two collections of Mayence-Grande-Chartreuse and Mayence-Lorsch to the habits of the original stenographers, while Van den Hout (1955:297) comments that some readings in the Vallicelliana A 14 manuscript of the *Tractatus in Iohannem* can only be explained as errors of stenography. See further Chapter 6 below.

The topic must be examined with a variety of verbal illustrations: people who declaim a sermon prepared and learnt word for word in advance are unable to do this.

He compares his sermon preparation with the process of incarnation:

ecce ego qui uobiscum loquor, antequam ad uos uenirem, cogitaui quod uobis dicerem. quando cogitaui quod uobis dicerem, iam in corde meo uerbum erat. non enim uobis dicerem nisi ante cogitarem. inueni te latinum, latinum tibi proferendum est uerbum. si autem graecus esses, graece tibi loqui deberem, et proferre ad te uerbum graecum. illud uerbum in corde nec latinum est, nec graecum: prorsus antecedit linguas istas quod est in corde meo . . . sicut uerbum meum assumpsit sonum, per quem audiretur, sic uerbum dei assumpsit carnem, per quam uideretur. (*Sermo* 225.3.3)

Look, I who speak with you thought about what I would say to you before I came to you. When I thought what I would say to you, the word was already in my heart, because I would not speak to you unless I thought about it in advance. I encountered Latin speakers, so it was necessary to produce Latin words. But if you were Greek, I would have had to speak to you in Greek and produce Greek words. The words in my heart are neither Latin nor Greek: what is in my heart directly precedes those languages . . . Just as my word took on sound, through which it was heard, so the Word of God took on flesh, through which it was seen.

While he may have meditated on his words in advance, there is no indication that Augustine relied on written notes.[19] Instead, he normally bases his address on the scriptural texts read earlier in the service, alluding to the liturgical readings with phrases such as:

modo cum euangelium legeretur audistis. (*Sermo* 251.3.3)

You have just heard when the Gospel was read.

non audistis quid dixerit cum eadem lectio hodie legeretur?

(*Sermo* 294.13.14)

Did you not hear what he said when the same reading was read today?

[19] Similar passages to *Sermo* 225 appear at *Sermo* 187.3.3 and *Tractatus in Iohannem* 14.7. For the absence of written preparation, see Deferrari 1922, especially 118 and 217. Stock 1996:5–6 has suggested that Augustine sometimes paused while delivering the sermon in order to meditate upon the scriptural text, but the evidence he adduces is not compelling: *Tractatus in Iohannem* 69 was dictated, and refers to the opening verses of John, while *Epistula* 73.5 also has no connection with a liturgical context.

Such comments have been used to try to reconstruct the cycle of readings which made up Augustine's lectionary. Although there is some evidence by the end of the fourth century for fixed passages, especially on major feasts, the selection was often left to the bishop's discretion. This enabled Augustine to preach series of sermons on the Psalms or the Gospel according to John.[20] In fact, when the *lector* reads the wrong psalm, Augustine responds by preaching on the reading rather than what he expected:

maluimus nos in errore lectoris sequi uoluntatem dei quam nostram in nostro proposito. (*Enarratio in Psalmos* 138.1)

We prefer to follow God's will in the lector's mistake, rather than our own in the original plan.

On another occasion, Augustine decides that the readings will be repeated at the next service so that he can finish his exposition:

omnia quae hic adhuc discutienda arbitror hodie non discuto; sed iterum nobis in nomine domini diebus paucis reddendi sermonis eadem lectio recitabitur et diligentius, illo adiuuante, tractabitur. (*Tractatus in Iohannem* 46.8).

I think that I will not discuss today everything which is still to be discussed here, but in a few days the same reading will be recited for us to preach a sermon in the Lord's name, and with his help it will be considered in greater detail.[21]

This is also the case when he brings his sermon to a premature conclusion because he sees that the congregation is tired of standing, or suffering because of excessive heat (*Sermones* 355.2 and 319.8.7).

It is clear that for most if not all of his expository sermons, Augustine preached from a biblical codex. This can be seen not only from his citation technique (compare p. 58 below), but from many direct and indirect comments, including the following description of Christian teaching:

[20] The classic study on this subject is Willis 1962. La Bonnardière 1965:89 notes that the raising of Lazarus (John 11) and 1 Thessalonians 4:13–18 were the customary readings at funerals (cf. *Sermo* 139A.1). On the thematic relationship of readings, it is interesting to note that Psalm 34, with its reference to *flagella* in verse 15, appears to have been read at the same service as the account of the cleansing of the Temple, featuring the word *flagellum* in John 2:15 (*Tractatus in Iohannem* 10.4).

[21] The promise is kept in the next sermon, in which Augustine notes that shorter sermons were preached on Sundays (*Tractatus* 47.9). Similar examples occur in *Sermo* 68.1 and *Enarratio in Psalmos* 90.s2.1.

ire in ecclesias aut codicem legere aut legentem praedicantemque hominem audire. (*De doctrina christiana* proem.5)

Go into churches either to read a manuscript or to hear a man reading and preaching.

The singular *hominem* and co-ordinated participles suggest that the preacher was himself reading. Augustine uses the phrase *gestare in manibus* at the beginning of several sermons to indicate that he is holding a copy of the Scriptures:

et hoc quod gestamus in manibus, scriptura scilicet quam uidetis, commendat nobis inquirendam et laudandam mulierem quamdam de qua paulo ante cum legeretur audistis. (*Sermo* 37.1)

And this which we are holding in our hands, the Bible, clearly, as you see, mentions this woman for our consideration and praise, about whom you heard a moment ago when it was being read.

hoc lectum est, et hanc lectionem tractandam gestamus in manibus.
(*Tractatus in Iohannem* 15.1)

This was read, and we are holding this passage for commentary in our hands.

de sancto euangelio secundum Iohannem, quod gestare nos uidetis in manibus, iam multa audiuit caritas uestra. (*Tractatus in Iohannem* 40.1)[22]

Concerning the holy Gospel according to John, which you see us holding in our hands, you have already heard much, dear friends.

Unlike the sermons which had to be abbreviated through lack of time, there is one occasion on which Augustine continues his exposition beyond the passage read by the *lector*:

non quidem huc usque peruenit lector, sed tamen aliqui recordantur; et qui non recordantur, audiant a me breuiter. (*Enarratio in Psalmos* 96.13)

The *lector* did not get this far, although some will remember it, and those who do not remember it may hear it briefly from me.

The number of quotations which follow suggest that he was reading from a codex. Furthermore, if this were the same one used by the *lector*, it confirms that the readings were taken from continuous text

22 Note that Willems' edition unfortunately reads *quod gestare* ***non*** *uidetis*; the error is noted in Alexanderson 1999.

manuscripts rather than a specialized lectionary which only contained the liturgical passage. In *Tractatus in Iohannem* 36, Augustine quails before the exegetical task ahead of him and imagines an objector suggesting he lay down the codex and finish his sermon:

et tamen etiam nos humi repentes, infirmi et uix ullius momenti inter homines, audemus tractare ista et ista exponere; et putamus nos aut capere posse cum cogitamus aut capi dum dicimus. quare ista dixi? forte enim post haec uerba quisquam mihi iuste dicat: pone ergo codicem. quod excedit mensuram tuam, quid sumis in manum tuam? quid ei committis linguam tuam? (*Tractatus in Iohannem* 36.5)

And yet even we, who creep on the ground, weak and of scarcely any importance among humans, dare to comment on and expound these matters, and we think that we can understand when we ponder it, or can be understood while we are speaking. Why have I spoken thus? Well, perhaps after these words someone may rightly say to me: 'Put down the manuscript. Why do you take in your hand something which exceeds your capability? Why do you entrust your tongue to it?'

Another imaginary opponent risks receiving rougher treatment from the preacher:

quid, si dicat alius: 'hoc Christus non dixit'? unde conuincis, unde probaturus es? codicem aperturus, lectionem inuenturus, homini demonstraturus, immo cum magna fiducia pectoris resistenti codicem impacturus. 'tene, attende, lege, euangelium portas.' 'quid ergo, rogo te, quid conturbas paululum? noli urgere, dic planius, tranquillius.' 'ecce euangelium porto et quid hinc?' Ille: 'euangelium loquitur Christum dixisse quod negas.' 'et ideo credes hoc dixisse Christum, quia loquitur euangelium?' 'ideo plane' inquit. 'ego multum miror, quomodo dicas mentiri Christum et non mentiri euangelium. sed ne forte, cum dico euangelium, codicem attendas, membranam et atramentum cogitas euangelium, quid dicat uide graecum nomen: euangelium est 'bonus nuntius' uel 'bona annuntatio'. (*Sermo* 133.6)

What if someone were to say: 'Christ did not say this'? How do you show him, from where will you prove it? You will open the codex, find the reading, show it to the man, yes, with great confidence of heart you will force the book on the objector. 'Hold on, wait, read, you are carrying the Gospel. Why then are you getting worked up over a little matter, I ask you? Do not force it, speak more plainly, more calmly.' 'See, I am carrying the Gospel. What of it?' He says: 'The Gospel tells that Christ said what you deny.' 'And you believe that Christ said it for this reason, namely that the Gospel says it?' 'Exactly, this very reason,' he says. 'I am greatly surprised, then, at how you say Christ lies and the Gospel does not lie. But just in case you expect a codex when I say "Gospel", and you think the Gospel is ink on parchment, consider what the Greek word signifies: "Gospel" is a good messenger or good news.'

Forcing the book on the objector might earn Augustine the title of the first 'bible-basher'! Despite the polemic, this scene shows how a gospel book of 'ink on parchment' was an indispensable accessory for the preacher.[23] Again, at the close of another sermon, Augustine anticipates the departure of the congregation when he puts the codex away and finishes preaching:

depositurus sum et ego codicem istum, discessuri estis et uos quisque ad sua. bene nobis fuit in luce communi, bene gauisi sumus, bene exsultauimus; sed cum ab inuicem recedimus, ab illo non recedamus.

(*Tractatus in Iohannem* 35.9)

For my part, I will put down this manuscript, and you for yours will each return to your homes. It was good for us to share this day, good to rejoice, good to sing praise. But even though we have parted from each other, we will never part from him.

On a few notable occasions, it is explicitly recorded that Augustine took up a codex during his sermon, as in the middle of *Sermo* 362:

sed ex ipso codice audite. propterea enim non tantum disputatoris sed etiam lectoris fungor officio, ut sermo iste noster sanctarum scripturarum auctoritate fulciatur, non humanis suspicionibus super arenam aedificetur, si forte aliquid non memoriter occurrerit. audite ergo euangelium secundum Iohannem. (*Sermo* 362.22.25)

But hear it from the manuscript itself. For I am fulfilling not only the role of the expositor, but also the *lector*, so that our sermon may be supported by the authority of the holy Scriptures and not be built on the sand of human suggestions, should relying on memory perhaps result in leaving something out. Hear, then, the Gospel according to John.[24]

23 Similar imaginary scenes occur at *Enarratio* 21.s2.29 and *Sermo* 72A.5, where Augustine threatens to suffocate his Manichaean objector with the gospel book! There is a hint that the passage in *Sermo* 133 is also directed against the Manichees, as the reference *ille qui promittebat se docturum me ueritatem* (*Sermo* 133.5) appears to reflect the Manichees' use of John 16:13. This topic also forms part of the discussion in *Contra Faustum*.

24 It is a matter of debate whether the liturgical reading of the Gospel was undertaken by a *lector* or a deacon (see, for example, Dulaey and Klöckener

Augustine's frequent emphasis on the exact wording of the passage read earlier in the service implies that he was relying on the same manuscript which had been used for the liturgical proclamation of the Gospel. At the beginning of *Sermo* 356 it is explicitly recorded that the deacon handed the codex to Augustine, who repeats the passage:

cumque Lazarus diaconus recitans episcopo codicem tradidisset, Augustinus episcopus dixit: et ego legere uolo. plus enim me delectat huius uerbi esse lectorem quam uerbi mei disputatorem. (*Sermo* 356.1)

And when Lazarus, the deacon who declaimed, had handed the manuscript to the bishop, Augustine the bishop said: 'I too want to read. For I take greater pleasure in being a reader of this word than an expounder of my own.'

Again, in *Sermo* 374 (*Dolbeau* 23), Augustine takes a codex of Isaiah for his sermon, lamenting his inability to recall the Bible as well as classical poetry:

ecce lego uobis, ne forte aliquid memoriam meam fugiat. ego enim, fratres, ab adolescentia litteras istas non didici et alia, quod peius est, superflua possum memoriter recitari. ista uero quibus non a pueritia studui, nisi codices inspiciam, pronuntiare non possum. aut forte magis utile est quod non ex ore meo, sed ex diuino libro, auditis quod salubriter noueritis.

(*Sermo* 374.19 [*Dolbeau* 23])

See, I read to you in case anything should, by chance, escape my memory. You see, brothers, I have not studied these writings from my youth, and, what is worse, I can recite other irrelevant texts from memory. Yet in the case of writings which I have not studied from my boyhood, I cannot speak out unless I consult the manuscripts. Besides, perhaps it is more useful that you hear this profitable knowledge not from my mouth but from the sacred book.

2002:1149). Comments such as this do not provide strong evidence, as Augustine always contrasts the activities of reading and preaching (e.g. *iam non disputator, sed lector factus sum* in *Sermo* 374.21). As deacons had various other duties, to use *diaconus* in such circumstances would fail to convey the intended emphasis; conversely, statements about the involvement of deacons in the gospel reading are more significant (e.g. *Sermo* 356.1, cited below, or *Sermo* 139A.1). Paoli-Lafaye 1986:66 sets much store by the phrase *uox lectoris et tractatoris* at *Tractatus in Iohannem* 22.2, but this seems to be another loose conjunction of two activities rather than proof that lectors read the Gospel; she herself admits that lectors in North Africa did not preach.

Finally, Augustine describes in *Epistula* 29 to Alypius how, on one occasion early in his ministry when asked to preach on a particularly difficult topic by his bishop Valerius, he used several codices for the same address, quoting first from Exodus and then 1 Corinthians and Galatians, while on the next day he cited the Epistles of Peter. This was presumably an exceptional case: none of his mature sermons mention such a flurry of textual activity, although he would have been able to refer to the collection of biblical manuscripts available in the church.

As Augustine was reading from a biblical codex and his words were being recorded by a stenographer, this suggests that, as in the case of the debates, the scriptural citations in his sermons reflect the manuscript which he used. Of course, this would only be true of the passage which is the subject of his exegesis: illustrative quotations from other parts of the Bible are likely to have been produced from memory.[25] Even so, there are indications that the biblical references in Augustine's sermons have been transcribed exactly as spoken. For example, in *Sermo* 72A.3 he expounds a passage from Matthew 12, stating in the middle of a five-verse citation *euangelium sequor* ('I am following the Gospel'): despite the date assigned to this sermon of 417–18, this long passage has a distinctly Old Latin text form and consistent renderings not preserved in any surviving codex.[26] Furthermore, in the initial citation Augustine appears to misread the text of Matthew 12:47, quoting it with *foris sunt* rather than the customary *foris stant* which appears two paragraphs later. A similar example is found in *Sermo* 129 on John 5:39–47, which features a double form of John 5:44:

> *quae fuit doctrina Pharisaeorum nisi quam modo audistis? gloriam ab inuicem quaerentes, gloriam ab inuicem expectantes, et gloria quae a solo deo est non quaerentes.* (*Sermo* 129.2)

What was the teaching of the Pharisees except what you have just heard? Seeking glory from each other, looking for glory from each other, and not seeking the glory which comes from God alone.

25 See further the discussion of 'flattening' on pp. 68–70.

26 In place of *quaerentes* Augustine has *uolentes* in Matthew 12:46 and *uolunt* in 12:47; where all manuscripts have *dixit* he reads *nuntiauit* in 12:47 and *ait* in 12:49; in both 12:49 and 12:50 he has the dative of possession, *mihi*, rather than a possessive adjective.

The initial use of *quaerentes* ('seeking') appears to be a mistake, anticipating *quaerentes* later in the verse, which Augustine immediately corrects to *expectantes* ('looking for'), the form of text he uses throughout this sermon. The stenographer, however, has recorded both forms and they have remained unaltered. There are numerous such non-standard forms of text in Augustine's sermons. In addition, some variants in the biblical citations may be characteristic of particular churches, because Augustine probably used local copies of Scripture when preaching away from Hippo.[27] Nonetheless, his propensity for paraphrase and reliance on memory mean that not all citations in sermons are equally valuable as sources for the scriptural text: the task of determining the probable reading of the codex used by Augustine requires careful analysis. To anticipate a conclusion from later in this work, the initial citation of each verse of a lectionary passage seems to be the most likely to represent the text of Augustine's manuscript, after which he reverted to memory.

Augustine tells us that he used scribes while composing his other theological works (e.g. *Retractationes* 1.26). His method of working was usually to dictate a passage, which his secretary then produced in longhand. This was then read back to the author, or he went over the draft himself, writing alterations directly onto the copy. It has been claimed that the earliest surviving manuscript of *De doctrina christiana* contains two corrections in the author's hand.[28] Although Augustine treats *dictare* and *scribere* as equivalent, there is some evidence for his own writing: Possidius mentions a sheet in the library at Hippo written by Augustine:

> *quaternio unus quam propria manu sanctus episcopus Augustinus initiauit.*
>
> (Indiculus X^3.n.15)

[27] See Hombert 2000:329. Unfortunately, there are rarely enough citations from the same passage to permit more than a tentative suggestion, and the location and date of many sermons remain unknown. Characteristics of the biblical text in Carthage and Thagaste are suggested in Chapter 6 below.

[28] Green 1962:229, who suggests that the reading ***omnes*** *prophetae* in Matthew 22:40 is peculiar to Augustine, and no-one but he would have added the word at *De doctrina christiana* 1.26.27 and 1.30.31 in the oldest surviving manuscript. On the writing practices of Latin Church Fathers, see Dekkers 1952:127–39: although Jerome copied certain manuscripts, Dekkers concludes that Ambrose was the only Father who made a habit of composing his own works in writing.

One fascicle which the holy bishop Augustine began with his own hand.

Not all works in sermon form were delivered in public. Augustine describes his *Sermones ad populum* as *alios dictatos, alios a me dictos* (*Retractationes* 2.epilogus).[29] The discovery of *Epistula* 23A* indicates that the later sermons in the *Tractatus in Iohannem* were dictated rather than preached:

et ut faciam de Iohannis quoque euangelio ea quae restant, dictare iam coepi populares tractatus non prolixos mittendos Carthaginem.

(*Epistula* 23A*.3.6)

And in order also to do what remains for the Gospel of John, I have already begun to dictate short congregational sermons to be sent to Carthage.

Sermons composed by dictation have a noticeably higher proportion of references to variants in biblical translations and Greek readings, which may indicate that Augustine consulted volumes from his library during the process of composition. In fact, a line in the *Quaestiones in Heptateuchum* following a reference to Aulus Gellius may be an instruction to an assistant to check the exact form of the quotation which was mistakenly incorporated into the text:

sed considerandum est quemadmodum hoc dicat A. Gellius, et diligenter inserendum. (*Quaestiones de Genesi* 30)

But it is necessary to consider the manner in which Aulus Gellius says this, and incorporate it carefully.

In the case of shorter references to the Bible and classical authors, citations are likely to have been drawn from memory.[30] A codex would have been used for the longer passages, as demonstrated not just by the length and accuracy of the extracts, but also by the sequence in which they appear. For example, in the review of Jewish prophecies in *De ciuitate dei* 17, Augustine cites up to ten verses at a time from Jeremiah, 1 Samuel, 2 Samuel, the Psalms, and Wisdom.

[29] Compare also the statement: *psalmos ceteros . . . partim sermocinando in populis, partim dictando exposui* (*Enarratio in Psalmos* 118. prol). Some prefer the reading *dictatas* in *Retractationes* 2, which they apply only to the *Epistulae* (e.g. Deferrari 1922:99); however, a strong case is made at Pontet 1946:3 for *dictatos*, which is also the text of Mutzenbecher's edition.

[30] On classical texts, see O'Donnell 1980; this is also borne out by the textual character of Augustine's citations from John (see Parts II and III).

The section on the Last Days in *De ciuitate dei* 20 also has lengthy citations from the Gospels, Revelation, and the Epistles in that order, followed by discussions of Isaiah, Daniel, and Malachi. The chapters on Revelation read as a commentary, as Augustine treats the whole of Revelation 20 in sequence in *De ciuitate dei* 20.7–16, and it is inconceivable that such a detailed exegesis could have been composed without reference to the written text. Similarly, in book one of *De trinitate*, there are clusters of citations from four passages of John (5:22–9, 12:47–50, 14:17–28, and 16:22–8) which probably indicate the use of a manuscript.[31]

The codex format made it easier to look up a passage, but there does not seem to have been a consistent scheme for giving references. Modern chapter and verse divisions are not replicated in biblical manuscripts from antiquity, and Old Latin Gospels show different ways of dividing the text. Some have traces of chapters, while smaller sense-units are indicated by lines extending into the left margin or other types of punctuation.[32] Augustine's only use of *uersus* occurs in the *Speculum quis ignorat*, a collection of biblical *testimonia* which, it has been suggested, he created by marking up the texts in a codex before handing it to a copyist. The citations appear in the same sequence as in the original scriptural book, with an occasional reference to the number of *uersus* which separate them, although it is not clear whether these refer to sentences, sense-lines, or indented text.[33] Words for chapter, *caput* and *capitulum*, appear more frequently. At *Contra Fortunatum* 19, Augustine refers to *capita* in the Epistle to the Romans, while a section of the letter of Mani is designated by *caput* at *Contra Felicem* 1.16. *Capitulum* is used for scriptural citations in Augustine's debates with Faustus and

[31] It is possible that this may have been a collection of *testimonia* rather than a biblical manuscript (cf. *De trinitate* 1.6.13), but this is immaterial for the present discussion; see pp. 153–6 below.

[32] A helpful summary is provided at Bogaert 1988:286–8 with references to earlier work. Petitmengin (1985:100–3) suggests that there are indications of chapters in Codex Vercellensis, one of the earliest surviving Old Latin manuscripts; a few later codices have the system of eighteen *kephalaia* in John also present in the Greek tradition.

[33] For a detailed discussion of the use of *uersus* in the *Speculum*, see Petitmengin 2003:7–14; the use of a codex is suggested at Burkitt 1910:266–7. For more on this work and its scriptural text, see pp. 174–5.

Adimantus, but comes to indicate the argument which they were used to support rather than the biblical text itself: for example, Augustine alludes to Pelagius' *Liber capitulorum* and the *capitula* of Caelestius.[34] References to *capitulum* in sermons usually indicate a liturgical lection. At the opening of the second *Tractatus in Iohannem*, before quoting the first five verses of the Gospel he says:

capitulum primum praeterito die dominico tractatum esse meminimus.

(*Tractatus in Iohannem* 2.1)

We remember that the first *capitulum* was expounded on the previous Sunday.

The length of these texts can vary considerably: in *Tractatus* 28 it covers the opening thirteen verses of John 7 (cf. *Sermo* 133.1), while in *Tractatus* 96 it only comprises two verses from John 16. Even when citing from memory, however, Augustine often demonstrates a high level of accuracy regarding the relative position of citations, using phrases such as *paulo post* or *post aliquantulum* ('shortly after') to indicate their degree of separation in the original text.[35]

A couple of other features may provide indications that Augustine has drawn his text from a manuscript. The first is the use of the phrase *audi quod sequitur* ('hear what follows') or some other form of *sequi* before citations. This occurs frequently in *Sermo* 374, when Augustine is demonstrably using a manuscript of Isaiah, as well as throughout the *Tractatus in Iohannem*; similarly, *deinde sequitur* appears before one of the Old Latin citations of Matthew taken from a codex in *Sermo* 72A.2. Another detail, primarily in theological works, is the amount of information supplied about the source in the introduction to the citation. Although general references to the Evangelists are unlikely to be significant, Augustine takes great care at *De gratia et libero arbitrio* 2.4 to specify the addressees of the Pauline

[34] e.g. *De gestis Pelagii* 14.30, 30.55. On the anti-Manichaean works, see Decret 1970:66. For more on *capitula* of the Bible and in Augustine's own works, see Petitmengin 1994:1033–4.

[35] For example, *paulo post* separates John 4:21 and 4:23 in *Sermo* 198.11, and John 17:11 and 17:20 in *Epistula* 238.4.28 and *Contra Maximinum* 2.22.1; *post aliquantulum* is found between these verses in *Contra Maximinum* 1.12 and between John 6:44 and 6:60 in *De praedestinatione sanctorum* 8.15. For more examples, see Petitmengin 2003:9.

Epistles from which he is quoting. This may mean that he is using either a scriptural codex or a book of *testimonia* in which the extracts are identified by title: it is also a feature of the *testimonia* in *De peccatorum meritis* 1.27.40–52 and his lengthy citations in the last three books of *De ciuitate dei* which were clearly read from an exemplar.[36]

Some of Augustine's works include verbatim quotations from other authors drawn from manuscripts in his possession (e.g. Cyprian's *Sententiae episcoporum* at *De baptismo* 6.6 or Porphyry at *De ciuitate dei* 19.23). There are also several occasions on which he quotes his own works. His practice of reproducing large portions from his opponents' writings in his polemical works means that, ironically, he is often their only surviving source. On the other hand, excerpting these texts may have allowed Augustine to define the argument on his own terms rather than sending enquirers back to the original. Indeed, he is criticized by Gaudentius for setting his work against Petilianus, *Contra litteras Petiliani*, in the form of a dialogue by turning his opponent's written text into an imaginary interlocutor. This practice is also employed in *Contra Faustum*. Augustine may also have been motivated by a practical concern to prevent his opponents eluding his rebuttals by later emendation of their work. There was additionally the perennial problem of mistaken attribution and poor copies: Augustine discovered after writing his first work against Julian of Eclanum, *Contra Iulianum*, that his manuscript was partial and corrupt. On receiving a complete text, he found he had to begin again, citing large sections of his opponent in the unfinished refutation *Contra Iulianum opus imperfectum*. One concomitant feature of these quotations is that Augustine often preserves the biblical citations of his opponent in their original form, providing important evidence for a range of versions of Scripture which no longer survive.

In sum, biblical manuscripts circulated freely in Augustine's world and he had a substantial collection himself of both Greek and Latin codices which he frequently consulted. When preaching, he would refer during his sermon to the text which had been used for the

[36] This concern for detail may also represent the growing importance of references and sources in the Church in Augustine's final years: see Vessey 1998.

liturgical lection, and sometimes repeat it from the same copy. Augustine's sermons and public debates were usually transcribed by teams of stenographers attached to the church: even though official copies were kept in the library at Hippo, there is also evidence for the circulation of unauthorized versions. Many of his sermons do not seem to have been revised by Augustine, which means that incidental details of historical significance are sometimes preserved: unfortunately, much of this apparently trivial information may have been removed by later excerptors. Nonetheless, the text of certain biblical citations in these stenographic records seems likely to represent the manuscripts used by Augustine. Longer citations from the Bible, especially those which appear in sequence, and other texts in his theological writings were probably also drawn directly from an exemplar. Augustine made full use of his secretarial team and network of friends to publicize and distribute his own writings and to acquire works of other authors, ensuring that Hippo was one of the best-stocked libraries in the African Church.

3

Augustine's Biblical Exposition and Citation Technique

Augustine's first encounter with the Christian Scriptures was profoundly negative, as he tells us in *Confessiones* 3.5.9.[1] In comparison with the texts of the classical canon which he had learnt at school and which provided the models for his career as a rhetorician, he found the unadorned style and occasional infelicities of these translations quite off-putting. He was next introduced to the Bible when he became a Manichaean *auditor*, although the original texts were mediated through the works of Mani and exegesis was jealously guarded by the higher class of initiates, the *electi*.[2] It was only when he discovered the allegorical approach of Ambrose in Milan that Augustine felt he had found a satisfactory hermeneutic which he could employ to identify spiritual truths behind the problems of the contradictory façade. The predominantly literary nature of his conversion is reinforced by the famous scene in *Confessiones* 8.12.29, in which he hears the command '*tolle, lege*', 'take and read'.[3]

[1] *Non enim sicut modo loquor, ita sensi, cum attendi ad illam scripturam, sed uisa est mihi indigna, quam Tullianae dignitati compararem. tumor enim meus refugiebat modum eius et acies mea non penetrabat interiora eius.* See further O'Donnell 1992 *ad loc.*, who quotes similar passages at *De utilitate credendi* 6.13 and *Sermo* 51.5.6.

[2] Stock 1996:46 and Lancel 2002:53–4 note that only the higher ranks of Manichees knew the canonical Scriptures. Several writers, however, suggest that Augustine's interpretation of Scripture as sign may owe something to Manichaean teaching: see Vessey 1993:204, Margerie 1983:46.

[3] Bochet's fine recent work on the development of Augustine's exegesis includes a section on the historicity and significance of this scene (2004:266–93); Dulaey 2003:62–3 also argues that Romans 13:13 had a genuine impact on Augustine at this point given its appearance in *Epistula* 22.

Once a Christian, Augustine began to apply his rhetorical training to the Bible. A programme of biblical study formed part of his catechumenate.[4] He also spent a period of retreat at Cassiciacum before his baptism, exploring the doctrines of his new-found faith from a predominantly neo-Platonist stance. It has often been noted how few scriptural citations are found in his works from this period. Despite composing some early apologetic works, Augustine's engagement with Scripture seems to have become a more pressing concern when faced with the pastoral and homiletic task of Christian ministry. Following his ordination as priest in 391, Augustine asked his bishop, Valerius, for time to study the Bible (*Epistula* 21.3). This request appears to have been granted, and Augustine's gradual assimilation of the text of Scripture can be seen in the increasing proportion of citations in his works and his biblical commentaries. In the *Retractationes*, he acknowledges his early lack of familiarity with the Scriptures when correcting a citation made in *De moribus* (387–8):

mendositas nostri codicis me fefellit minus memorem scripturarum in quibus nondum assuetus eram. (*Retractationes* 1.7.2)

The faultiness of our codex was less of a hindrance to me than the remembrance of the Scriptures, with which I had not yet become familiar.

Similarly, his account of an early sermon in *Epistula* 29, looking up relevant passages in his codex of Paul's Epistles, offers a vivid picture of an exegete still learning his craft. Augustine continued to devote considerable time to biblical study: in *Epistula* 73.5, he complains to Jerome that his ecclesiastical duties hindered his research. His admission on taking up a codex of Isaiah in *Sermo* 374.19 that he could not recall the scriptural text with the same accuracy as secular works has already been quoted above.[5] It was also noted that the appointment of Eraclius as his assistant towards the end of Augustine's ministry was intended to give the bishop more time to devote to the study of Scripture (*Epistula* 213.5). Possidius, however, tells us that even on his deathbed, Augustine

4 See Duval 1985:270–7 and La Bonnardière 1975:151–3.

5 Page 36 above.

asked for certain psalms to be copied out so that he could meditate on them.[6]

Augustine would have encountered the Bible most frequently in the course of attending Christian worship, not just in the form of lectionary readings, but in the repetition of key verses in responses and canticles. This regular exposure to Scripture assisted memorization, although it is going too far to suggest that the congregation knew all the lessons and associated psalms off by heart.[7] The collections of *testimonia* which circulated, such as Cyprian's *Testimonia ad Quirinum* or Ambrose's *De spiritu sancto*, also provided an armoury of key biblical illustrations and proof-texts.[8] Learning these would have been an important tool in preaching and debates. In controversies between different sectarian groups, both sides had recourse to Scripture as the ultimate authority. Augustine developed his own dossier of biblical verses to counter his opponents' collection of proof-texts, and the same verses are found in combination across a number of his works, which often assists with determining their chronology.

Augustine's attitude to Scripture combines dogmatism with pragmatism. While he maintains that the Bible is the inspired word of God, whose authority is not to be contested, he also provides the classic statement of the validation of Scripture by the the Church:

[6] *Nam sibi iusserat psalmos dauidicos, qui sunt paucissimi de poenitentia, scribi, ipsosque quaterniones iacens in lecto contra parietem positos diebus suae infirmitatis intuebatur, et legebat* (Possidius *Vita Augustini* 31.2).

[7] Thus La Bonnardière 1986:57; the only illustration of this is the resistance to Jerome's revised text of Jonah mentioned in *Epistula* 71. She also observes that more than half of Augustine's biblical citations occur during the context of Christian worship, something she terms 'la Bible liturgique' (see La Bonnardière 1975 and 1986:56). Both references to memorization in Augustine listed by Petitmengin 1994:1036, *De catechizandis rudibus* 3.5 and *Enarrationes in Psalmos* 102.25, deny the importance of committing large portions of Scripture to memory; *De doctrina christiana* 2.9.14, however, emphasizes the benefit of committing biblical books to memory 'or at least having some acquaintance with them' (*legendo tamen uel mandare memoriae uel omnino incognitos non habere*).

[8] Augustine refers to a *testimonia* collection at *De trinitate* 1.6.13, and he quotes the prologue of Ambrose's work in *De doctrina christiana* 4.21.46: see further La Bonnardière 1965:83–7 and Saxer 1985b:350–1. Pelagius also compiled a set of *testimonia*: see Plinval 1943:76 and 106. The brief proofs from prophecy in *De ciuitate dei* 22.3 may also derive from an earlier collection. Albl 1999 considers early Christian *testimonia* collections in detail.

ego uero euangelio non crederem nisi me catholicae ecclesiae commoueret auctoritas. (*Contra epistulam fundamenti* 5.6)

In truth, I would not believe the Gospel unless the authority of the Catholic Church prompted me.[9]

The continuous involvement of the Church in the transmission of the written records safeguards their accuracy, as Augustine explains in a comment on John 17:20:

quotquot enim postea crediderunt in eum per uerbum apostolorum sine dubio crediderunt, et donec ueniat, credituri sunt; ipsis enim dixerat *et uos testimonium perhibebitis quia ab initio mecum estis*; et per hos euangelium ministratus est et antequam scriberetur; et utique quisquis in Christum credit, euangelio credit... quoniam ipsi qui cum illo tunc fuerunt quod ab illo audierunt ceteris praedicauerunt; atque ita uerbum eorum ut etiam nos crederemus ad nos usque peruenit, ubicumque est eius ecclesia, et peruenturum est ad posteros. (*Tractatus in Iohannem* 109.1)

For as many as believed in Jesus later did so, without doubt, through the words of the apostles, and they will go on believing until he comes. For he had said to the apostles '*You too will bear witness, because you were with me from the beginning*' and through them the Gospel was passed on even before it was written. Assuredly, anyone who believes in Christ, believes the Gospel... since the same people who were with him then preached to others what they heard from him, and thus, wherever his Church is, their words have reached as far as us, so that we too would believe, and will reach future generations.

The idea of Scripture as a temporary vehicle of revelation until the return of Christ is often asserted by Augustine, most fully at *Tractatus in Iohannem* 35.9:

quando ergo dominus noster Iesus Christus uenerit... non legetur nobis propheta, non aperietur codex apostoli, non requiremus testimonium Iohannis, non ipso indigebimus euangelio. ergo omnes scripturae tollentur de medio.

(*Tractatus in Iohannem* 35.9)

[9] Some commentators consider that Augustine has used the imperfect subjunctive here in place of the pluperfect and is therefore referring to his own spiritual journey: 'I would not *have believed* the Gospel...' See further Polman 1961:178 and 198–208, who argues that this citation has to be understood within its polemical context. For more on the importance of the Church, see *De utilitate credendi* 14.31 and *De ciuitate dei* 15.26.2.

When, therefore, our Lord Jesus Christ shall have come . . . the prophet will not be read by us, the codex of the apostle will not be opened, we shall not need the witness of John, we shall not require the Gospel itself. All Scriptures will therefore be removed from before us.

Similarly, in *Sermo* 57 he asks rhetorically:

numquid angelis codices sunt necessarii, aut disputatores, aut lectores?

(*Sermo* 57.5.5)

Are codices, or preachers, or readers necessary for the angels?

Instead, he describes the Bible as a form of divine accommodation to human limitations, or a continuation of the Incarnation through which God continues to speak to his followers. This, and the accompanying position that true understanding of Scripture can only be achieved with God's assistance, plays an important part in his approach to exegesis.[10]

Much has been made of Augustine's use of the same techniques for biblical exposition which he had employed as a teacher of rhetoric.[11] The recent research of Dulaey, however, has shown that his development as an exegete was based on a careful reading of earlier Latin Christian writers, including Ambrose, Ambrosiaster, Tertullian, Cyprian, Optatus, and translations of Origen. In a series of articles, she charts the correspondences between Augustine's observations and surviving works, as well as identifying shared sources which are no longer extant, such as Latin commentaries on Genesis and Matthew.[12] As Augustine only seems to have become fluent in Greek later in his career, he was initially dependent on translations. References to the significance of biblical places or names were culled from *onomastica* such as Jerome's *Liber interpretationis Hebraicorum nominum*.[13]

[10] For Scripture as accommodation, see Polman 1961, especially 105 and 126; his whole study offers a readable introduction to Augustine's attitude to the Bible. Margerie 1983:25 and Norris 1993 also refer to the incarnational aspect of the Bible. Further references to codices are supplied in Petitmengin 1994:1035–7.

[11] Lawless offers illuminating comparisons of Augustine's exposition of John 9 in *Tractatus in Iohannem* 44, the construction of *Tractatus in Iohannem* 124, and the techniques of the Roman *grammaticus* (Lawless 1996 and 1992 respectively). See also Drobner 2004, and, on Augustine's use of rhetorical figures, Marrou 1938:79–83.

[12] See Dulaey 2002, 2003, and 2005 which cover works written between 386 and 394.

[13] Augustine appears to have taken the etymology of Lazarus from Jerome (*Quaestiones euangeliorum* 2.38.1; Berrouard 1969:829), although Dulaey 2002:293–4

Augustine's use of technical vocabulary for exegesis also reflects different stages in his apprenticeship: prior to his ordination, he makes a binary division between *historia* and *prophetia* in *De Genesi contra Manichaeos*, while in two works from 393 he presents a four-fold scheme of *historia*, *allegoria*, *analogia*, and *aetiologia* which he seems soon to have discarded.[14] Instead he moves towards an approach which is less inspired by rhetoric and more in keeping with the particular problems of biblical interpretation, the theme of much of *De doctrina christiana*.

The composition of this handbook of biblical interpretation gives an indication of Augustine's increasing authority as an exegete, although he left the work unfinished for almost three decades. Its concern with the practical results of biblical interpretation also demonstrates his recognition of the connection between the roles of preacher and pastor following his consecration as bishop. Peter Brown observes that the contemporary *Confessiones*, sometimes seen as a companion work to *De doctrina christiana*, were a turning point at which Augustine 'had come to believe that the understanding and exposition of the Scriptures was the heart of a bishop's life'. Similarly, Gerald Bonner states that 'The most important feature of Augustine's biblical exegesis is its ecclesial quality'.[15] For Augustine, the Bible had to be read within the context of the Church which produced and transmitted it.

Augustine's principal exegetical concern is what constitutes a valid reading of a biblical text and how it might be applied. The first step is

suggests that both writers depended on a common source. It is generally agreed that Augustine had not read Origen's *Commentary on John*, as it had not been translated into Latin (Berrouard 1988:420–1 and Altaner 1952:209; see also Comeau 1930:29–39), although Augustine reproduces some of Origen's explanations and mentions him by name at *De ciuitate dei* 15.27.3. It is only Augustine's latest works, such as *Contra Iulianum* in 421/2 and the translation of *De haeresibus* in 428–9, which demonstrate his ability to read a patristic Greek text; see further the description of his library on p. 26 above and Altaner 1952.

[14] *De Genesi ad litteram opus imperfectum* and *De utilitate credendi* 3.5; see Dulaey 2005:22–5. Her suggestion that this stilted classification may have originated with Augustine's bishop, Valerius, is highly plausible.

[15] Brown 2000:155 and Bonner 1970:561 (see also Hardy 1974:184, Loewen 1981:203–7, and Pontet 1946:157); on the *Confessiones* and *De doctrina christiana* as a diptych composed against the scholastic tendencies of a Hieronymian approach to exegesis, see Vessey 1993. Young 1997:271 notes how the latter combines Augustine's earlier rhetorical training with a distinctively Christian approach.

to understand the whole passage rather than excerpting phrases which appear to support a particular argument:

quia testimonium, quod profertur, de contextione totius psalmi debet habere suffragium, ut certe nihil sit quod ei refrageretur, si non omnia suffragantur, ne more centonum ad rem, quam uolumus, tamquam uersiculos decerpere uideamur. (*De ciuitate dei* 17.15)

... because the example which is brought forward must have support from the context of the whole psalm, that if not everything is in favour there may be nothing which definitely opposes it, so that we do not appear to be plucking verses to support the position we wish, in the style of patchwork.

Similarly, at *De peccatorum meritis* 1.30.59, he cites a long passage from the Gospel according to John in order to give the background (*circumstantia*). Without this, an interpreter may fail to observe the identity of the speakers:

sed quando inquirentes probari nobis aliquid uolumus testimonio sanctorum eloquiorum, non nobis dicatur credendum esse etiam quod in euangelio scriptum esse, si forte euangelista eum hoc dixisse commemorat, cui fides habenda non est. (*Ad Orosium contra Priscillianistas* 9.12)

But when we want to prove something to ourselves by seeking the evidence of the holy writings, let it be stated that we do not have to believe even what is written in the Gospel, as the evangelist may have recorded the words of someone who should not be trusted.

Augustine illustrates this with the comment of the Jews at John 8:48, *Samaritanus es tu et daemonium habes*, which could supply a scriptural mandate indicating that Jesus was both a Samaritan and demon-possessed![16] A second concern is for a consensus of interpretation:

sic et in ceteris interpretationibus figurarum per uniuersum textum diuinae scripturae licet considerare et conparare sensus eorum, qui Christum ibi intellegunt, et eorum, qui praeter Christum ad alia quaelibet ea detorquere conantur. (*Contra Faustum* 12.39)

Thus, too, in the other explanations of figures throughout the whole text of Holy Scripture, we must consider and contrast the ideas of those who

[16] For more examples of the importance of context to Augustine, see Polman 1961:62–3.

understand Christ to be intended, and those who, instead of Christ, try to twist it round to something else entirely.

This reliance on an interpretative community brings scriptural exegesis firmly within the domain of the Church. Indeed, Augustine describes one of his key exegetical principles as the *regula sana catholica* ('sound catholic rule'; *Tractatus in Iohannem* 18.2): when interpreting texts concerning Christ, it is necessary to determine to which of his two natures they apply, the divine or the human.[17] A common shorthand way of expressing this is to take Philippians 2:6–7 as a hermeneutic principle, enabling material to be categorized as *forma dei* ('in the form of God') or *forma serui* ('in the form of a servant'). In the Gospel according to John, with its varied expressions of the relationship of the Father to the Son, this distinction is frequently invoked by Augustine in order to maintain scriptural unity.[18]

The principle of the unity of Scripture is a corollary of its divine inspiration. At *Contra aduersarium legis* 1.17.35, Augustine explicitly calls God the 'author of both testaments' (*auctor amborum testamentorum*), while elsewhere he describes the activity of the Holy Spirit on the biblical writers:

quoniam uidebo coelos tuos, opera digitorum tuorum. legimus digito dei scriptam legem, et datam per Moysen sanctum seruum eius: quem digitum dei multi intellegunt spiritum sanctum. quapropter si digitos dei, eosdem ipsos ministros spiritu sancto repletos, propter ipsum spiritum qui in eis operatur, recte accipimus, quoniam per eosdem nobis omnis diuina scriptura confecta est; conuenienter intellegimus hoc loco coelos dictos libros utriusque testamenti. (*Enarratio in Psalmos* 8.7)

Since I will see your heavens, the works of your fingers (Psalm 8:4). We read that the Law was written by the finger of God and given through his holy

[17] See Berrouard 1977:123, 731–2 and Lienhard 1996:14; this principle is also set out as the *regula catholicae fidei* at *De diuersis quaestionibus* 69.1 and the *regula intellegendarum scripturarum de filio dei* at *De trinitate* 1.11.22 (see further Polman 1961:209–13). Berrouard observes that Augustine later introduces a third class of text at *De trinitate* 2.1–4, which express Christ's power over humanity without implying any inequality with the Father.

[18] e.g. *Tractatus in Iohannem* 99.1. Norris 1993 gives a good summary of Augustine's hermeneutical principles in the *Tractatus in Iohannem*, drawing out the theme of Scripture as a continuation of the Incarnation.

servant Moses: many understand this 'finger of God' to be the Holy Spirit. Therefore we may correctly take the fingers of God as those very servants filled with the Holy Spirit, because of the Spirit at work in them, since through them all divine Scripture was accomplished for us; we fittingly understand that the books of each Testament are called 'heavens' in this place.

This provides an example of the distinction made by Augustine between the role of ministers, who are always identified with the preposition *per* ('through'), and the divine source, indicated by a plain ablative (e.g. *digito dei*). Elsewhere, he speaks of the Bible being 'delivered through humans' (*per homines ministratae sunt scripturae*).[19] Despite the potential for inconsistency between writers, Augustine takes it as axiomatic that holy Scripture nowhere contradicts itself (*scriptura sancta in nulla parte discordat*; *Sermo* 82.9). The most famous summary of this is found in the *Quaestiones in Heptateuchum*:

. . . quamquam et in Vetere Nouum lateat, et in Nouo Vetus pateat.

(*Quaestiones in Exodo* 73)

. . . although the New may lie hidden in the Old, and the Old be revealed in the New.

Another significant image is found at *Tractatus in Iohannem* 9.5 where Augustine speaks of Christ turning the water of the Old Testament into the wine of the New.[20]

One of Augustine's most common hermeneutical devices, the principle of *scriptura sui interpres*, Scripture as its own interpreter, relies on this doctrine of the unity of the Bible. It is based on the assumption that the best way of clarifying obscurity or ambiguity is to compare similar expressions elsewhere in the same work, and has

[19] *Tractatus in Iohannem* 1.6; see also *De doctrina christiana* 3.27.38 and *De consensu euangelistarum* 3.7.30, while in *De consensu* 1.35.54, the process might almost be described as divine dictation: *quidquid enim ille de suis factis et dictis nos legere uoluit, hoc scribendum illis tamquam suis manibus imperauit.* Augustine's understanding of biblical inspiration is further considered in Polman 1961:39–54 and Bochet 2004 (especially pp. 44–50).

[20] See also, among other references, *De ciuitate dei* 5.18.3 and 20.4, and *Contra aduersarium legis* 1.17.35. The relationship between the Old and New Testaments in Augustine is treated at length in Pontet 1946:305–83 and Margerie 1983:55–9; see also Bochet 2004:466 ff. on Augustine's use of the New Testament to illuminate the Old.

parallels in ancient readings of Homer as well as Jewish rabbinic techniques: one commentator has dubbed it the 'concordance method' of exegesis.[21] Augustine summarizes the idea in another pithy tag:

sic est expositio diuinarum scripturarum sicut sunt ipsae diuinae scripturae.

(*Sermo* 125.1)

The explanation of the Holy Scriptures is just as the Holy Scriptures are themselves.

By treating the whole Bible as the product of divine inspiration, illustrations may legitimately be drawn from any canonical book. Augustine explains this theory when he examines two apparently contradictory texts containing the word *timor* (fear), 1 John 4:18 *(perfecta caritas foras mittit timorem)* with Psalm 18:10 *(timor domini castus, permanens in saeculum saeculi)*:

spiritus unus est, etsi codices duo, etsi ora duo, etsi linguae duae. hoc enim dictum est per Iohannem, illud dictum est per Dauid; sed nolite putare alium esse spiritum. si unus flatus inflat duas tibias, non potest unus spiritus implere duo corda, agitare duas linguas? sed si spiritu uno, id est uno flatu, impletae duae tibiae consonant; impletae duae linguae spiritu dei, dissonare possunt? est ergo ibi quaedam consonantia, est quaedam concordia, sed auditorem desiderat. ecce inspirauit et impleuit duo corda, duo ora, mouit duas linguas spiritus dei. (*In epistolam Iohannis* 9.5)[22]

There is one spirit, even if there are two books, two voices, two tongues: the first was spoken through John, the second through David, but do not think that it was a different spirit. If one breath blows two pipes, cannot one spirit fill two hearts, move two tongues? But if when filled with one spirit (that is one breath) the two pipes are in concord, can the two tongues filled by the spirit of God discord? Therefore there is a certain concord, a certain harmony here, but it requires someone to listen. See, the spirit of God has breathed out and filled two hearts, two mouths, and set two tongues in motion.

[21] Lienhard 1996:18; for classical texts, see also Fredouille (1985:41) and Marrou (1938:481, 495 ff.). The Hebrew practice of *gezerah shewa* or 'inference by analogy' is described at Young 1997:92 and Barrett 1970:393; Albl 1999:41 mentions its use by Christians in creating collections of *testimonia.*

[22] The reference to *codices duo* does not indicate that the entire Old Testament and New Testament were contained in two volumes, but rather that the two writings under discussion were found in separate books.

The vindication of this doctrine requires the reconciliation of inconsistencies in the biblical text, which occupies a considerable amount of Augustine's energy and ingenuity. Apparent contradictions occur even within the same book:

quamquam et ipsum euangelium potest putari sibi esse contrarium. quo modo enim uerum est quod in eo dicitur *qui me uidit uidit et patrem* si *deum nemo uidit umquam*? (*Epistula* 147.5.13 on John 14:9 and 1:18)

... although even the Gospel can be thought to be contrary to itself, for how can *Who sees me, sees the Father also* be a true saying if *No one has ever seen God*?

In most cases, the problem is resolved by careful attention to the exact form of the text before him. In response to the puzzle of John 14:24 (*qui non diligit me, sermones meos non seruat. et sermonem quem audistis non est meus, sed eius qui misit me patris*) Augustine suggests:

ecce suos dixit esse sermones; numquid sibi ipse est contrarius, ubi rursus dixit: *et sermo quem audistis non est meus*? et fortasse propter aliquam distinctionem, ubi suos dixit, dixit pluraliter, hoc est *sermones*; ubi autem *sermonem*, hoc est uerbum, non suum dixit esse, sed patris, seipsum intellegi uoluit.

(*Tractatus in Iohannem* 76.5)

See, he has said that his words are his own; surely he contradicts himself, when in turn he says: *and the word you have heard is not mine*? But perhaps there is some sort of distinction: when he refers to his own words, he uses the plural, *sermones*, but when he says that the *sermo*, word, is not his own but the Father's, he wishes it to be understood as himself.

Augustine is similarly exercised by Jesus' apparent inconsistency in attending the festival of John 7:8 after initially denying that it was his intention. A solution is to be found in a minor detail of the original statement, *ego non ascendo ad diem festum* ***istum*** ('I do not go up to **this** festival'). By suggesting in *Sermo* 133.7 that the festival lasted a number of days, Augustine clears Jesus of mendacity. Forced though such explanations may seem to modern readers, they indicate Augustine's fidelity to the text of Scripture: rather than proposing a conjectural emendation to resolve these difficulties, he follows the grammarians' practice of establishing the text before beginning the commentary, and not deviating from it in the exegesis.[23]

The express purpose of *De consensu euangelistarum* is to show how the four Gospels can be harmonized with each other. On several occasions, Augustine resorts to rather contrived arguments to affirm the accuracy of each source. For example, in the case of the timing of the crucifixion, where John has *hora quasi sexta* (John 19:14) and Mark *hora tertia* (Mark 15:25), Augustine offers two solutions, first invoking a metaphorical sense of *crucifixus*:

hora tertia crucifixus est dominus linguis iudaeorum, hora sexta manibus militum. (*Tractatus in Iohannem* 117.1)

The Lord was crucified at the third hour by the tongues of the Jews, at the sixth hour by the hands of the soldiers.

Alternatively, he suggests different starting points for the two evangelists:

hora tertia secundum Marcum, non praeparationis, sed diei; eademque sexta non diei, sed praeparationis, sex utique horis a noctis nona usque ad diei tertiam computatis. (*Tractatus in Iohannem* 117.2)

The third hour, according to Mark, was not of the festival but of the day; the sixth hour was not of the day but of the festival, since six is the total of the hours from the ninth of the night to the third of the day.

His concern with such discrepancies manifests itself even at the level of phrasing, as in the discussion as to whether John the Baptist is worthy to carry or loose the sandals of the Messiah comparing Matthew 3:11 and John 1:27:

itaque si ad rem pertinet aliquid aliud intellegere ex eo quod dictum est *calciamenta portare* et aliquid aliud ex eo quod dictum est *corrigiam calciamenti soluere* quid aliud accipiendum recte existimaueris nisi Iohannem utrumque dixisse, siue aliud alio tempore siue contextim? potuit enim sic dicere 'cuius non sum dignus corrigiam calciamenti soluere nec calciamenta portare' ut unus euangelistarum hinc aliud alii uero aliud omnes tamen uerum narrauerint. (*De consensu euangelistarum* 2.12.29)

Therefore, if it is relevant to understand one thing by the saying *to carry his sandals* and another by the saying *to loose the strap of his sandal*, would you

23 See the references to ancient reading techniques on p. 18 above.

rightly think that any other explanation should be received except that John the Baptist said both, either at different times or on the same occasion? For he could have said the following: 'the strap of whose sandal I am not worthy to loose, nor to carry his sandals', with the result that one of the evangelists related one part and the others the other part, but all told the truth.

Again, Augustine's solution preserves the integrity of the accounts as they have been transmitted to him. In fact, it has been observed that in such situations, he regularly presents two possible explanations rather than one: by leaving the choice open, in good dialectic style, he draws his audience into the dialogue of biblical exegesis.[24]

Augustine cites Scripture in a variety of ways. The most common introduction to scriptural citations is the impersonal formula *scriptum est* ('it is written'). The majority of his references to *codices* or *exemplaria* indicate the Bible.[25] Individual citations may be described by a variety of nouns: *uoces euangelicae* (*De duabus animabus* 9), *illum intellectum euangelicum* (*Enarratio in Psalmos* 55.9), and *illa euangelica tuba* (*Sermo* 331.1.1). A flavour of Augustine's appreciation of metaphors, often with biblical overtones, is given by some of his introductions to the first verse of John, which he describes as *plenitudo mensae* (*Sermo* 194.2.2), *solidus cibus* (*Sermo* 335K.5), and *patriam* (*Sermo* 92.3), picturing it also as divine thunder (*per quamdam nubem suam ipse intonuit*; *Enarratio in Psalmos* 29.s2.1) or a finely woven garment (*texuit pretiosissimum illud pallium laudis*; *Sermo* 37.17). Occasionally Scripture is personified: *euangelium loquitur* (*Sermo* 2.2), *euangelium respondet* (*Enarratio in Psalmos* 49.1), *docet scriptura* (*Contra Adimantum* 5), and *euangelium diuina uoce testatur* (*Sermo* 362.13.13).[26] Most frequently, however, Augustine

[24] See Harrison 2001:160 and Lienhard 1996:21; Wiles 1970:456 and 476 observes that Origen uses the same device. On Augustine's approach to exegesis as a dialogue, see also McCarthy 2007, especially 327 and 333. This is not the place to consider the thorny question of whether Augustine believed that Scripture contained a multiplicity of literal senses: a sympathetic discussion may be found at Margerie 1983:61–108.

[25] See further the figures and evidence in Petitmengin 1994, who notes that of the 636 instances of *codex* in Augustine, 551 refer to biblical manuscripts: it is qualified by *diuinus* on fourteen occasions, *sanctus* nineteen times, *dominicus* six times, and *canonicus* once (*Epistula* 44.14). *Exemplaria* (always in the plural) indicates the Bible on forty-five occasions.

[26] See also *scriptura testatur* (*De Genesi ad litteram* 5.13 on John 1:1); *praedicat scriptura* (*Sermo* 341 on John 1:14); *non tacuit euangelium* (*De dono perseuerantiae* 14.35 on John 12:37). Barrett 1970:391 notes that the personification of Scripture was

identifies the speaker as divine (e.g. *dixit dominus*): this is not restricted to words of Jesus in the Gospels, but also introduces prophetic and poetic citations from the Old Testament.[27] Certain abstract nouns are synonymous with God, especially 'wisdom' (e.g *De moribus* 1.16.28) and 'truth' (e.g. *Retractationes* 1.4.3). The writers of biblical books are less frequently mentioned by Augustine, and he rarely uses an abbreviated form such as 'the Gospel of John', emphasizing that it is the Gospel of Christ mediated by the evangelists.[28] When referring to biblical books by name he sometimes uses the Greek titles, as in *Sermo* 1.1 where he even borrows the preposition *κατά* for the gospel writer:

ipsa principia libri Geneseos et euangelii **cata** Iohannem. (*Sermo* 1.1)

The very beginnings of the book of Genesis and of the Gospel according to John.[29]

It has been suggested above that certain citations which are introduced by the title of their source may have been made with reference to a manuscript.[30]

also a Hebrew custom. It is rare to find *euangelium* qualified by an adjective other than *sanctum* (see Dulaey and Klöckener 2002:1147), although this phrase is by and large restricted to the liturgical context of Augustine's sermons.

27 Cyprian also identifies the first-person narrator of the Psalms with Christ (Fahey 1971:48); for Augustine's practice, see further Comeau 1930:291–8 and Knauer 1955:148, 183–5.

28 *De consensu euangelistarum*, where the evangelists have to be distinguished, is an exception. For other examples of his use of a 'short' gospel title, see *Contra Faustum* 17.3 and 28.2, *De haeresibus* 30, *Sermones* 239.1.1 and 259.2 and, of course, the title of the *Tractatus in Iohannis euangelium*, as noted in *Epistula* 23A*.3.6. Augustine identified the evangelist John with the author of the Johannine epistles and Revelation (e.g. *In epistolam Iohannis* 1.1, *Tractatus in Iohannem* 13.2 and 36.5): *euangelista* and *apostolus* are used interchangeably before citations of these books (as at *Epistula* 214.1, *De duabus animabus* 9, *Contra Iulianum opus imperfectum* 3.106). For the identification of John with the beloved disciple, see Dideberg 1986.

29 *Geneseos* here is a Greek genitive. The only other use of *κατά* I have found in Augustine is also *Contra epistulam fundamenti* 10: the Latin *secundum* is his customary form (e.g. *De doctrina christiana* 2.8.13). Running titles in Old Latin biblical manuscripts sometimes use *cata* (Parker 1992:13). In the *Itinerarium Egeriae*, it is used both of the evangelists and more generally (Löfstedt 1911:175). Another characteristic of Old Latin versions is the use of *Regnorum* ('Kingdoms') for the books known in the Vulgate as *Regum* ('Kings').

30 See pp. 41–2. Although Augustine often gives details when quoting other Christian sources, particularly in later works (see Vessey 1996 and 1998, Rebillard 2000), he prefers to cite classical authors in an allusive fashion, in keeping with

Augustine's longest citations, as already noted, are drawn from a codex. His expository sermons often begin with a reference back to the liturgical readings, which sometimes gives the impression of the preacher finding his place in the gospel book:

ad euangelicam lectionem, quae recens sonuit in auribus nostris, aduertat caritas uestra dum pauca loquimur quae dominus donat. ad Iudaeos dominus loquebatur Iesus, et dicebat eis: *scrutamini scripturas, in quibus putatis uos uitam aeternam habere; ipsae testimonium perhibent de me.* deinde post paululum: *ego,* inquit, *ueni in nomine patris mei et non accepistis me; si alius uenerit in nomine suo, illum accipietis.* deinde post paululum: *quomodo potestis mihi credere, gloriam ab inuicem exspectantes, et gloriam quae a deo solo est, non quaerentes?* ad extremum ait: *non ego uos accuso apud patrem; est qui uos accusat Moyses, in quem uos speratis. si enim crederetis Moysi, crederetis forsitan et mihi; de me enim ille scripsit. cum autem uerbis illius non creditis, quomodo potestis mihi credere?* ad haec proposita nobis diuinitus, ex ore lectoris, sed ministerio saluatoris, audite pauca non numeranda, sed appendenda. (*Sermo* 129.1; see also *Sermones* 29 and 356)

Dear friends, pay attention to the gospel reading which has just sounded in our ears, while we speak a few words which God grants us. The Lord Jesus was speaking to the Jews, and said to them: *Examine the Scriptures, in which you think you have eternal life: they bear witness to me.* Then, a little later, he says: *I have come in the name of my Father and you did not receive me: if another comes in his own name, you will receive him.* Then, a little later: *How can you believe me, hoping for renown from each other and not seeking the renown which comes from God alone?* At the very end, he says: *I do not accuse you in the presence of the Father: it is Moses who accuses you, in whom you place your hope. For if you believed Moses, perhaps you would also believe me, for he wrote about me. But since you do not believe his words, how can you believe me?* Concerning these statements of divinity to us from the mouth of the reader, but through the offices of the Saviour, hear a few more not to be counted among them, but added to the end.

There is occasionally a resumptive citation of several verses, which may also have assisted him in keeping his place in the manuscript during his sermon. Otherwise, Augustine normally treats the text in a linear fashion, quoting a single verse or a phrase at a time and analysing each clause and its constituent elements.

citation practice in antiquity. See further Müller 2003 and Hagendahl 1947. Stanley 1992:267–91 considers the textual characteristics of citations in Greco-Roman literature.

The most straightforward form of commentary is to interrupt the biblical text with brief explanations. An example of such glossing can be seen in his treatment of John 5:25:

amen dico uobis quia ueniet hora et nunc est quando mortui, id est infideles, *audient uocem filii dei,* id est euangelium, *et qui audierint,* id est qui obedierint, *uiuent.* (*Sermo* 127.6.9)

Amen I say to you that the hour is coming and now is when the dead, that is the unfaithful, *will hear the voice of the Son of God,* that is the Gospel, *and those who hear,* that is, who obey, *will live.*[31]

This decoding of the text has clear parallels with the method of allegory, although Augustine rarely builds up the sustained scheme required for this type of exegesis. Another of his favourite approaches dissects the scriptural text to show the logical consistency of its literal form. This is typified by the following treatment of John 6:45:

quid est *omnis qui audiuit a patre et didicit uenit ad me,* nisi nullus est qui audiat a patre et discat et non ueniat ad me? si enim *omnis qui audiuit a patre et didicit uenit,* profecto omnis qui non uenit non *audiuit a patre* nec *didicit*: nam si audisset et didicisset, ueniret. neque enim ullus audiuit et didicit et non uenit sed *omnis,* ut ait ueritas, *qui audiuit a patre et didicit uenit.* (*De praedestinatione sanctorum* 8.13)

What does *everyone who has heard from the Father and has learnt comes to me* mean, except that there is no one who hears the Father and learns and does not come to me? If, then, *everyone who has heard from the Father and has learnt comes,* clearly, everyone who does not come has not *heard from the Father* nor *learnt*: for if they had heard and had learnt, they would come. Nor, then, has anyone heard and learnt who does not come, but *everyone,* as the truth himself speaks, *who has heard from the Father and has learnt, comes.*

This explanation also demonstrates Augustine recasting the biblical text as a negative statement in order to focus attention on the precise wording and scope of the original. This can be extended in various ways. First, Augustine may draw attention to what is not said, relying heavily on the exact wording before him. The importance of the preposition in John 6:29 is shown by the change of meaning which would result from its absence:

31 For a more extended example, see *De trinitate* 1.10.20 on John 16:28.

hoc est enim opus dei ut credatis in eum quem ille misit. non dixit credatis ei aut credatis eum sed credatis in eum. (*Sermo* 130A.3 [*Dolbeau* 19])

For this is the work of God, that you should believe in him whom he sent. He did not say 'you should trust him' or 'you should believe him' but 'you should believe in him'.

This is often found repeatedly for the same verse: in no fewer than six works Augustine observes of John 3:36 *non ait ueniet sed manet.*[32] On other occasions Augustine cites the whole verse but with one crucial alteration, in order to emphasize the correct reading. Two versions of John 5:19 will suffice to illustrate the numerous examples of these 'imaginary citations', one including the canonical text and one not:

non enim ait: quaecumque pater iubet haec filius facit, sed ait: *quaecumque pater facit haec et filius facit similiter.* (*Contra sermonem Arrianorum* 22.18)

For he did not say 'Whatever the Father orders, the Son does', but he said *Whatever the Father does, this the Son does likewise.*

non ergo ait quaecumque pater facit talia filius facit, tamquam alia facit pater et alia filius. (*Sermo* 126.7.9)

Therefore he did not say 'Whatever the Father does, the Son does similar things', as if the Father and the Son did different things.

Apart from the substitution of the critical term, the wording of the rest of the phrase may still be useful as evidence for Augustine's text of Scripture. In certain schemes of classifying citations, the whole sentence might be described as an adaptation, although without explanation of the context and how the verse has been modified this could be misleading. Augustine's sensitivity to language and fondness for word play means that he frequently chooses to substitute words of a similar sound or shape to the true biblical term, such as *iubet* and *facit* in the example above.[33] The rhetorical power of this comes across in his clever use of the device against Pelagius:

[32] *Enchiridion* 10.33, *Contra Iulianum* 6.24.79, *De peccatorum meritis* 1.21.29, *Enarratio in Psalmos* 101.s1.11, *Sermo* 130A.7 and *Sermo* 294.14.14. See also Augustine's comment on John 17:11, *Christus autem non ait ut ipsi et nos unum simus, sed ait ut sint unum sicut et nos unum sumus* (*Contra Maximinum* 1.12 and elsewhere), *In epistolam Iohannis* 2.5 and *Sermo* 121.2 on John 8:58, and *De ordine* 1.11.32 on John 18:36.

[33] For Augustine's word play in the *Sermones*, especially this category of similar-sounding words, see Mohrmann 1932. Augustine's use of 'figures of sound' is also treated in Lawless' analysis of *Tractatus in Iohannem* 44 (1997:55–60).

dominus autem, ut responderet futuro Pelagio, non ait sine me difficile potestis aliquid facere, sed ait *sine me nihil potestis facere*, et ut responderet futuris etiam istis in eadem ipsa euangelica sententia non ait *sine me nihil potestis* perficere sed *facere*. (*Contra epistulas Pelagianorum* 2.8.18)

But the Lord, in order to reply to Pelagius as yet unborn, did not say 'without me, you are able to do something with difficulty' but he said *without me, you are able to do nothing.* And in order to reply to these later claims, in the same gospel statement he did not say *without me you are able to* complete *nothing*, but *to do nothing.*

The importance of the exact form of the biblical text for Augustine's exegesis cannot, therefore, be underestimated: his manipulation of these citations is predicated on the assumption that there is a single correct version which his audience will recognize.

Another common ploy is to use scriptural citations as the answer to questions. For example, Augustine uses John 13:34 to explain the word *mandatum*:

quod est hoc peccatum? facere contra mandatum. quod est mandatum? *mandatum nouum do uobis, ut uos inuicem diligatis.* (*In epistolam Iohannis* 5.2)[34]

What is this sin? To act against the commandment. What is the commandment? *I give you a new commandment, that you should love each other.*

Similarly, he introduces John 1:29 into his exposition of Jesus' commission to Peter to feed his sheep:

quomodo sibi fecit agnos agnus? *ecce agnus dei.* de illo dictum est: *ecce agnus dei.* et quomodo sibi fecit agnos? *ecce qui tollit peccatum mundi.*

(*Sermo* 229P.4)

How has the Lamb made a flock for himself? *Behold the Lamb of God.* It is said of him: *Behold the Lamb of God.* And how has he made a flock for himself? *Behold him who takes away the sin of the world.*

Sometimes, the whole phrase is presented as a rhetorical question in which the biblical text is put forward as the only possible answer:

quid est lex Christi nisi *mandatum nouum do uobis ut uos inuicem diligatis?* quid est lex Christi nisi *pacem meam do uobis pacem meam relinquo uobis?* (*Contra epistulam Parmeniani* 3.2.5)

[34] Later in the same series of sermons, he supplies this verse as the answer to the questions *lex imperatoris quae est?* (*In epistolam Iohannis* 9.11) and *quae sunt praecepta dei?* (*In epistolam Iohannis* 10.3).

What is the law of Christ except *I give you a new commandment, that you should love each other*? What is the law of Christ except *I give you my peace, I leave you my peace*?

A version of this has already been seen in Augustine's treatment of John 6:45 on p. 59, where the elements of the question are reversed. Christine Mohrmann calls this question-and-answer style *dialektikon*, observing that it is normally found in exegetical sermons and that it promotes a simple, straightforward identification of scriptural meaning. Indeed, it may draw on similar structures used in catechesis.[35] Augustine sometimes applies it to the sequence of biblical texts, as if to reconstruct the train of thought which inspired the author:

ideo Iohannes euangelista de domino ipso ait *erat lumen uerum,* et quasi quaereretur 'quid est lumen uerum?' *quod illuminat omnem hominem* inquit, non ergo quod illuminatur sed quod illuminat.

(*Sermo* 341.18 [*Dolbeau* 22])

Thus the Evangelist John said of the Lord himself, *It was the true light*, and as if someone had asked 'What is the true light?', he said: *which enlightens every man*; therefore it is not what is enlightened, but what enlightens.

This device is particularly common when Augustine expounds comments made by the evangelists *in propria uoce*, such as John 2:21. Given such a concentration on details, it is hardly surprising that he also finds significance in the precise word order of a passage or the tense of verbs. Such a method of explaining the Scriptures to his congregation has obvious parallels with the way Augustine the *rhetor* would have taught his pupils classical texts, examining the structure and sequence of each sentence and seeking to discern the meaning and intention underlying the form.

Augustine's adherence to the principle of *scriptura sui interpres* means that he frequently cites biblical material in order to supply verbal parallels for the occurrence of a particular word or concept in

[35] Mohrmann 1958:60 (see also Mohrmann 1961:364). Berrouard 1969:12 characterizes Augustine's commentary on John as a series of questions. Lawless 1997:63 compares Augustine's use of questions in his sermons to the Cynic diatribe, while Pontet (1946:81) identifies elements of the catechetical style in *Sermones* 265D.3 and 72A.8. For the construction of the argument of *De uera religione* on biblical *testimonia*, see Bochet 2004:368.

another passage. For instance, in *Tractatus in Iohannem* 10.3, Augustine considers the mention of Jesus' mother and brothers in John 2:12 alongside the reference to mother and brothers in Matthew 12:46–50; in the next paragraph, the word *flagellum* ('whip') in John 2:15 is discussed in conjunction with *flagella* in Psalm 34:15. The frequent occurrence of similar phrases in the Gospel according to John means that it is a prime candidate for this treatment. In *Tractatus in Iohannem* 31 Augustine draws on the evangelist's own repetition to elucidate each half of John 7:34, which has parallels with both John 13:34 and John 17:28, before relating the whole verse to John 13:36:

ideo ait: *ubi ego sum, uos non potestis uenire* [7:34]. nec dixit non poteritis sed non potestis; tales enim tunc erant qui non possent. nam ut sciatis non hoc ad desperationem dictum, et discipulis suis dixit tale aliquid: *quo ego uado, uos non potestis uenire* [13:33]; cum pro illis orans dixerit: *pater, uolo ut ubi ego sum et ipsi sint mecum* [17:28]. denique hoc Petro exposuit et ait illi: *quo ego uado, non potes me sequi modo. sequeris autem postea* [13:36]. (*Tractatus in Iohannem* 31.9)

Thus he said: *Where I am, you are unable to come.* And he did not say 'you will not be able' but 'you are not able'; for the men of that time were the sort who are not able. In order for you to know that this was not said to make us despair, he said something similar to his disciples: *Where I am going, you are not able to come*; and when praying for them, he said: *Father, I wish that where I am they too may be with me.* Finally, he explained it to Peter and told him: *Where I am going, you cannot follow me now. But you will follow later.*

This demonstrates to the full Augustine's ability to assemble Scripture to illuminate Scripture, relying strongly on the verbal form of each verse. A more straightforward sequence of illustrative citations can be seen in his explanation of the Beatitudes in *De sancta uirginitate*:

Beati pauperes spiritu: imitamini eum qui *propter uos pauper factus est cum diues esset* [2 Cor. 8:9]. *Beati mites*: imitamini eum qui dixit: *discite a me, quoniam mitis sum et humilis corde* [Matt. 11:29]. *Beati lugentes*: imitamini eum qui fleuit super Ierusalem [cf. Luke 19:41]. *Beati qui esuriunt et sitiunt iustitiam*: imitamini eum qui dixit: *meus cibus est ut faciam uoluntatem eius qui misit me* [John 4:34]. *Beati misericordes*: imitamini eum qui uulnerato a latronibus et in uia iacenti semiuiuo desperatoque subuenit [cf. Luke 10:30]. *Beati mundicordes*: imitamini eum qui *peccatum non fecit nec inuentus est dolus in ore eius* [1 Peter 2:22]. *Beati pacifici*: imitamini eum qui pro suis persecutoribus dixit: *pater, ignosce illis, quia nesciunt quid faciunt* [Luke 23:34]. *Beati qui persecutionem patiuntur propter iustitiam*: imitamini eum qui *pro uobis passus est relinquens uobis exemplum ut sequamini uestigia eius* [1 Peter 2:22]. (*De sancta uirginitate* 28.28)

Blessed are the poor in spirit: imitate him, who *was made poor for you even though he was rich. Blessed are the meek*: imitate him who said: *Learn from me, for I am meek and lowly in heart. Blessed are those who mourn*: imitate him who wept over Jerusalem. *Blessed are those who hunger and thirst for righteousness*: imitate him who said: *my food is to do the will of him who sent me. Blessed are the merciful*: imitate him who helped the man wounded by robbers and lying half-dead and despairing in the road. *Blessed are the pure in heart*: imitate him who *committed no sin, nor was deceit found in his mouth. Blessed are the peacemakers*: imitate him who said on behalf of his tormentors: *Father, forgive them, for they know not what they do. Blessed are those who suffer persecution for righteousness' sake*: imitate him who *suffered for you, leaving you an example that you should follow in his steps.*

Modern exegetes may sometimes find certain parallels less than compelling, especially in the case of items of everyday vocabulary. Augustine often connects *transire* ('cross over') in John 13:1 with verses which include the noun *transitus* ('crossing'; see *Sermo* 104.6, *Sermo* 155.5.5, *Sermo* 179.6.6). Similarly, John 19:34 is linked with Genesis 2:22 on the basis of the shared word *latus*:

fit uiro dormienti coniux de latere: fit Christo morienti ecclesia de sacramento sanguinis, qui de latere mortui profluxit. (*Contra Faustum* 12.8)

A wife was made for the sleeping man from his side; the Church was made for the dying Christ from the sacrament of his blood, which flowed from the dead man's side.

Most examples of this derive from Augustine's propensity for treating passages of biblical narrative in an allegorical fashion.[36]

The pairing of citations is sometimes of textual interest, in cases when the common term is not normally read in one or other of the verses. In John 1:9, only four surviving Old Latin witnesses read *lumen* rather than *lux*, but the illustration of this verse in *Sermo* 299D.5 (and *De trinitate* 7.3.4) by Psalm 35:10, *quoniam apud te fons uitae et in* ***lumine*** *tuo uidebimus* ***lumen***, and in *Sermo* 341.18 by

[36] See Polman 1961:95–6 and Norris 1993:390–2.

Matthew 5:14 in the form *uos estis* ***lumen*** *mundi*, confirms that Augustine read *lumen* in this verse.[37] Again, of his two citations of John 1:26, *Tractatus in Iohannem* 4.9 reads *medius autem uestrum* but *Enarratio in Psalmos* 81.2 cites the verse with *in medio uestrum* as a parallel to the verse *in medio autem deos discernere* (Psalm 81:1). While it is possible that Augustine was misled by the similarity between the texts, particularly as he would be citing at least one reference from memory, *in medio* is found in a number of Old Latin sources which suggests that he did know both readings in John.

Verbal parallels can often be supplied from more than one verse, and Augustine frequently develops 'chains' of citations which share the same key word. For example, in *De continentia*, he compares John 1:14 with four other verses in which the word *caro* appears:

legimus *uerbum caro factum est et habitauit in nobis* [John 1:14]. quid hic caro intellegenda est nisi homo? *et uidebit omnis caro salutare dei* [Luke 3:6], quid potest intellegi nisi omnis homo? *ad te omnis caro ueniet* [Psalm 64:3], quid est nisi omnis homo? *dedisti ei potestatem carnis* [John 17:2], quid est nisi omnis hominis? *ex operibus legis non iustificabitur omnis caro* [Romans 3:20], quid est nisi nullus iustificabitur homo? (*De continentia* 4.11)

We read: *The word was made flesh and dwelt among us.* How should 'flesh' be understood here except by 'a man'? *And all flesh will see the salvation of God*: how can this be understood except 'every man'? What is *To you all flesh shall come*, if not 'every man'? What is *You gave him power over flesh*, if not 'over every man'? What is *All flesh will not be justified by the works of the Law* except 'no man will be justified'?

A similar 'chain' is found for the word *spiritus* in John 4:24 (*Epistula* 238.2.14). This practice may well be described as 'concordance exegesis' (cf. Lienhard 1996:18). As well as clusters based on verbal similarity, groups of citations may be related by theological topic or polemical concern. Some of these probably pre-date Augustine, deriving from earlier thematically arranged collections of biblical *testimonia*.[38] He was, however, responsible for assembling others:

[37] Knauer 1955:113, however, notes that *lux* and *lumen* can appear in the same 'associative group', as in *Confessiones* 8.10.22.

[38] Knauer identifies three categories of 'associations' among Augustine's citations (word associations, content associations, and exegetical associations), and describes groups of citations in the *Confessiones* as 'Zitatnester' (Knauer 1955:111 ff.). On earlier groups of citations by Novatian and Cyprian, see Saxer 1985b:350–4.

omnia haec quae uelut catenatim conexui habent uoces suas in scripturis sanctis. (*De spiritu et littera* 30.52)

All these which I have joined together as in a chain have their utterances in the Holy Scriptures.

Catenatim here seems to function as a technical term. In certain cases the 'chains' are held together not by a keyword but by a similar rhetorical structure, as in the following list of nine verses which Augustine claims the Pelagians ignored:

ita namque illis tumor ipse aures cordis obstruxit, ut non audiant *quid enim habes quod non accepisti?* [1 Cor. 4:7] non audiant *sine me nihil potestis facere* [John 15:5], non audiant *caritas ex deo est* [1 John 4:7], non audiant *deus partitus est mensuram fidei* [Romans 12:3], non audiant *spiritus ubi uult spirat* [John 3:8], et *qui spiritu dei aguntur, hi filii sunt dei* [Romans 8:14], non audiant *nemo potest uenire ad me nisi fuerit ei datum a patre meo* [John 6:65], non audiant quod Esdras scribit, *benedictus est dominus patrum nostrum qui haec dedit in cor regis clarificare domum suam quae est in Hierusalem* [1 Esdras 8:25], non audiant quod per Ieremiam dominus dicit, *et timorem meum dabo in cor eorum ut a me non recedant et uisitabo eos ut bonos eos faciam* [Jer. 32.40]. (*Contra epistulas Pelagianorum* 4.6.14)

For this swelling has so obstructed the ears of their heart that they do not hear *What do you have that you have not received*; they do not hear *Without me you can do nothing*; they do not hear *Love is from God*; they do not hear *God has distributed the measure of faith*; they do not hear *The spirit blows where it wills* and *Those who are led by the spirit of God, these are the children of God*; they do not hear *No one can come to me unless it is granted him by my Father*; they do not hear what Esdras writes, *Blessed is the Lord of our fathers who placed this idea in the mind of the king to glorify his house which is in Jerusalem*; they do not hear what the Lord said through Jeremiah, *And I will put my fear in their hearts so that they will not withdraw from me and I will visit them to make them good.*

It seems more than likely that Augustine drew such references from a list of verses prepared in advance: the mention of Esdras and Jeremiah by name would support this.

Anne-Marie La Bonnardière has observed that a number of these doctrinally organized clusters, or *nœuds scripturaires*, were developed in response to particular issues.[39] She claimed not only that their

[39] First presented in La Bonnardière 1965, where she terms them *groupes scripturaires* (page 16); in the *Biblia Augustiniana* each verse is presented with its *orchestra-*

genesis could be traced, as Augustine gradually added references to his armoury, but that the presence of similar combinations in multiple works indicates that Augustine was working on them simultaneously. For example, almost all of Augustine's citations of the figure of the dove from John 1:32–3 come from early works, where it is found in combination with Song of Songs 6:8, Matthew 3:14, Matthew 3:16, and Genesis 8:8–11. Two later works, *Tractatus in Iohannem* 61 and *De trinitate* 15, both treat John 13:24 in the same way and, uniquely, connect it with Wisdom 2:1. Citations of the first half of John 5:19 are mostly in anti-Arian texts, while the second half of this verse is cited in later texts to support a trinitarian doctrine. These ingenious observations enabled her to redate the *Tractatus in Iohannis euangelium* and some of the *Enarrationes in Psalmos*, and have been more recently applied by Pierre-Marie Hombert to review the dating of works written between 397 and 407, the *Sermones Dolbeau* and several other sermons. Similarly, Isabelle Bochet has applied a similar technique to show how the use of biblical citations can illuminate Augustine's argument in contemporary works.[40]

The development of such associative groups reflects the importance of memory in Augustine's citation practice, which also has implications for the biblical text. The majority of his citations, especially of illustrative material, were probably made from memory. Even in sermons, with the manuscript in front of him, it is unlikely that he used it for anything other than the lectionary passage. Citing by memory does not necessarily produce an inaccurate text of Scripture. Ancient education involved a considerable degree of learning by rote and this may have resulted in a corresponding ability to recall extensive passages word for word.

Nonetheless, Augustine himself admits in several places that his memory of the biblical text was not perfect (e.g. *Sermo* 374.19, *Retractationes* 1.7.2, *Sermo* 362.22.25). Furthermore, except in those cases where the exact wording of Scripture is a key part of the argument, complete accuracy was not important. Given that many

tion scripturaire. At Hombert 2000:vi, they are described as *nœuds* or *chaînes scripturaires.* For the following examples, see La Bonnardière 1965:29 ff. (John 1:32–3), 79–80 (John 13:24), 110 ff. (John 5:19).

[40] See Bochet 2004 (summary at pp. 501–2); the significance of theological similarities is also recognized by Bardy 1954:21.

citations are used simply to illustrate an idea or term common to both, the details are often immaterial so long as this principal function is fulfilled. The fact that a phrase is introduced as a quotation is a stronger indication that the preacher is invoking scriptural authority than a direct correspondence with any exemplar. Because of this treatment of citations as independent, self-contained units, verses quoted from memory normally appear in a discrete form devoid of the contextual reference or grammatical connections found in the original: this may be described as Augustine's 'mental text' of the Bible.[41]

The process of arriving at this universally applicable form of a biblical verse for use out of context I will call 'flattening'. It may or may not be a conscious alteration. The original text is often abbreviated, in order to concentrate on relevant material and perhaps ignore complicating features. Other contextual elements may also be adapted, such as the substitution of nouns for pronouns or the omission of connectives. In some cases, the syntax is changed to enhance parallelism or give a more natural sequence. The resulting form is normally extremely stable, and is therefore frequently reproduced regardless of the original text.[42] There are numerous examples of this among Augustine's citations of John. For example, all Latin biblical manuscripts of John 5:22 have a text identical or very similar to the following:

neque enim pater iudicat quemquam sed iudicium omne dedit filio.

For nor does the Father judge anyone, but he has given all judgement to the Son.

The vast majority of Augustine's citations read:

pater non iudicat quemquam sed omne iudicium dedit filio.

The Father does not judge anyone, but he has given all judgement to the Son.

[41] The phrase 'mental text' was suggested to me by Philip Burton.

[42] Gryson's observation is to the point: 'la mémoire s'attache de préférence aux mots significatifs et accorde une moindre attention aux outils grammaticaux, auxquels se substituent plus facilement des équivalents' (1978:48). On the omission of phrases, see also Fee 1971:172. Rhetorical considerations sometimes also lead to the re-casting of citations: Knauer shows that anaphora, parallelism, and tricolon are among the many devices employed to shape biblical text in the *Confessiones* (1955:177 ff.).

Each of the alterations is indicative of flattening. The connective element of *neque* and the word *enim* have been omitted, as there is no prior reference. The subject, *pater*, has been fronted for emphasis, as the verse is used to demonstrate the different roles of the Father and the Son. The change in word order to *omne iudicium* may also have been made for emphasis although the position of *omne* is more likely simply to reflect current Latin usage: the sequence is paralleled in other Church Fathers. The fact that none of these variants is preserved in a biblical manuscript further supports the conclusion that this form of text is entirely due to Augustine's memory. Similarly, the canonical text of John 10:17–18 is:

propterea me pater diligit, quia ego pono animam meam ut iterum sumam eam. nemo tollit eam a me sed ego pono eam a me ipso. potestatem habeo ponendi eam et potestatem habeo iterum sumendi eam.

For this reason the Father loves me, because I lay down my life in order that I may take it up again. No one takes it from me, but I lay it down of my very own accord. I have power to lay it down and I have power to take it up again.

Augustine usually has a shorter form, changing the sequence and incorporating elements of both verses:

potestatem habeo ponendi animam meam et potestatem habeo iterum sumendi eam. nemo tollit eam a me sed ego eam pono a me et iterum sumo eam.

I have power to lay down my life and I have power to take it up again. No one takes it from me, but I lay it down of my own accord and I take it up again.

The replacement of the pronoun *eam* by *animam meam*, and the loss of the purpose clause so that *sumo* is co-ordinated with *pono*, are both hallmarks of flattening. The result is a clearly defined saying of general application, which stands by itself out of context.

The process of flattening can sometimes be seen at work within a single sermon. For instance, Augustine expounds John 8:24 in *Tractatus in Iohannem* 38. The initial citation begins the second half of the verse in the same way as all surviving biblical manuscripts:

si enim non credideritis quia ego sum moriemini in peccatis uestris.

(*Tractatus in Iohannem* 38.7)

For if you shall not have believed that I am, you will die in your sins.

The next three citations, which only quote this phrase, omit the connective *enim*. After this, every time these words are cited, it is in the form *nisi credideritis quia ego sum*. What is more, this is also the text which appears in the next sermon, *Tractatus in Iohannem* 39. It seems that, for his initial citation of this verse, Augustine relied on a biblical manuscript, but gradually changed the form of text during his exposition as he cited from memory rather than referring back to the codex. Although some have suggested that the initial form of text might have been brought into agreement with biblical manuscripts by copyists during the transmission of the work, this pattern of gradual alteration is so common in Augustine that it seems most plausible to derive it from his own rhetorical practice.[43]

Another variation in the form of biblical texts which is attributable to memory is that of conflation. These are composite citations in which elements from two or more verses have been fused together. Augustine's 'citation', *ego sum uitis, uos estis sarmenta, pater meus agricola*, despite being introduced on most occasions as a verbatim quotation of the words of Jesus, is clearly an amalgam of two overlapping statements:

John 15:1 ego sum uitis uera et pater meus agricola est

John 15:5 ego sum uitis, uos palmites [*or* sarmenta]; qui manet in me et ego in eo hic fert fructum multum.[44]

It is usually the similarity between verses which leads to their conflation.[45] In *Contra Adimantum*, Augustine completes John 17:5 with John 12:28, misled by the appearance of *clarificare* in both verses:

[43] See further the discussion of the *Tractatus in Iohannem* on pp. 113–17. The alteration of *si enim non* to *nisi* is also found in six of Augustine's citations of John 16:7.

[44] John 15:1 reads 'I am the true vine and my Father is the farmer'; John 15:5 reads 'I am the vine, you the branches: the one who remains in me and I in him, he bears much fruit.' Augustine's 'citation' is: 'I am the vine, you are the branches, my Father is the farmer.'

[45] Gryson (1978:64) notes that harmonization between different verses is almost inevitable when citations are made from memory; Fee (1995:203) observes this tendency with particular reference to the Synoptic Gospels. More conflations of Johannine verses may be seen at *De correptione et gratia* 21 (John 3:15 and 6:39), *Contra aduersarium legis* 2.5.19 (John 5:39 and 8:19), *De peccatorum meritis* 1.23.33 (John 6:53 and 3:36), *Sermo* 12.1 (John 10:9 and 14:6).

cum ipse dominus dixisset *pater clarifica me ea claritate qua fui apud te priusquam mundus fieret* [John 17:5] sonuit uox de caelo *et clarificaui et clarificabo* [John 12:28]. (*Contra Adimantum* 9)

When the Lord himself said 'Father, glorify me with that glory in which I was with you before the world began', a voice sounded from heaven 'I have glorified and I will glorify.'

While the verbal parallelism of John facilitates many such confusions, there are also conflations with the other Gospels. This can even be seen in his commentary on John, when Augustine twice replaces *ambula* in John 5:8 (*surge tolle grabatum tuum et ambula*) with *uade in domum tuam* from the parallel pericope in Mark 2:11.[46] On one occasion, Augustine doubly interweaves Jesus' words from John 2:16 (in bold type) and Luke 19:46:

auferte ista hinc. *scriptum est domus mea domus orationis uocabitur. uos autem fecistis eam* ***domum negotiationis*** *uel speluncam latronum.*

(*Quaestiones euangeliorum* 2.48B)

Take these from here. It is written: My house will be called a house of prayer. But you have made it **a house of business** or a den of robbers.

A more common sort of conflation can be seen in the combination of John 13:16 (*non est seruus maior domino suo neque apostolus maior eo qui misit illum*) and Matthew 10:24 (*non est discipulus super magistrum nec seruus super dominum suum*):

non est seruus maior domino suo et non est discipulus super magistrum.

(*Enarratio in Psalmos* 36.s1.9)

A slave is not greater than his master, and a pupil is not above his teacher.

As with several composite citations, the plausibility of the compound means that the two separate elements were not even identified by the modern editors of this work.[47] Furthermore, certain harmonizations

[46] In fact, Augustine's citations here reproduce the Marcan text, but the context and reference to the *quinque porticus* show that the intended reference is to the Johannine passage (see *Tractatus in Iohannem* 20.2).

[47] Dekkers and Fraipont in *Corpus Christianorum* 38. Compare the conflation of John 17:2 and John 3:15 in *De diuersis quaestionibus* 80.2. Other composite citations involving more than one Gospel occur in *De moribus* 1.16.28 (John 1:18 and Matt. 11:27), *Epistula* 26.5 (John 7:37 and Matt. 11:28), *Enarratio* 102.3, *Sermo* 313C.1 and *Sermo* 313D.1 (John 12:25 and Mark 8:34–5/Matt. 16:25), *Enarratio* 40.8 (John 15:20 and Matt. 10:24).

are even present in biblical manuscripts. At John 13:38, Codex Palatinus reads:

respondit Iesus: animam tuam pro me ponis? amen dico tibi, ***priusquam gallus cantet, ter me negabis.***

Jesus replied 'You lay down your life for me? Indeed I say to you, **before the cock crows, you will deny me three times.'**

The words in bold type are taken from Matthew 26:34: the customary Johannine reading is *non cantabit gallus donec me ter neges.* However, as the conflated form is found in five of Augustine's sermons, this presents a problem in determining his source: did he rely on Codex Palatinus, or is this an independent, identical error? Given that none of these sermons covers this lection, the likelihood is that Augustine was citing from memory.

Except in cases where an altered form can clearly be attributed to him, Augustine may not always be responsible for the abbreviated text in a biblical citation. If he drew his references from a collection of scriptural extracts or *testimonia*, these might already have been presented in a decontextualized form. Again, Augustine could have been influenced by the work of another Church Father who also cited a particular text in a flattened or conflated version. For example, Cyprian also has a shortened form of John 15:15 (*Epistula* 63.14, *De catholicae ecclesiae unitate* 2) and Augustine's text of John 14:2 is found in a number of other Fathers, both Greek and Latin. On the other hand, the same types of alteration may have been made independently by different authors. A similar text is not always a sure sign of dependence: a better indication that Augustine relied on *testimonia* or another author is a similar sequence of biblical citations, or verbal correspondence outside the scriptural elements.

In Augustine's polemical works, however, it is clear that the form of his biblical reference is sometimes directly influenced by the text of his opponent. When quoting the *Sermo Arrianorum*, Augustine always reproduces the scriptural citations verbatim, despite the fact that they correspond to an Old Latin text-type which he does not appear to have used since composing the first book of *De trinitate* almost two decades earlier. Although his response includes some biblical references in his customary form of text for this period, in others he reverts to the older text-type, with its distinctive renderings such as *aduocatus* in John 14:16 and John 16:7, and *honorificare* in John 16:14, 17:4, and 17:5. In both of these cases, the final verse is not among those cited in the *Sermo Arrianorum*, which suggests that Augustine may deliberately have extended his use of this text-type in order to accord with the work he is refuting. Similarly, in *Contra Gaudentium*, Augustine prefers the rendering *saeculum* to *mundus* in keeping with Gaudentius' citations but against his own practice.[48] Augustine's comments in *Contra litteras Petiliani* suggest that he was sensitive to the variants in the biblical text of his opponents but made a conscious choice to ignore minor verbal discrepancies in order to focus on matters of exegesis:

> *ubi forte aliter dicis testimonia scripturarum quam sese habent et ad rem quae inter nos agitur non pertinet non nimis curo; ubi autem impediunt quod tractamus nisi ueraciter proferantur, non te arbitror succensere debere si quemadmodum scriptum sit te commemoro.*
>
> (*Contra litteras Petiliani* 2.61.138)

> When you happen to give scriptural citations in a different form from how they are and it does not affect the matter under discussion, I am not overly concerned. However, when they obstruct our exegesis if they are not correctly quoted, I do not think that you will be offended if I remind you of how it is written.

Nonetheless, there are several instances of Augustine criticizing the form of text used by his adversaries, especially the Donatists whose text often corresponds to the renderings found in the 'African' versions of the *Vetus Latina*.[49] As with the forms noted above, other departures from Augustine's customary text of scriptural verses may indicate that he is reliant on another source.

This analysis of the form of Augustine's biblical material has for the most part concentrated on examples which may be termed 'citations proper': scriptural texts usually introduced by a quotation formula or pragmatically distinguished in some way. Elsewhere, I have made a case for dividing these between *primary citations*,

[48] See the citations of John 14:27 and 15:18 at *Contra Gaudentium* 2.12.13 and 1.26.29. Augustine's citation of John 16:3 at *Contra Gaudentium* 1.23.26 also seems to be influenced by Gaudentius, although none of these repeat his opponent's text verbatim.

[49] See pp. 81–4 below.

which are most likely to have been drawn from a codex, and *secondary citations*, which probably derive from memory.[50] Together these constitute the majority of Augustine's scriptural references, since his appeal to the authority of the Bible entails that it should be clearly identified as his source. He also refers to biblical texts in a more allusive manner, although these are less easy to isolate. As a Christian writer, his religious vocabulary derives in large part from the Latin translations of Scripture, which at times seem also to influence his phraseology. The *Confessiones* stand out as a special case in which Augustine deliberately employs a scriptural idiom whilst making comparatively few verbatim citations. Knauer has shown how this effect is achieved by fusing together elements from different texts, usually psalms, in order to create a deliberate type of conflation which he calls *Pasticciozitate*.[51] Nonetheless, allusions to particular passages and reminiscences of biblical style in other works can also be significant for understanding his interpretative associations and identifying the extent of his familiarity with Scripture.

Did Augustine ever deliberately alter the text of the Bible when making a citation? The account given above of his exegetical methods and concern for the exact wording of Scripture implies that this is unlikely. Nonetheless, it was common in antiquity to make minor alterations to a quoted source.[52] One frequent practice is the adaptation of a citation to fit its context: the omission or alteration of conjunctions has already been mentioned in the discussion of flattening. Again, a passage may be cited selectively, leaving out words which contradict the intended application of the text: it is often difficult to show that this is deliberate, given the tendency to abbreviate or re-order citations from memory in order to emphasize the points of correspondence. Furthermore, the variety of Latin versions of the Bible means that it is hard to prove that a particular variant is due to Augustine: his reading may have been present in a witness no longer preserved. For example, the form of John 13:10 which he uses

[50] See Houghton 2008.

[51] Knauer 1955:84.

[52] The citation practice of the Apostle Paul, Greco-Roman literature, and early Judaism is compared in Stanley 1992; see especially his summary on pp. 343–9, where he concludes that over half the citations in each of these sources have been subject to adaptation.

against the Donatists' practice of rebaptism has two words not found in the majority of Latin manuscripts, *semel* and *iterum*, both of which contribute to the force of his argument.[53] Although it is tempting to hold him responsible for this amplification of the scriptural saying, both terms appear in earlier Fathers and *semel* occurs in two manuscripts (the fifteen-verse Fragmentum Milanense and the very late Codex Colbertinus), so the case dissolves. More general changes which may clarify the meaning of a verse, widen the scope of a saying, improve the style or language of the original, or harmonize conflict or contradiction, are all paralleled in surviving biblical codices and may also have appeared in collections of *testimonia*.

On the other hand, there are a handful of instances in the text of John where Augustine deviates from the canonical text, most of which occur in quotations of speech. Some add immediacy to the biblical account, and might be classed as a free reworking of the text, such as the addition of the vocative in *mulier, da mihi bibere* in John 4:7 (*Enarratio in Psalmos* 61.9, *De diuersis quaestionibus* 64.4); similarly, most of his citations of John 21:15–17 have *Petre* rather than the formal *Simon Iohannis*. On several occasions, Augustine uniquely has *ecce* (e.g. John 7:25 and 14:30); he also seems to prefer the use of *iste* as a derogatory pronoun (e.g. John 4:18, 7:27, 8:48, 9:16, 9:17, 9:29, and 11:48). There are a few examples of verses where the action seems to have been 'speeded up' with the replacement of 'walking' by 'running' (John 4:28, 12:19, and 12:35).[54] Sometimes the variant reading appears to have arisen from Augustine's exegetical association of two texts, resulting in the sort of conflation already seen to affect parallel passages: in John 4:7 he includes the verb *sitio* on three occasions (*Enarratio in Psalmos* 61.9, *Enarratio in Psalmos* 68.s1.14, *Sermo* 99.3.3), which enables him to compare Jesus' thirst by the well with his thirst on the cross (John 19:28). The appearance of *inclinato capite* in certain citations of John 8:6 or 8:8 is used to connect this pericope with John 19:30. Most of his citations of John 20:22 feature the detail *insufflauit in faciem eorum* which may stem from the linking of this text and Genesis 2:7. It could be that Augustine was

[53] *qui lotus est* ***semel*** *non habet necessitatem* ***iterum*** *lauandi* ('the one who is washed **once** has no need of being washed **again**'); see p. 305.

[54] Bastiaensen 2003:23–6 identifies *currere* as characteristic of Augustine.

familiar with these readings from biblical versions no longer extant, but as these verses frequently feature together in his exegesis it is also possible that he was responsible for the variation in the text. At any rate, there is no indication that these alterations were made consciously: all are characteristic of the types of variation which arise when citing from memory or freely paraphrasing the passage.

Another selection of unusual readings from direct speech demonstrates that Augustine was not always concerned for total accuracy even when quoting the words of Jesus. Editors have connected the citation in *Contra Faustum* 6.9, *ego fallere non didici: quod sentio loquor*, with John 8:28, *sicut docuit me pater, haec loquor*, but the resemblance is superficial. Similarly, while *si inuenistis in me peccatum, dicite* (*Enarratio in Psalmos* 50.9) has been claimed as a citation of John 8:46, *quis ex uobis arguit mihi de peccato?*, closer correspondences may be suggested.[55] In John 16:33, one citation adds an entirely new phrase:

dominus dixit *haec loquor uobis ut in me habeatis pacem.* ***pacem in terra uobis non promitto.*** (*Enarratio in Psalmos* 33.s3.19)

The Lord said: *I tell you this so that you may have peace in me.* ***I do not promise you peace on earth.***

In keeping with many such *agrapha*, this seems to be a 'homiletic invention'.[56] These sorts of alterations and paraphrases attributable to Augustine's citation technique should be distinguished from textual revision carried out against a Greek exemplar or internally within the Latin tradition, evidence for which is considered in Chapter 4.

To summarize, Augustine's biblical awareness is entirely consistent with his having started afresh at the time of his conversion to catholic Christianity. He himself tells us that he could not remember the Scriptures as reliably as the secular works which he had learnt as a boy. Nonetheless, despite using a codex on some occasions, the

[55] This same text is found in *Sermo* 26.10 and, with *arguite*, in *Sermo* 44.6 (an amalgam of extracts from sermons of Augustine by Caesarius of Arles). Compare also *Tractatus in Iohannem* 33.6, *in me peccatum non inuenisti.* The closest parallel in sense seems to be Psalm 16:3, *igne me examinasti, et non est inuenta in me iniquitas*, or Malachi 2:6, *lex ueritatis fuit in ore eius et iniquitas non est inuenta in labiis eius.*

[56] See Elliott 1993:349. The sentiment is similar to Luke 12:51, although there is little verbal correspondence.

majority of his citations are likely to have been made from memory. Many of these follow a form described as his 'mental text', often slightly simplified or abbreviated by a process termed 'flattening' in order to adjust a biblical verse for use out of context. Such memorized forms may also involve conflation of two or more verses from different books. All, however, is treated as Scripture, regardless of its exact textual form, and is accorded the highest authority in Augustine's argument. His doctrine of biblical inspiration comprises both divine initiative and human agency, and identifies the Church as the proper location for the reading and exegesis of the Bible. Although various hermeneutic schemes are found in Augustine's earlier works, one of his most characteristic practices is 'concordance exegesis', based on the principle of *scriptura sui interpres*, which gives rise to chains of citations sharing the same key word. While some of these may have been taken from other sources, many are original and bear witness to Augustine's ever-increasing command of biblical material. He also applied his rhetorical training to the Bible, subjecting it to detailed verbal analysis usually with the goal of reconciling apparent inconsistencies in order to prove the inspiration of the whole. The exposition of Scripture was not, however, for him an exercise in literary theory but a pastoral task at the heart of his episcopal ministry, building up the faithful in his congregation and serving the needs of the Church both in his own lifetime and for generations to come.

4

Augustine as a Witness for the Text of the New Testament

The final stage in this introductory section considers the text of Augustine's biblical citations, drawing on the observations of previous chapters. The aim here is to offer an overview of the different types of evidence and their relationship to the textual traditions of the New Testament, in particular the Gospel according to John (to which the rest of the book is devoted). The distinction between primary and secondary citations is central to assessing the significance of Augustine's readings: although the latter also include interesting forms, these cannot be ascribed to biblical manuscripts with the same degree of confidence. Similarities with the text of other Church Fathers may indicate dependence or use of a shared source: as noted above, however, the same types of alteration due to flattening may be made independently, and it is also important to remember that many of the earlier works available to Augustine are no longer extant. One of the difficulties in handling Latin material from this period is the differentiation between Old Latin and Vulgate text-types, given the way in which these co-existed and were subject to mutual contamination. In keeping with the standard practice set out earlier, Augustine's divergences from the modern editorial text of the Vulgate will be treated as Old Latin except in primary citations for which he was clearly relying on Jerome's revision: this may be anachronistic, but it is one of the few ways to impose stability on a diverse tradition.[1] As for the Greek Bible, it should be borne in mind that a translation does not necessarily reproduce every feature of the

[1] See p.10; the Vulgate text taken as standard is Weber–Gryson.

original, and a single underlying word may be rendered in a number of ways. Patristic evidence needs to be analysed carefully, but it is still a key element of New Testament textual criticism as it supplies readings from an identifiable time and place, some of which may not be preserved in surviving manuscripts.

The most compelling evidence for the biblical text comes from a sub-set of primary citations which explicitly mention variants Augustine has encountered in different biblical manuscripts. For instance, he was aware of the 'African' rendering *sermo* in the opening verse of John, even though all surviving biblical codices have *uerbum*:

graecum quippe euangelium λόγος habet, quod etiam ibi legitur ubi dictum est: *in principio erat uerbum et uerbum erat apud deum et deus erat uerbum* ... unde et hic poni potuit, et in quibusdam codicibus positum est: *uerbum tuum ueritas est*; sicut in quibusdam codicibus etiam ibi scriptum est: *in principio erat sermo.* in graeco autem sine ulla uarietate et ibi et hic λόγος est. (*Tractatus in Iohannem* 108.3)

The Gospel in Greek has *logos*, which is also present in the saying: *In the beginning was the Word, and the Word was with God, and the Word was God*... For this reason, this verse could read—as it does in several manuscripts—*your word* [*uerbum*] *is truth*, just as in certain manuscripts in the other verse is written: *In the beginning was the Word* [*sermo*]. However, in the Greek in both places, without any variation, is *logos.*

Several similar comments in the *Retractationes* have already been quoted.[2] Alteration of these observations by later editors is almost inconceivable; the only question is whether Augustine had verified these readings from personal inspection or simply reproduced them from other sources. In fact, Augustine's method of dealing with variant readings is often to run the alternatives together. He is aware of two forms of John 16:13, both of which are preserved in gospel manuscripts:

docebit uos omnem ueritatem, uel, sicut alii codices habent, *deducet uos in omni ueritate.* (*Tractatus in Iohannem* 96.4)

He will teach you all truth, or, as other manuscripts have, *He will lead you in all truth.*

[2] e.g. Genesis 2:5 and Matthew 20:17 (*Retractationes* 1.10.3 and 2.12.1) on pp. 17–18. For a list of references to variant biblical readings in a number of Church Fathers see Metzger 1979:188–90, which includes fourteen from Augustine.

In his commentary, however, he combines both:

quid est quod dominus ait de spiritu sancto, cum eum uenturum esse promitteret et docturum discipulos eius omnem ueritatem uel eos deducturum in omni ueritate? (*Tractatus in Iohannem* 99.1; see also *Tractatus* 96.4 and 100.1)

What is it that the Lord said of the Holy Spirit, when he promised that it would come and teach his disciples all truth, or would lead them in all truth?

In the Old Testament, his quotation of the Latin translations from Hebrew alongside those of the Septuagint reflects this approach.[3] Such an easy acceptance of alternatives demonstrates the limitations of Augustine's textual scholarship, but it does confirm that he had access to several different versions and that he transmits readings from more than one form of text.

Comments on the presence or absence of specific passages also form part of these explicit references. As mentioned above, he discovered that the omission of a phrase from Sirach 34:30 was characteristic of African codices (*Retractationes* 1.21.3). Although Augustine himself has no doubt about the authenticity of the *Pericope Adulterae* (John 7:53–8:11), missing from many early witnesses, he is aware of codices without these verses:

sed hoc uidelicet infidelium sensus exhorret, ita ut nonnulli modicae fidei uel potius inimici uerae fidei, credo, metuentes peccandi impunitatem dari mulieribus suis, illud quod de adulterae indigentia dominus fecit auferrent de codicibus suis, quasi permissionem peccandi tribuerit qui dixit *iam deinceps noli peccare.* (*De adulterinis coniugiis* 2.7.6)

But apparently the sensibility of the unfaithful shudders at this, to such an extent that several of limited faith, or rather, enemies of the true faith, I believe, afraid that their wives may be given freedom to sin, remove from their manuscripts the Lord's action in respect of the failing of the adulteress, as if the Lord had granted permission to sin, who said *Now henceforth do not sin.*

His assumption that the longer text is original and that later generations have removed the passage is characteristic of his explanation of textual differences based on content. Similarly, although he recognizes

[3] See La Bonnardière 1986:306 on the *Quaestiones in Heptateuchum.*

that John 20:30–1 reads like a conclusion, he never suggests that John 21 was originally lacking:

ad hoc itaque commendandum ualere arbitror, quod tamquam finis interpositus est libri, quod esset etiam secuturae narrationis quasi proaemium, quod ei quodammodo faceret eminentiorem locum. (*Tractatus in Iohannem* 122.1)

I think, therefore, that these verses serve to emphasize the following, because they are inserted in the book like an ending, but they would also be a kind of preface for the following narrative and give it some sort of greater importance.

A further, related, group is made up of Augustine's comments about the biblical text cited by his opponents. Despite his statement in the pseudo-dialogue with Petilianus that he is not concerned with textual differences where they are not germane to his argument, he offers several observations of this nature, such as the distinction between 'life' and 'livelihood' in Matthew 16:25:

Petilianus dixit: . . . siquidem dominus dicit: *qui perdiderit substantiam suam, centuplum recipiet eam.*

Augustinus respondit: et hoc ad rem pertinet commonere quemadmodum scriptum est. nam ubi nihil impedit intentionem meam si quid de scripturis fallis aut falleris nihil curo. non ergo ita scriptum est: *qui perdiderit substantiam suam,* sed: *qui perdiderit animam suam propter me.*

(*Contra litteras Petiliani* 2.99.227)

Petilianus said: . . . since the Lord said: *whoever shall have lost his livelihood will receive it a hundredfold.*

Augustine replied: Here, too, it is relevant to remember exactly what is written. You see, when it does not obstruct my meaning I do not care if you make a mistake or are misled concerning the Scriptures. In this case, then, it is not written as: *whoever shall have lost his livelihood,* but: *whoever shall have lost his life for my sake.*

As with many of the variants in the Donatist writings, the alternative reading is not found in surviving manuscripts.[4] The text which

[4] Other examples of Augustine correcting Petilianus' biblical text are found at *Contra litteras Petiliani* 2.13.30 (John 8:44), 2.61.138 (Matthew 5:19–20) and 2.62.140 (1 Corinthians 6:18). For Petilianus' unique readings in John, see *Contra litteras Petiliani* 2.8.17 (John 17:12), 2.12.27 (John 10:37), 2.32.72 (John 20:22), 2.75.167 (John 13:34), 2.89.196 (John 12:24).

Augustine criticizes is often marked by the phrase *non sic* (or *ita*) *scriptum est*, as in the following discussion of Galatians 4:10:

et quod dicit: *dies obseruatis et sabbata et solemnitates; timeo uos ne frustra laborauerim in uobis*, non sic scriptum est ut Adimantus ponit. non enim nominat ibi sabbatum Apostolus. dicit enim: *dies observatis et annos et tempora; timeo uos ne frustra laborauerim in uobis.* (*Contra Adimantum* 16.3)

And what he says: *You observe days and sabbaths and festivals; I fear for you, that my work among you may have been in vain*, is not written in the way that Adimantus puts it. For the Apostle does not name the sabbath there. He says: *You observe days and years and seasons: I fear for you, that my work among you may have been in vain.*

These comments demonstrate not just that Augustine was sensitive to variations in the form of biblical citations, but also that he had a concept of a 'correct version' which he was prepared to cite in response. As these are all works for which he had opportunity to check the reference, it seems highly likely that Augustine confirmed his text in a codex, particularly given the level of detail involved and the length of certain examples:

adhibuit enim apostolum testem eo quod dixerit: *uide Israel carnaliter nonne qui edunt hostias, participes sunt altaris? quid ergo? dico, quod idolum sit aliquid? sed qui sacrificant, daemonibus sacrificant.* quod non ita scriptum est, sed ita: *uidete Israel secundum carnem: nonne qui de sacrificiis manducant, socii sunt altaris? quid ergo? dico quia idolis immolatum est aliquid, aut idolum est aliquid? sed quia quae immolant daemoniis, et non deo immolant.* (*Contra aduersarium legis* 1.19.38)[5]

For he cites the Apostle Paul as a witness, in that he said: *Behold Israel; surely those who eat the offerings in the manner of flesh are sharers in the altar? What, then? Do I say that an idol has any significance? But those who sacrifice, sacrifice to demons.* Yet this is not written in this way, but as follows: *Behold Israel according to the flesh: surely those who consume parts of the sacrifices are companions of the altar? What, then? Do I say that what is offered to idols has any significance, or that an idol has any significance? But it is because what they sacrifice they sacrifice to demons and not to God.*

It is noteworthy that Augustine's version of 1 Corinthians 10:18–20 here, like Galatians 4:10 above, presents an Old Latin form of text. By

[5] See also *De natura et origine animae* on p. 172.

contrast, his standard for the Gospels in the same work was the Vulgate:

sed lex, inquit, *per Moysen data est; ueritas autem ab Iesu Christo est.* non ita scriptum est, sed ita: *lex per Moysen data est, gratia et ueritas per Iesum Christum facta est.* (*Contra aduersarium legis* 2.3.10)

But the law, he said, *was given through Moses; truth, however, is from Jesus Christ.* It is not written thus but as follows: *The law was given through Moses, grace and truth were made through Jesus Christ.*

The omission of *autem* from John 1:17 is distinctive of the Vulgate, and there are further similar examples in works of this period.[6] The sole exception to forms preserved in biblical codices is Augustine's text of John 16:2 in response to Gaudentius:

ueniet hora quando qui uos occiderint putent se officium facere deo, aut sicut tu hoc testimonium posuisti, *putent se uictimam dare deo.* (*Contra Gaudentium* 1.23.26)

The hour will come when those who kill you shall think they are performing a duty for God, or, in the form you gave this reference, *shall think they are offering a victim to God.*

On the other hand, *officium facere* is the text of the majority of Augustine's references and appears in several other Fathers, so the likelihood is that it appeared in a version no longer extant. When Augustine does invoke the authority of a codex against Julian of Eclanum, a Greek manuscript of 1 Corinthians 12:23 would hardly have contained the Latin words he quotes:

lege diligenter et inspice codicem graecum et inuenies apostolum *inhonesta* dixisse, quae '*uerecundiora*' tu dicis. (*Contra Iulianum opus imperfectum* 4.36)

Read carefully and consult a Greek manuscript and you will find that the Apostle called '**less honourable**' what you call '**more shameful**'.

There are, however, some readings in his opponents' biblical text on which we might expect Augustine to comment, such as Faustus' reference to the 'Flying Jesus' at Luke 4:29–30 (*Contra Faustum*

6 e.g. *Contra aduersarium legis* 2.4.16 and *De natura et origine animae* 3.11.15–17, although in these cases the majority of Old Latin manuscripts have the same reading as the Vulgate.

26.2) or Petilianus' version of John 20:22 with *sibilauit* rather than *insufflauit* (*Contra litteras Petiliani* 2.32.72). It seems more likely that Augustine decided to ignore these, rather than failed to notice them: the explicit corrections quoted in this paragraph are the exception rather than the rule.[7]

Augustine's biblical text in the bulk of his primary citations, made with reference to a codex, corresponds closely to surviving witnesses. Most correspondences with Old Latin Gospels occur in his early works before he encountered Jerome's Vulgate text. The text of Matthew 5–7 in *De sermone domini in monte* from 394/5 has been analysed in detail in Mizzi 1954: it is clearly Old Latin. Augustine's longest single citation of John from an Old Latin manuscript is the discussion of John 4 in *De diuersis quaestionibus* 64; other parts of this work, composed between 388 and 395, also feature non-Vulgate forms. The first book of *De trinitate* is the other principal source for Old Latin readings: Augustine began writing this around 400, while books two to fifteen were composed between 411 and 422, and there is a noticeable change in the affiliation of the biblical citations during the course of the work. A number of Augustine's sermons on John are based on Old Latin lections, such as *Sermo* 129 on John 5:39–47. This often seems to be a particular characteristic of sermons preached in Carthage, including *Sermo* 133 (John 7:2–10) and *Sermo* 145 (John 16:24). Even after he began to use Jerome's version in Hippo, Augustine still drew his text from local Old Latin manuscripts when preaching in other churches.[8]

Augustine does not seem ever to have been familiar with the versions of the Epistles, Acts, or Revelation which became part of the Vulgate. The citations of Acts and 1 Timothy read out of different

[7] For the possible origin of Faustus' text in the Diatessaron, see pp. 19–20 above and the discussion of *Contra Faustum* on pp. 149–51 below. Augustine's customary silence concerning his opponents' scriptural texts is noted by Decret (1970:154).

[8] These three sermons were dated to the end of the fourth century in Frede 1995; however, in Gryson 2007, *Sermo* 129 is placed in 405/9, *Sermo* 133 in 405, and *Sermo* 145 in 412/5. Just as Augustine appears to have extended the text-type of his opponents to his own citations in his polemical works, there are also distinctly Old Latin readings in John in sermons preached on a different lection outside Hippo (e.g. *Enarrationes in Psalmos* 39, 40, 58.s1, 95, 98, and 102): it is, however, possible that John had been the liturgical Gospel of the day.

manuscripts in *Contra Felicem* 1.4–8 are both in Old Latin forms, as are those from Ephesians and Romans in *Contra Fortunatum.* Augustine's commentaries on Romans and Galatians also use an Old Latin exemplar, while his sermons on the First Epistle of John, delivered around 407, are based on an older text than the majority of his citations.[9] The corrections Augustine makes to his opponents' citations of the Epistles quoted above do not correspond to the Vulgate; neither do the twelve paragraphs of *testimonia* from ten Epistles, Acts, and Revelation in *De peccatorum meritis* 1.27.41–52. Similarly, the citations of extended passages from Revelation 20, 2 Peter, 1 and 2 Thessalonians, 1 Corinthians and Ephesians in the final three books of *De ciuitate dei* (422–6) all diverge more or less from the form of text which appears in the Vulgate. The only occasion on which the later text of these books does appear is in the collection of biblical *testimonia* known as the *Speculum quis ignorat,* which was altered by a subsequent editor.[10]

The earliest primary citations which accord with Jerome's revision of the Gospels occur throughout *De consensu euangelistarum* and at *Contra Felicem* 1.3, where a long citation of Luke was read out from a manuscript and recorded by stenographers. *Sermo* 362, now believed to have been delivered in 403, includes John 5:24–9 read from a codex with a Vulgate form of text. Augustine also used this version for his sermon-commentary on John (*Tractatus in Iohannis euangelium*), which he began in 406/7. *De peccatorum meritis* 1.30.59, composed a few years later, contains an uninterrupted citation of John 3:1–21; although there are some variant readings corresponding to Old Latin witnesses, the overall character is Vulgate as shown by two distinctive readings found only in this version. In later works, all extended gospel references conform to this text-type, such as the citations of Matthew 13:37–43, Matthew 25:31–41, and John 5:22–9 in *De ciuitate dei* 20.5. The minor variations found in primary citations of the Vulgate probably reflect the exemplars used by Augustine: although most, if not all, are paralleled in surviving Old Latin manuscripts and might therefore be dismissed as contamination, it is also possible that, as one

[9] See Thiele 1972:101.

[10] See pp. 174–5 and the references provided there.

of the first witnesses to Jerome's version, Augustine may sometimes give a text closer to the original.[11]

The form of the primary citations indicates that most of the biblical references in Augustine's writings have not undergone later revision or adaptation. It has often been suggested that copyists consciously or subconsciously made scriptural citations conform to the text best known to them: the subsequent prevalence of the Vulgate may have resulted in the eradication of many Old Latin features in the biblical references of early Church Fathers. There is some evidence for this in the works of other authors, as well as the *Speculum quis ignorat* noted above.[12] Although it remains possible that individual citations may have been corrupted, especially in works preserved in a single manuscript or handful of copies, in the majority of cases we can be fairly confident that we have the original scriptural text: as I have already observed, Augustine's citations follow a general pattern of Old Latin readings in his early works, and Vulgate forms in those composed after 404. Furthermore, not only are there inconsistencies between different works (and sometimes within the same work), but Augustine's citations also feature several readings in John which do not correspond to any surviving biblical manuscript: it is reasonable to assume that a redactor would correct the text towards the Vulgate. Some modern editions of Augustine do include one or two witnesses in which the influence of the Vulgate can be detected, but these are among the latest and least significant for the text. In contrast, Old Latin readings which have not been adopted by the editor are sometimes found in the critical apparatus, and may be worthy of further consideration.[13]

[11] Gribomont (1985:62) goes so far as to claim that no Vulgate copy of the New Testament is free from Old Latin readings. The text of the Vulgate in modern editions, based on manuscripts from the sixth to eighth centuries, may owe more to Cassiodorus or later scholars than Jerome himself.

[12] Petitmengin 2003:7 mentions the alteration of the biblical text in commentaries on Paul by Pelagius and Ambrosiaster. See also Frede 1972:469–70 and Bogaert 2006:149.

[13] For examples of both types of witness, see the section on *De diuersis quaestionibus* on pp. 140–3 below. Elliott 1986:140 notes the need for textual criticism of patristic sources before using them as evidence for the Bible. Criticisms of the biblical text presented in certain editions of the Church Fathers are voiced at Frede 1972:470–2 and Willis 1966.

There do not seem to be any indications that scriptural citations are any more or less liable to alteration than the rest of the text within which they are set, implying that, in Augustine's works at least, 'vulgatizing' tendencies may be less widespread than generally supposed.

The majority of Augustine's secondary citations do not correspond as closely to biblical exemplars as the longer quotations, but display abbreviations and other alterations characteristic of flattening. This confirms that they have been drawn from memory. Nonetheless, there are a number of cases when it is very difficult to decide whether a shorter citation was made with reference to a manuscript or not, particularly when it is textually distinctive. For example, some verses of John quoted in *De praedestinatione sanctorum* and *De dono perseuerantiae* have Old Latin similarities even though these works were written in the last three years of Augustine's life. In such cases, it is possible that Augustine either referred to a different copy of the Gospels from usual, or that he took his text from an intermediate source, such as a collection of *testimonia* or another patristic writing. The overall pattern of the secondary citations conforms to that identified in the previous paragraph, beginning with Old Latin forms and gradually moving towards the Vulgate. However, there is a slight delay in the influence of the Vulgate on this material, which further suggests that Augustine was quoting from memory. In later works, the Vulgate even displaces the version which Augustine has cited on all previous occasions. For example, in the *Quaestiones in Heptateuchum* of 419, Augustine abandons his usual form of John 14:30–1, citing a Vulgate text for the only time outside *Tractatus in Iohannem* 79 (*Quaestiones de Deuteronomio* 55), while the text of John 7:37–9 in *Quaestiones de Iudicibus* 36 is closer to the Vulgate than any of his other citations. Likewise, in *De gratia et libero arbitrio* from 426, Augustine prefers the Vulgate form of John 3:27, 13:34, and 13:35 to his customary form of these verses. It is therefore possible to chart the differing rate at which Augustine adopted the Vulgate according to whether he was citing from a codex or from memory.[14]

[14] As well as Part II below, a summary of this is presented in Houghton 2008.

The form (or forms) of Augustine's mental text can usually be determined for commonly cited verses. Indeed, the more frequently Augustine quotes a verse and the more stable his text, the less likely it is to derive directly from a biblical manuscript. This form of text is already found for some verses in his earliest works, proving that it reflects Old Latin versions with which he was familiar. As details such as auxiliary words and sentence structure are likely to have been affected by flattening, his mental text is primarily valuable for the rendering of key words and phrases. Again, it can be problematic to decide whether a frequently appearing reading not attested elsewhere derives from a version now lost or is a feature of Augustine's mental text. For example, *tunc* in John 8:36 is found in twenty-eight of Augustine's thirty-two citations:

si uos filius liberauerit, ***tunc*** *uere liberi eritis.*

The omission of *ergo* before *uos* is typical of flattening, and it is simple to see *tunc* as a secondary addition which highlights the antithesis of the verse. Even so, the weight of attestation is remarkable. Likewise, in John 5:19, where surviving manuscripts have either *haec* or *eadem*, Augustine reads a double form on thirteen occasions, as in:

quaecumque enim pater fecerit ***haec eadem*** *et filius facit similiter.*

(*Tractatus in Iohannem* 20.1)

There are also examples of flattening in this text, such as the replacement of the pronoun *ille* by *pater*, but the fact that this form appears in his commentary on this verse is significant. Of course, even if a particular variant characteristic of memory is paralleled in a biblical codex, this may be purely coincidental. Another indication of Augustine's mental text comes when he is reading from a manuscript and encounters a form of text which does not correspond to what he was expecting. His response is to gloss the unexpected term with the more familiar form, as in the third sermon of his commentary on John:

in propria uenit, id est in sua uenit, *et sui eum non receperunt.*

(*Tractatus in Iohannem* 3.6)

He came to what was his, that is he came to his own, *and his own did not receive him.*

In keeping with several Old Latin Gospels, most of Augustine's citations of John 1:11 read *in sua propria uenit*; only the Vulgate has *in propria uenit*. It is hardly surprising that in this, one of the earliest sermons in his commentary, Augustine supplies the Old Latin form he knew by heart. The same phenomenon occurs in a number of the *Tractatus in Iohannem*, as when he glosses *sub ficu* in John 1:48 with *id est, sub arbore fici*, the Old Latin rendering, at *Tractatus* 7.20. Similarly, in two sermons Augustine gives an alternative form for John 21:11 which is common in his citations but unique to him, *tanti, id est tam magni* (*Sermones* 251.3.3 and 252.1.1).

There is no surviving biblical manuscript which offers an exact match for Augustine's citations in any one work, let alone across his entire output. Such a correspondence would be extraordinary, given the scarcity of codices which have been preserved from the time of Augustine. The Matzkow–Jülicher–Aland edition of the Old Latin version of John is based on the main twelve manuscripts, which are more or less complete, and six fragments of no more than four pages: most were copied after Augustine's death, although they may preserve text-types current in his day. Burton groups these into two classes, the first of which comprises the oldest surviving manuscripts, while the second includes the Vulgate and a number of witnesses often described as 'mixed texts'.[15] It is perhaps only to be expected that the majority of Augustine's Old Latin readings corresponds to members of the first group, since these have been defined against the Vulgate. Even so, it is important not to overlook the considerable variation within each group. The Old Latin vocabulary in Augustine's mental text usually corresponds to the agreement of three or four of the principal older manuscripts, with renderings such as *mandatum* rather than *praeceptum* for ἐντολή, *caritas* and not *dilectio* for ἀγάπη, and *occidere* rather than *interficere* for ἀποκτείνω. These matches are impossible to predict, however, because neither Augustine nor the gospel codices are consistent. Furthermore, even within the same citation different variants often correspond to mutually exclusive groups of witnesses.

15 Burton 2000:62–74; for more detailed descriptions of the surviving Old Latin manuscripts and their texts see pp. 104–6 below.

On the other hand, in certain citations, a variant or combination of variants may only be paralleled in a single Old Latin manuscript. This is partly due to the haphazard preservation of different text-types; nonetheless, it still provides points of orientation. For example, a large proportion of Augustine's non-Vulgate readings are also present in Codex Monacensis, including those in a number of primary citations, such as *Sermones* 133 and 145 and parts of the long passage from John 4 in *De diuersis quaestionibus* 64.[16] Unexpectedly, the best match for the latter is Codex Rehdigeranus, which Burton places in his second group, and it is possible that its text-type in John 4 is closer to the earlier versions. The biblical lection in *Sermo* 127 resembles Codex Usserianus, a member of the first group; this manuscript has a number of similarities to Codex Monacensis, and provides the only sustained agreement for the text of John 12:47–50 in the first book of *De trinitate.* Other readings in *De trinitate* 1 are only found in Codex Vercellensis, the oldest surviving manuscript, and Codex Monacensis. Codex Palatinus, the principal Old Latin witness for 'African' readings in John, corresponds to certain features of primary citations in *Sermones* 14A, 126, and 129, as well as secondary citations in other sermons and theological works (e.g. *Sermones* 5, 210, and 239, many of the *Enarrationes in Psalmos*, the *Adnotationes in Iob* and *De catechizandis rudibus*). This patchwork of parallels shows the complexity of trying to match Augustine's biblical text with the Old Latin versions still extant.

Despite the scarcity of Old Latin gospel manuscripts, it is remarkable that, although extended correspondences are rare, the vast majority of Augustine's non-Vulgate readings are paralleled in the codices which have survived to the present day. This suggests that the versions which have been preserved are a fairly representative sample of what was available to him in North Africa at the end of the fourth century (even though many were copied after this date). Even in cases when Augustine's reading does not appear in an exemplar at that point, the same rendering may be found elsewhere in the tradition. For example, at John 1:23 and 3:14, Augustine has *eremo*

[16] Gryson 1978 has shown that the biblical text of Augustine's opponent Maximinus is even closer to Codex Monacensis: his study is a model of the close analysis of Old Latin affiliations in one or two patristic texts, but such a detailed approach is impracticable for the much larger body of evidence considered here.

for ἐρήμῳ in Greek. In neither verse does this feature in the extant Old Latin manuscripts, but at John 6:49 this rendering occurs in Codex Usserianus, indicating that it may well have been more widespread. Again, although the use of *glorificare* to render δοξάζειν is found in biblical tradition at John 17:5 and 17:10, Augustine also has it independently at John 17:4 and John 21:19. In certain cases, contextual considerations may have governed the choice of rendering: in John 11:14 when Jesus 'openly' announces the death of Lazarus, παρρησίᾳ is translated by *manifeste*, as alternatives such as *in auctoritate*, *constanter*, or *audenter* would not suit the occasion.[17] However, there is no obvious constraint for the rendering of this term at John 16:25, where *De trinitate* 1.10.21 has the only surviving instance of *manifeste*; Codex Palatinus reads *euidenter* here, and this in turn supplies a parallel for Augustine's unique use of *euidenter* in John 7:10, where φανερῶς is rendered in most Old Latin witnesses as *manifeste*. While it remains possible that Augustine may have substituted an equivalent term when citing from memory, it is reasonable to consider the majority of these variants as evidence for readings which once featured in the manuscript tradition.

Some readings absent from the manuscripts may be attested by other Latin Fathers. Although it is often the case that this may indicate dependence, it is also possible that both may preserve evidence from exemplars which no longer exist, particularly if the rendering corresponds to known Greek texts. One of the best examples of this is Augustine's reading *officium facere* in John 16:2, quoted above in his criticism of Gaudentius' text of this verse. Not only is this a plausible translation of the Greek λατρείαν προσφέρειν, but it is found in four other Fathers: Augustine's opponent Petilianus, Tyconius (another Donatist), Cyprian, and Lucifer of Cagliari. Even if the two Donatists might have derived their text from Cyprian, the appearance of this form outside Africa in Lucifer's *De Athanasio* is a strong argument in favour of its inclusion in a version now lost. As the manuscript evidence for the text of John used in Africa is comparatively slight, correspondences between Augustine and Cyprian may reflect this tradition. For instance, the rendering of

[17] For this example, I am grateful to Philip Burton; he identifies other key renderings and contextual constraints in Burton 2000:29–74.

$\mu\alpha\rho\tau\acute{\upsilon}\rho\eta\sigma o\nu$ by *exprobra* in John 18:23 occurs in three of Augustine's five citations and three times in Cyprian, but not in any surviving biblical codex. Similarly, Cyprian also cites John 3:14 with *eremo.* Even though Augustine is known to have used Cyprian and other African Fathers when composing his theological works, if these similarities feature in the context of sermons or other occasions when he was not able to refer to earlier sources then it is more likely that they offer independent witness to a form no longer preserved in an Old Latin manuscript.

In contrast with the remnants of the Old Latin Gospels, it has been estimated that over ten thousand manuscripts of the Vulgate survive. Modern critical editions are based on a selection of the most important witnesses, which can be split into groups according to country of origin or recension.[18] Weber–Gryson gives the readings of fourteen manuscripts and two editions in the Gospels: again, while many of the variants in Augustine's primary citations based on Jerome's version are paralleled in their critical apparatus, there is no significant pattern of correspondence with any one witness. Most of these forms are also found in Old Latin sources, anyhow, and so are not distinctive of the Vulgate. The most extensive collation of Latin biblical manuscripts is Fischer's comparison of over four hundred and fifty gospel codices dated before the tenth century across four test passages in each Gospel. The data provided for John bring to light a number of parallels for readings in Augustine's citations not found in the Old Latin tradition or principal Vulgate sources. Some are found in a number of witnesses, such as the word order *datum fuerit ei* in John 3:27 (a characteristic of Irish manuscripts), *dicit* in John 7:33, *nescio* in John 20:2, and *scripturas* in John 20:9. Others only appear in a single codex: Fischer's manuscript **Wb**, a Spanish lectionary from around the beginning of the tenth century, alone matches *intrabit* rather than *potest intrare* in John 3:5; **Jy**, an early Vulgate manuscript from an Italian *scriptorium* reads *discesserunt* for *recesserunt* in John 8:9; **Ce**, copied in Belgium or north-east France at the beginning of the ninth century, provides the sole example of *insufflauit in faciem eorum* at John 20:22. These parallels demonstrate

[18] The most detailed analysis is Berger 1893, but a convenient summary may be found in Elliott 1992:220–35.

the continuity in the Latin versions of the Gospels, often characterized as the appearance of Old Latin readings in otherwise Vulgate texts. Certain witnesses normally described as Vulgate may, in fact, preserve substantial sections of Old Latin material: the only manuscript example of *opus non habebat* in John 2:25, **Jc**, has been identified as an Old Latin witness in John 1–6, and the same is true of the ninth-century Breton manuscript **Bw**, which also parallels some of Augustine's variants.[19] On the other hand, it is also possible that what appear to be fossilized Old Latin forms may have been reintroduced into the manuscript tradition through glosses or following comparison with the text of patristic citations or commentaries. Despite the wealth of information presented by Fischer, a few readings remain unique to Augustine, such as *hoc autem* in John 2:21 and *fratribus* in John 20:17.

The principal evidence for Augustine's use of a Vulgate text of John comes from *De consensu euangelistarum* and the *Tractatus in Iohannem.* As noted in Chapters 5 and 8, the citations most likely to have been drawn from manuscripts are the initial citations in the commentary and the sequential treatment of the Gospels in *De consensu.* It appears that Augustine used different manuscripts of John for these two works, as they rarely feature the same variant reading. The following are common to both: the omission of *uobis*, and *uenit* (for *uenturus est*) in John 1:15, the addition of *ecce* in John 1:29, *missus erat* (for *missus fuerat*) in John 3:24, the addition of *autem* in John 8:35, *etiamsi* (for *et si*) in John 11:25, *in cor* (for *in corde*) at John 13:2, *quaeritis* (for *quaeretis*) in John 13:33, *ad Caipham* in John 18:28, *impleretur* (for *impleatur*) in John 19:24, the omission of *iam* in John 19:28, *uidit* (for *uidet*) in John 20:14, *dixit* (for *dicit*) in John 20:22, *resurrexisset* (for *surrexisset*) in John 21:14, and the omission of *si* in John 21:22 and 21:23. All of these appear in witnesses listed in the critical apparatus of Weber–Gryson.[20] There

19 Gryson 1999 identifies fourteen Old Latin witnesses to John not included in Matzkow–Jülicher–Aland: portions of seven manuscripts (including **Jc**), three lectionaries, three canon tables and a set of glosses. Until the publication of the new *Vetus Latina Iohannes*, these are not easily accessible and so have not been cited in this study except for the passages given in Fischer 1991.

20 Burkitt 1910:457 offers a list of readings in Matthew where *De consensu euangelistarum* is of interest in agreeing with early Vulgate manuscripts.

are also several readings shared by the commentary text of the *Tractatus* and certain manuscripts of *De consensu euangelistarum.* For example, *panibus meis* in John 6:26, unique to Augustine, occurs in *Tractatus* 25.10 and one manuscript of *De consensu* 4.10.15. In John 19:13, *autem* rather than *ergo* is present in *Tractatus* 116.8 and certain manuscripts of *De consensu* 3.8.35. This is found in some Vulgate witnesses, as are *utique* in John 18:36, *congregati* in John 20:19, and *suis* in John 21:14, also featuring in the *Tractatus* and the apparatus of *De consensu euangelistarum.* A full list of differences between the initial citations in the *Tractatus* and the editorial text of Weber–Gryson is provided in Chapter 5: the majority appear in other Vulgate manuscripts or the Old Latin tradition although, again, a handful are not even paralleled in Fischer's collation, including *rursum* in John 8:8 and *deinceps* in John 8:11.

Augustine's citations are at two removes from the Greek text of the Gospels, being both patristic and versional evidence. Nonetheless, the Old Latin tradition has been identified as a source for what is sometimes known as the 'Western' text, a strand of biblical transmission marked by a number of additions and peculiar readings. Recent advances in the classification of witnesses have cast doubt on theories of an early separation of Greek manuscripts into geographical text-types, but Latin support for readings traditionally grouped under this name remains important.[21] Augustine's citations contain three of the four 'Greater Interpolations' identified by Burkitt in the 'Western' text of John, namely the *Pericope Adulterae* (John 7:53–8:11), the addition of *quoniam deus spiritus est* in John 3:6 and the angel at the pool in John 5:4, which Augustine clearly knows although he does not quote verbatim. He gives no indication, however, of the additional phrase about receiving the body of the Son of Man as the bread of life in John 6:56.[22]

[21] The classic exposition of the theory of geographical text-types is at Westcott and Hort 1882:108–35, with a description of 'Western' characteristics on 120–6. The Vulgate seems to have been revised against an 'Alexandrian' Greek text (see Westcott and Hort 1882:152; Metzger 1977:355–9). The theory of geographical text-types has been called into question by the development of the Coherence-Based Genealogical Method: see the report of a recent presentation by Wachtel and Strutwolf in Foster 2006.

[22] For the 'Western' interpolations in the Gospels, see Burkitt 1896:46–53. Augustine's works also support two of the six 'Smaller Interpolations' in John, with the

Most of the readings significant for the Greek text in Augustine are shared with Latin biblical manuscripts. For example, all Old Latin witnesses have the present tense *uita est* in John 1:4, as do about half Augustine's citations; the Greek present is found in Codex Sinaiticus and Codex Bezae. Similarly, in John 1:34, only Codex Sinaiticus has ὁ ἐκλεκτός but four Old Latin witnesses include *electus*, which appears in Augustine's *Sermo* 308A.4. The majority of his citations of John 14:30 read *nihil inueniet*, based on a similar text to that underlying Codex Brixianus, only extant in a few Greek manuscripts. In John 16:21, *Sermo* 210.5.7 has *dies* rather than *hora*, like ἡμέρα in P^{66} and Codex Bezae. Others appear in Vulgate witnesses, such as *filium* rather than *nomen* in John 12:28 (*Sermo* 12.5 and *De trinitate* 2.10.18), corresponding to υἱόν in Greek, although this may be an independent harmonization between this verse and John 17:1. Augustine is cited by name on two occasions in the critical apparatus of Nestle–Aland. In John 10:8, *ante me* (πρὸ ἐμοῦ) is missing from all three of his own citations (*Tractatus* 45, *Contra aduersarium* 2.4.16, and *Enarratio* 90.s1.1) although he repeats it from his opponents' text at *Contra Faustum* 16.12 (based on 16.2) and *Contra aduersarium* 2.4.16. In John 6:59, however, the evidence for his addition of *sabbato* is less convincing: it does not occur in his one citation of John 6:59 (*De correptione et gratia* 22), but only features in the title of *Tractatus in Iohannem* 27, which was probably added by a later editor.[23]

There are two readings in the *Pericope Adulterae*, both in John 8:9, for which Augustine appears to constitute the earliest surviving evidence. The first is the addition at the beginning of the verse referring to the consciences of the accusers, which appears as καὶ ὑπὸ τῆς συνειδησέως ἐλεγχόμενοι in four later Greek majuscules and several minuscules. The only examples of this in Latin seem to be Augustine's *illi autem considerantes conscientias suas* in *Sermo* 272B.5 and *unusquisque iam interrogans conscientiam suam* at *Enarratio* 102.11, with *unusquisque* corresponding to ἕκαστος in some

reading *qui est in caelo* in John 3:18 and the inclusion of *sabbato* in John 6:59 (on which see the following paragraph).

[23] Tischendorf also cites Augustine at these places: although he gives more details about the attestation, he does not mention *Enarratio* 90.s1 or *De correptione et gratia*.

witnesses. The other is the inclusion after 'beginning from the eldest' of the phrase 'until the youngest': Augustine reads *usque ad minores* in *Sermo* 16A.4 and *usque ad minorem* in *Sermo* 272B.5.[24] This corresponds to ἕως τῶν ἐσχάτων in five later Greek majuscules, as well as numerous minuscules; there are also two later Latin gospel manuscripts which read *usque ad iuniorem* (Fischer's **Bw**, ninth-century) and *usque in ultimis* (Fischer's **Sx**, tenth-century), but apart from these the phrase does not occur elsewhere in the Latin tradition.

In a very small number of instances, the Latin tradition has a variant without a parallel in surviving Greek manuscripts. Although the retroversion of a Latin citation into Greek can only be a hypothesis, this may be justified in a few cases when the evidence is sufficiently consistent. One of the best-known examples is the singular in John 1:13, *natus est* rather than ἐγεννήθησαν, present in Codex Veronensis and Tertullian. Two of Augustine's citations support this reading, *Confessiones* 7.9.14 and *De peccatorum meritis* 2.24.38, even though the majority of his references to this verse have the plural. Of the two versions of John 16:13 known to Augustine from Latin codices, *docebit uos omnem ueritatem* and *deducet uos in omni ueritate*, only the latter corresponds to Greek manuscripts, which read ὁδηγήσει. Despite a connection sometimes made between *docebit* and the patristic reading διηγήσεται, it is more likely to derive from διδάξει.[25] Augustine's unique reading *feret* in John 21:18 presents a similar case. This corresponds to the standard Greek reading οἴσει, which suggests that *ducet* in the rest of the Latin tradition may reflect a different term, perhaps comparable to ἀπάγουσιν in Codex Bezae (the Latin side of which has *ducent*).

It has sometimes been suggested that Augustine's citations contain readings from the Diatessaron. Even though this version was also current among various Manichaean groups, Augustine's earlier affiliation with this sect is unlikely to have provided him with any significant knowledge of this harmony: he never progressed beyond

[24] One manuscript of *Sermo* 16A.4 reads *minorem* rather than *minores omnem*.

[25] The equation between διηγήσεται and the Vulgate *docebit* appears in Nestle–Aland. John 14:26 demonstrates the equivalence of *docere* and διδάσκειν, although the variant may be internal to the Latin tradition given the similarity of *ducere* and *docere* (see Weber-Gryson). See further p. 317 below.

the grade of *auditor*, and the gradual development of his familiarity with the biblical text after his baptism is entirely consistent with his having started from scratch at his conversion. Furthermore, most of the alleged 'Diatessaronic' readings in his citations appear in later works and none corresponds to the oldest Latin harmony manuscript, the sixth-century Codex Fuldensis.[26] Instead, the same variants are also present in Old Latin witnesses, which are much more likely to have been Augustine's source. The extra phrase in John 13:9, which has been claimed to reflect the Tatianic baptismal practice of full immersion, appears in Codex Vercellensis, while others are minor conflations which could even have arisen independently, such as the insertion of *amicus noster* from John 11:11 into verse fourteen, or the repetition of *uado* in John 20:17. Given these parallels with Old Latin manuscripts, it is possible that some are further interpolations characteristic of the 'Western' text.[27]

It has already been judged unlikely on external grounds that Augustine made a systematic revision of the text of the New Testament. This can also be shown from a comparison of the variant readings in his citations with Greek manuscripts: although we cannot know for sure the reading of the Greek versions available to Augustine, revision normally brings a translation into greater correspondence with its source.[28] If such emendation had taken place, traces would be most likely to appear in the *Tractatus in Iohannem.* These do feature a couple of readings which are not found elsewhere in the Latin tradition but resemble forms in Greek. *Tractatus* 61 and 62 have uncompounded forms of *tingere* on both occasions in John 13:26,

[26] For the history of the Latin gospel harmony tradition, see Schmid 2003 and 2005, who shows that there is no evidence that the existing Latin manuscripts rely on an Old Latin gospel harmony prior to Codex Fuldensis (Schmid 2005:33). In his major study of the Diatessaron, Petersen remarks of Augustine that 'one might presume that had he known the Diatessaron, he would have mentioned it, or that more blatant Diatessaronic readings would have surfaced in his copious œuvre' (1994:336).

[27] On John 13:9, see Petersen 1994:380–4; Augustine offers a loose reference with *et totum* at *Enarratio* 92.3. Examples of minor additions corresponding to Codices Vercellensis or Bezae include *ante me* in John 10:8, *et ego* in John 15:12, and *in eos* in John 20:22.

[28] Gribomont (1985:52) observes that the custom of revisers was to reinforce the parallelism of Latin Bibles with Greek, both in structure and vocabulary; Burton comments that the Vulgate is more literal than the Old Latin Gospels (2000:79).

which correspond to βαπτίζειν in the majority of Greek manuscripts; *intingere* in all other Latin witnesses matches the variant ἐμβαπτίζειν. In John 14:24, *Tractatus* 76 reads ***sermo** quem audistis non est meus*: in Latin Bibles *sermo* has been attracted into the accusative of the relative clause, but in Greek it remains nominative: ὁ λόγος ὃν ἀκούετε οὐκ ἔστιν ἐμός. However, these are the only parallels with Greek which are unique to the initial citations in the *Tractatus in Iohannem*.[29] By contrast, Augustine's text features several discrepancies which have no support in Nestle–Aland, such as the plural *quaecumque* in John 14:13 (all Greek witnesses have the singular), ***ad** Caipham* in John 18:28 (the Greek has ἀπό), and the addition of *rex iudaeorum* at John 19:20. The most significant is the perpetuation of the reading *discumbentium* ('recliners') in John 21:12 (*Tractatus* 123), where all Greek witnesses have τῶν μαθητῶν ('disciples'). The Latin variant probably arose through an early misreading of *discentium* ('learners'): comparison with the Greek would result in the correction which does appear to have been made by Jerome, although some Vulgate manuscripts (including that used by Augustine) continue to read *discumbentium*. This seems to confirm that Augustine did not revise the text of John himself, but relied on a version of Jerome's revision.[30]

In conclusion, Augustine's citations are of considerable value for the history of the New Testament. His prime importance is for the Latin tradition, both Vulgate and Old Latin, although these early translations can also have a bearing on the Greek text. The explicit comments he makes about variant readings and his primary citations constitute the most significant evidence, as there is a high probability

[29] Others are also found in Vulgate manuscripts, such as the omission of *ipsum* in John 18:2, where the Greek has been misunderstood by several Latin translators; compare also *illud* in John 6:39 and John 19:40, although this may be an internal change as the strict antecedent in Latin both times is also neuter. Resemblances to Greek manuscripts in illustrative citations are more difficult to explain, and may simply be coincidence. The most remarkable example of this is John 9:39, where all Latin Bibles render the Greek participles by relative clauses, but *Tractatus* 33.1 preserves them: *ut non uidentes uideant et uidentes caeci fiant*.

[30] The biblical text of *Tractatus* 17 and 24, discussed on pp. 117–20 below, is exceptional in that it appears to have been altered in order to read more smoothly. However, this is an internal improvement to the Latin, and there is no evidence that it is due to Augustine. His explicit comment on John 12:32 at *Tractatus* 52.11 also implies that he had not consulted a Greek codex.

that these transmit the text of manuscripts known to him. Old Latin forms are found in his secondary citations as well, but as most of these were made from memory they may include alterations or errors. The distinctive overall pattern which has emerged of Augustine's textual affiliation indicates that his scriptural citations have for the most part been transmitted accurately. It also reflects his increasing familiarity with the gospel text and his adoption of the version now known as the Vulgate. The fact that the majority of Augustine's non-Vulgate readings are paralleled in surviving Old Latin manuscripts suggests that these provide a fairly complete cross-section of the versions available to him: the principal exceptions are the variants shared with other African Church Fathers. The overall conclusion must be that although Augustine's text of John often has clear affinities with the Vulgate, it illustrates clearly the continuity in the Latin Bible and the ongoing transmission of Old Latin elements within the revised version. This textual evidence reveals much about Augustine's own use of the Bible which should be borne in mind when considering his own exegesis and the textual history of his works. The later parts of the present book offer more detailed accounts of the biblical citations in individual works and a commentary on Augustine's text of John to assist with further historical and text-critical research.

Part II

Augustine's Citations of John: Analysis of Selected Works

Introduction: Sources and Dates

By analysing the text of all the citations of the Gospel according to John in Augustine's writings, it is possible to gain an idea of the patterns of affiliation between his biblical text and surviving manuscripts. The overall shape has already been described: correspondences with Old Latin witnesses in earlier works give way to readings from Jerome's revision of the Gospels. The results are immediate in citations made with reference to a codex, and much more gradual in Augustine's mental text. In Part II, these conclusions are illustrated by a detailed study of the text of John in selected works, beginning with the *Tractatus in Iohannem* and other sermons based on this Gospel, and then considering other writings in broadly chronological order.[1] Treating each work separately allows for the possibility of anomaly, either in the source Augustine used for his biblical text or in the later transmission of that work. It also gives an indication of Augustine's consistency within each piece, which is essential for distinguishing primary and secondary citations.

The dating of Augustine's works is often highly contested. His own list in the *Retractationes*, which appears to be in roughly chronological order, provides a point of departure. Certain letters, such as *Epistulae* 23A* and 169, include details of his current projects. Writings which do not feature in such lists, such as individual sermons and letters, are sometimes assigned a date on the basis of allusion to historical events, such as the passing of a law or death of a bishop. Similarities with other works are also important in terms of mapping Augustine's theological development. Several studies have shown that his exegesis of certain verses changes over time: even the *orchestration*

1 A representative selection of works is also presented in Houghton 2008.

scripturaire, the combination of scriptural texts to illustrate a particular idea, is significant in this respect.[2] For the sake of convenience, dates have been taken from the latest edition of the index of Church Fathers published by the Institut Vetus Latina (Gryson 2007), unless otherwise specified. This index also gives details of the most recent editions for each of Augustine's works, which are usually those cited in this study.[3] References are cited using the standard system of sections and paragraphs.

The standard text for the Gospel according to John is provided by the editorial form of the Weber–Gryson Vulgate. When Augustine's citations differ from this, they are characterized in terms of their relationship to the surviving Old Latin manuscripts presented by Matzkow–Jülicher–Aland. Along with many editions of the Bible, this uses a system of lower-case letters to indicate Old Latin manuscripts: these are being superseded by a numerical classification (Gryson 1999), and both designations are given in the rest of this section. Elsewhere, however, manuscripts are referred to by name. The two Old Latin text-types have already been described above, but it may be useful here to provide further details about individual witnesses.[4]

Burton's first group in John consists of seven witnesses which often differ markedly from the Vulgate. **Codex Palatinus** (e, 2) contains the greatest proportion of 'African' renderings, but this fifth-century manuscript has been overlaid with a European text and it has been suggested that it was copied in North Italy rather than Africa.[5] **Codex**

[2] On the *orchestration scripturaire*, see La Bonnardière 1965 and Hombert 2000. Berrouard and Dulaey, amongst others, consider the treatment of single verses, details of which are given in Part III below.

[3] The exceptions are the *Enarrationes in Psalmos*, where the *Corpus Christianorum* edition of Dekkers and Fraipont has been used throughout, and the *Sermones ad populum*: the most convenient edition of *Sermones* 51–396 is the online text at www.augustinus.it which reproduces Migne's *Patrologia Latina* along with the supplementary sermons (apart from the *Sermones Dolbeau*). The dates given in Gryson 2007 correspond largely to the complete chronology of Augustine's works assembled in Anoz 2002: the latter also gives references to secondary literature to explain the chosen date and provides a further list featuring every work in chronological order. Many of the revised datings differ markedly from Frede 1995, especially in the case of the sermons, and I have sometimes mentioned alternatives previously suggested.

[4] See p. 89 above, based on Burton 2000. I also rely on Burton 2000:16–28 for the following descriptions, which may be supplemented by the bibliographies in Gryson 1999:21–45, Metzger 1977:295–308, and Elliott 1992:203–12.

[5] Fischer 1972:32; on the difficulty of classifying Codex Palatinus in John, see Burton 2000:17.

Vercellensis (a, 3), an Italian manuscript from the second half of the fourth century, has a number of unique and important early readings, although its deterioriation means that scholars often have to rely on previous editions. **Codex Veronensis** (b, 4) is a fine fifth-century Italian codex with silver and gold ink on purple vellum and one of the best 'European' witnesses for the Synoptic Gospels. In John, however, its affiliation changes around the beginning of chapter 11, when it becomes part of the second group. **Codex Bezae** (d, 5) is the oldest surviving bilingual gospel manuscript, with Greek on the left-hand page and Latin in the privileged position on the right. Despite a predominantly European text-type, it seems likely that the manuscript was produced in Africa. The Latin and the Greek sides of Codex Bezae are independent in origin, although there has been some cross-contamination: it is the main Greek witness for the interpolated 'Western' text.[6] Two manuscripts from the sixth or early seventh century, which often provide parallels for Augustine's non-Vulgate readings, may form a distinct sub-group in John: these are **Codex Monacensis** (q, 13), copied in Illyria or North Italy but with a text-type very similar to Augustine's Arian opponent Maximinus, and **Codex Usserianus** (r^1, 14), the principal 'Gallo-Irish' witness.[7] **Codex Sarzanensis** (j, 22) actually consists of two different Old Latin manuscripts; the larger portion, covering the first half of the Gospel, has a text close to Codex Veronensis. Burton includes two fragments within this group, the **Fragmentum Sangallense** (p, 20) and the **Fragmentum Mediolanense** (ρ, 24). In addition to these, the **Folium Vindobonense** (v, 25) also occasionally corresponds to readings in Augustine.

The second group is of Old Latin manuscripts which have a text closely linked to that of Jerome's revision of the Gospels. **Codex Corbeiensis** (ff^2, 8) is a fifth-century witness, which in John 'forms the basis of the Vulgate text' (Burton 2000:20). Two manuscripts are related to this, **Codex Rehdigeranus** (l, 11) from the first half of the eighth century, and **Codex Colbertinus** (c, 6), the most recent Old Latin manuscript, dating from the twelfth century. The latter changes

6 The principal study of Codex Bezae is Parker 1992; its production is considered on 269 ff., and the relationship of the two versions on 198 ff. and 250 ff. Burton 2000:22 includes an example of the influence of the Latin side on the Greek.

7 The biblical text of Maximinus is analysed in Gryson 1978.

affiliation, like Codex Veronensis, becoming less similar to the Vulgate from chapter 7 onwards.[8] In contrast with these three 'basically Old Latin' codices, the sixth-century **Codex Brixianus** (f, 10) and the eighth-century **Codex Aureus** (aur, 15) are 'basically Vulgate' and are classified as Vulgate by Fischer.[9] The textual history of the Vulgate is even more complicated than that of the Old Latin witnesses: the differences between early 'mixed texts' were amplified into distinct local traditions, before reformers such as Theodulf and Alcuin attempted to impose some unity. Most critical editions only draw on a handful of manuscripts: fourteen are cited for John in the Weber–Gryson Vulgate, including the earliest surviving Vulgate gospel book, the fifth-century Codex Sangallensis 1395 (S), Codex Mediolanensis (M) and the gospel harmony Codex Fuldensis (F) from the sixth century, and the famous Codex Amiatinus (A) produced in Northumbria at the beginning of the eighth century. These may be supplemented with manuscripts considered in the four test passages of Fischer 1991.

Given that Old Latin readings are characterized by their disagreement from the Vulgate, particular attention will be paid to such forms in Augustine's citations. It is more difficult to demonstrate correspondences with the Vulgate, as many of these are shared with Old Latin manuscripts from both groups. A representative selection of '**distinctive Vulgate readings**' in John has been defined as those which appear in the Vulgate and up to one extant Old Latin manuscript. There are eighty-five readings only attested in the Vulgate, and a further two hundred and twenty-one which are shared with an Old Latin exemplar.[10] This list is unlikely to represent all readings distinctive of Jerome's version: more than half of the agreements with one manuscript are in either Codex Brixianus or Codex Aureus, and it is likely that the conformity of these and other manuscripts from the second group is also characteristic of the Vulgate. However, these criteria provide a manageable set of readings which can be used to trace the use of the Vulgate by Augustine.

[8] Burton 2000:27.

[9] Fischer 1991, where they have the sigla **Jg** and **Ea** respectively. The subdivision of this group comes from Burton 2000:71.

[10] These figures are based on the information given in Matzkow–Jülicher–Aland, although the Vulgate text has been amended to bring it into conformity with Weber–Gryson.

5

Tractatus in Iohannis Euangelium

Augustine's commentary on the Gospel according to John in the form of one hundred and twenty-four sermons is the first surviving Latin exposition of this text, and held the field for several centuries.[1] He appears to have begun it as a set of sermons in 406/7: the first fifty-four tractates, covering chapters one to twelve, are lengthy and bear many of the marks of extempore preaching. From John 13 onwards, the individual pieces are much shorter, more regular in their division of the gospel text, and at times rather repetitive. Despite a few traces of oral style, it has long been assumed that these were dictated in order to complete the sequence. This was confirmed by the discovery of *Epistula* 23A* in 1975, in which Augustine tells Possidius that the sermons were being sent to Carthage for publication:

et ut faciam de Iohannis quoque euangelio ea quae restant, dictare iam coepi populares tractatus non prolixos mittendos Carthaginem ea conditione ut, si uult idem senex noster sibi ceteros mitti, <dicat> neque cum dixerit edere differat. iam sex dictaui; noctes enim sabbati et dominici ipsis proprie deputaui. (*Epistula* 23A*.3.6)

[1] The most recent edition is Willems (*Corpus Christianorum series latina* 36; 1954), which is based primarily on previous editions rather than surviving manuscripts (see Van den Hout 1955): Wright's preliminary work on the textual tradition shows that it is more diverse than previously thought (Wright 1972, 1981). Willems' edition also contains over two hundred misprints (listed in Verheijen 1976:4–5, supplemented by Alexanderson 1999). The precise date assigned to each sermon is now untenable (see La Bonnardière 1965:64). A new CSEL edition was announced in 2001, but has not yet appeared. The translation and commentary by Berrouard (1969–2003), who reverts to the Maurists' text, are worthy of special mention; the introductory material from each volume has been reprinted in Berrouard 2004.

And in order that I should also finish off what remains from the Gospel of John, I have already begun to dictate short congregational sermons to be sent to Carthage on the condition that if our old man [Bishop Aurelius] wants the rest to be sent to him, he should say, and not delay publishing them once he has spoken. I have already dictated six, as I have set aside Saturday and Sunday nights specifically for these.[2]

On the basis of the other works mentioned in the same letter, tractates 55–124 have been dated to 419–20. The earlier sermons can be divided into several groups: the currently accepted dating places *Tractatus* 1–16 in 406–7, 17–19 and 23–54 in 414, and 20–2, later inserted into the sequence, in 419.[3]

Almost the whole of the Gospel can be reconstructed from his commentary, but it is important to distinguish between different types of biblical text.[4] These correspond to Augustine's expository technique, as described in Chapter 3. The **continuous text** consists of the citations of the Gospel in order during the commentary. Within these, the ***initial citation*** of each verse, most likely to have been drawn from a codex, has been taken as the definitive form of each verse. In the course of his exposition, Augustine is often inconsistent when repeating words or phrases, resulting in ***sequential variants*** to this text as a result of relying on memory. The overlap between sermons means that some verses appear as continuous text in more than one sermon, sometimes in a different form which may reflect a change of exemplar.[5] **Non-sequential citations** are illustrative material cited from

[2] I follow Berrouard's translation of the last phrase (in *BA* 46B); others have suggested that it indicates that Augustine was following a lectionary which set these passages for Saturdays and Sundays, but this seems less likely.

[3] This corresponds to the final position of Berrouard (1977:26–46), differing from La Bonnardière (1965:43 ff.), who places *Tractatus* 17–23 after 418 and 24–54 even later. The problems with *Tractatus* 20–2 are set out in Wright 1964. Full accounts of earlier proposals are given in La Bonnardière (1965:63–5), Berrouard (1969:30–4), and Milewski (2002:65–8); Anoz 2002:262–5 assigns *Tractatus* 55–124 to specific Saturdays and Sundays between November 419 and July 420.

[4] All the omissions occur in the first eleven chapters, and are likely to be due to the nature of extempore preaching. Five passages are missing or partial (John 2:5–11, 4:49–5:10, 5:31–8, 5:47–6:8, 7:40–5), fourteen single verses are not cited at all (John 2:22, 3:11, 3:16, 3:20, 4:36, 4:45, 5:45, 6:12, 6:41, 6:59, 6:71, 8:53, 10:14, 11:18) and numerous half-verses featuring narrative or introducing direct speech are also ignored.

[5] Examples of inconsistencies occur in the initial citations of John 5:19 in *Tractatus* 7 and 18, John 8:16–17 in *Tractatus* 36 and 37, and John 9:41 in *Tractatus* 44 and 45. There are also several minor variations in the tractates covering John 13–21.

Table 5.1 Comparison of the continuous text (CT) of the *Tractatus in Iohannem* with selected Vulgate readings

	Total readings	Not cited in *Tractatus*	CT identical to Weber–Gryson	CT identical to other Vulgate mss	CT does not agree with any Vulgate
Vulgate only	85	3	56 (68%)	19	7
Vulgate + Vercellensis	2	—	—	2	—
Vulgate + Aureus	80	1	64 (81%)	5	10
Vulgate + Veronensis	20	1	11 (58%)	4	4
Vulgate + Colbertinus	36	13	14 (61%)	4	5
Vulgate + Bezae	18	—	13 (72%)	4	1
Vulgate + Palatinus	1	—	—	1	—
Vulgate + Brixianus	38	2	33 (92%)	1	2
Vulgate + Corbeiensis	5	—	2 (40%)	3	—
Vulgate + Sarzanensis	4	—	4 (100%)	—	—
Vulgate + Rehdigeranus	4	1	1 (33%)	1	1
Vulgate + Frg. Sangall.	1	—	1 (100%)	—	—
Vulgate + Monacensis	3	1	1 (50%)	—	1
Vulgate + Usserianus	6	—	3 (50%)	3	—
Vulgate + Fol. Vindob.	3	—	1 (33%)	—	2
Total	**306**	**22**	**204 (72%)**	**47 (16%)**	**33 (12%)**

memory, either out of the order of the Gospel or from elsewhere in the Bible. Finally, scriptural verses are included in the title of each sermon, indicating the extent of its lection. Although these were probably added later, they are still of textual interest as they do not always reproduce the form of text in the following sermon.

All commentators observe that the gospel text of the *Tractatus* follows the text-type of Jerome's revision.[6] This is clearly mapped in Table 5.1, which compares the continuous text with the list of 'distinctive Vulgate readings' (see p. 106 above). The table shows that the Vulgate character of the continuous text is incontrovertible: Augustine's citation accords with the editorial Vulgate text in fifty-six of the eighty-two possible places where the Vulgate is distinct from all surviving Old Latin manuscripts (68%), while in nineteen of the remaining twenty-six instances, Augustine's reading is present

[6] Thus Frede 1971:460, Burkitt 1896:59, and Comeau 1930:52. In his introduction (page xi), Willems describes it as *uersionem Vulgatam ab ipso aliquantulum emendatum.*

somewhere in the Vulgate tradition. As for the readings shared by the Vulgate and one surviving Old Latin manuscript only, Augustine's continuous text agrees with Weber–Gryson on 148 of the total possible 202 occasions (73%), with twenty-eight more examples of readings found elsewhere in the Vulgate. In total, of the 284 places in the *Tractatus in Iohannem* when Augustine's citations can be compared with these distinctive readings, 204 (72%) have the editorial Vulgate text and a further 47 (16%) are paralleled in other Vulgate manuscripts. It is not surprising that Augustine's citations do not correspond exactly to a composite modern editorial text, although the high proportion of overlap with readings shared with either Codex Aureus or Codex Brixianus may be indicative of an early form of Jerome's revision.

Of course, not every variant has the same value. Minor variations in word order (e.g. *uobis dabit* or *dabit uobis* in John 6:27 and *misit me* or *me misit* in John 9:4), alternative forms of connectives or pronouns (e.g. *quia* or *quod* at John 8:25, and *eis* in John 11:4) and changes in verb voice or tense (e.g. *stetit* or *stat* in John 1:26) could easily have arisen independently. The possibility of a 'distinctive Vulgate reading' appearing in an Old Latin witness now lost can never be entirely discounted. Even so, there is a sufficient number of major agreements involving a distinctive form of text to confirm the Vulgate as Augustine's source in the *Tractatus*. Among some notable readings only found in the Vulgate, we may note *gratias agente domino* in John 6:23 (where the Old Latin tradition has *quem benedixerat dominus*), *qui maneat uobiscum* in John 14:16 (rather than *qui uobiscum sit in aeternum*), the addition of *et eduxerunt* in John 19:16 and the phrase *cum . . . fores essent clausae* in John 20:19, where the majority of Old Latin witnesses have an ablative absolute of the form *ostiis clusis*. The treatment of οἱ Ἕλληνες in John 7:35 and John 12:20 may be considered diagnostic: Fischer (1991) shows that only the eight Old Latin codices render this by *Graeci*, while almost four hundred other manuscripts have *gentes*, which also appears at *Tractatus* 31.10 and 51.8. Other distinctive renderings include *ligatum* in John 18:24 (Old Latin *uinctum*) and *partiti sunt* rather than *diuiserunt* in John 19:24.

Defining the level of agreement between the continuous text and the Vulgate on the basis of 284 distinctive readings in the

Weber–Gryson text also risks overlooking at least 318 occasions on which they differ.[7] Most of the variant readings, especially in the first part of the work, are paralleled in surviving Old Latin witnesses:

John 1:4 *illo, est*; 1:8 *lumen*; 1:9 *hunc*; 1:14 *gratia, ueritate*; 1:15 om. *uobis, uenit*; 1:22 *tu*; 1:26 *nescitis*; 1:27 *uenit*; 1:29 *ecce*; 1:38 *se*; 1:42 *duxit, Iohannis*; 1:45 *dixit*; 1:50 *arbore fici*; 2:15 *resticulis*, 3:4 *iterum*; 3:6 *de, de*; 3:8 *nescis, aut, et*; 3:10 *in*; 3:15 *eum*; 3:19 *mala opera eorum*; 3:23 *ibi, ueniebant*; 3:24 *erat*; 3:26 *illum*; 4:3 *terram*; 4:5 *filio suo Ioseph*; 4:13 *biberit*; 4:14 *ego*; 4:23 *ueniet*; 4:25 *ueniet*; 4:29 *et, mihi dixit*; 4:32 *non scitis*; 4:40 *apud eos*; 4:42 *nos*; 4:43 *biduum*; 4:44 *patria sua*; 5:11 *ipse*; 5:29 *male, fecerunt*; 6:17 *nauiculam*; 6:21 *eum accipere, in*; 6:24 *uidissent turbae, in*; 6:27 *dabit uobis*; 6:35 *uenit*; 6:36 *credidistis*; 6:37 *uenerit*; 6:39 *resuscitabo illud in*; 6:53 *habebitis*; 6:63 *est*; 6:66 *ambulauerunt*; 6:67 *ire*; 7:4 *enim*; 7:6 *uenit*; 7:8 *hunc*; 7:20 *occidere*; 7:23 *irascamini, saluum*; 7:24 *personaliter*; 7:25 *quaerebant*; 7:26 *illi*; 7:27 *nouimus*; 7:28 *nescitis*; 7:31 *facturus est*; 7:36 *quaeritis*; 7:38 *dicit*; 7:39 *nondum, datus, erat*; 7:52 *scripturas*; 8:7 *prior*; 8:9 *omnes recesserunt*; 8:12 *lumen*; 8:13 *testimonium dicis*; 8:20 *Iesus*; *nondum*; 8:22 *dixit*; 8:24 *peccatis uestris*; 8:27 *intellexerunt, de patre, diceret*; 8:31 *crediderant, uerbo*; 8:35 *autem*; 8:38 *meum*; 8:49 *inhonorastis*; 8:50 *quaerat, iudicet*; 8:55 *noui*; 9:2 *eius, an*; 9:3 *manifestentur*; 9:10 *tui*; 9:18 *uocarent*; 9:28 *eius sis*; 9:30 *oculos meos*; 10:5 *fugiunt*; 10:6 *illis*; 10:13 *est ei cura*; 10:27 om. *ego*; 10:29 *est omnibus*; 10:31 *illum*; 10:32 *bona opera*; 10:37 *mihi credere*; 10:39 *adprehendere*; 10:40 *ibi*; 11:1 *sororum*; 11:3 *eius*; 11:10 *in nocte*; 11:11 *excitem*; 11:13 *quod*; 11:15 *quia*; 11:16 *et, illo*; 11:25 *dicit, etiamsi*; 11:31 *illa*; 11:32 *autem*; 11:33 *illa, semetipsum*; 11:45 *Iesus*; 11:48 om. *et*; 11:52 om. *et*; 11:54 om. *in, suis*; 11:56 *inter se, uenit*; 12:6 *et*; 12:8 *habebitis, habebitis*; 12:9 *Iesus*; 12:23 *glorificetur*; 12:24 om. *ipsum*; 12:27 *hac hora, hanc horam*; 12:29 *dicebat*; 12:30 *haec uox*; 12:40 *cor eorum, illos*; 12:50 om. *ergo*; 13:1 *hora eius*; 13:2 *cor*; 13:7 *dixit*; 13:8 *habebis*; 13:10 *semel, habet necessitatem, nisi pedes lauare*; 13:18 *panem mecum, leuabit super*; 13:27 *panem*; 13:31 *ait*; 13:33 *quaeritis*; 13:35 *in*; 13:38 *pones, ter me*; 14:1 *credite*; 14:7 *cognouistis, cognouistis*; 14:9 *uidet me uidet*; 14:13 *haec*; 14:14 om. *me*; 14:17 *cognoscetis*; 14:19 *uidebitis*; 14:23 *mansionem*; 14:26 *commemorabit uos*; 15:6 *arescet, eum, mittent, ardet*; 15:15 *faciat*; 15:19 *essetis*; 15:22 *eis fuissem*; 15:27 *perhibebitis*; 16:2 *extra*; 16:3 *uobis, cognouerunt*; 16:5 *nunc autem*; 16:11 *huius mundi*; 16:15 *accipiet*; 16:20 *in gaudium erit*; 16:22 *tollet*; 16:30 *nosti*; 16:33 *habebitis*; 17:1 *ut et*; 17:5 *claritate*; 17:14 *eos odio*; 17:22 *illis, et nos*; 17:23 *ut*; 17:25 om. *et*; 17:26 *quam*;

[7] These figures are not as precise as they may appear: it is sometimes difficult to decide whether Augustine is paraphrasing narrative material or quoting directly.

18:2 om. *ipsum*; 18:3 *principibus*; 18:4 *dixit*; 18:9 *eis*; 18:10 *principis sacerdotum*; 18:12 *autem*; 18:14 *dedit*; 18:18 *calefaciebant se*; 18:19 *discipulis eius*; 18:28 *ut manducarent*, *ad Caipham*; 18:32 *morte esset*; 18:36 *utique*; 18:37 *meam uocem*; 18:38 *dixit*; 19:6 *eum*; 19:8 *hoc uerbum*; 19:12 *enim*; 19:13 *autem*; 19:24 *impleretur*; 19:28 om. *iam*; 19:35 *testimonium eius*; 19:36 *impleretur*; 19:40 *illud*, *est Iudaeis*; 20:1 *uidit*; 20:5 *uidit*; 20:6 *uidit*; 20:11 *cum*; 20:14 *uidit*; 20:19 *congregati*; 20:20 *cum hoc*; 20:22 *dixit*; 20:23 *et*, *retenta*; 21:8 om. *a*; 21:12 *discumbentium*, *est*; 21:13 *accipit*; 21:14 *suis*, *resurrexisset*; 21:18 *tu*; 21:20 *tradet*; 21:22 om. *si*; 21:23 *inter*, om. *si*.

A large proportion of these are also found in Vulgate manuscripts, which offer the only parallels for four other variants: the word order *carnem suam nobis dare* in John 6:52, *liniuit* in John 9:6, the word order *ponat quis* in John 15:13 and *fixuram* in John 20:25. Again, not all variants are of the same importance: the most significant are renderings such as *lumen* at John 1:8 and 8:12, *resticulis* at John 2:15, *occidere* at John 7:20, and *commemorabit* at John 14:26, or longer phrases, including *non est ei cura de ouibus* in John 10:13 (also found in Codices Rehdigeranus and Usserianus). Most of these forms may be considered as typical of the 'mixed text' tradition. There are sixty-seven readings in the initial citations of the *Tractatus* which are not attested in surviving Old Latin manuscripts or the Vulgate witnesses in Weber–Gryson:

John 1:26 *et dixit*; 2:20 *dicis*, *excitabo*; 3:14 *eremo*; 3:27 *quidquam accipere*; 4:18 *iste*; 4:25 *demonstrabit*; 4:28 *cucurrit*, *ad*; 4:39 *Samaritani*; 4:40 *autem*; 4:47 *rogare coepit*; 5:29 *bene*; 5:39 *scripturam in qua*; 6:15 *uenerant*; 6:26 *meis*; 6:31 *manna*; 6:42 *dixerunt*; 6:60 *itaque*; 6:64 *in*; 7:3 *tu*; 7:24 *rectum*; 7:27 *istum*; 7:33 *dicit*, *tunc*; 8:3 *illi*; 8:8 *rursum*; 8:11 *deinceps*; 8:17 *quod*; 8:36 *tunc*; 8:48 om. *tu*; 9:1 *exiens*; 9:27 *iam uobis*; 9:29 *istum*; 9:36 *ait*; 10:16 *ut sit*; 10:38 *illo*; 11:7 *dicit iterum*; 11:33 *erant*; 11:39 *remouete*; 11:44 *manus et pedes*; 11:56 *loquebantur*; 12:2 *ibi cenam*; 12:3 *uero*; 12:6 *illum*; 12:16 *scripta erant*; 12:22 *dicunt*; 12:32 *post me*; 12:34 *et*; 12:44 om. *autem*; 13:10 *habet opus*; 13:14 *debetis et uos*; 13:24 om. *huic*; 13:26 *tinctum*, *tinxisset*; 14:13 *quaecumque*; 14:24 *sermo quem*; 15:25 *adimpleatur*; 16:2 *synagogas*; 16:25 *meo*; 18:16 *alius discipulus*; 19:4 om. *uobis*; 19:15 *enim*; 19:37 *confixerunt*; 21:3 *apprehenderunt*; 21:10 *apprehendistis*; 21:24 *ille*.

Fischer 1991 provides seven parallels for the twelve variants above which fall within his test passages (John 3:14, 3:27, *dicit* in 7:33, 12:32, 12:34, 12:44, 21:3): no doubt a full collation of these witnesses would supply others elsewhere. Nonetheless, even these manuscripts do not agree with Augustine's text in the rest of the verse. Some variants remain intractable, such as *dicis* and *excitabo* in John 2:20; a few of these may be errors of memory (despite his normal use of the codex), such as *demonstrabit* in John 4:25 and *uero* in John 12:3. Both the Old Latin parallels and these unique readings tell against suggestions that the biblical citations in this work have been changed by later copyists to accord with the text known to them. Similarly, the discrepancies between the initial citations of the same verse in different sermons, mentioned above, reduce the likelihood that the unified work was subject to editing.

The sequential variants in the continuous text also cast doubt on the likelihood of later revision, although at first glance they may appear to support it: Bogaert observes that citations within the body of the commentary are more resistant to change than the lemma.[8] Most of the sequential variants are paralleled in Old Latin manuscripts, and in cases such as *Tractatus* 42, where only the initial citation of John 8:37 reads *quaeritis me interficere* and all three subsequent references have *quaeritis me occidere*, the immediate impression is that the first citation has been made to conform to the Vulgate. This pattern, however, is better explained as Augustine lapsing into the Old Latin forms of his mental text after citing the initial passage from a codex. Distinctive Vulgate readings are grammatically incorporated into Augustine's exposition as well (such as *gentes* in *Tractatus* 31.11 and 51.8), which confirm that he was using this version. The remaining distribution of Old Latin readings would require the hypothetical editor to have been zealously interventionist in one sentence while remarkably careless in the next. This can be illustrated from the citations of John 3:12 in *Tractatus in Iohannem* 12.7.[9] The initial citation in line 1 reads:

si terrena dixi uobis et non creditis quomodo si dixero uobis caelestia credetis?

[8] Bogaert 1988:150; for examples of the alteration of *lemmata*, see Petitmengin 2003:7. There are four cases when the initial citation seems to have been made from memory and is followed by a sequential variant which corresponds to the Vulgate: see John 3:33, 4:25, 6:50, and 10:31.

[9] This passage, as well as a similar example concerning John 7:10 in *Tractatus* 28.8 are both quoted in full in Houghton 2008.

The Vulgate form *terrena* is also found in a citation in line 8, and is repeated in Augustine's argument in lines 3, 4, 5, 7, 10, 13, 19, and 22. However, in line 23 a final citation has *terrestria*, as found in six Old Latin manuscripts. It seems inconceivable that someone who had deliberately changed an original Old Latin text to the Vulgate in the two earlier citations and altered various reflexes of this word eight times in Augustine's argument would have overlooked the distinctive word in the citation in the next line. More plausibly, Augustine himself reverted to *terrestria* at the end of his exposition when citing from memory, perhaps influenced by its similarity to *caelestia* later in the verse. Likewise, the sole appearance of the Old Latin *escam* in John 6:27 at *Tractatus* 25.12 amidst thirteen occurrences of *cibum* in the same sermon is more likely to be due to Augustine than overlooked by a reviser.[10]

Reliance on memory can also be seen in sequential variants which are not found in any surviving biblical manuscripts. A handful of these may have derived from translations now lost, such as the form *de propriis* in John 8:44 at *Tractatus* 42.12 (all surviving witnesses read *ex suis propriis* or *de suo*), but others bear the hallmarks of memory lapse, especially when they have no parallels in the Greek tradition. For example, the initial citation of John 4:38 in *Tractatus* 15 reads:

ego misi uos metere quod uos non laborastis. alii laborauerunt et uos in laborem eorum introistis.

The sequential variant at *Tractatus* 15.32 has:

misi uos metere quod non seminastis. alii seminauerunt et uos in labores eorum introistis.

The replacement of *laborare* by *seminare* is undoubtedly due to the influence of *seminare* in both the preceding verses. Again, in *Tractatus* 25, John 6:38 (*quia descendi de caelo non ut faciam uoluntatem meam*) appears in three sequential variants as *quia* ***non ueni facere*** *uoluntatem meam*, an abbreviation which exemplifies the process of

[10] This discrepancy was in fact noticed in the later manuscript tradition of the *Tractatus*: in the Vatican manuscript Palatinus 207, a corrector has underlined *escam* on folio 7r and written *cibum* above the line.

flattening. The frequent repetition of these altered forms diminishes the significance of reiterated sequential variants with Old Latin readings.

The non-sequential citations were also made from memory, following Augustine's customary practice. Many reproduce his mental text, such as the citations of John 12:31 and John 14:30 throughout the work. They often include Old Latin readings: *Tractatus* 55.2 and 61.5 have a version of John 15:13 with *caritatem*, like the 'first group' of Old Latin manuscripts, but the commentary text in *Tractatus* 84 and 85 reads *dilectionem*. There are also paraphrases or conflations, as in the three citations of John 3:17 which replace *non enim misit deus filium suum in mundum* with *non uenit filius hominis* (*Tractatus* 87.2, 95.4, and 110.2). Although Augustine introduces the verse *tolle grabatum tuum et uade in domum tuam* as a citation of John 5:8 in *Tractatus* 20.2, the words he quotes actually correspond to Mark 2:11. The text of John 14:25–6 in *Tractatus* 104.1 unusually reads *et suggeret uos* in conformity with the Vulgate, unlike the commentary in *Tractatus* 77 which has *et commemorabit uos.* Although it has been suggested that this is a correction, this would have been more likely to affect the treatment of the verse in sequence: instead, the second version may reflect Augustine's growing familiarity with the Vulgate.[11]

The title includes part of the opening and closing verses of the passage covered in each sermon. No variants are recorded in the edition, but a brief survey of some of the manuscripts reveals a number of different traditions and readings. They were probably not added by Augustine but a later redactor, since their biblical text does not always correspond to the commentary which follows, as is shown in Table 5.2 (overleaf). The fact that the title supplies text missing from the sermon on twenty-two occasions demonstrates that it is from an independent source: the fewer occurrences of this in the second set of sermons reflect the more methodical treatment of the biblical passages. On the other hand, the number of agreements between the title and the continuous text indicates a degree of influence. The clearest example of this is in John 5:19, where the title of each sermon corresponds to the continuous text, reading

[11] For the correction, see Berrouard 2003:45.

Table 5.2 Textual affinities of titles in *Corpus Christianorum* edition of *Tractatus in Iohannem*

Tractates	Title supplies text not in CT	Supplied text differs from Vg	Title agrees with Vg against CT	Title agrees with CT against Vg	Title differs from both Vg and CT
1–54	20	8	15	10	13
55–124	2	1	7	14	7

quaecumque enim ille fecerit haec et filius similiter facit in *Tractatus* 18, but *quaecumque enim pater facit haec eadem et filius facit similiter* in *Tractatus* 20. The differences from the Vulgate suggest that the titles originated comparatively early in the transmission of the work. Some have Old Latin parallels, as in the addition of *sabbato* in the title of *Tractatus* 27, but there is no pattern of correspondence with any surviving biblical manuscript, and further study of the titles in the manuscript tradition of the *Tractatus in Iohannem* may yield important information both for the biblical text and also perhaps for the transmission of this work.

A detailed analysis of specific readings in the *Tractatus in Iohannem* is better deferred until the publication of a critical edition of the manuscripts. At any rate, it is unlikely to furnish primary evidence for the Old Latin tradition apart from the explicit observations which Augustine makes about variant readings in different codices.[12] It is, however, worth drawing attention to a few anomalies. These all occur around the beginning of the continuation of the first group of sermons (*Tractatus* 17 onwards, into which *Tractatus* 20–2 were interpolated), which may be significant. Although Augustine normally uses the Vulgate for the gospel passage, some of these tractates have a text which also resembles an Old Latin witness. The most striking is *Tractatus* 30, where his citations have a high proportion of variants from the Vulgate probably due to reliance on memory. Augustine begins by quoting the first half of John 7:20 with *quis te*

[12] *Tractatus* 96.4 and 99.1 (on John 16:13; cf. *Tractatus* 96.4 and 100.1) and 108.3 (on John 1:1 and 17:17) are quoted on pp. 79–80. See also *Tractatus* 82.1, 100.1, and 104.3 on *claritas* and *gloria*, *Tractatus* 83.2 on John 15:12, and *Tractatus* 120.6 on John 20:2.

quaerit interficere before a brief explanation in which the word *occideretis* appears. When he goes on to cite the second half of the verse, it has the Old Latin *quis te quaerit occidere*, an inconsistency not paralleled in any biblical manuscripts. Similarly, the initial citation of John 7:23 runs:

ergo nec mihi irascamini, quia saluum feci totum hominem sabbato; si circumcisionem, inquit, *accipit homo in sabbato, ut non soluatur lex Moysi* (aliquid enim per Moysen in illa constitutione circumcisionis salubriter institutum est), *mihi operanti salutem in sabbato quare indignamini?*

It is immediately clear that this is a paraphrase, starting with the second clause and becoming closer to the biblical text at the interjection *inquit*. The final clause after the explanation is loose too but, unlike the earlier version of this part of the verse, features the Vulgate forms *in sabbato* and *indignamini*. It is therefore difficult to determine the reading of Augustine's codex: the Old Latin *saluum feci*, *sabbato*, and *irascimini* also occur a couple of paragraphs later. Finally, all the citations of John 7:24 in this sermon read:

nolite iudicare personaliter, sed rectum iudicium iudicate.

This combines the term *personaliter*, only paralleled in Codices Monacensis and Palatinus, with *rectum*, unique to Augustine. (*Personaliter* and *rectum* also appear in four secondary citations of this verse.) Furthermore, readings in the commentary such as *personaliter iudicatis, ueritatem adtendite* and *iudicate inter nos, sed uerum iudicium iudicate* could even be taken to support *uerum iudicium*, even though all Latin Gospels read *iustum iudicium*. The best explanation is that Augustine is, for some reason, reverting to his mental text rather than closely following a codex on this occasion.

Two biblical passages in these sermons stand out for the concentration of variants they contain: John 5:13–16 in *Tractatus* 17 and John 6:9–11 in *Tractatus* 24. The differences emerge clearly when placed alongside the Vulgate (variations from the Vulgate are in bold type, and absent material is indicated by [ ]):

Vulgate *5:13* is autem qui sanus fuerat effectus nesciebat quis esset. Iesus enim declinauit turba constituta in loco. *5:14* postea inuenit eum Iesus in templo et dixit illi: 'ecce sanus factus es; iam noli peccare ne deterius tibi aliquid contingat.' *5:15* abiit ille homo et nuntiauit Iudaeis quia Iesus esset qui fecit eum sanum *5:16* propterea persequebantur Iudaei Iesum quia haec faciebat in sabbato.

Tract. 17 *5:13* **sed** qui sanus **erat factus** nesciebat quis esset. Iesus **autem** declinauit **ab eo in turba** [] *5:14* **uidit eum** postea Iesus in templo [] 'ecce **iam** sanus factus es noli peccare ne **quid tibi** deterius contingat' *5:15* abiit [] et nuntiauit Iudaeis quia Iesus esset qui **eum** sanum **fecerat** *5:16* [] persequebantur Iudaei **dominum** Iesum quia haec faciebat in sabbato.

Some of these are paralleled in Old Latin manuscripts: *autem* in John 5:13 (which corresponds to a Greek variant) and *ne quid tibi deterius* appear in several witnesses, while Codex Palatinus provides the only examples of *ab eo* and the omission of *loco* in the first verse, and the addition of *iam* in John 5:14. Several of the other variants appear to be corrections to the grammar, such as the simplification of the pleonastic *fuerat effectus,* the introduction of the more elegant pluperfect *fecerat* in John 5:15, and the removal of the redundant *in loco* and *ille homo.*[13] These are all unique to this citation, as is the addition of *dominum,* a standard devotional accretion. The two remaining differences improve the sense. Old Latin translators handle *καὶ διὰ τοῦτο* at the beginning of John 5:16 in a variety of ways, but the form *propterea* in the Vulgate is unfortunate, as it could imply that the man maliciously denounced Jesus to those who were already searching for him (despite the reference of *haec* to the current event): the deletion of this word resolves the ambiguity. Similarly, *uidit* rather than *inuenit* in John 5:14 is also only found here, and removes the inconsistency between Jesus' apparently deliberate disappearance into the crowd and his seeking out of the man in the temple.[14] None of these variants is paralleled in Greek, and the motivation which seems to underlie them suggests that they are internal to the Latin version. The same is true of part of the lection in *Tractatus* 24:

Vulgate *6:9* 'est puer unus hic qui habet quinque panes hordiacios et duos pisces, sed haec quid sunt inter tantos?' *6:10* dixit ergo Iesus 'facite homines discumbere.' erat autem faenum multum in loco. discubuerunt ergo uiri

[13] On the development of the passive in later Latin (and the justification for *fuerat effectus*), see Burton 2000:178–80. García de la Fuente 1994:195 considers the pleonastic use of *homo* in biblical Latin.

[14] Compare also *Sermo* 135.5.6, where Augustine supplies *uenit* in place of *inuenit* in the introduction to John 9:35.

numero quasi quinque milia. *6:11* accepit ergo panes Iesus, et cum gratias egisset distribuit discumbentibus; similiter et ex piscibus quantum uolebant.

Tract. 24 *6:9* 'est **hic puer quidam** qui habet quinque panes [][15] et duos pisces, sed haec quid sunt **ad** tantos?' *6:10* **et ait** Iesus 'facite homines discumbere.' erat autem **ibi** foenum multum **et** discubuerunt **ferme** quinque millia **hominum.** *6:11* accepit **autem dominus** Iesus panes, **gratias egit** [] et **de** piscibus quantum **sufficiebat.**

Stylistic alterations include *quidam* for *unus* (6:9) and *ibi* for *in loco* (6:10), which are both more classical in idiom.[16] The alteration of *uiri numero quasi quinque milia* to *ferme quinque milia hominum* removes the unnatural emphasis on *uiri*, the redundant *numero*, and the possibility of interpreting *quasi* as potential ('as if') rather than approximate ('about'). The substitution of both instances of *ergo* improves the narrative flow and avoids unexpected logical connections: the presence of grass, the seating of the crowd and Jesus' actions are not dependent on each other. As in John 5:16 above, the introduction of *dominus* is clearly secondary, while the replacement of *uolebant* by *sufficiebat* may be theologically motivated, demonstrating that Jesus, rather than the crowd, keeps the initiative (alternatively, it may have been influenced by John 6:7). The majority of these forms do not correspond to any variants in Greek or Latin biblical manuscripts, and the normal Vulgate text of these verses is found at *De consensu euangelistarum* 2.46.95. The question remains as to whether Augustine was responsible for these variants, or whether they appeared in his codex. Even though it has been observed that most of Augustine's interventions usually affect direct speech, he also paraphrases narrative material.[17] The initial citation of John 6:9 is immediately followed by a reworking, which implies that the previous version was read from his exemplar; the context of John 6:11, however, shows Augustine expanding the text, while the status of the intervening verse remains unclear. The treatment of the lection in *Tractatus* 17 seems less likely to be a paraphrase, and it is conceivable that, when recommencing his commentary after a

[15] *Hordeaceos* appears three lines later in a sequential variant: its omission here seems to be an oversight (Berrouard 1977:412).

[16] On the development of *loco* to mean *ibi* in later Latin, see Löfstedt 1911:143–5.

[17] See pp. 75–6 above.

seven-year gap, he might have reviewed the biblical text in advance. There are few comparable changes elsewhere in the *Tractatus*, and the peculiarities of this handful of sermons are exceptional.[18]

In conclusion, there is more to the gospel text of the *Tractatus in Iohannis euangelium* than has previously been observed, and more still to come following the publication of a critical edition based on the manuscripts. The overall Vulgate character of the text used by Augustine for his commentary has been confirmed, but individual sermons may have been preached from different exemplars. The transmission of the biblical citations appears to have been accurate, including a number of Old Latin features and even some forms unique to Augustine which are not paralleled in any Latin Gospel from the first millennium. The initial citation (the 'continuous text') is the one most likely to have been drawn from a codex; inconsistencies when these verses are repeated in the body of the sermon ('sequential variants') represent Augustine's reversion to his mental text rather than fossilized Old Latin readings overlooked by a later editor. The titles, although unlikely to have been added by Augustine, give the extent of the lection for each sermon, and are worthy of study in their own right: they may shed more light on the compilation and dissemination of this series of sermons, which became the most influential Latin commentary on John in antiquity.

[18] The only other similar variation occurs in *Tractatus* 33, affecting a single verse (John 7:46): the text *non enim quisquam sic loquitur homo* could be a paraphrase or an Old Latin version which is no longer preserved. *Tractatus* 44 also seems to have been preached from a codex less similar to Jerome's version than the rest of the *Tractatus*: see the discussion of John 9 on p. 271 ff.

6

Other Sermons

Alongside the one hundred and twenty-four *Tractatus in Iohannem*, at least eighty-four of Augustine's other surviving sermons are based on readings from the Gospel according to John. Forty-one occur in the sequence of *Sermones ad populum* numbered 117-47A, another twenty-four were preached on feast days, and thirteen more can be identified from references to John as the preceding lection.[1] Six of the *Enarrationes in Psalmos* also followed a liturgical reading of John indicated in this way, although they do not have any extended citations of the passage: this may indicate that Augustine was only preaching from the psalm codex.[2] Other sermons feature multiple citations from John which may have been taken from a codex.[3] The same concepts of the 'initial citation' and 'sequential variants' used in the analysis of the

[1] In addition to the thirty-one sermons numbered **117–47**, there are ten supplementary items: *Sermones* **125A** (Mai 128), **130A** (Dolbeau 19), **132A** (Mai 129), **136A** (Mai 130), **136B** (Lambot 10), **136C** (Lambot 11), **139A** (Mai 125), **140A** (Mai post 174), **145A** (Casinensis 2.136), and **147A** (Denis 12). (Note also that *Sermo* 142 has been augmented by Wilmart 11 and Dolbeau 7.)

Drobner 2000 and Verbraken 1976 list twenty-six for feast days: *Sermones* **1**, **170**, **217**, **229K–P**, **243–53** (including **252A**), **259–60**, **342**, **369**, and **375C**; however, neither 260 nor 369 cite the supposed lectionary passage. It seems that in both cases the Johannine lection of the previous sermon has been incorrectly reproduced in the next entry (368 is inauthentic).

A further thirteen not listed by Drobner or Verbraken but which refer to a lection or codex of John are: *Sermones* **14A**, **16A**, **173**, **178**, **294**, **299**, **299A**, **299B**, **319**, **329**, **340A**, **362**, and **376** (the indications in *Sermones* 294 and 362 are quoted on pp. 31 and 35 above). Berrouard 1977:860 treats *Sermo* 13 as a lectionary sermon on John 7:53–8:11, but there is no explicit mention of the liturgical Gospel.

[2] *Enarrationes* **35**, **62**, **65**, **83**, **90.s1**, and **139** refer to a lection from John.

[3] The following are treated in this chapter: *Sermones* **5**, **13**, **210**, **293**, **352**, and **379**; *Enarrationes* **3**, **39**, **40**, **44**, **50**, **52**, **58.s1**, **65**, **68.s2**, **92**, **95**, **98**, **102**, and **138**. Many of these were preached outside Hippo.

Tractatus can be applied to any of Augustine's expository sermons. Although it would be illuminating to consider these works in chronological order, very different dates have sometimes been proposed for the same piece, while others lack any suggestion.[4] The place of delivery is also significant, but this too is not known in many cases. For ease of reference, the sermons will be treated in numerical order, followed by the *Enarrationes.* Only those with an extended or particularly noteworthy biblical text are considered in this chapter: other readings are discussed by verse in the Commentary.

SERMONES AD POPULUM

It is not clear what gospel reading preceded ***Sermo*** 5, preached in Carthage in 403: it includes verses from both Matthew and John with Old Latin features characteristic of an early date.[5] The text of John 19:30 is unusual for Augustine:

perfectum est, ait, et inclinauit caput et dimisit spiritum. (*Sermo* 5.3)

Although *perfectum* is part of his mental text, he normally reads *inclinato capite* and *tradidit* or *reddidit.* The rendering *dimisit* is unique to this sermon, although it appears to be supported by Tertullian *Apologeticum* 21; some manuscripts of the sermon have *emisit* here, which also occurs in the reminiscence a few lines later. Codex Palatinus contains *perfectum* and *inclinauit caput*: the implication is that this citation reflects an African version of John.

The *Pericope Adulterae* (John 7:53–8:11) features in ***Sermo*** 13, delivered in Carthage possibly in 418. Augustine alludes to the whole episode, but only quotes a few phrases verbatim. He gives John 8:7 twice as *qui sine peccato est, prior in illam lapidem mittat*: no surviving Old Latin manuscripts omit *uestrum* although three have *prior. Coepit scribere* in the next verse and *unus post alterum*

[4] Dates and locations are taken from Gryson 2007 unless otherwise stated, but many of these differ considerably from Frede 1995; details of earlier suggestions are set out in Verbraken 1976 and Drobner 2000.

[5] The date suggested in Frede 1995 is 408/11; Hombert 2000 puts the sermon even earlier, in 394/5.

discesserunt in John 8:9 are also unique to Augustine and appear in some of his other citations. It is possible that he is citing from memory, in keeping with the introductory line *euangelicum capitulum recolamus*, which makes no reference to a codex.

***Sermo* 14A** (*Dolbeau* 20), probably also from Carthage but in 415, followed readings from Psalm 17 and John 6. It was preached a few days after *Sermo* 130A (*Dolbeau* 19), also on John 6: they share the text *quem ille misit* in John 6:29 with Codices Palatinus, Brixianus, and Monacensis. Augustine cites John 6:40 five times in whole or part:

haec est uoluntas patris ut qui uiderit filium et crediderit in eum habeat uitam aeternam et ego suscitabo eum in nouissimo die.

Further points of contact with Codex Palatinus alone are provided by *uiderit* and *crediderit.* However, the omission of *enim* and *omnis* in the first half of the verse are not paralleled in any Old Latin manuscript, and nor is *ego suscitabo*, for which all read *resuscitabo ego* or *resuscitem ego*: Augustine's consistency is remarkable.

***Sermo* 16A** was delivered in Carthage in 411 and, like *Sermo* 13, features the *Pericope Adulterae.* Again, many of the cited verses appear to be paraphrased, although this time Augustine explicitly refers to the gospel lection. A few readings correspond to Old Latin manuscripts, such as *comprehensa* in John 8:4 (only in Codex Bezae) and *lapidauit* in John 8:10 (only in Codex Corbeiensis). In John 8:7 Augustine reads *qui se scit uestrum sine peccato esse* instead of *qui sine peccato est uestrum*: this is similar to *Enarratio* 50.8 from Carthage in 413, although it omits *uestrum* and has *primus* and *iaciat* rather than *prior* and *mittat* later in the verse.

Unlike Augustine's other sermons on the opening verses of John, ***Sermo* 121** has variations from his mental text. Although it does read *per eum* in John 1:10 (only found in Codices Veronensis and Monacensis) and *in sua propria* at John 1:11, it has the canonical *his qui credunt* in John 1:12 rather than his customary *credentibus.* The addition *non ex carne*, another feature of Augustine's mental text, is lacking from John 1:13, although this sermon uniquely transposes *uiri* and *carnis*, reading *neque ex uoluntate uiri nec ex uoluntate carnis.*[6] It also has Old Latin readings in its citations of John 8:39–40, but has been dated to 414.

[6] Poque's *Sources Chrétiennes* edition reads *non* for *neque.*

***Sermo* 122** is surprisingly inconsistent in its citations, reading both *arbore fici* and *ficu* in John 1:48, *maiora horum* and *maius his* in John 1:50 and *ad* and *super* in John 1:51. Both *arbore fici* and *ficu* are embedded in the first paragraph of the sermon; the latter, which occurs more frequently, is only preserved in the Vulgate and Codices Aureus and Colbertinus. Similarly, *maius his* is peculiar to the Vulgate and Codex Colbertinus, but this only appears once, towards the end of the sermon: the Old Latin *maiora horum* features in the initial citation and the following question, *quae sunt ista maiora?* The best indication of dating, however, is provided by John 1:51: Berrouard 1962 has shown that Augustine read *ad filium hominis* in works written before 400, when he first encountered *super filium hominis* and changed his exegesis to match. Although *Sermo* 122 has *super* in its initial citation, by the time Augustine comes to expound this verse in the penultimate paragraph, he has reverted to *ad* with his earlier explanation. This implies that this sermon was preached before *Tractatus* 7, in which the subsequent text and exegesis is established, giving a date of before 406: while the Vulgate readings could have been present in other manuscripts or even introduced by copyists, it is less likely that Augustine would have returned to an older explanation.[7] The date of *Sermo* 122 affects ***Sermo* 123**, which was preached on the following day. In the latter, Augustine recalls John 1:50–1, presumably from memory, with the forms *maius his* and *ad filium hominis.* He only cites John 2:11 from that day's lection, which gives no further indication of his text-type.

***Sermo* 125** is frequently included in the manuscripts of the *Tractatus in Iohannem* as part of the problematic sequence of *Tractatus* 19–23.[8] The verbatim citations extend beyond the lection of John 5:2–5 listed in the indexes, as shown by the introductions to John 5:7 (*consideremus uerba ipsius*) and John 5:18 (*quod modo legebatur*; a paraphrase follows). The only two verses cited verbatim both feature non-Vulgate readings. The initial citation of John 5:7 reads:

[7] The presence of *ficu* in Tertullian *Aduersus Praxean* 21 indicates that it may have featured in an Old Latin version. No date is supplied for this sermon or *Sermo* 123 in Gryson 2007.

[8] See Wright 1972:99.

hominem non habeo, ut cum mota fuerit aqua deponat me in piscinam; cum enim uenio, descendit alius. (*Sermo* 125.3)

Deponat is unique to Augustine, as is the abbreviated form of the end of the verse. Despite the Old Latin *mota*, there is substantial use of *turbata* (found in Codex Palatinus as well as the Vulgate and related manuscripts) in the commentary. Again, the first two citations of John 5:17 have *usque nunc*, only paralleled in Codex Vercellensis, but Augustine later reverts to *usque modo*. These readings indicate an Old Latin text-type. The date of the sermon, however, is highly contested: most commentators give 416–17; Hombert's dating of 400–5, which the Old Latin readings would support, has been generally adopted, but this has been criticized on the grounds of Augustine's exegesis.[9]

***Sermo* 126** is based solely on John 5:19. The main interest here lies in the second half of the verse, introduced in the middle of the sermon:

attende et quod sequitur: *quaecumque enim facit pater, eadem et filius facit.* (*Sermo* 126.6.8)

The initial formula indicates the use of a codex. Both Augustine's subsequent citations have the peculiar double form of his mental text, *haec eadem*, but none of these three has *similiter* at the end of the verse. The only surviving manuscript without *similiter* is Codex Palatinus, which, like Codex Sarzanensis, also reads *pater* rather than *ille*: both, however, have *quae* rather than *quaecumque* and differences in word order in the first half of the verse, so are ruled out as exact parallels for Augustine's text in this sermon. The date given for this sermon is 416/17, but no location is suggested: the Old Latin features indicate that it may have been preached outside Hippo.

The situation is similar in ***Sermo* 127**, whose location is unknown although it has been dated to 415/18. The continuous text is as follows:

5:25 amen dico uobis quia ueniet hora, et nunc est, quando mortui audient uocem filii dei, et qui audierint uiuent. 5:26 sicut enim pater habet uitam in semetipso, sic dedit filio habere uitam in semetipso. 5:27 et potestatem dedit ei

[9] Dulaey (2006b:312) casts doubt on Hombert's analysis by drawing attention to similarities between *Sermo* 125 and *Tractatus* 17; Berrouard (1977:93) had earlier observed that the treatment in the former appears to predate the *Tractatus*. Unfortunately, John 5:7 is paraphrased in *Tractatus* 17, which reads *usque modo* in John 5:17.

Table 6.1 Selected readings in *Sermo* 127 and Old Latin manuscripts

Verse	*Sermo* 127	Codex Usserianus	Codex Monacensis	Codex Palatinus	Weber–Gryson Vulgate
5:25	ueniet	[lacuna]	ueniet	ueniet	uenit
5:26	sicut	[lacuna]	sicut	quomodo	sicut
5:26	in semetipso	in se	—	in se	in semetipso
5:26	dedit filio	[*et filio d*]edit	dedit et filio	dedit et filio	dedit et filio
5:26	habere uitam	habere uitam	uitam . . . habere	habere uitam	uitam habere
5:27	ei	ei	illi	illi	ei
5:27	facere	faciendum	faciendi	facere	facere
5:27	quoniam	quoniam	quia	quia	quia
5:28	ueniet	ueniet	ueniet	ueniet	uenit
5:28	quando	in qua	in qua	in qua	in qua
5:28	hi	omnes	omnis	omnes	omnes
5:28	qui sunt in monumentis	qu[*i sunt in monumen*]tis	qui fuerint in monumento	qui in monumentis sunt	qui in monumentis sunt
5:29	prodient	prodient	prodient	exiant	procedent
5:29	omnes	—	et	—	—
5:29	egerunt (1)	gesserunt	gesserunt	faciunt	fecerunt
5:29	autem	autem	autem	—	uero
5:29	egerunt (2)	gesserunt	—	egerint	egerunt

et iudicium facere, quoniam filius hominis est. 5:28 nolite mirari hoc, quia ueniet hora quando hi qui sunt in monumentis audient uocem eius, 5:29 et prodient omnes. qui bona egerunt, in resurrectionem uitae; qui autem mala egerunt, in resurrectionem iudicii.

The introductory formula *audi quod sequitur* shows that Augustine was reading from a codex, and there are also several sequential variants, mostly involving word order. The best match for Augustine's text is Codex Usserianus, as shown in Table 6.1, but even this does not provide an exact fit, as can be seen from the table: *quando* and *hi* in John 5:28 are not found in surviving manuscripts, although Codex Colbertinus does read *egerunt* twice in John 5:29. Even at this comparatively late date, Augustine appears to be relying on a codex with an Old Latin text-type.

The summary of the lection in the opening paragraph of ***Sermo* 129** has already been cited in full above.[10] This clearly demonstrates the Old Latin character of Augustine's text, which on this occasion

[10] Page 58. The stenographer's record of an apparent slip in a citation at *Sermo* 129.2 is quoted on p. 37 above.

shows similarities with Codex Palatinus and Cyprian *Ad Quirinum* 1.18 (e.g. *quaerentes* in John 5:44, *uos accuso* in John 5:45, the omission of *forsitan* in John 5:46). There are a couple of sequential variants: *putatis* and *speratis* in John 5:39 and *accepistis* and *suscepistis* in John 5:43. In both cases, the second term is not found in any biblical manuscript, which may suggest an error of memory on the part of Augustine. The date 405–9 has recently been proposed for this sermon, but earlier commentators suggested it was in the range 393–405.[11]

***Sermo* 130A** (*Dolbeau* 19) expounds John 6:27–9. The text of John 6:27 in the title is slightly different from that in the body of the sermon.[12] The latter reads:

operamini escam quae non perit, sed quae permanet in uitam aeternam
(*Sermo* 130A.1)

Escam confirms that this is an Old Latin form of text: the word order is closest to Codex Usserianus, which also does not repeat *escam* later on. Furthermore, this is one of only three works which do not have Augustine's mental text *non corrumpitur* (the others are *Tractatus* 25 and *De consensu* 4.10.15). The form *opus dei* in the next verse may be an anticipation of John 6:29; it does not feature in any biblical manuscripts. The non-sequential citations, for example John 8:58 and 14:1, also have an Old Latin form of text, although a convincing argument has been put forward for a date of 415 based on Augustine's exegesis.[13]

***Sermo* 131** was delivered in Carthage in 417. The gospel text is perplexing: in John 6:53 (6:54 in the Vulgate) Augustine combines *habebitis*, the majority Old Latin reading, with his customary form *carnem meam... sanguinem meam. Escam* rather than *cibum* in the adaptation of John 6:55 (6:56) suggests an Old Latin source, but both citations of John 6:62 (6:63) have *si ergo uideritis*, a reading distinctive of the Vulgate and Codex Colbertinus; *ubi erat prius* is also only found in manuscripts close to the Vulgate. All except one of the

[11] Hombert 2000 suggests 405–9. The only other instance of an identical form of John 5:43 appears in *Enarratio* 117.21, which he dates to 403–4.

[12] Dolbeau has restored the title from Possidius; on inaccuracies in the titles of Augustine's sermons, see Wright 1979.

[13] See Hombert 2000:527–40; although he prefers Hippo, he leaves open the possibility that it may have been preached at Carthage.

citations of John appear in the first two paragraphs: the rest of the sermon is taken up with an exposition of the psalm. It may therefore be that Augustine was quoting John from memory, with the psalm codex in front of him.

***Sermo* 133** is not only located in Carthage, but dated to 405.[14] These considerations would lead us to expect an Old Latin lection, but the passage features two distinctive Vulgate readings, *opera tua* in John 7:3 and *mundo* without *huic* in John 7:4. However, each of these is shared with one extant Old Latin manuscript, Codex Brixianus and Codex Bezae respectively, and in this case the definition of readings also found in one other witness as 'distinctively Vulgate' appears to be misleading: the sole unique Vulgate form in this pericope, *quippe* in John 7:4, does not appear in this sermon. Instead, there are numerous Old Latin features, the most notable of which is *quasi occulte* in John 7:10. This is paralleled by Codex Monacensis alone, whose text corresponds to a number of non-sequential citations too (e.g. John 1:4 and 1:14; compare *Sermo* 145): as usual, no manuscript provides an exact match, but most of Augustine's readings appear in surviving witnesses.

The lections for ***Sermones* 136, 136A, 136B,** and **136C** all come from John 9, and reproduce none of the distinctive Vulgate readings in this chapter: for example, all four sermons omit *autem* and read *exaudit* rather than *audit* in John 9:31. There are several Old Latin parallels: *Sermo* 136 has the only citation of John 9:2 outside *Tractatus* 44, displaying similarities with Codices Palatinus, Veronensis, and Usserianus; *Sermones* 136A, 136B, 136C, and Codex Palatinus all refer to the pool in John 9:7 as *piscina* rather than *natatoria* (neither word features in *Sermo* 136); *Sermo* 136A corresponds to Codex Vercellensis with *et ideo* for *propterea* in John 9:23. There are also a number of forms unique to Augustine, which are considered in Part III. The analysis of Augustine's exegesis by Dulaey (2003:51) offers the greatest precision for *Sermones* 136A and 136C, suggesting a date of 406–18; despite their Old Latin readings, Gryson assigns *Sermones* 136 and 136B to 416/18 and 412 respectively.

Augustine appears to be citing from memory in ***Sermo* 137** (cf. *Sermo* 131): he reverses the order of John 10:1 and 10:2, in keeping

[14] Other commentators suggest 397.

with the flattened form also found in *Enarratio* 95. Furthermore, he gives no fewer than three versions of John 10:1: *ex alia parte, per alteram partem*, and *per aliam partem*. Remarkably, each is preserved somewhere in the Old Latin tradition, although most witnesses have *aliunde*. His mental text includes several Old Latin features, such as *non est ei cura de ouibus* in John 10:13 and *unus grex* in John 10:16, which also occur in ***Sermo* 138**. This was probably delivered in Carthage in 411; *Sermo* 137 was preached some time between 410 and 420. ***Sermo* 139A** (dated 420–30) appears to have been abbreviated: the sole parallel for both *putet* and *quadriduanus* in John 11:39 is Codex Bezae.

Although the title of ***Sermo* 142** only refers to John 14:6, subsequent discoveries (*Wilmart* 11, *Dolbeau* 7) have increased its scope. It was preached outside Hippo in 404/6; its citations are typical of Augustine's mental text, with *qui me uidet, uidet et patrem* in John 14:9. ***Sermo* 143**, dated to 410/12, repeats the whole lection in the first paragraph. There are just three variants from the Weber–Gryson text, all of which are paralleled in other Vulgate witnesses: *ego abiero* in John 16:7, *crediderunt* in John 16:9, and *huius mundi* in John 16:11. There is no unique Vulgate reading in this passage, but *enim* in John 16:7 is only found in the Vulgate and Codices Aureus and Bezae: Augustine is undoubtedly following Jerome's version. Furthermore, the sequential variants later in the sermon are consistent with citations from memory. ***Sermo* 144** also cites all four verses of its lection in the opening sentences. Like *Sermo* 143, it has *crediderunt* in John 16:9 and *huius mundi* in John 16:11, but combines these with some distinctive Old Latin forms: *ipse*, found in all three citations of John 16:8, is only found in Codex Vercellensis; Codex Usserianus alone transposes *uero* and *autem* in John 16:10–11; Codices Monacensis and Veronensis also add *iam* in John 16:11. Despite these readings, it has been assigned a later date than *Sermo* 143, around 416.

Only John 16:24 is cited from the gospel reading preceding ***Sermo* 145**. In the title and initial citation, it takes the following form:

usque nunc nihil petiistis in nomine meo. petite et accipietis ut gaudium uestrum sit plenum.

This corresponds exactly to Codex Monacensis, and only differs in one word from Codices Bezae and Palatinus. Later variations have *modo* or *adhuc* in place of *nunc*. The sermon has been located in Carthage (compare *Sermo* 133), but estimates of date differ widely: Hombert (2000:253–64) prefers 412–15 because of the apparent influence of the Pelagian controversy, but Bochet (2004:196–7) maintains that the use of Romans 7:22–5 indicates that this work precedes the *Confessiones*, supporting the traditional date of 397.

In the brief ***Sermo*** **147**, from after 412, Augustine makes a special feature of the words *plus his* in John 21:15, only found in the Vulgate and Codex Brixianus:

non enim simpliciter dominus dixerat *diligis me* sed *plus his diligis me*. (*Sermo* 147.2.2)

The form *cinget* in John 21:18 is also peculiar to these two witnesses. However, *ibas quo uolebas*, *alter* rather than *alius*, and the addition of *tu* in this verse are all Old Latin readings which are probably part of Augustine's mental text, as is the form *feret*, unique to him. If he was using a Vulgate text-type, he must have reverted to memory in the final paragraph.

Although ***Sermo*** **170** introduces John 6:39 as one of the day's readings, a conflated form is given from memory. ***Sermo*** **173** includes John 11:25–6 from its lection. The text is identical to Codex Corbeiensis, which alone has *licet moriatur*, apart from the omission of *omnis* from John 11:26; this is paralleled by the Fragmentum Sangallense. Gryson suggests a date of after 418, and no location. Augustine's comments in ***Sermo*** **178** show that it too followed a reading from John, of which he quotes one verse:

nolite iudicare **personaliter** *sed iustum iudicium iudicare*. (*Sermo* 178.1.1)

This corresponds exactly to John 7:24 in Codex Palatinus and Codex Monacensis. As Augustine's mental text of the verse seems to have been *rectum iudicium*, he could have been relying on a codex: he barely cites the advertised lection from Titus.[15] This sermon has been assigned a date after 396, and the location is unknown.

[15] For *rectum iudicium*, see the discussion of *Tractatus* 30 on p. 117 above, and also p. 252 below.

In one paragraph of ***Sermo* 210**, Augustine quotes four consecutive verses. The first group comprises John 16:19–20 and 22:

16:19 pusillum, inquit, *et non uidebitis me, et iterum pusillum et uidebitis me. 16:20* haec est hora de qua dixit *uos tristes eritis, saeculum autem gaudebit. 16:22 sed iterum,* inquit, *uidebo uos, et gaudebit cor uestrum, et gaudium uestrum nemo auferet a uobis.* (*Sermo* 210.5.7)

Four sentences later comes the missing verse:

16:21 et *mulier cum parturit,* ait dominus, *tristitia est illi, quoniam uenit dies eius, sed cum pepererit fit gaudium magnum, quoniam natus est homo in saeculum.* (*Sermo* 210.5.7)

The omissions and paraphrases suggest that Augustine is relying on memory, but there are numerous Old Latin readings: *pusillum* rather than *modicum, tristes eritis* in the next verse and *auferet* (or *aufert*) in John 16:22 are found in most of the 'first group' of witnesses. In addition, Codex Palatinus alone has *saeculum* in John 16:20, while *parturit* in John 16:21 is confined to Codices Vercellensis and Monacensis. Gryson 2007 gives no date, but this text-type indicates that it may be early. Anoz 2002:280 records Hill's proposal of 391–6. Berrouard suggested 405 on the basis of the non-Vulgate character of the citations and specifically Augustine's failure to include *quia uado ad patrem* in the initial verse, which he identifies as John 16:16. However, if this is taken as John 16:19, where the phrase does not appear, it cannot function as an indication of date.

Several Easter sermons have a lection from the last two chapters of John (***Sermones* 229K–P** and **243–53**). Most were delivered around 412, and contain few citations: these appear to reflect Augustine's mental text and do not contain any forms characteristic of the Vulgate in their gospel passage.[16] Three are dated later, two of which do feature distinctive Vulgate readings: ***Sermo* 229O**, from 420/2, includes *plus his* in John 21:15, while ***Sermo* 229P**, from 418, has not just this, but also *agnos* in John 21:16 and *tu omnia scis* in John 21:17. ***Sermo* 244**, also from 418, does not have any such

[16] The only exception is *Sermo* 252A, where a sequential variant to John 21:6 reads *rete*; however, the initial citation has *retiam*, and both feature the Old Latin *partem*, so this does not appear to be indicative of the Vulgate.

indications. Its initial citation of John 20:9, in fact, has three non-Vulgate forms:

nondum enim nouerant scripturas quia oportebat eum a mortuis resurgere.

(*Sermo* 244.1)

Codex Aureus is the only manuscript with both *scripturas* and *oportebat*, which appear in all four lectionary sermons which quote this verse (*Sermones* 229L, 244, 245, and 246); *nouerant* is unique to this citation, although *nouerat* is found in Codices Palatinus and Usserianus as well as *Sermo* 246. ***Sermo* 247** (410/12) only features an adapted form of John 20:19, but the forms *cum sero factum esset*, *ostia*, and *timorem Iudaeorum* all point to an Old Latin form of the lection. ***Sermo* 252** has been assigned to 396, but this is not reflected in its gospel citations. The only feature of note is that, while four of these sermons have Augustine's mental text, *cum tam magni essent*, in John 21:11 (*Sermones* 229M, 249, 250, and 252A), the initial citations of *Sermones* 251 and 252 have the canonical text, *cum tanti essent*, glossed with his customary form. On the other hand, in the next phrase *Sermones* 229M and 252 both read *retia non sunt disrupta*, also characteristic of Augustine's memory, while the other four sermons have *non est scissum rete*, paralleled in biblical manuscripts.

***Sermo* 293**, delivered in Carthage on the Feast of St John the Baptist, 24 June 413, provides Augustine's only citation of the final words of John 3:29 outside *Tractatus* 14. The form *completum*, in *hoc gaudium meum completum est*, is paralleled by Codices Veronensis and Usserianus; it is not clear whether this was part of the lection or not. Three days later, in the same church, Augustine preached ***Sermo* 294** on baptism against the Pelagians, for which he clearly relied on a manuscript for his discussion of John 3. The citations of John 3:5 and 3:6, however, follow Augustine's customary text of the verse, reading *intrabit* rather than *potest intrare* and *nascitur* rather than *natum est*: the latter only occurs out of sequence, several paragraphs later, while the former precedes Augustine's first reference to his codex and so may have been cited from memory. In the verses read from a manuscript, there are several Old Latin readings, most notably *eremo* rather than *deserto* in all three citations of John 3:14, an African form used by Cyprian; other parallels include *sic oportet exaltari* later in the same verse, *qui credit in eum* in John 3:15, and *crediderit* in John 3:18 (only found in Codices Palatinus and Sarzanensis). Once again, the distinctive text-type of the Gospels used by Augustine in Carthage is evident.

Three of Augustine's sermons on the feast of St Peter are based on John 21:15–25. ***Sermo* 299** was delivered only two days after *Sermo* 294: it has Augustine's customary forms of John 21:18 and 19, not paralleled in any surviving manuscript. ***Sermo* 299A** was preached somewhere outside Hippo in 404. Its citations of John 21:15–17 are paraphrased, reading *Simon Petre* rather than *Simon Iohannis* and not remarking on the differences between the three questions and answers. The latest of these sermons, ***Sermo* 299B**, is dated some time after 417. Like the Easter sermons noted above, it has the distinctive Vulgate reading *plus his* in John 21:15. It also appears to mark the distinction in this verse between Jesus' question, with *diligis*, and Peter's response, with *amo*. Although it has most features of Augustine's mental text of John 21:18–19, it reads *ubi uolebas* in the former, in keeping with most biblical manuscripts, and also differs from *Sermo* 299 by featuring *glorificaturus* rather than *clarificaturus* in John 21:19.[17]

***Sermo* 342** is on the opening of John. Despite the familiarity of this passage, there is one indication that Augustine may have been referring to a codex: the initial citation of John 1:5 has *lux in tenebris lucet*, even though he reverts to his customary *lux lucet in tenebris* two sentences later. Furthermore, this sermon has an unusual feature shared only with *Sermo* 379: Augustine has the Old Latin pronoun found only in Codices Veronensis and Monacensis combined with the distinctive Vulgate verb, reading *in eo uita erat* in John 1:4. No date has been suggested for either sermon. Most of the Old Latin readings are also found in his mental text, and in John 1:16, the flattened word order indicates that he is citing from memory; the same is also probably true of the version of John 1:13 beginning *non ex carne, non ex sanguine*. ***Sermo* 352** on penitence does not appear to have followed a liturgical reading from John, but has several illustrative citations in an Old Latin form in keeping with the assigned date

[17] The observation at Pellegrino 1967:404 that putting Augustine's citations of John 21:15–19 in chronological order has little significance appears, therefore, only to apply to their exegesis.

of 404; it was also preached outside Hippo. In John 6:49, it reads *manna in eremo* rather than *panem in deserto* on all three occasions: Codices Monacensis, Brixianus, and Aureus have *manna*, while Codex Usserianus alone reads *deserto*. This last also agrees with *prodi* in John 11:43, although it is lacunose where *Sermo* 352.3.8 has *putet* in John 11:39.

The information that Augustine used a codex to cite John 5:24–9 in the middle of ***Sermo* 362**, a lengthy sermon on the resurrection of the dead, has already been cited above.[18] Although it does not feature a distinctive Vulgate reading, the form of the whole passage is indicative of Jerome's version. The variants in the initial citation from the Weber–Gryson editorial text are *transitum fecit* in John 5:24 and *monumento* in John 5:28, both of which are later replaced by sequential variants. *Transitum fecit* appears three times, however, before Augustine switches to *transiit*, and it seems likely that this form, unique to him, did appear in his manuscript. Prior to the discovery of the *Sermones Dolbeau*, this sermon used to be dated to 410–11. However, Dolbeau's arguments to locate it in Carthage in December 403 have been widely accepted.[19] This early date and the character of the text of John in the other sermons preached in Carthage make the Vulgate similarities surprising: gospel citations outside this passage in *Sermo* 362 do not offer any confirmation, as most display evidence of flattening. Nonetheless, the connection made by Hombert (2000:82–4) between *Sermo* 51, preached in the same month, and *De consensu euangelistarum*, for which Augustine used the Vulgate, suggests that he may have had a copy of Jerome's revision with him.

***Sermo* 375C** was preached some time between 402 and 404. Most of the references to its lection of John 20:24–31 seem to be paraphrases reproducing Augustine's mental text. This sermon also offers an early example of his unique present-tense form of John 20:29, *beati qui non uident et credunt*. The lection of ***Sermo* 379** (augmented by *Lambot* 20) was from Luke, but it has extensive citations from the opening verses of John. The sequential treatment of this passage, together with the command *audi Iohannem* and the verb *sequitur*,

[18] Page 35 above.

[19] Dolbeau 1996:66–9, adopted in Hombert 2000, Anoz 2002, and Gryson 2007.

might suggest that he turned to this page. The text is very similar to *Sermo* 342, with the only other example of the unusual combination *in eo uita erat* in John 1:4, and *lux in tenebris lucet* on all three occasions in the next verse.

ENARRATIONES IN PSALMOS[20]

***Enarratio* 3** is the only work apart from *Tractatus* 47 in which Augustine cites John 10:17 and 10:18 in their biblical order, as opposed to the sequence in his mental text. There is no evidence in this very early sermon (392/4) that Augustine is relying on a codex. His text is closest to Codex Bezae, which also reads *quoniam* in John 10:17 and does not include the phrases *pro ouibus* and *sed ego pono eam a meipso* in the next verse. There are several differences, however: Augustine has *propterea* and *sumam* in John 10:17 where Codex Bezae reads *propter hoc* and *accipiam*. This sermon also has a rare citation of John 13:27, in the form *quod facis cito fac*: this too resembles Codex Bezae. At this early date, Augustine's secondary citations clearly reflect Old Latin witnesses known to him.

***Enarrationes* 39** and **40** share a form of text in John 9:27–8 which is very close to Codex Palatinus:

Vulgate *numquid et uos uultis discipuli eius fieri? maledixerunt ei et dixerunt 'tu discipulus illius es'.*

Codex Palatinus *numquid et uos uultis discipulus eius* ***esse?*** *maledixerunt* ***illi dicentes*** *'tu* ***sis*** *discipulus* ***eius****'.*

Enarr. 39, 40 *numquid et uos discipuli eius uultis* ***esse? et illi*** *maledixerunt ei* ***dicentes*** *'tu* ***sis*** *discipulus* ***eius****'.*

There is also a selection of unusual readings in John 11:47–51 in *Enarratio* 40, although conflations and other errors indicate that they have been paraphrased. *Enarratio* 39 has been located in Carthage in 413, while *Enarratio* 40 was preached some time between 400 and 410. ***Enarratio* 44** was preached in Carthage in 403. In an excursus on

20 Dates for the *Enarrationes* have been taken from Anoz 2002:255–62, as indicated by Gryson 2007.

Jacob's ladder, Augustine cites John 1:47–51. He makes no mention of a manuscript; the citations have Old Latin forms including *arbore fici* in both John 1:48 and 1:50 and *maiora horum* in John 1:50, although no surviving exemplar parallels *credidisti* in John 1:50 (possibly under the influence of John 20:29?). This sermon is one of the first to read *super* rather than *ad* in John 1:51, along with the accompanying change in exegesis.[21] Furthermore, it has the earliest example in Augustine of the distinctive Vulgate form in John 1:4, *quod factum est in ipso uita erat* (*Enarratio* 44.5). The context supports the reading *erat* in the citation, so perhaps this reflects Jerome's newly arrived version of the Gospels (despite the Old Latin readings in other citations from John).

The citations of the *Pericope Adulterae* in ***Enarratio* 50** have already been mentioned in the discussion of *Sermo* 16A. Augustine's text here has a number of similarities with Codex Colbertinus, reading *iaciat* and *primus* in John 8:7, adding *de illa* in John 8:5 (Codex Colbertinus adds *de ea*), and citing John 8:11 with *condemnabo*, the majority Old Latin reading, rather than his mental text of *damnabo*. As in *Enarratio* 44, this is an excursus, with no indication that Augustine was relying on a codex, but it is possible that he had made a note of the passage in advance. The sermon was delivered in Carthage in 413.

Among the thirteen citations of John 11:48 in the *Enarrationes*, only ***Enarrationes* 52** and **68.s2** read *regnum* rather than *gentem*. This is not found in any surviving biblical manuscript. *Enarratio* 68.s2 has been located in Thagaste in 414–15; the same place has been suggested for *Enarratio* 52 (405–11), and it is tempting to see this as a distinctive reading from an exemplar which Augustine used in his birthplace. There are no other citations of John in *Enarratio* 52, while *Enarratio* 68.s2 gives Augustine's mental text for John 5:39 and 8:39, so it may just be an error of memory.[22] The gospel citations in ***Enarratio* 58.s1** (the first sermon on Psalm 58), preached in Carthage in 413, were also made from memory. Augustine summarizes John 7:45–9 with numerous variants, although there are some similarities with Codex Palatinus. This sermon also features his mental text of

[21] See Berrouard 1962:489–93 and pp. 200–1 below.

[22] Anoz 2002 only situates *Enarrationes* 34 and 68 in Thagaste, but this location has been proposed by Zarb for *Enarrationes* 93 and 139 as well (see below).

John 14:9, *patrem non nostis*, and an accusative and infinitive in John 19:21. ***Enarratio* 65**, from 412, followed a lection which included John 10:30 but is more remarkable for its citations of John 1:41–7, 2:18–20, and 9:40–1: *interpretatur* in John 1:41 and *uerus* in 1:47 both appear only in Codex Monacensis; John 2:19, unusually for Augustine, corresponds to the Vulgate, although in the next verse he reverts to *triduo*; John 9:40–1 appear to be paraphrased, but feature the additional *in uobis* peculiar to Codices Vercellensis and Veronensis.

***Enarratio* 90.s1** (Augustine's first sermon on Psalm 90, delivered in 412, possibly in Carthage) was preceded by a gospel reading from John. The cited verses, John 10:7–8, read *ianua* and *omnes qui uenerunt*: the only surviving manuscript with both these is Codex Sarzanensis. ***Enarratio* 92**, for which a date of 404 has been suggested, cites much of John 13:5–14 as a gloss on *praecinctus* in Psalm 92:1. There are numerous Old Latin features, including *habebis* in John 13:8, *pedes tantum* in John 13:9, the addition of *et totum* in 13:9, *habet necessitatem lauandi* in 13:10, and *dicitis* rather than *uocatis* in 13:13. Many of these are paralleled by Codices Vercellensis, Palatinus, and Monacensis. The liturgical Gospel at the service, however, was from Luke 3. Other examples of Augustine's mental text in John corresponding to the four manuscripts mentioned in this paragraph are found in ***Enarratio* 95** (John 10:2), ***Enarratio* 98** (John 6:63 and 6:65), and ***Enarratio* 102** (John 14:9, 15:13 and 16:33); ***Enarratio* 138** has readings unique to Augustine in John 12:35 and 16:32. All these sermons are believed to have been preached outside Hippo.[23]

***Enarratio* 139**, from 415, contains a version of John 14:21 not found in any of Augustine's other citations of this verse:

qui audit praecepta mea et custodit ea, ipse est qui diligit me: et qui diligit me, diligetur a patre meo, et ego diligam eum et ostendam illi meipsum.

(*Enarratio* 139.18)[24]

Elsewhere, Augustine has *mandata* rather than *praecepta* over thirty times; *audit* also appears in this citation alone. While *praecepta* and *audit* are paralleled in Codices Aureus, Veronensis, and Colbertinus,

[23] Anoz 2002:259–61 lists Carthage for *Enarrationes* 98 and 102 (dated to 403/4), and Utica for *Enarratio* 138 (dated to 412).

[24] Gori's edition has two minor variants: *diligitur* for *diligetur* and *illum* for *eum*.

custodit only features in Codices Monacensis and Vercellensis (which, along with Codex Bezae, also have *ostendam illi meipsum*), Codex Brixianus is the sole surviving source with *ipse*, and *et qui* rather than *qui autem* is unique to Augustine. It seems unlikely, therefore, that this citation has been altered. What is more, the introduction to this verse, albeit in the last paragraph of the sermon, shows that it came from the day's lection. The best explanation for Augustine's unusual text here, then, is that it reflects the manuscript of the Gospel he used that day.[25]

To summarize, the citations of John in Augustine's other sermons are much more diverse than the *Tractatus in Iohannem*. Old Latin readings appear in sermons on the Gospel according to John throughout Augustine's career. This is particularly marked when he preached in Carthage (or Thagaste). It is not always possible to tell whether Augustine was relying on a codex; the citations of John in the *Enarrationes in Psalmos* suggest that he may sometimes have made a selection of illustrative passages in advance, since he is likely to have used a copy of the Psalter during his sermon. Although his biblical text rarely corresponds to any one surviving manuscript, many of his variations from the Vulgate are paralleled in the Old Latin tradition, particularly in Codices Monacensis, Usserianus, Vercellensis, and Palatinus. Most readings peculiar to Augustine can be attributed to paraphrase or errors of memory, but some are worthy of fuller consideration. The effect of Augustine's use of the Vulgate on his mental text can be seen in the appearance of distinctive Vulgate readings in sermons delivered in 418 or later. Given that much of the lection is often omitted and sustained citations are rarely found, Augustine's sermons are not a consistent source for his gospel text, although certain pieces do preserve important evidence.

[25] Zarb suggested that this sermon was preached in Thagaste (cf. *Enarratio* 68.s2 above).

7

Early Works (before 403)

There are very few citations of the Gospel according to John in Augustine's writings before his ordination in 391.[1] Nonetheless, some of Augustine's earliest citations already feature the customary form of his mental text as found in numerous later works. For example, ***De moribus ecclesiae catholicae et de moribus Manichaeorum*** 2.11.22 (387/9) reads *si uos filius liberauerit tunc uere liberi eritis* in John 8:36, with Augustine's characteristic word order and addition of *tunc*. In the same work, John 17:3 appears as:

haec est uita aeterna, ut cognoscant te uerum deum, et quem misisti Iesum Christum. (*De moribus* 1.25.47)

There is no parallel in Latin or Greek Gospels for the omission of the term before *uerum*, although it is also lacking from ***De libero arbitrio*** 2.2.6 (391–5). Augustine soon begins to cite this verse with the addition of *solum*, the reading of most biblical manuscripts, as in *De duabus animabus* 10 (392) and *De diuersis quaestionibus* 35.2 (388–95).

DE GENESI CONTRA MANICHAEOS (388/9)

This work has another early instance of Augustine's mental text, with *escam quae non corrumpitur* for John 6:27 at 2.9.12. On the other

[1] The following works have no citations of John: *Contra academicos, De dialectica, De immortalitate animae, De quantitate animae, De magistro, De musica.* The *Soliloquia* have four allusions but no citations. Three citations or fewer are found in *De ordine, De beata uita, De libero arbitrio,* and *De utilitate credendi.*

hand, *De Genesi contra Manichaeos* 1.7.11 does not have his customary form of John 16:12, *non potestis illa portare modo*, but omits *illa* in keeping with several biblical witnesses. The citations in this work correspond to members of the 'first group' of Old Latin manuscripts in John: for example, *usque **nunc*** in John 5:17 (1.22.33 twice; Codex Vercellensis only); *principium **quod*** in John 8:25 (1.2.3); ***de suo** loquitur* in John 8:44 (2.14.20, 2.16.24 twice), ***quae** audiui* and *nota **uobis feci*** in John 15:15 (1.7.11) and ***hunc** mundum* in John 16:28 (2.24.37). Augustine makes corrections to the Old Testament citations of this work in *Retractationes* 1.10.3, but does not alter his gospel text.

DE DIUERSIS QUAESTIONIBUS (388–95)

The eighty-three *Quaestiones* are Augustine's earliest major theological work with numerous citations of John. Most have a mixture of Old Latin readings and Augustine's customary forms, such as the versions of John 6:44 and 16:13 in ***Quaestio* 38**.[2] ***Quaestio* 80** shares a form of John 15:13 with *De mendacio* 6.9 which is halfway to Augustine's mental text: *quam* is added and *quis* omitted, but it reads *dilectionem* with the majority of Old Latin witnesses rather than *caritatem*. The citation of John 17:2 in the same work is conflated with John 3:15:

sicut dedisti ei potestatem omnis carnis, ut omne quod dedisti ei non pereat sed habeat uitam aeternam. (*Quaestio* 80.2)

This shows that Augustine was already relying on his memory for gospel citations, with corresponding errors.

The critical edition of this work by Mutzenbecher includes variant readings in the manuscript tradition which affect biblical citations. There are surprisingly few examples of alterations which harmonize Augustine's text with the Vulgate, and these are confined to witnesses

[2] Other examples of Augustine's customary form of text can be seen in *Quaestio* 68 (John 1:12 and 15:15), *Quaestio* 69 (John 8:31, 14:28, and 19:11), and *Quaestio* 71 (John 13:35).

from the thirteenth century onwards, chiefly manuscripts E (thirteen occasions), H (eight occasions), and I (seven occasions). There is no evidence for the systematic alteration of Augustine's biblical text, and even these manuscripts transmit most of his Old Latin or peculiar readings without variation. Three variants in John deserve special consideration. All appear in manuscript G, one of the two oldest witnesses, which Mutzenbecher usually follows for the editorial text. In the citation of John 10:18 at *Quaestio* 80.2, most manuscripts read *iterum sumendi eam*, but G and Z have *iterum* ***accipiendi*** *eam*. Although this is not found in Augustine's other citations, it is the form of text used by Fortunatus at *Contra Fortunatum* 32, also from this period, and is paralleled in Codex Rehdigeranus (which has a text-type similar to *Quaestio* 64). In John 16:12, cited at *Quaestio* 53.4, manuscript G includes *adhuc* in the second half of the verse, *non potestis* ***adhuc*** *portare illa*. Although there is no instance of this among the biblical witnesses, a similar citation in another contemporary work, *De sermone domini* 2.20.67, offers an important parallel. Finally, in John 16:13 most manuscripts of *Quaestio* 38 read *ipse uos in omnem ueritatem inducet* but manuscript G has *ipse uos inducat in omnem ueritatem*, the same word order as found in all four of Augustine's other verbatim citations with *inducet*, all of which are in his early works.[3]

Three of the *Quaestiones* have significant Old Latin readings in their biblical text of John. In its discussion of John 4:1–2, ***Quaestio*** **62** has the imperfect indicative, *baptizabat*, in both verses: Codex Corbeiensis supplies a parallel for this in John 4:1, while four manuscripts have it in John 4:2.[4] In the latter verse, however, there is no surviving witness with *quamuis* (for *quamquam*), or the omission of *Iesus*. John 7:39 is cited in Augustine's customary form in *Quaestio* 62, which differs from the form he gives in *Quaestio* 64.4: the inconsistency is unsurprising, as he himself tells us that these *Quaestiones* were composed individually (*Retractationes* 1.26).

[3] It is also comparable to Codex Palatinus, the only biblical witness with *inducet*. Note that manuscript C features a gloss with the reading of Codex Rehdigeranus and the Vulgate: *ipse uos in omnem ueritatem inducet, id est docebit*. This is probably due to a copyist.

[4] Manuscript C of *Quaestio* 62 reads *baptizauit* on both occasions; this is not found in surviving manuscripts. Compare also *Epistula* 265.5, discussed below.

***Quaestio* 64**, *De muliere Samaritana*, cites much of John 4 sequentially: Augustine was clearly working from a codex, even though there are a few paraphrases and omissions of half verses. The initial *puteus Iacob* in John 4:6 matches Codices Sarzanensis, Rehdigeranus, and Usserianus, although other manuscripts have *puteum* later in the verse. Augustine is unique in reading *perrexerant* instead of *abierant* in John 4:8, where *cibos* rather than *escas* implies that, unusually, his text-type does not correspond to the majority of older witnesses; this is further demonstrated by his inclusion of the additional sentence at the end of John 4:9 absent from most of these manuscripts. Both, however, are found in Codices Usserianus and Rehdigeranus, which along with Codex Sarzanensis also have *magis* in John 4:10. Codex Rehdigeranus is the only one of the three to read *ab eo* later in John 4:10, while it is joined by Codex Sarzanensis in adding *mihi* and *dare* in 4:11. Despite further coincidences with this manuscript over the next few verses, Augustine does not have the phrase *et pueri eius* in John 4:12, and the sole parallel for *de aqua ista* in John 4:13 is Codex Monacensis.[5] The only surviving examples of *in sempiternum* in John 4:14 are Codices Veronensis and Usserianus: Codex Rehdigeranus does not contain this part of the verse. Nonetheless, *alterutrum* in John 4:33 is peculiar to these three manuscripts, which also have *esca* in John 4:32 and 4:34, although Augustine changes to *cibus* in the latter. Overall, Augustine's text in this, one of his longest continuous citations of a passage of John, most resembles Codex Rehdigeranus, although it is also close to Codex Usserianus.[6]

In ***Quaestio* 65**, *De resurrectione Lazari*, there are two variants which are characteristic of Augustine's later citations of John 11:39. The first is *auferte*, where all Old Latin manuscripts have *tollite*; the second is *putet*, shared with Codex Bezae and the Fragmentum Sangallense. At the end of this verse, where Augustine elsewhere

[5] It is worth observing that *Quaestio* 64 shares the readings *biberit*, *ista*, and *dedero* in John 4:13 with Codex Palatinus and Cyprian, although there are other readings in Cyprian's *Epistula* 63.8 which do not correspond to Augustine's text (e.g. *aeternum* rather than *sempiternum* in the next verse).

[6] Codex Rehdigeranus is assigned by Burton to his 'second group' of Old Latin witnesses, based on the whole of the Gospel, although he detects 'an overlay from a Group 1 tradition' (2000:71). The parallels with Codices Usserianus and Sarzanensis suggest that in this passage it may belong to the 'first group'. Part of the text of *Quaestio* 64 is reproduced in Houghton 2008.

has *quadriduanus* or *quadriduum*, *Quaestio* 65 has *quarta dies*, paralleled only by Codex Palatinus. The quotations of John 11:44 in *Quaestio* 65 include the Old Latin forms *exiit* and *ire*, along with two words not found in the surviving manuscripts, *inuolutis* and *tecta*. These *Quaestiones* therefore confirm that Augustine was not using a Vulgate text at this point, and constitute a valuable source of Old Latin readings.[7]

DE UERA RELIGIONE (390)

There are three noteworthy gospel citations in *De uera religione*. In John 2:4 at *De uera religione* 16.31, Augustine adds the line *recede a me mulier* before *mihi et tibi quid est? nondum uenit hora mea*. There is no support for this in any biblical manuscripts and it is possible that Augustine has confused the situation with *noli me tangere* in John 20:17. *De uera religione* 31.58 already shows Augustine's customary form of John 5:22, *pater non iudicat quemquam sed omne iudicium dedit filio*. Another reading unique to Augustine is *diem* rather than *lucem* in John 12:35:

> *ambulemus dum diem habemus*, id est dum ratione uti possumus... *ne nos tenebrae comprehendant*. (*De uera religione* 42.79)

It seems most likely that Augustine substituted *diem* under the influence of *tenebrae*, but the recurrence of this form of text twenty years later in *Enarratio in Psalmos* 138 shows its persistence.

CONTRA FORTUNATUM (392)

Most of the citations of John in Augustine's earliest recorded debate are on the lips of his opponent, Fortunatus the Manichee. These feature some Old Latin readings and some conflations, which appear

[7] Dulaey's study of *Quaestiones* 44 and 58–60 promises a further article on *Quaestiones* 61, 64, and 65 (see Dulaey 2006a:114), which has not yet appeared at the time of writing.

to be typical of Manichaean citations. In *Contra Fortunatum* 3, Fortunatus combines John 5:24 and John 8:52, and produces the following mixture of John 10:9 and John 14:6:

ego sum uia, ueritas et ianua, et nemo potest ad patrem peruenire nisi per me.

He also has a repetitive form of John 15:22 at *Contra Fortunatum* 21: all these variants probably derive from memory. Augustine's citation of John 10:18 (*Contra Fortunatum* 34) in this work is one of the very few in which he omits the adverb *iterum*. Although this is also missing from Codices Palatinus and Corbeiensis, it is more likely that Augustine has been influenced by Fortunatus' citations in the two preceding paragraphs. This work is remarkable for its long citations of the Pauline Epistles: Fortunatus reads Ephesians 2:1–18 (*Contra Fortunatum* 16), while three paragraphs later Augustine quotes Romans 1:1–4. Both feature minor variations from the text of Weber–Gryson. Given that the origin of the Vulgate Epistles is unknown and Augustine's citations of Paul rarely correspond to this version, these references are of particular interest. The stenographer's reference to *omnia quae in Apostoli codice scripta sunt* (*Contra Fortunatum* 19) suggests that a single codex is being used.

CONTRA ADIMANTUM (394)

In *Contra Adimantum* Augustine expounds a sequence of biblical verses against his Manichaean opponent. It seems probable that Augustine quotes the initial citations in each paragraph from Adimantus. For example, the citation of John 1:10 in the opening paragraph has the unusual word order *et mundus factus est per ipsum* as well as the sole example of *illum non cognouit* among Augustine's citations. This practice would also explain the unusual form of John 1:18 and John 5:37–8 in *Contra Adimantum* 9:

insidiantur ergo Manichaei et dicunt omnia contraria esse nouo testamento, quoniam dominus dicit: *deum nemo uidit umquam nisi unicus filius qui est in sinu patris ille adnuntiauit uobis de eo.* et iterum quod dicit Iudaeis: *nec uocem illius aliquando audistis nec faciem eius uidistis, nec uerbum eius habetis in uobis manens quia ei quem ille misit non credidistis.* quibus respondemus eo ipso, quod in euangelio scriptum est: *deum nemo uidit umquam, nisi unicus filius qui est in sinu patris ipse adnuntiauit uobis de eo,* totam ipsam solui posse quaestionem.

These are the only instances of John 1:18 in all Augustine's writings with *unicus* rather than *unigenitus*, although he also has this rendering in John 3:16 in *De catechizandis rudibus* (see p. 210). Interestingly, the only surviving gospel manuscript with *unicus* in John 1:18 is Codex Vercellensis, which also reads *illum* in John 1:10: it is possible that Adimantus had a codex of this type.[8] However, there are no parallels for the addition of *uobis de eo* at the end of the verse, and it does not occur in any of Augustine's other citations. Similarly, this is the only time Augustine cites the second half of John 5:37 and it features several unique readings: *nec*, *illius*, *aliquando* (all biblical codices read *umquam*) and *faciem* (rather than *speciem* or *figura*). These are repeated later in the paragraph, before Augustine finishes with a conflation of John 12:28 and 17:5 which is probably an error of memory.

The other citations of John in this work display Old Latin readings which correspond to Augustine's mental text, such as *heremo* rather than *deserto* in John 3:14 (*Contra Adimantum* 21) or the absence of *forsitan* from John 5:46 (*Contra Adimantum* 5). While these were probably made from memory, Augustine's extensive citations from the Pauline Epistles must have been drawn from a codex (e.g. 1 Corinthians 15:39–50 in *Contra Adimantum* 12.4, Romans 14:1–23 in *Contra Adimantum* 14.2, 1 Corinthians 10:19–31 in *Contra Adimantum* 14.3).

DE SERMONE DOMINI IN MONTE *(394/5)*

This is Augustine's first major work on the Gospels, and has a substantial number of citations from John.[9] Many correspond to Augustine's

[8] It is suggestive that numerous manuscripts of this work (and Migne's edition) read *usque* ***nunc*** *operatur* in the initial citation of John 5:17 in *Contra Adimantum* 2.1; this too is unique to Codex Vercellensis, although Zycha's edition has the more common *usque modo operatur.*

[9] Its text of Matthew 5–7 is analysed in detail in Mizzi 1954, who concludes that it is Old Latin, with no trace of the Vulgate.

preferred form of each verse, including John 5:22 and 6:27 at *De sermone domini* 1.11.32 and 2.7.26–7 respectively. Augustine's earliest citation of John 8:11 appears at *De sermone domini* 1.16.43, in the form *uade, uide deinceps ne pecces.* None of the last four words are found in Old Latin manuscripts, but four citations in Ambrose read *uade et amodo uide ne pecces.* Conflation is apparent in John 7:12 at *De sermone domini* 1.5.14, probably with John 7:40. Augustine's citation of John 16:12 at *De sermone domini* 2.20.67 includes his customary addition of *illa* (missing from *De Genesi contra Manichaeos*), although unlike the rest of his citations, *adhuc* seems to have been repeated from the beginning of the verse and *modo* omitted.[10] Along with the contemporary *De mendacio*, *De sermone domini* 1.19.58 has the phrase *exprobra de malo* in John 18:23, an Old Latin form also found in Cyprian.

DE MENDACIO (395)

There are four verses of John cited verbatim in *De mendacio.* John 15:12 at *De mendacio* 6.9 is identical to Codex Vercellensis, but the following verse appears in the same form as *Quaestio* 80, similar to Augustine's mental text. The brief citation of the first part of John 3:21 (*De mendacio* 17.35) corresponds to the 'second group' of manuscripts with *lucem* rather than *lumen.* Finally, as noted above, *De mendacio* 15.27 has one of only three citations of John 18:23 made by Augustine outside the Vulgate-influenced *De consensu euangelistarum* and the *Tractatus in Iohannem.* All three have *exprobra* rather than *testimonium perhibe*, which is not paralleled in surviving manuscripts but appears in three of Cyprian's letters. Given that Augustine uses it in three different places, it is probable that he knew this reading from a biblical codex. Alternatively, he may have taken it from Cyprian or elsewhere: the inconsistencies in the affiliation of the gospel text of *De mendacio* suggest that Augustine may have relied on a variety of sources.

[10] It is possible that *adhuc* is a translation of ἄρτι in place of *modo* but this seems less likely: note also the appearance of *adhuc* in this phrase in manuscript G at *Quaestio* 53.4, discussed on p. 141.

EARLY LETTERS

The corpus of Augustine's letters includes those written by his correspondents as well as his own. When dictating his letters, he seems normally to have quoted scriptural verses from memory: there are examples of his customary text of John across the whole collection. Longer citations are an exception, and two early letters deserve a mention. ***Epistula* 243** to Laetus is dated by Hombert to 394–5. Augustine quotes Luke 14:26–32, clearly from an Old Latin codex, at *Epistula* 243.2: there are numerous readings only paralleled in Codex Palatinus. The form of John 12:25 in *Epistula* 243.5, however, is conflated with the Synoptic parallels. ***Epistula* 265** to Seleuciana contains several verses of John rarely cited by Augustine, and is included here because of its Old Latin affiliation.[11] In *Epistula* 265.5, Augustine begins by referring to John 4:1–2 apparently from memory, with *baptizabat* in both verses (cf. *Quaestio* 62). He then cites John 3:22 in an Old Latin form, reading *exiit* and *morabatur*, before giving a full citation of John 4:1–3:

ut ergo cognouit Iesus quia audierunt Pharisaei quod Iesus plures discipulos haberet et baptizaret quam Iohannes, quamquam Iesus ipse non baptizaret, sed discipuli eius, reliquit Iudaeam terram, et abiit iterum in Galilaeam.

This is identical to Codex Sarzanensis except for *quod* in John 4:1 and *terram* in John 4:3: it is quite possible that Augustine consulted a manuscript after his initial reference with *baptizabat.* Later on in the same paragraph, there is one of Augustine's few citations of John 13:10 with Old Latin parallels, reading *non indiget nisi ut pedes lauet* as found in Codices Veronensis, Corbeiensis, and Rehdigeranus. Augustine gives two citations of John 3:5 in *Epistula* 265.4, which differ despite their proximity: the first begins *si quis non*, while the second has *nisi quis* (the rest of the text follows his customary form). The version of John 20:22 at *Epistula* 265.2 also does not correspond to Augustine's mental text, with *sufflauit* rather than *insufflauit* and

[11] Gryson 2007 gives no date for *Epistula* 265; Anoz 2002:254 notes Mandouze's suggestion of 405–8, but proposes 420 on the basis of the similarity of the citation of John 13:10 to *Tractatus* 80.3. The Old Latin parallels in the other citations seem more compelling, particularly as *Tractatus* 80.3 is a non-sequential citation.

the word order *eorum faciem.* It may be, then, that in this discussion of baptism and penitence Augustine drew on a collection of *testimonia* or another source: in *Epistula* 265.3 he refers to differences in manuscripts of Paul, which implies that he had consulted some codices.

CONFESSIONES (397–403)

In the *Confessiones,* Augustine's biblical references are predominantly allusions or reminiscences. The psalm citations, which considerably outnumber those from the New Testament, have been thoroughly analysed by Knauer. Similar conflation or paraphrase is found in some of the gospel citations, as in the following version of John 14:30, resembling Luke 23:15:

princeps huius mundi non inuenit quidquam morte dignum.

(*Confessiones* 7.21.27)

Some of the allusive references are to John, such as:

in Ambrosii ora suspendi ad fontem salientis aquae in uitam aeternam.

(*Confessiones* 6.1.1; cf. John 4:14)

Most of the verbatim citations come from John 1, with the Old Latin readings typical of his mental text. Despite the parallels with Codices Veronensis and Monacensis, it is likely that Augustine was citing from memory. However, the allusion to John 12:35 at *Confessiones* 10.23.33 omits *tempus* after *modicum.* This reading is peculiar to the Vulgate and Codex Aureus, but as the citation is loose it could simply be an oversight.

CONTRA FAUSTUM (400/2)

Augustine reproduces extensive quotations of Faustus, the Manichaean Bishop of Milevis, in this work which is presented as a dialogue even though he is working from a written source. His opponent's citations of John have a marked preference for 'African' renderings: *μαρτυρεῖν* is always translated by *testificari* in John 8:13, 8:14, and 8:18, which is more consistent than any surviving biblical manuscript. In John 15:10, Faustus quotes:

si feceritis mandata mea, manebitis in mea caritate. (*Contra Faustum* 5.3)

Both *mandata* and *caritate* are 'African' renderings which are found in this verse in Codices Palatinus and Bezae, although no manuscript has *feceritis.* A further similiarity with Codex Palatinus is the absence of *forsitan* from all of Faustus' citations of John 5:46, although he rejects the whole verse as an interpolation made by Judaizers (*Contra Faustum* 16.2). Other readings are only preserved in witnesses related to the Vulgate, such as *non potest uidere* in John 3:5 (Codex Aureus) or *nam* in John 8:17 (Codex Brixianus). There are several unique forms which may be errors of memory or derive from an African version no longer preserved, such as *semper* rather than *usque modo* in John 5:17 (*Contra Faustum* 16.6), and *processi* for *exiui* in John 16:28 where all manuscripts have *exiui* (*Contra Faustum* 12.1). Faustus quotes John 16:13 as:

ipse uos inducet in omnem ueritatem et ipse uobis adnuntiabit omnia et commemorabit uos. (*Contra Faustum* 32.6)

This would have been a key verse for Manichees, who believed that Mani was the promised Paraclete. The final four words are a conflation with John 14:26, another reference to the Paraclete, in the form found in Codices Vercellensis and Usserianus.[12] It is interesting that Felix the Manichee also has a conflated form of this verse (*Contra Felicem* 1.2). Suggestions that Manichees used the Diatessaron do not seem to be borne out by Faustus' citations of John, although it is well known that he refers to the episode of the 'Flying Jesus' in Luke

[12] Decret (1970:287) suggests that Augustine's response to this citation, using a shorter form of text, is meant as a correction to this conflation: *deinde paracletus sic est promissus, ut diceretur: ipse uos inducet in omnem ueritatem* (*Contra Faustum* 32.16). He also remarks (1970:161) on the reading *inducet* in these citations and *Contra Felicem* 1.2, which is shared by some of Augustine's other references and Codex Palatinus.

4:29–30 (*Contra Faustum* 26.2), which is believed to be peculiar to this version.[13]

When Augustine refers to one of Faustus' citations, he normally reproduces his opponent's biblical text without alteration or comment, even when it goes against his customary reading. For example, his only citation of John 10:38 with *creditis* rather than *uultis credere* (*Contra Faustum* 13.5) is identical to Faustus' text at *Contra Faustum* 12.1, while many of the distinctive features of John 8:13 and 8:17 reappear in *Contra Faustum* 16.13. The majority of Augustine's own citations of John follow his mental text. This includes some parallels with Old Latin manuscripts, such as *interpretatur* in John 1:41 (*Contra Faustum* 12.44) and *os eius* in John 19:36 (*Contra Faustum* 12.30), which both appear in Codex Monacensis. Several variants are paralleled in Augustine's other citations but not found elsewhere, such as *quamdiu* in John 10:24 (*Contra Faustum* 12.4 and *Sermo* 293D.4), or *oportebat mori* in John 11:51 (*Contra Faustum* 16.23 and *Enarratio* 40.1). *Contra Faustum* 17.3–4 includes citations of John 21:20, 24, and 25 with numerous Old Latin parallels, which suggest that they may have been drawn from a codex: in fact, John 21:25 is almost identical to Codex Usserianus.

It is therefore all the more remarkable to discover the following text of John 5:25–7 in one of the earlier books:

> uno loco in euangelio secundum Iohannem ita scriptum est: *amen amen dico uobis quia uenit hora et nunc est quando mortui audient uocem filii dei et qui audierint uiuent. sicut enim pater habet uitam in semet ipso sic dedit et filio uitam habere in semet ipso. et potestatem dedit ei et iudicium facere quia filius hominis est.* (*Contra Faustum* 5.4)

This is the earliest of only three of Augustine's citations of John 5:26–7 which correspond exactly to the Vulgate; the others are *Tractatus in Iohannem* 19 and *Sermo* 362. On the other hand, many of these readings also appear in surviving Old Latin manuscripts, especially the 'second group'. This may not, therefore, be a Vulgate reference, but it is unclear why Augustine prefers this form of text to his customary readings at this point. As he gives the title of the book

[13] See further Baarda (1986:330). Much has been made of this, and Augustine's failure to comment on the allusion, but as he seldom criticizes his opponents' biblical text, this silence is not significant.

it could be that he is drawing it from a written source rather than from memory: alternatively, these verses may have been altered during the work's transmission, but this is impossible to prove.

CONTRA LITTERAS PETILIANI (400–5)

As with *Contra Faustum*, Augustine set his response to the letter of Petilianus of Constantine in the form of a debate. As noted above, Augustine makes several corrections to his opponent's biblical text.[14] These include the alteration of *accusator* to *homicida* in John 8:44 (*Contra litteras Petiliani* 2.13.30). Petilianus' citations include several such unique forms which may have been characteristic of versions of the Bible used by the Donatists: for instance, he has *sibilauit in faciem eorum* for John 20:22 (*Contra litteras Petiliani* 2.32.72). Most of his non-Vulgate readings are differences in rendering which correspond to 'African' forms paralleled elsewhere in Codex Palatinus or Codex Bezae, such as *facta* in place of *opera* in John 10:37 (*Contra litteras Petiliani* 2.12.27) or *quomodo* for *sicut* (John 13:34, *Contra litteras Petiliani* 2.75.167). Agreements with one or both of these manuscripts include *putet* in John 16:2 (*Contra litteras Petiliani* 2.92.202), *facere* rather than *accipere* in John 3:27 (*Contra litteras Petiliani* 2.31.70), and *pacem meam dimitto uobis* in John 14:27 (*Contra litteras Petiliani* 2.22.49). On the other hand, a comparison between John 17:12 in Codex Palatinus and Petilianus reveals several differences:

c. Pet. 2.8.17 *quos dedisti mihi omnes seruaui et ex illis nullus periit nisi filius perditionis ut impleretur scriptura.*

Cod. Palatinus *quos dedisti mihi custodiui et nemo ex is perit nisi filius perditionis ut scriptura impleatur.*

This suggests that if Petilianus cites accurately, he could be an important source for African biblical texts which have not been preserved. The majority of Augustine's own citations of John in *Contra litteras Petiliani* conform to his mental text, although he

[14] See p. 81 above.

sometimes reproduces readings from Petilianus, such as John 8:44 at *Contra litteras Petiliani* 2.13.30 and John 16:2 at *Contra litteras Petiliani* 2.92.206.

ADNOTATIONES IN IOB (400/5)

These notes on Job include several Old Latin features typical of Augustine's mental text, such as *lumen uerum* in John 1:9, *tamquam* in John 1:14, *populum* in John 7:12, and *in quo princeps huius mundi nihil inuenit* in John 14:30. An adaptation of John 3:21 in *Adnotationes* 36 puts it into the plural:

ipsi ueniant ad lucem ut manifestentur opera eorum quoniam in deo sunt operata.

Quoniam and *operata* are paralleled by Codices Veronensis, Palatinus, Bezae, and Usserianus. Other references correspond to a form of text preserved in Codex Palatinus alone, such as *facta . . . facite* in John 8:39 (*Adnotationes* 30), *cum exaltatus fuero omnia traham ad me* in John 12:32 (*Adnotationes* 39), and *saeculo* in John 17:15 (*Adnotationes* 38):

non peto ut tollas eos de saeculo sed ut tollas eos a malo.

Both *peto* and the second *tollas* are unique to this citation and seem to be errors of memory (*peto* has been substituted for the manuscripts' *rogo*, and *tollas* repeated instead of *serues*). In short, although Augustine is probably citing from memory, his text shows the influence of a text-type similar to Codex Palatinus and no appearance yet of Vulgate forms. It is interesting to note that, in the *Retractationes*, Augustine wished to disclaim authorship of the work and left it unrevised.[15] The fact that its biblical text corresponds to that of contemporary writings tells against any suggestion that Augustine was in the habit of revising or making silent alterations to biblical citations in his early works.

[15] *Postremo tam mendosum conperi opus ipsum in codicibus nostris ut emendare non possem nec editum a me dici uellem, nisi quia scio fratres id habere, quorum studio non potuit denegari* (*Retractationes* 2.13).

DE TRINITATE (400–3, 411-POST 422)

De trinitate is included in this chapter because it was begun in 400; it is principally of interest for the citations in Book I, which was finished in 403. Augustine started on Book II in 411, and the full fifteen books, including some revisions to the earlier books, were completed soon after 422.[16] The clear distinction between Book I and the rest of the work is shown by the Old Latin affiliation of its gospel citations. These consistently read *aduocatus* rather than *paracletus*, as shown by three of the four verses in which this appears:

et ego rogabo patrem et alium aduocatum dabit uobis ut uobiscum sit in aeternum. (John 14:16; *De trinitate* 1.8.18 (twice), 1.9.19)

aduocatus autem ille spiritus sanctus quem mittet pater in nomine meo, ille uobis declarabit omnia. (John 14:26; *De trinitate* 1.12.25)

sed ego ueritatem dico, expedit uobis ut ego eam. nam si non abiero, aduocatus non ueniet ad uos. (John 16:7; *De trinitate* 1.8.18)

Only Codex Monacensis has *aduocatus* in all three verses, although it is joined by Codices Palatinus and Vercellensis on two occasions. *Ut uobiscum sit* in John 14:16 is also characteristic of the Old Latin tradition, but no surviving manuscript has *declarabit* in John 14:26. These verses are not cited in later books, but the citation of John 15:26 in Book II does not feature the rendering *aduocatus*:

cum autem uenerit paracletus, quem ego mittam uobis a patre, spiritum ueritatis qui a patre procedit, ille testimonium perhibebit de me.

(*De trinitate* 2.3.5)

Many of the citations of John in Book I appear in four clusters of verses: John 14:16–23 in *De trinitate* 1.9, John 16:22–8 in *De trinitate* 1.10, John 12:47–50 in *De trinitate* 1.12, and John 5:22–9 in *De trinitate* 1.13. They may have been drawn from a codex or a collection

[16] For dating, see Hombert 2000:45–80 and 638; he draws heavily on the earlier treatment by La Bonnardière 1965:69–77 and 165–77, which tries to determine the extent of Augustine's additions to earlier books. Thse later revisions explain the dating of the opening chapters in *De trinitate* 1–4 after 420 (e.g. Hombert 2000:535–7).

of *testimonia*: Augustine refers to such assemblies of verses on the theme of the Holy Spirit at *De trinitate* 1.6.13. It is worth observing that all these Old Latin readings occur in the second half of Book I: this fits with La Bonnardière's suggestion that the *prooemium* which Augustine later added to this book extends as far as the end of *De trinitate* 1.6.[17] The citations of John in the first six chapters have no clear Old Latin affiliation, but correspond to Augustine's customary form of text: John 5:19 appears in an almost identical form in the prologues of both Books I and II (*De trinitate* 1.6.11 and 2.1.3). Most remarkable is the treatment of John 17:3. Throughout the first half of Book I and all of Book II, every reminiscence of this verse includes the word *solus*, either as *unus et solus deus* (*De trinitate* 1.6.9, 1.6.10) or *unus et solus et uerus deus* (*De trinitate* 1.2.4, 1.6.10, cf. 1.6.11). This does not appear in any of the verbatim citations in the second half of Book I (*De trinitate* 1.8.17, 1.13.30, 1.13.31). As Augustine seems to have known two forms of this verse (see p. 333), this detail too seems to reveal the different stages of composition.

The principal similarities of the Old Latin citations in Book I are with the first group of Old Latin manuscripts, often combining readings preserved in different witnesses. For example, *De trinitate* has Augustine's only citation of John 16:25 outside the *Tractatus in Iohannem*:

haec uobis locutus sum in similitudinibus. ueniet hora quando iam non in similitudinibus loquar uobis sed manifeste de patre nuntiabo uobis.

(*De trinitate* 1.10.21)

Codex Vercellensis is the sole parallel for *similitudinibus* rather than *prouerbiis*, while only Codex Palatinus prefers *quando* to *cum*. Both have *nuntiabo* for *adnuntiabo*, as does Codex Monacensis, yet although *manifeste* renders παρρησίᾳ elsewhere it is not extant in any manuscript here. The reading *custodit illa* in John 14:21 is only preserved in Codices Vercellensis and Monacensis, while the latter alone reads *ostensurus es* in the next verse and *mansionem apud illum* in John 14:23 (*De trinitate* 1.9.18). The form of John 14:17 also has similarities with these three manuscripts:

[17] La Bonnardière 1965:85–6.

quem hic mundus accipere non potest quoniam non uidet illum. nostis illum uos quia uobiscum manet et in uobis est. (*De trinitate* 1.9.19)

Unusually, *nostis* and *uobiscum* are also found in Codex Colbertinus, from the second group. The cluster of citations in *De trinitate* 1.12 has a particular affinity (but not identity) with Codex Usserianus, which shares readings such as *saluum faciam* in John 12:47, *uerbum quod* in John 12:48, and *mandatum* in John 12:50 with other manuscripts and provides the only surviving parallels for *audit* in John 12:47 and *ipsum* in John 12:48 (cf. also *ille* in John 12:49). The rendering *ita ut* rather than *sicut* (or *secundum quod*) in John 12:50 is not found in any Old Latin exemplar; *ita* also appears, again without manuscript parallel, in the two citations of John 5:26 at *De trinitate* 1.12.26 and 1.13.30, although *De trinitate* 1.11.22 has *sic* here.[18] The form of John 5:29 in this cluster is also distinctive:

et prodient qui bona gesserunt in resurrectionem uitae, qui mala gesserunt in resurrectionem iudicii. (*De trinitate* 1.13.30)

Apart from the absence of *autem* at the beginning of the second clause, this is identical to Codex Usserianus and very close to Codices Rehdigeranus and Monacensis.

When the same verse of John is cited in later books, it is in a different form. The version of John 14:21 at *De trinitate* 1.9.18 has *custodit* and *ostendam*, but Augustine reads *seruat* and *manifestabo* for this verse at *De trinitate* 4.19.26 in keeping with the Vulgate. Similarly, John 14:23 has *mansionem facere* in *De trinitate* 1.9.18 but *habitare* in 7.6.12, while John 14:28 is cited with *quia* in *De trinitate* 1.9.18 but *quoniam* in 2.1.3 and 6.9.10. The disjunction between Books I and II has already been noted above, with *aduocatus* and *paracletus*, although there is an Old Latin form of John 10:36 identical to Codices Veronensis and Usserianus at *De trinitate* 2.5.9, and several examples of Augustine's mental text.[19] Book III also corresponds to Augustine's customary form of text (e.g. John 3:14–15 at

[18] Three Old Latin manuscripts have *ita* in John 5:21, while it is also present in citations of John 5:26 in Tertullian (*Aduersus Praxean* 21) and Ambrose (*De fide* 5.36).

[19] La Bonnardière 1965:169–76 suggests, however, that the paragraphs preceding *De trinitate* 2.7.13 are also a later addition by Augustine.

3.9.20 and John 5:46 at 3.10.26), but the closest match for the citation of John 17:20–3 at *De trinitate* 4.8.12 (composed in 414–15) is the Vulgate. This change in text-type becomes even more pronounced in Book XIII, written some time after 420: when Augustine diverges from citations in earlier books he almost invariably prefers the Vulgate reading, even in the opening verses of John where *De trinitate* 13.1.2 has *ipso* in John 1:4 (*illo* four times in *De trinitate* 4.1.3) *lux uera quae* in John 1:9 (*lumen uerum quod* in *De trinitate* 7.3.4), and *in propria* in John 1:11 (*in sua propria* in *De trinitate* 2.5.7). On the other hand, some citations still follow Augustine's mental text, such as *credentibus* in John 1:12 at *De trinitate* 13.9.12 (despite *his qui credunt* at *De trinitate* 13.1.2 and 13.2.5), and the form of John 14:30–1 at *De trinitate* 13.14.18. *De trinitate* 15 also agrees frequently with Jerome's revision, including a distinctive Vulgate reading in John 13:24 at *De trinitate* 15.10.19. The biblical text in *De trinitate* therefore corresponds to the composition of this work over a period of time, fitting the chronology which has already been suggested on other grounds. Furthermore, not only do the biblical citations in such a well-known work appear to have been transmitted without alteration, but even Augustine did not remove the inconcinnities between Book I and the rest of the work, and within Book I itself, when revising the text.

8

Middle Period (403 to 419)

Augustine began to cite the Vulgate text of the Gospels from around 403 when he wrote *Epistula* 71 to Jerome expressing his approval of the new version. This does not, however, authorize the assumption that after this date he used nothing but the Vulgate. Not only are Old Latin forms still transmitted in his mental text in the *Tractatus in Iohannem* and other works, but the analysis of the sermons has shown that he continued to preach from manuscripts of the earlier version for over a decade. His anti-Donatist writings, anticipating and following the Conference of Carthage in 411, have already been identified as a source for the African Old Latin tradition. The debates in this period recorded by stenographers also transmit important primary citations from the biblical codices known to Augustine, while the text-type of his citations from memory shows the extent to which his use of Vulgate affects his mental text.

DE CONSENSU EUANGELISTARUM (403/4)

It has been recognized since Sabatier's edition of Old Latin manuscripts that the gospel text in *De consensu euangelistarum* corresponds to Jerome's revision of the Gospels, and this work may plausibly be connected with the comparison of this version with the Greek which Augustine mentions in *Epistula* 71.6.[1] The date of

[1] Sabatier is quoted in Burkitt 1896:59; Burkitt (1896:72–8 and 1910:447–58) also demonstrates the Vulgate character of the gospel text. *Epistula* 71.6 is quoted on p. 13 above.

Table 8.1 Comparison of *De consensu euangelistarum* with distinctive Vulgate readings

	Total readings	Present in *De consensu*	*De consensu* identical to Weber–Gryson	*De consensu* identical to other Vulgate mss	*De consensu* does not agree with any Vulgate
Vulgate only	85	29	25 (86%)	3	1
Vulgate + Vercellensis	2	1	1 (100%)	—	—
Vulgate + Aureus	80	20	14 (70%)	2	4
Vulgate + Veronensis	20	10	8 (80%)	1	1
Vulgate + Colbertinus	36	5	4 (80%)	—	1
Vulgate + Bezae	18	2	—	2	—
Vulgate + Palatinus	1	—	—	—	—
Vulgate + Brixianus	38	7	5 (71%)	2	—
Vulgate + Corbeiensis	5	2	2 (100%)	—	—
Vulgate + Sarzanensis	4	1	1 (100%)	—	—
Vulgate + Rehdigeranus	4	1	1 (100%)	—	—
Vulgate + Frg. Sangall.	1	—	—	—	—
Vulgate + Monacensis	3	—	—	—	—
Vulgate + Usserianus	6	—	—	—	—
Vulgate + Fol. Vindob.	3	1	1 (100%)	—	—
Total	**306**	**79**	**62 (78%)**	**10 (13%)**	**7 (9%)**

the work is contested: estimates have ranged from 399 to 415, but the consensus has settled around 403.[2] It is inconceivable that this detailed investigation in four books of the text of the canonical Gospels could have been written without reference to at least one codex: Augustine practically creates his own synopsis, quoting extensively from all four evangelists. The Vulgate character of the biblical text is clearly demonstrated by comparison with the list of distinctive Vulgate readings in John, presented in Table 8.1.[3]

Although only seventy-nine of the possible points of comparison are cited in this work, *De consensu euangelistarum* accords with a

[2] See Hombert 2000:82–7, which responds to the date of 410–15 suggested by O'Donnell 1980:173–4 on the basis of the similarity of the classical citations with *De ciuitate dei.* Weihrich, in his 1904 edition, proposed 399–400, while De Bruyne 1931:595 hazarded 405 or 410, only to be refuted by Zarb 1938:312.

[3] As Augustine is sometimes inconsistent in multiple citations of the same verse in *De consensu euangelistarum*, any single agreement with a distinctive reading (normally from the sequential treatment of the Gospel) has been included as an agreement in Table 8.1.

distinctive Vulgate reading in sixty-two (78%). Furthermore, twenty-five (86%) of these are preserved in the Vulgate alone, without parallel in any surviving Old Latin witness. In each case, this is a higher figure than the *Tractatus in Iohannem*: there are nine occasions when *De consensu* has a distinctive Vulgate reading which is not found in the *Tractatus*, including the name *Iohanna* rather than *Iohannis* in John 1:42 and *sermone* rather than *uerbum* in both citations of John 8:31.[4] *De consensu* also accords with the Vulgate (and certain Old Latin witnesses) in some other verses when the *Tractatus in Iohannem* have a non-Vulgate reading, such as *sororis* in John 11:1 (*De consensu* 2.79.154; *Tractatus* 49.4 reads *sororum*), and *huic* in John 13:24 (*De consensu* 3.1.3; missing from *Tractatus* 61.6). Nonetheless, there are many agreements between the biblical texts of the *Tractatus* and *De consensu*, the vast majority of which correspond to the Vulgate in contrast to Augustine's citations in other works.[5]

The critical apparatus of Weihrich's edition includes much information about the manuscript tradition of *De consensu*, but most of the distinctive Vulgate readings are uncontested: for instance, no witness includes *simul* in John 18:15 or *ille* in 18:16 or varies from *istius* in 18:17 (*De consensu* 3.6.19–23), and the text *eo quod esset discipulus* for John 19:38 is invariant at *De consensu* 3.22.59. Sometimes a variant does have Old Latin parallels, such as a group of manuscripts which reads *palmas* rather than *alapas* in both citations of John 19:3 (*De consensu* 3.8.35 and 3.9.36). The same group also has *foras habens* and not *portans* in the first citation of John 19:5 (*De consensu* 3.8.35), but not in the later citation of this verse at *De consensu* 3.13.46. However, not only are these witnesses inconsistent, but they also belong to Weihrich's fourth and weakest class, a group of ninth-century manuscripts with many interpolations. The Vulgate readings in these verses are present in the earliest and most important manuscript of *De consensu* from the sixth century.[6]

[4] See also John 2:1, 3:4, 14:1, 17:25, 18:19, 18:36, and 18:37. Conversely, there are nine occasions when the continuous text of the *Tractatus* has a Vulgate reading not found in *De consensu*, although in four of these the Vulgate reading is present in the manuscripts of *De consensu*, while two others involve repeated words.

[5] The sixteen instances where *De consensu* and the *Tractatus* agree against the editorial text of Weber–Gryson have been listed above on p. 93.

[6] Weihrich sometimes lists agreements with Old Latin manuscripts in his apparatus, but these should be treated with caution: Burkitt (1910:456–7) notes one

Augustine's citations are closest to the Vulgate when he follows the sequence of the Gospel: as in his commentary, he is more likely to have taken these from his codex. Inconsistencies in the text of the same verse are comparable to the sequential and non-sequential variants cited from memory. For example, the non-sequential citation of John 5:19 at *De consensu* 1.4.7 reproduces his mental text, featuring three non-Vulgate readings, but he agrees with the Vulgate when he treats the verse in context at *De consensu* 4.10.13. The initial citation of John 2:19 at *De consensu* 4.10.12 corresponds to the Vulgate, but is replaced by Augustine's customary text in a sequential variant eight lines later. This phenomenon also comprises distinctive Vulgate readings, such as John 6:1, cited in sequence at *De consensu* 2.45.94 but out of context at *De consensu* 3.25.79 (which corresponds to Codices Vercellensis and Monacensis), or John 19:10–16 at *De consensu* 3.8.35 and 3.13.46. The continuing Old Latin character of Augustine's mental text is also evident. In a narrative summary of several chapters, he gives John 6:5 in the form:

tunc leuatis oculis et uisa multitudine maxima pauisse eam.

(*De consensu* 2.45.94)

Only Old Latin manuscripts have the first ablative absolute, *leuatis oculis*. The verbatim citation of this verse in the next paragraph, however, is almost identical to the Vulgate:

cum subleuasset ergo Iesus oculos et uidisset quia multitudo maxima uenit ad eum. (*De consensu* 2.46.95)

This suggests that Augustine has produced it from his exemplar.

The distribution of both Old Latin and Vulgate forms also tells against later alteration of the biblical citations. The reading *fores*, unique to the Vulgate, appears in Augustine's initial citation of John

misreading of the apparatus of Wordsworth–White at Matthew 26:52–4 and there are at least two errors concerning John: at *De consensu* 2.46.95, Weihrich cites Codex Vercellensis as a parallel for the omission of *ergo* after *discubuerunt* in John 6:10 and Codex Veronensis in support of the alternative *autem*; in fact, these refer to the connective after *dixit* earlier in the verse. Also, at *De consensu* 3.2.5, Weihrich claims that '*nonnulli codd. euang.*' omit *sicut... inuicem* from John 13:34. According to the Weber–Gryson apparatus, two Vulgate manuscripts omit the whole phrase; all Old Latin witnesses in Matzkow–Jülicher–Aland have *sicut ego dilexi uos*, although two witnesses omit *ut... inuicem*.

20:19 and throughout the subsequent discussion (*De consensu* 3.25.74–75), where an editor is unlikely to have changed the text.[7] When Augustine refers to this verse out of sequence, ten paragraphs later, he reverts to an Old Latin version with *clausis ostiis* (*De consensu* 3.25.85). Alongside the Vulgate readings, there are numerous examples of Augustine's mental text, including *non noueram* in John 1:33 (*De consensu* 2.15.32), *bene fecerunt* and *male fecerunt* in John 5:29 (*De consensu* 2.30.71), *concupiuit* in John 8:56 (*De consensu* 4.10.16), and his usual versions of John 10:16 and John 21:11 (*De consensu* 3.4.14 and 4.9.10). There are Old Latin parallels as well, such as *inmisisset in cor* in John 13:2 (*De consensu* 3.1.4), present in both Codex Bezae and Codex Aureus, and *quid quaeritis?* rather than *quem quaeritis?* in John 18:4 (*De consensu* 3.5.15) which is only paralleled by Codex Palatinus. As this occurs as part of a six-verse citation of John 18 in sequence, it has a strong claim to be the reading of Augustine's codex. Likewise, the Old Latin *ad Caifan* in John 18:28 is likely to have appeared in Augustine's copy of the Vulgate, given his comments on it at *De consensu* 3.7.27. A comparison with Fischer's collation of John 20 reveals manuscript correspondences for many of Augustine's variants in this work, and it is probable that most of his 'non-Vulgate' readings in John 18 and 19 too are present in other witnesses.

There are very few occasions on which *De consensu* has a unique reading in a citation of the Gospel according to John. Most fall into the category of impromptu adjustments made by Augustine or peculiarities of his codex. For example, all three citations of John 13:33 lack *uos* even though it is found in all biblical manuscripts (*De consensu* 3.2.5–6). The initial *autem* is also missing from John 18:15 at *De consensu* 3.6.19, while *alius* is repeated later in the verse; later in this book, *ergo* is added in John 18:17 (*De consensu* 3.6.23) and *ut* in John 18:39 (*De consensu* 3.8.35). Augustine's text of John 6:26 at *De consensu* 4.10.15 has several variants:

amen amen dico uobis quaeritis me non quia signa uidistis sed quia edistis de panibus et satiati estis.

[7] This is one of eleven such proofs of Augustine's use of the Vulgate in this work listed by Burkitt (1910:451–4): he also draws attention to Augustine's explicit comment on the reading *fugit* in John 6:15 at *De consensu* 2.47.100, although this occurs in several Old Latin manuscripts as well.

Codex Veronensis and Codex Palatinus also read *satiati* rather than *saturati*, and the latter has the word order *signa uidistis*, but *edistis* rather than *manducastis* is peculiar to Augustine. One manuscript of *De consensu*, however, reads *quia manducastis ex panibus meis*. This is one of Weihrich's third class of witnesses, and while the Vulgate harmonization is to be expected, the addition of *meis* is intriguing: it is not found in Old Latin Gospels or the Vulgate manuscripts listed in Weber–Gryson, but appears in Augustine's only other citation of this verse, at *Tractatus in Iohannem* 25.10.

In conclusion, a detailed study of the text of John supports the other arguments for the authorial use of the Vulgate in *De consensu euangelistarum*. The identification of citations likely to have been made by memory, in contrast to the sequential use of a Vulgate text, explains many of the inconsistencies and variant readings. The mixed text characteristic of early versions of the Vulgate also accounts for parallels with Old Latin manuscripts. The manner in which distinctive readings are embedded in Augustine's commentary reduces the probability of later alteration, and although there are variations in the manuscript tradition of this work, most of the important citations are unchallenged. Despite the unique nature of *De consensu euangelistarum*, with its close attention to the words of the evangelists, it seems probable that, as with Augustine's other works, its biblical text has been transmitted largely intact.

CONTRA EPISTULAM PARMENIANI (403/4)

In this treatise against the Donatists, Augustine quotes brief extracts from a letter of Parmenianus, the former Donatist bishop of Carthage who died in 391. Citations of his opponent's biblical text therefore reproduce an Old Latin version, as shown in John 9:31:

deus peccatores non audiet sed si quis dominum coluerit et uoluntatem eius fecerit illum audiet. (*Contra epistulam Parmeniani* 2.8.15)

Parallels for most of these readings, including *si quis deum coluerit* and *fecerit*, are found in Codex Palatinus and Cyprian *Epistula* 65.2. Augustine's own citation of this verse two paragraphs later is slightly different, but seems to have been influenced by his opponent's text. Most of the other citations in this work correspond to Augustine's mental text, but several other unusual readings may also have been influenced by a passage from Parmenianus' letter not quoted by Augustine. *Contra epistulam Parmeniani* 2.14.32 is the only one of Augustine's twenty citations of John 5:21 to read *excitat* rather than *suscitat*: the latter is the reading of all surviving Latin Gospels. Similarly, *Contra epistulam Parmeniani* 2.15.34 provides the sole example of *ideo* in John 16:15 alongside six citations with *propterea*. Two neighbouring citations of John 20:22 vary from Augustine's text elsewhere:

haec cum dixisset insufflauit et ait illis accipite spiritum sanctum.

(*Contra epistulam Parmeniani* 2.11.24)

Although the initial *haec* is found in the majority of Old Latin witnesses, Augustine normally has *hoc*, while on all other occasions except one, he reads *dixit eis* or *dicens*; his customary addition, *in faciem eorum*, is absent as well. The case for attributing this form of text to the influence of Parmenianus is supported by its exact correspondence to Codex Palatinus, the witness closest to the African versions used by the Donatists.

CONTRA FELICEM MANICHAEUM (404)

Although the stenographer indicates the current consul at the beginning of these minutes, at least three different identifications have been proposed for the year, of which 404 is generally accepted.[8] This debate is chiefly notable for the long biblical citations recorded as they were read from codices: Luke 24:36–49 in *Contra Felicem* 1.3 corresponds to the Vulgate, while the Acts of the Apostles and Pauline epistles in later paragraphs were taken from Old Latin exemplars. Only one verse from John is quoted on the first day of the conference, which features in Felix's first biblical citation:

[8] Monceaux 1923:80 suggested 398, while Frede 1995 hesitated between 404 and 409.

et sanctitas tua mihi probet quod in euangelio scriptum est, Christo dicente: *uado ad patrem, et mitto uobis spiritum sanctum paracletum, qui uos inducat in omnem ueritatem.* (*Contra Felicem* 1.2)

This is a conflation of multiple verses, like the similar reference at *Contra Faustum* 32.6: *uado ad patrem* appears in John 16:10, the promise personally to send the Paraclete is John 15:26, only John 14:26 contains both *spiritus sanctus* and *paracletus*, and the final clause corresponds to John 16:13. Augustine does not repeat the whole text, but only *mitto uobis spiritum sanctum paracletum* which he identifies as John in *Contra Felicem* 1.3. There are a few citations from John 1 on the second day, but apart from the Old Latin word order *lux lucet in tenebris* in Felix's citation of John 1:5 (*Contra Felicem* 2.16) there is no indication of textual affiliation.

DE BAPTISMO (404)

Augustine draws heavily in this work on proof texts assembled from Cyprian's *Sententiae episcoporum*, composed almost one hundred and fifty years earlier. Their Old Latin form is exemplified by Lucius of Membressa's citation of John 9:31 as *deus peccatorem non audit* (*De baptismo* 7.26.50). Augustine has the same text at *De baptismo* 5.20.28, even though it contrasts with his mental text. Likewise, he only reads *inspirauit* in John 20:22 at *De baptismo* 3.18.23: this is not found in any surviving manuscript, but appears in Cyprian *Epistula* 73.7. The *sententiae* often involve harmonizations: six of the seven citations of John 3:5 in *De baptismo* read *non intrabit in regnum caelorum* (cf. Matthew 5:20), which is also found in Codex Palatinus. The process of flattening can be seen in action in the eight references to John 20:23 in *De baptismo*. Each time, there are minor differences which enhance the parallelism of the verse. The final outcome is:

si cui dimiseritis dimittentur, si cui tenueritis tenebuntur.

(*De baptismo* 5.21.29)

Although each word can be found in an Old Latin manuscript, not one corresponds with the Vulgate form of this verse. This is an extreme example of the effect of rhetorical alteration on biblical citations.

IN EPISTOLAM IOHANNIS AD PARTHOS TRACTATUS DECEM (407)

In the opening sentence Augustine indicates that he delivered these sermons after beginning the *Tractatus in Iohannis euangelium*, but their gospel text does not correspond to the Vulgate used in his commentary. Most verses are cited in his customary form, such as John 8:58 at *In epistolam Iohannis* 2.5, or John 12:31 at *In epistolam Iohannis* 4.1. There is occasionally inconsistency between sermons: for John 15:13, *In epistolam Iohannis* 5.12 and 6.13 read *maiorem (hac) caritatem nemo habet* while *In epistolam Iohannis* 7.2 and 7.7 have *maiorem dilectionem nemo potest habere.* Again, this is probably due to memory.

LETTERS TO MACROBIUS AND HONORATUS *(410, 412)*

Two letters from around this time feature notable citations of John. ***Epistula* 108**, written to Macrobius in 410, has several parallels with Codex Vercellensis. The first is *auferebat* in John 12:6, although Augustine appears to be paraphrasing (*Epistula* 108.3.8). More compelling is the following form of John 13:35:

in hoc scient omnes quia discipuli mei estis si ueram dilectionem habueritis in uobis. (*Epistula* 108.6.17)

This is the only instance of *ueram* in Augustine's twelve citations of this verse, which include a couple of early references: among surviving manuscripts it is peculiar to Codices Colbertinus and Vercellensis. The latter is far closer to Augustine's text, only differing in the word order *mei discipuli* and *inter uos* at the end of the verse. Augustine's customary form of John 10:16, with *ut sit unus grex,* also appears in the same paragraph. ***Epistula* 140** to Honoratus is a lengthy response to five questions, and includes an exposition of John 1:1–14 and Psalm 21 both cited in their entirety. It is possible that Augustine produced these from memory, but his detailed sequential exposition may have been made with reference to a codex. Although the citations of John 1:8–12 have the Old Latin forms characteristic of his mental text, including *lumen* and *credentibus,* this work has the distinctive Vulgate reading *in ipso uita erat* in John 1:4 (*Epistula* 140.3.6) as well as the standard version of John 1:13 found in most manuscripts (*Epistula* 140.3.9). However Augustine was citing, this marks a departure from most earlier citations of these verses.[9]

DE PECCATORUM MERITIS ET REMISSIONE ET DE BAPTISMO PARUULORUM (411/12)

There is an uninterrupted citation of John 3:1–21 at *De peccatorum meritis* 1.30.59. Its text for the most part agrees with the Vulgate, including two of the four distinctive readings found in this passage: alongside the word order *senex sit* in John 3:4 and *opera eius* in John 3:21, it has the Old Latin forms *descendit de caelo* and *in eum* in 3:13 and 3:15 respectively. There are several other non-Vulgate forms, including the following text of John 3:4:

numquid potest in utero matris suae iterum introire et nasci?

(*De peccatorum meritis* 1.30.59)

Utero is the majority Old Latin reading: *iterum* (which also features in *Tractatus* 11) is found in certain Vulgate manuscripts as well as Codex Vercellensis. While *testificamur* in John 3:11 is another Old Latin form, *credidistis* in the next verse is only paralleled by eight manuscripts in Fischer's collation. Uniquely among Augustine's citations, this work reads *deserto* in John 3:14 and also agrees with biblical manuscripts in John 3:17 against Augustine's usual text. These characteristics indicate that Augustine's citation comes directly from a codex with a Vulgate text-type, and has been transmitted without alteration.

References to John 3 outside this paragraph normally correspond to Augustine's mental text, although the citation of John 3:36 at *De*

[9] See further pp. 187–93 below: the Vulgate form of John 1:4 is rare in Augustine and only appears in four other works.

peccatorum meritis 1.20.28 includes the distinctive Vulgate reading *incredulus est*. Some of his other citations feature Old Latin readings paralleled in Codex Palatinus, such as *dedero* and *saeculi* in John 6:51 (*De peccatorum meritis* 1.20.27 and 1.24.34) and John 12:46:

ego lux in saeculum ueni ut omnis qui crediderit [*credit* 1.25.38] *in me non maneat in tenebris.* (*De peccatorum meritis* 1.24.35, 1.25.38)

These are Augustine's only citations of this verse outside the *Tractatus in Iohannem*: no surviving manuscript has *saeculum* here, not even in Fischer's collation, but *crediderit* is preserved in Codex Palatinus alone, which also has the word order *non maneat in tenebris.* The form of John 10:27–8 in this work varies from Augustine's mental text:

qui de ouibus meis sunt uocem meam audiunt, et ego noui illas, et secuntur me; et ego uitam aeternam do illis et non peribunt in aeternum.

(*De peccatorum meritis* 1.27.40)

There are similarities with individual Old Latin manuscripts but no exact correspondence: *qui de ouibus meis sunt* appears in Codex Corbeiensis (and with a minor variation in Codex Palatinus, which also reads *illas*, *secuntur*, and *illis*), while only Codex Usserianus has *noui*. This departure from his customary form suggests that Augustine was relying on another source, but not the exemplar he used three chapters later for the long citation from John 3. In fact, this verse occurs in a series of *testimonia* from the Gospels, followed by twelve chapters of lengthy citations from other New Testament books, so it may have been taken from a compilation. In sum, despite the Vulgate text-type in the longer citation, there are still a number of significant Old Latin readings in citations of John in this work.

EPISTULAE 187, 193, AND 194 (417/19)[10]

These three letters include several examples of distinctive Vulgate readings. The lengthy ***Epistula* 187** to Dardanus, also known as *De*

10 Dates from Frede 1995 and Anoz 2002; these letters are not mentioned in Gryson 2007.

praesentia dei, was written in 417. The longer citation of John 11:50–2 (*Epistula* 187.12.37) accords with the Vulgate against Augustine's mental text (including distinctive readings in the two outer verses), although John 15:15 and 16:12 appear in his customary form (*Epistula* 187.8.27). ***Epistula* 193** to Mercator has the reading *incredulus est* in both its citations of John 3:36, peculiar to the Vulgate and Codex Colbertinus and also noted in *De peccatorum meritis* (*Epistula* 193.2.3–4). ***Epistula* 194** is a treatise against the Pelagians, sent to the priest Sixtus in 418 or 419. It includes the distinctive Vulgate word order *locutus fuissem eis* in John 15:22 (*Epistula* 194.6.26), which does not even feature in the *Tractatus in Iohannem.* Unusually for Augustine it also has a Vulgate form of John 6:44, in a sequence of citations from John 6 at *Epistula* 194.3.12.

CONTRA GAUDENTIUM DONATISTARUM EPISCOPUM (418/19)

Despite Augustine's success in securing condemnation of the Donatists at the Conference of Carthage in 411, the sect persisted. Augustine responded in two books to letters from the Donatist bishop Gaudentius, which he quoted at length. Gaudentius' text of John features the 'African' renderings already observed in Donatist writings: *saeculum* rather than *mundus* is found in citations of John 14:27 (*Contra Gaudentium* 1.23.26) and John 15:18 (*Contra Gaudentium* 1.26.29), which both have further variants only preserved in Codex Bezae. There are also similarities with Codex Palatinus, such as *ponit*, *suis*, and the omission of *qui non est pastor* in John 10:11–12 (*Contra Gaudentium* 1.16.17) and the following form of John 16:2–3:

ueniet hora ut omnis qui interficit uos putet se uictimam dare deo: sed haec facient quia non cognouerunt patrem neque me. (*Contra Gaudentium* 1.20.22)

Apart from his unique reading *uictimam dare*, this is almost an exact match with Codex Palatinus.[11] Augustine challenges this as an

[11] The other exception is the phrase *interficit uos* rather than *uos occiderit*. Although the former is a distinctive Vulgate reading, given the variants in the rest of the

inaccurate citation, replacing it with the form quoted above on p. 83 (*Contra Gaudentium* 1.23.26). This is the only explicit repetition of one of Gaudentius' citations by Augustine, but his opponent's text seems to have influenced the form of several biblical references within his discussion: he too reads *saeculum* in John 14:27 and 15:18 (*Contra Gaudentium* 2.12.13 and 1.26.29) despite having *mundus* elsewhere, and he reads *sed* and *cognouerunt* in John 16:3 (1.23.26). Augustine's citation of John 15:2 (*Contra Gaudentium* 2.8.9) has Old Latin features typical of his customary text, and *Contra Gaudentium* 1.16.17, his only citation of John 10:10 outside *Tractatus in Iohannem* 45, reads *occidat* with the majority of manuscripts, rather than the distinctive Vulgate *mactet.*

CONTRA SERMONEM ARRIANORUM (419)

After his confrontations with the Donatists, Augustine became aware of the threat posed by Arianism. The text of an Arian sermon has been transmitted alongside Augustine's refutation. It features several citations of John with an Old Latin text-type very close to Codices Monacensis and Vercellensis, as well as certain readings paralleled only in other Arian sources, such as *neminem* in John 5:22.[12] When citing the sermon, Augustine reproduces its form of text exactly: its versions of John 5:22, 5:30, and 8:28 are found at *Contra sermonem Arrianorum* 11.9 and 34.32. Elsewhere, he usually reverts to his customary text of these and other verses. On a couple of occasions the biblical text of the sermon seems to have influenced Augustine outside his direct quotations. For example, at *Contra sermonem* 30.28 he cites John 16:7 with *aduocatus*, a rendering which has not appeared in his writings for twenty years. The sermon has *aduocatum* in John 14:16, which Augustine reflects at *Contra sermonem*

verse it is most likely that Gaudentius knew this from a biblical manuscript which is no longer preserved. His citation of John 10:11–12 has neither of the distinctive Vulgate features in these verses.

12 For more on the text of John in Arian writings, see *Contra Maximinum* below and Gryson 1978.

Arrianorum 19.9, but does not quote John 16:7. The reading *cum ego iero* in this verse (*Contra sermonem* 4.4, cf. 19.9) is another reading which Augustine has not used since Book I of *De trinitate.* Similarly, *honorificare* in John 16:14 and John 17:4 (*Contra sermonem* 23.19) parallels these verses in the sermon, but Augustine extends this into John 17:5 too a few lines later, the only example of *honorifica* in his citations of this verse. (He reverts to *glorifica* at *Contra sermonem* 31.29.) It seems unlikely that Augustine is relying on another source for his refutation: instead, he has either deliberately or subconsciously returned to the text-type he used in his earlier works, in harmony with the sermon.

9

Later Works (after 419)

The previous chapter has shown that between 403 and 419 an increasing proportion of Augustine's citations of John conform to the Vulgate, identifiable by distinctive readings. This affinity is first seen in longer citations, but gradually affects shorter references too. The displacement of Old Latin features from Augustine's mental text in favour of the Vulgate continues in his later works. Even so, his biblical text is never entirely predictable, not only because of the influence of the scriptural citations of his opponents in polemical works, but also perhaps due to his use of other sources.

QUAESTIONES IN HEPTATEUCHUM (419/20)

There are few citations of John in the *Quaestiones in Heptateuchum*, but they demonstrate further the influence of the Vulgate on Augustine's mental text. At *Quaestiones de Deuteronomio* 55, instead of his usual form of John 14:30–1 Augustine has a Vulgate reading for the only time outside *Tractatus in Iohannem* 79. Similarly, the text of John 7:37–9 at *Quaestiones de Iudicibus* 36 is closer to the Vulgate than any of his other citations. *Quaestiones de Deuteronomio* 10 features John 4:21–4 with a text identical to the Vulgate. Although shorter references normally appear in Augustine's customary form (e.g. *qui sic soluit sabbatum* in John 9:16 at *Quaestiones de Iudicibus* 49), in the longer passages his affiliation is with the Vulgate.

DE NATURA ET ORIGINE ANIMAE (419/20)

Further evidence of Jerome's revision of the Gospels appears in this work, which has the only instances of John 3:4 and 13:10 in Augustine's writings which are identical to the Vulgate, including the distinctive word order *cum senex sit* in the former (*De natura et origine* 3.11.17 and 3.9.12 respectively). Augustine also makes two corrections to Vincentius Victor's citations of John, firstly replacing *apud patrem meum* in John 14:2 with *in domo patris mei* (*De natura et origine* 3.11.15). Not only is *apud patrem meum* widespread among Church Fathers, but it features in three of Augustine's other six citations of the verse (*Enarratio* 60.6, *Sermo* 239.2.2, *De sancta uirginitate* 26.26). His knowledge of the Gospel by this stage is clearly sufficient to recognize even this form as inexact. He also corrects his opponent's text of John 3:5 in keeping with most Latin Bibles:

> ipsum dominum audi, qui non ait: *si quis non renatus fuerit ex aqua et spiritu non potest intrare in regnum caelorum*, sed *non potest*, inquit, *intrare in regnum dei.* (*De natura et origine* 3.11.17)

Vincentius' citations actually read *qui non renatus fuerit ex aqua et spiritu sancto non intrabit in regnum caelorum* (e.g. *De natura et origine* 2.12.16, 3.13.19), a text which Augustine himself has in no fewer than twenty-two of his earlier citations of this verse. This is a further indication of the change in his mental text, although given that Augustine cites John 3:3–5 in this paragraph, it is possible that he made the correction with reference to a codex.

CONTRA ADUERSARIUM LEGIS ET PROPHETARUM (420)

Augustine's correction of the version of John 1:17 given by his anonymous opponent has already been quoted on p. 83, where it was noted that the text he supplies includes a distinctive Vulgate reading (*Contra aduersarium* 2.3.10). He also draws attention to the citation of John 10:8 as *omnes alii quotquot ante me uenerunt fures sunt et latrones*, giving instead the text of the Vulgate and most other witnesses (*Contra aduersarium* 2.4.16). Augustine's other citations, however, tend to correspond to his customary text. These include John 2:25 at *Contra aduersarium* 1.20.41, with three variants peculiar to him, and the only citation of John 8:19 outside *Tractatus in Iohannem* 37, where *Contra aduersarium* 2.5.19 reads *nostis* with the majority of Old Latin manuscripts. This is likely to be his mental text, because it appears in a sequential variant in his commentary. Nonetheless, *Contra aduersarium* 1.24.52 and *Tractatus in Iohannem* 26 are the only occasions on which Augustine reads *cibus* with the Vulgate rather than *esca* in John 6:55 (6:56 in the Vulgate).

CONTRA IULIANUM (421/2)

Augustine also cites a Vulgate form in place of his mental text of John 6:44 and 6:65 at *Contra Iulianum* 4.8.44 and John 15:17–19 at *Contra Iulianum* 6.2.4; the latter paragraph also has the only citation of John 12:31 outside *Tractatus in Iohannem* 52 with the Vulgate *eicietur*. There is some inconsistency between books: at *Contra Iulianum* 2.6.18, Augustine produces a similar text of John 3:5 to that which he criticized in *De natura et origine animae*, reading *non introibit in regnum caelorum*, but in later books he has *non potest intrare in regnum dei* (*Contra Iulianum* 3.2.8 and 6.4.10). Conversely, while the Vulgate form of John 6:44 appears at *Contra Iulianum* 4.8.44, Augustine's mental text with *potest uenire* is found at *Contra Iulianum* 5.4.14. There is one reading in this work unique to Augustine, *exsuscitabo* in John 2:19 (*Contra Iulianum* 6.14.42): this could be explained as a conflation of the Vulgate *excitabo* with Augustine's preferred term, *suscitabo*, showing once again the influence of the Vulgate on his memory.

DE CIUITATE DEI (412–26)

Like *De trinitate*, *De ciuitate dei* was composed over a number of years, although in this case the most interesting citations occur towards the end of the work: in Book XX, written some time after 422, there are lengthy citations from the books of the New Testament drawn from a codex. The citations of John 5:22–4 at *De ciuitate dei* 20.5.5 and John 5:25–9 in the next paragraph are almost identical to the Vulgate. In later citations of these verses, however, Augustine partially reverts to his customary forms (e.g. John 5:25 at *De ciuitate dei* 20.9.4), although two citations of John 5:29 feature *bona* and *mala* rather than *bene* and *male* (*De ciuitate dei* 20.23.2 and 21.1). The only verse which reveals a difference between books is John 3:5:

si quis non renatus fuerit ex aqua et spiritu, non intrabit in regnum caelorum. (*De ciuitate dei* 13.7)

nisi quis renatus fuerit ex aqua et spiritu, non intrabit in regnum dei. (*De ciuitate dei* 21.27.3)

The form *intrabit* is characteristic of Augustine's mental text, which presumably also supplies the Old Latin reading *usque nunc operatur* in John 5:17 twice in *De ciuitate dei* 22.24.2.

SPECULUM QUIS IGNORAT (427/8)

Two collections of biblical *testimonia* with the title of *Speculum* are attributed to Augustine. The *Speculum quis ignorat* is generally accepted as authentic: it is too late to be listed in the *Retractationes*, but is mentioned by Possidius at *Vita Augustini* 28.3. One of the features adduced in the debate over its authorship is the fact that the biblical text of the excerpts corresponds more closely to the Vulgate than any of Augustine's other works. Although it has been claimed that Augustine was responsible for the current form of the work, the fact that it cites both the Old Testament and the Pauline Epistles according to the Vulgate, which he never uses elsewhere, suggests that the text has been updated by a later editor: traces of the earlier version remain in certain doublets.[1]

[1] A history of scholarship on the *Speculum* together with arguments for its authenticity is presented in Mutzenbecher 1984:63–71; the doublets are identified in Vaccari 1961. Burkitt 1910:264–8 suggested that Augustine marked the verses

Fourteen extracts from John appear in *Speculum* 28. Of the twenty-nine verses cited, six provide the sole instance of the Vulgate text for those verses in Augustine's writings (John 8:11, 12:26, 13:14, 14:21, 15:6, and 15:13), while in a further four the *Speculum* is joined by *De consensu euangelistarum* or the *Tractatus in Iohannem* as the only witnesses to the Vulgate (John 8:31, 12:43, 13:34, and 13:35). There are five minor variations from Weber–Gryson: two differences in word order (John 8:51 and 15:10); *enim* rather than *etenim* in John 13:13; *diligit* and *mansionem* in John 14:23. All of these forms are widely attested in the Vulgate tradition. Although the Vulgate version of John 15:13 is cited in the section on John, the preface to the extracts from the Song of Songs reads:

maiorem hac caritatem nemo habet quam ut animam suam ponat pro amicis suis. (*Speculum* 9)

This occurs in twenty-four of Augustine's twenty-nine citations, and the addition of *quam* is not paralleled in any biblical manuscript. Such a clear example of his mental text seems to confirm that Augustine was the author of the prefaces, and that they have been transmitted without alteration.

DE PRAEDESTINATIONE SANCTORUM (428)

De praedestinatione 8.15 cites several verses from John 6:60–5 which, apart from the omission of *autem* in John 6:61, correspond to the Vulgate. The version of John 6:65 immediately following this sequence reads *uenit* instead of *potest uenire*, a reversion to Augustine's mental text. Similarly, at *De praedestinatione* 17.34 the initial citation of John 15:16 has the Vulgate word order *ego elegi uos*, but all subsequent repetitions read *ego uos elegi*. A citation of John 6:28–9 has some Old Latin features:

to be copied in a Vulgate codex; Petitmengin 2003:7–14 agrees with this method of composition but states that the stichometry indicates Old Latin originals. La Bonnardière 1986:408 raises questions about the selection of verses, which includes some rarely cited by Augustine.

dixerunt enim ad eum Iudaei, 'quid faciemus ut operemur opus dei?' respondit Iesus et dixit illis, 'hoc est opus dei ut credatis in eum quem misit ille.'

(*De praedestinatione* 7.12)

This is quite similar to Codex Palatinus, with the addition of *Iudaei* and the reading *illis*. Both *enim* and the first instance of *opus* are not paralleled in surviving manuscripts: the former may be an adaptation by Augustine, while the latter probably anticipates the following singular, even though it also appears in *Sermo* 130A.

COLLATIO CUM MAXIMINO AND *CONTRA MAXIMINUM* (428/9)

The biblical text of the Arian bishop Maximinus has been examined in detail by Gryson, who draws attention to its remarkable similarity to Codex Monacensis.[2] This is apparent both in his debate with Augustine and the portions quoted in *Contra Maximinum.* The parallels between Maximinus and the anonymous sermon transmitted with Augustine's *Contra sermonem Arrianorum* have been mentioned above: only these two Arian texts read *neminem* in John 5:22 (*Collatio* 18, Sermon 9), and they also have versions of John 16:13 and 14:16 very close to Codex Monacensis (*Collatio* 5, 12; Sermon 20, 34). Inconsistencies in Maximinus' text suggest that he cited from memory, while Augustine's own mental text appears during the debate in John 5:26 (*Collatio* 13–14) and John 16:15 (*Collatio* 11).

The majority of Augustine's citations of John in *Contra Maximinum* correspond to either his customary form or the Vulgate. He also reproduces some of Maximinus' *testimonia* from the *Collatio*, which at times influence his own text. For instance, after quoting his opponent's form of John 10:18 at *Contra Maximinum* 2.14.9 (cf. *Collatio* 14), Augustine continues to use *praeceptum* throughout the paragraph instead of his usual reading *mandatum.* A handful of other non-Vulgate readings could have been inspired by Maximinus' biblical text or may simply be due to memory, such as the only example

[2] The analysis of John appears at Gryson 1978:69–76.

of *ipse* rather than *ille* in John 15:26 (*Contra Maximinum* 2.22.3), *eam* for *uadam* in John 16:7 (*Contra Maximinum* 2.26.14), and *quoniam* in John 16:32 (*Contra Maximinum* 2.18.6): even though none of these verses is cited by Maximinus, all are paralleled in Codex Usserianus and other Old Latin manuscripts. As with *Contra sermonem Arrianorum*, it is impossible to determine whether this is a deliberate reversion to an earlier form of text or simply subconscious variation.

CONTRA SECUNDUM IULIANI RESPONSIONEM OPUS IMPERFECTUM (428–30)

Augustine did not live to complete his second work against Julian of Eclanum. There are agreements with the Vulgate, such as John 1:13 at *Opus imperfectum* 3.51, but there are still examples of Augustine's customary text, such as John 3:5, 3:36, 8:36, 14:30, and 15:13 at *Opus imperfectum* 6.12, 4.128, 6.15, 4.78 and 6.27 respectively. He even has *mittitur* in John 12:31 (*Opus imperfectum* 2.181 and 4.77; cf. 5.64) despite his use of the Vulgate *eicietur* in this verse in *Contra Iulianum* 6.2.4. Among the extracts from Julian's writings quoted by Augustine is a commentary on John 8:31–41 (*Opus imperfectum* 1.87). This features three of the six distinctive Vulgate readings in this passage: *sermone* and *Iudaeos* in John 8:31, and *filii Abrahae* in John 8:37. However, there are Old Latin elements too, including *quoniam* in John 8:34 and *autem* added in 8:35, while *audiui* rather than *uidi* in John 8:38 is unique to him. Julian's biblical text also features forms which are otherwise found only in Augustine. Some occur in his citations of Augustine's earlier works, but others appear on his own lips, such as *tunc* in John 8:36 in *Opus imperfectum* 1.87, or *suscipietis* in John 5:43 (*Opus imperfectum* 1.93). He may have known these from an exemplar, but the possibility of influence on Julian from Augustine's biblical text should not be ruled out. Julian also quotes the Epistle of Mani (*Opus imperfectum* 3.172 onwards), which features some unusual readings in John:

quod nascitur de carne, caro est et, quod de spiritu, spiritus est.

This is identical to the form of John 3:6 given by Faustus the Manichee at *Contra Faustum* 24.1, but unparalleled in biblical manuscripts. Augustine, however, responds with a text much closer to surviving witnesses:

quod natum est ex carne caro est et quod natum est de spiritu spiritus est. (*Opus imperfectum* 3.172)

His words here and in the next paragraph (*iam dixi quomodo nos accipiamus haec uerba euangelica*; 3.173) give the impression that he is repudiating not just the interpretation but the text itself. Perhaps this is an example of a specifically Manichaean reading, in which the present tense corresponds to their ideas of 'generation'. Later, Julian quotes John 3:20 from a Manichaean source:

omnis enim, qui male agit, odit lucem et non uenit ad lumen, ne manifestentur opera eius. (*Opus imperfectum* 3.187)

This does have Old Latin parallels, in particular with Codex Monacensis, the only surviving manuscript to read *ne manifestentur.* These citations may provide some evidence for the form of the Gospels used by the Manichees; it is worth observing that *ne manifestentur* is not found in any of Augustine's citations of this verse.

DE DONO PERSEUERANTIAE (429)

De dono perseuerantiae is most notable for the following text of 12:37–40:

12:37 cum autem tanta signa fecisset coram eis, non crediderunt in eum; 12:38 ut sermo Isaiae prophetae impleretur, quem dixit: domine, quis credidit auditui nostro, et brachium domini cui reuelatum est? 12:39 et ideo non poterant credere, quia iterum dixit Isaias: 12:40 excaecauit oculos eorum et indurauit cor illorum, ut non uideant oculis nec intellegant corde, et conuertantur et sanem illos. (*De dono perseuerantiae* 14.35)

This has five variations from Weber–Gryson, of which only two are paralleled in Old Latin witnesses: *crediderunt* in John 12:37 and *illos* in John 12:40. Two more, however, appear in one manuscript in

Fischer's collation: **Bw** is the only one of over four hundred Gospels with *ideo* rather than *propterea* in John 12:39 and *cor illorum* in the next verse. (It also has *crediderunt* and *illos*, but not *nec*.) As noted above, parts of this manuscript have an Old Latin affiliation.[3] Given that *Tractatus* 53 has the regular Vulgate form (with the exception of *illos*), Augustine seems to have reverted to a different codex for this late work, which features Old Latin readings.

CONCLUSION

This detailed survey of the text of John across Augustine's entire output has revealed a clear pattern in the affiliation of his gospel citations. In his early writings, he relies on Old Latin versions similar, but not identical, to surviving witnesses. He begins to cite Jerome's revised text in primary citations from around 403: this featured in his exemplars for both *De consensu euangelistarum* and the *Tractatus in Iohannis euangelium*, and also appears in sermons and debates. In other sermons, however, especially in Carthage, he continues to preach from an Old Latin text of the Gospel for at least fifteen years. Meanwhile, his secondary citations, usually made from memory, continue to include Old Latin forms until around 418. From this point, Vulgate readings begin to displace his customary versions in these references, although even in his latest works there are still features characteristic of his mental text.

The gospel text is not in itself a sufficient basis to establish the date of a work, but it may help to confirm other chronological suggestions. Inconsistencies within a text can often be explained by closer reference to the context in which a citation appears: initial citations made from a biblical codex are frequently followed by a different form of text produced from memory. Other variations from the expected pattern may be due to Augustine's reliance on another source: in his polemical works, he frequently reproduces the version of Scripture given by his opponents, and he also drew on collections of *testimonia* and earlier Christian writings.

[3] See p. 93 above.

This analysis has shown that most of Augustine's biblical citations seem to have been transmitted without alteration. Apart from the *Speculum quis ignorat*, whose form lends itself to such re-writing, all his works correspond to the same broad pattern and share characteristic readings. There is some evidence for changes towards a Vulgate version in late manuscripts of certain works, but even here the process is intermittent. The faithful transmission of all the variant readings, some of which are paralleled in a few surviving biblical manuscripts while others appear to be unique to Augustine, makes it possible to assess how Augustine cited the Gospels and what sorts of versions were available to him.

Part III

The Gospel According to John in Augustine: A Textual Commentary

Introduction

The following commentary presents and discusses most of the variations within Augustine's citations of John and the differences between his text and the Vulgate. Its principal function is to assess the significance of Augustine's readings for the history of the biblical text, drawing on the chronological developments demonstrated in Part II and the description of his citation practice in Chapter 3. Augustine has often been cited alongside other Church Fathers in support of a particular form of a verse or contested passage, but the nature and context of his citations and conflicting material elsewhere is sometimes ignored or discounted. This survey seeks to offer an assessment based on all Augustine's citations of John. It is not an attempt to reconstruct a single form of text for each verse: it has already become clear that Augustine used many biblical codices and quoted different forms from memory. Instead, it is intended to describe and account for the nature and range of variations in Augustine's text of John, and may also serve as a basis on which to justify the inclusion of Augustine in a critical apparatus to an edition of the Gospel.

The *Tractatus in Iohannis euangelium* and *De consensu euangelistarum* are mentioned whenever their sequential treatment of the Gospel differs from the Weber–Gryson Vulgate. Other primary citations and lectionary sermons are indicated: the majority of non-Vulgate readings occur in secondary citations and may be attributed to memory, although they could reflect versions which no longer survive. In frequently cited verses, an indication has been given where possible of his mental text. Verses which do not feature in the commentary have little of textual interest: they normally correspond to the Vulgate and are often cited in the *Tractatus in Iohannem* alone.

I have tried to give an indication of the number of works which support a particular reading in addition to a qualitative assessment of Augustine's variants, but considerations of space mean that it is not possible to list every citation, let alone give the full text of each. Nonetheless, the fresh collection of data on which this study is based has demonstrated that the *Vetus Latina Database* is a reliable guide to Augustine's citations: this card catalogue held at the Institut Vetus Latina in Beuron is also available as digital images on CD-ROM and online. For the citations of John, however, this will soon be superseded by the database of patristic material currently in preparation for the new edition of the *Vetus Latina Iohannes* in conjunction with the *Editio Critica Maior* of the International Greek New Testament Project.[1]

The principal focus of this commentary is Augustine's biblical text, but this is often closely bound up with his exposition. Although this work is neither intended as nor claimed to be a guide to Augustine's exegesis of John, brief comments on his use of particular verses have been included along with references to some secondary literature.[2] In the absence of a monograph in English on Augustine's treatment of this Gospel, it is hoped that these will provide a point of entry for those who wish to explore his use of the Bible more fully. There are also numerous cross-references between verses, where parallels for features of Augustine's text and exegesis are found within the Gospel.

The commentary has been written with the intention that a user should be able to make sense of it with reference to the Weber–Gryson Vulgate alone, and find sufficient explanation for each verse to relieve them from the burden of reading every one. For concepts such as 'primary' and 'secondary' citations, 'flattening' and 'sequential variants', the reader is referred to the explanations already given above. A 'lectionary sermon' is one which was preceded by a liturgical reading from John, while Augustine's 'commentary' means the *Tractatus*. Note that, unless other patristic material is explicitly

[1] The *Vetus Latina Database* is published by Brepols (www.brepolis.net/vld). The IGNTP electronic editions of John are hosted at the website www.iohannes.com, and there is further information on the *Vetus Latina Iohannes* at www.vetuslatina.org.

[2] My debt to the magisterial seven-volume edition of the *Tractatus in Iohannem* by Berrouard (1969–2003) is obvious. I have also drawn on the books of Comeau 1930 and Pontet 1946, as well as several essays and articles.

mentioned, 'witness' in the commentary refers to a gospel codex. Similarly, manuscripts are also indicated by 'biblical tradition' and 'Latin Gospels'. Greek evidence has usually been taken from Nestle–Aland, supplemented by Tischendorf.[3] The Old Latin tradition consists of manuscripts included in Matzkow–Jülicher–Aland, and the Vulgate is represented by the editorial text of Weber–Gryson. The collations of over 450 Latin manuscripts in Fischer 1991 have been used for his four test passages: John 2:18–3:31; John 7:28–8:16; John 12:17–13:6; John 20:1–21:4. Further information about gospel codices and the conventions used for Augustine's works is provided on pp. 103–6. Other Latin Fathers have normally been cited from the *Vetus Latina Database*, in conjunction with individual studies of some authors.

[3] Through the kindness of my colleague Dr R. L. Mullen, I have also been able to consult the database of Greek patristic citations in preparation for the IGNTP.

Commentary

JOHN 1:1

Augustine's comment at *Tractatus* 108.3 (quoted on p. 79) shows that, like Tertullian, he was aware of manuscripts which read *in principio erat **sermo***. Although Augustine treats this as an acceptable translation of λόγος, he does not use *sermo* in any of his citations of this verse. *Tractatus* 76.5 (quoted on p. 54), where Augustine suggests that Jesus might use the singular *sermo* of himself, indicates that he had no theological objection to this rendering even though *uerbum* became the customary term. He also alludes to a 'heretical punctuation' before the final word of the verse:

> iam nunc exempla considera. illa haeretica distinctio: *in principio erat uerbum et uerbum erat apud deum et deus erat*, ut alius sit sensus: *uerbum hoc erat in principio apud deum*, non uult deum uerbum confiteri.
>
> (*De doctrina christiana* 3.2.3)

However, there is no trace of this in other anti-Arian writings and it has been suggested that Augustine is offering a hypothetical example.[1] For the variety of formulae used by Augustine to introduce this key verse, see pp. 56–7.

[1] Simonetti, quoted in Moreau 1997 ad loc. Augustine's famous reference to Simplicianus' story of the Platonist who believed that the opening of John should be written in gold letters and placed in a prominent position in all churches occurs at *De ciuitate dei* 10.29.2.

JOHN 1:3–4

A large number of Augustine's citations of John 1:3 have *per* **quod** *facta sunt omnia*: the word order and relative pronoun are not paralleled in the surviving manuscripts. This is an adaptation: the pronoun normally refers to *uerbum*, understood as the antecedent from John 1:1, although the subject is sometimes *filium*, in which case *quem* is used (e.g. *De catechizandis rudibus* 22.39), or *sapientiam* with *quam* (e.g. *De gratia Christi* 2.35).[2] The latter is an image from the Hebrew Scriptures which Augustine closely associates with this passage about God's creative force, often referring to Jesus as God's wisdom (cf. *Sermo* 53A.13; further references at Comeau 1930:296). The punctuation of these verses varied in antiquity. Augustine ended the first sentence with *nihil* and treated the next seven words as a unit, as the following comment makes clear:

> non ergo ita pronuntiari oportet *quod factum est in illo uita est* ut subdistinguamus *quod factum est in illo* et deinde inferamus *uita est*... distinguit de quali uita loquatur cum addit *et uita erat lux hominum*. sic ergo distinguendum est ut cum dixerimus *quod factum est* deinde inferamus *in illo uita est*... nec praetermittendum est quod emendatiores codices habent *quod factum est in illo uita erat* ut sic intellegatur uita erat.
>
> (*De Genesi ad litteram* 5.14)[3]

The past tense *erat* in the final citation is unique to the Vulgate (although Jerome's version has *ipso* rather than *illo*). The earliest appearance of this form is in *Enarratio* 44.5 (identical to the Vulgate) and possibly also *Sermo* 341.2 (with *illo*), both from 403: the augmented version of the latter in *Sermo Dolbeau* 22.3 has *est* where

[2] See also the two citations of John 1:10 in *De doctrina christiana* 1.12.12 with *sapientia* as subject.

[3] This observation is considered in Hockey 1976. Compare also *Tractatus* 1.16: *non te abducant: pronuntia sic 'quod factum est'; hic subdistingue et deinde infer 'in illo uita est'.* Simonetti 1994:127 and Berrouard 1969:843–4 discuss the various punctuations of this verse in the early Church: Cyprian appears to place the full stop after *quod factum est* (*Ad Quirinum* 2.3), and others, including Hilary of Poitiers and Ambrose, insert a comma before *uita*. This was also a characteristic of Manichaean readings: see further Decret 1978:147 (vol. 2). On the similar problems of the punctuation of these verses in Greek, compare Metzger 1994:166–7.

Migne reads *erat*, suggesting that scribal interference may be responsible for the Vulgate reading in some citations. Although *Tractatus* 1 and 2 both read *in illo uita est*, *Tractatus* 3 has *in ipso uita erat*. The present tense *est*, paralleled by Codex Sinaiticus and the Greek side of Codex Bezae, occurs in the majority of Augustine's references to John 1:4, usually with *illo* or *eo*: the former (paralleled by Codices Vercellensis and Palatinus, as well as Cyprian *Ad Quirinum* 2.3) appears on sixteen occasions; *eo*, present in Codices Veronensis and Monacensis, is only found at *Confessiones* 7.9.13 and *Sermones* 133.6, 341A.1, 342.1, and 379.4: the latter two are lectionary sermons, which suggests that Augustine may have read *in eo uita erat* in a codex. If so, *erat* may have appeared in an Old Latin version no longer preserved.

JOHN 1:5

Augustine's preferred word order, *lux lucet in tenebris*, is shared with Codices Veronensis, Monacensis, and Palatinus, his opponent Felix (*Contra Felicem* 2.15) and Cyprian (*Ad Quirinum* 2.3), although it is not found in the initial citation of either *Sermo* 342 or 379. It does appear in later citations in *Sermo* 342. The imperfect *lucebat*, sometimes claimed as a Tatianic reading, occurs in three citations: *Tractatus* 36.3, 47.14, and *Sermo* 195.3.[4] As the first and the last of these also read *comprehendebant*, it is likely that Augustine has spontaneously recast the whole verse as imperfect: the present tense of *comprehendere* in five citations is another adaptation (*Epistulae* 130.2.5 and 187.3.7, *De consensu* 3.25.86, *Contra Faustum* 22.11, *De gratia et libero arbitrio* 19.40).

JOHN 1:6–7

Two citations of John 1:6 have *erat* rather than *fuit*, but both are likely to be from memory (*Tractatus* 35.3 and *Sermo* 379.7). They also

[4] For an imperfect in the Diatessaron, see Leloir 1962:12 and Quispel 1975:74, against whom Baarda (1993:213–14, 220) concludes that Tatian's own text of John 1:5 in the *Oratio ad Graecos* was the same as the majority of Greek manuscripts.

include variants in the next verse: *Sermo* 379 is one of four works which omit *in testimonium* through flattening, while *Tractatus* 35, *De ciuitate dei* 10.2, and *Epistula* 140.3.7 read *per eum*, like Codices Veronensis and Palatinus. The abbreviated citation at *Sermo* 133.6 has *per ipsum*.

JOHN 1:8–11

Augustine's preference for *lumen* (rendering φῶς) throughout John 1:8–9 is a clear indication of his Old Latin affinity in the opening verses of John. The only occurrences of *lux* are in *Tractatus* 2 and 3 and *De trinitate* 13, which cite both verses, and John 1:9 in *Enarratio* 25.s2.11. Similarly, the presence of the demonstratives in *hunc mundum* (John 1:9) and *hoc mundo* (John 1:10) is also characteristic of the Old Latin tradition: they are only missing from *Tractatus* 2 (both verses), *Tractatus* 35.3 (John 1:9), *Sermo* 121 (in Poque's *Sources Chrétiennes* edition), and *De trinitate* 13 (John 1:10). The reading *testimonium perhibebat* for John 1:8 in *Enarratio* 7.8 is an adaptation. Augustine's mental text of John 1:10, present in over forty citations, is *mundus per* **eum** *factus est*, only matched by Codices Veronensis and Monacensis. This occurs as early as *Enarratio* 6.5 and *De diuersis quaestionibus* 62, and is still his preferred form in *Contra Iulianum opus imperfectum* 4.18. It even appears in the initial citation of *Tractatus* 2, although the commentary immediately reverts to *ipsum*, found in seven other works. *Contra Adimantum* 1, with the word order *mundus factus est per ipsum*, is Augustine's only example of *illum non cognouit* (like Codex Vercellensis). The Vulgate reading *in propria* in John 1:11 is confined to a handful of works (*De trinitate* 13, *Tractatus* 3, *Sermo* 121 (only in a sequential variant), and *Sermo* 218.11.11). The gloss at *Tractatus* 3.6 (*in propria uenit, id est in sua uenit*) indicates that this was not Augustine's mental text (cf. John 1:48, 21:11): the majority Old Latin form *in sua propria* is found in fifteen citations, while *Sermo* 195.3 is the sole instance of *in sua uenit*, the reading of Codices Monacensis and Vercellensis.

JOHN 1:12

Augustine reads *credentibus* in fifteen citations of John 1:12, a literal rendering of τοῖς πιστεύουσιν paralleled only in Codex Veronensis. The appearance of this form twice in the lectionary *Sermo* 119 offers confirmation that Augustine knew it from a manuscript, while the early example in *De diuersis quaestionibus* 68.3 implies that Augustine did not introduce the correction on the basis of the Greek himself (cf. *uidentes* in John 9:39). The form in all other Latin Gospels, *his qui credunt*, occurs in six citations, including the commentary text of *Tractatus* 3 and *Sermo* 121. (*De trinitate* 13 initially has *his qui credunt* twice, but reverts to the participle at *De trinitate* 13.9.12.) Traces of the participle can also be seen in the appearance of *recipientibus* in conjunction with this verse (e.g. *Epistulae* 140.36.82 and 153.5.13 and *De peccatorum meritis* 2.6.7).

JOHN 1:13

In eight citations of John 1:13 Augustine adds an extra member to the beginning of the phrase:

qui ***non ex carne****, non ex sanguine, non ex uoluntate uiri, non ex uoluntate carnis nati sunt.* (*Sermo* 292.7)

It seems most likely that this form is due to Augustine's memory: not only does it have two balanced contrasting pairs, but the antithesis *carne/sanguine* is a commonplace, and the order of the last two units has been reversed (also found in *Epistula* 140.3.11 and the lectionary *Sermo* 121.4). The other references with *non ex carne* are *Confessiones* 7.9.14, *Tractatus* 3.6, *Contra Iulianum* 6.13.40, *De peccatorum meritis* 2.24.38, *Sermo* 342.5 (a lectionary sermon), and *Contra Secundinum* 5 (twice). All apart from *Tractatus* 3 have the singular *sanguine*, and most omit the initial *qui* (like Codices Monacensis and Vercellensis respectively). Augustine himself comments that the plural corresponds to the Greek against Latin usage, although he accepts it without emendation in his commentary:

sanguines non est latinum: sed quia graece positum est pluraliter, maluit ille qui interpretabat sic ponere... si enim diceret sanguinem singulari numero, non explicaret quod uolebat. (*Tractatus* 2.14)

Three of these citations appear to support the singular *natus est*, a significant reading found in Tertullian and Codex Veronensis which understands Christ as the subject. In *De peccatorum meritis* 2.24.38, this identification is made explicit:

nos non solum ex carne et sanguine uerum etiam ex uoluntate uiri et uoluntate carnis; ille autem tantum ex carne et sanguine, non ex uoluntate uiri neque ex uoluntate carnis sed ex deo natus est. (*De peccatorum meritis* 2.24.38)

However, it could be argued that the singular has been introduced here by Augustine for the sake of the antithesis. This is supported by the fact that the plural is found in the previous paragraph (*De peccatorum meritis* 2.23.37). *Confessiones* 7.9.14 and *Contra Secundinum* 5 present stronger cases, although as these too both have the variant form of the rest of the verse attributed to memory they are not strong evidence for the presence of this reading in a biblical manuscript.[5]

JOHN 1:14

The causal form *uerbum caro factum est* **ut habitaret** *in nobis* is an interpretative adaptation due to Augustine, appearing mainly in sermons (e.g. *Tractatus* 40.4 and 42.8, *Sermones* 27.2 and 265A.7). Nine citations read *tamquam* rather than *quasi*, paralleled by Codices Monacensis and Palatinus; this always precedes the Old Latin version with *plenum* plus the ablative (*Contra epistulam fundamenti* 37, *Adnotationes in Iob* 38, *Tractatus* 3.6, *De peccatorum meritis* 2.18.31, *Enarratio* 18.s2.2, *Sermo* 133.6, *Sermo* 174.2.2, *Sermo* 265D.7, *De spiritu et littera* 10.16.). Despite the appearance of *unici* rather than

[5] Augustine's text of this verse is discussed by Berrouard 1969:853–4, who considers *De peccatorum meritis* 2.24.38 as an adaptation but the other two passages as evidence for Augustine's use of the singular *natus est* before he adopted the plural form. A number of manuscripts of Augustine have *uoluptate* rather than *uoluntate*, a straightforward scribal error (e.g. *De trinitate* 13.1.2).

unigeniti in Codices Vercellensis, Palatinus, and Monacensis, Augustine always has the latter in citations of this verse, although he uses both words elsewhere (cf. John 1:18). At *Tractatus* 2.4 he claims that the concept of the *unigenitus filius* is also found in ancient philosophers.

JOHN 1:15

Augustine has the Old Latin text *qui post me uenit* in all thirteen citations of this verse, including *De consensu* 2.12.26 and *Tractatus* 3.7: the form *qui post me uenturus est*, peculiar to the Vulgate and Codex Aureus, does not appear in his writings (cf. John 1:27).

JOHN 1:16

Augustine treats John 1:16 as the words of John the Baptist, as shown by the introductions to this verse at, for example, *De baptismo* 5.9.10, *De ciuitate dei* 10.2, *De gratia et libero arbitrio* 9.21, and *Contra epistulam Parmeniani* 2.14.32, although he does not appear to extend the direct speech to the next two verses.[6] The word order *nos omnes de plenitudine eius accepimus* is found in all verbatim citations except the commentary at *Tractatus* 3.8: it appears to be a typical example of flattening, in which Augustine has fronted the subject to make a more logical sequence. There is no hint of this variation in any biblical manuscript, although it appears in two of Ambrose's three citations (*Expositio de Psalmo 118* 16.21, *Explanatio Psalmi* 48.23). Augustine's alternative form *nos* ***autem*** *de plenitudine* (*De gratia et libero arbitrio* 9.21, *Sermo* 67.5.9, and *Sermo* 308A.2; cf. *Sermo* 289.5 with *enim*) seems to indicate a fault in memory, as if he has forgotten the true reading but substituted an alternative disyllabic word to preserve the original rhythm; on the other hand, *Sermo* 292.8 combines both forms, reading *nos autem omnes*. At *Tractatus* 3.8,

[6] See further the references in Berrouard 1969:688–9 and 1988:152.

Augustine observes that the presence of *et* before *gratiam* is supported by Greek manuscripts. In the Latin tradition, this is only found in Codices Brixianus, Monacensis, and the Vulgate, but it features in both Augustine's complete citations of the verse (*Tractatus* 3 and *De gratia et libero arbitrio* 9.21). At *Epistula* 194.5.21, Augustine expands the antithesis, reading *non solum... sed etiam gratiam pro hac gratia* (cf. John 9:39). As well as offering the traditional exegesis of *gratiam pro gratia* as the New Testament following the Old (e.g. *Enarratio* 81.1), Augustine also uses the text to emphasize the idea of grace as a separate gift, following on from the earlier donation (see further *Tractatus* 3.8 and Berrouard 1969:859–60).

JOHN 1:17

Only the Vulgate and Codex Aureus omit *autem* from the phrase *gratia autem et ueritas*, although the large number of parallels in Augustine's citations suggests that it may have been missing from Old Latin witnesses no longer preserved. It is not found in *Ad Simplicianum* 1.1.17, his earliest reference. Only four works do include *autem*: *Epistula* 82.18 (which also has the Old Latin *quoniam*), *Tractatus* 3.2 (an anticipatory citation; the commentary at *Tractatus* 3.16 omits *autem*), *Enarratio* 123.14, and *Contra Faustum* 15–22 (in which *autem* is present in three and missing from four citations). Bochet (2004:410) notes that Augustine interprets this verse as a development rather than an antithesis: for him, the Law has *become* grace. This understanding would be assisted by the absence of *autem*, which emphasizes the disjunction.

JOHN 1:18

As noted on p. 145, *Contra Adimantum* 9 alone among Augustine's citations has *unicus* rather than *unigenitus* in this verse. I suggested above that this was probably due to the influence on Augustine of his opponent's writing, but it is also found in Codex

Vercellensis (see John 1:14 and 3:16 for wider attestation among the Old Latin witnesses). There is no parallel among surviving manuscripts for the text *ille/ipse adnuntiauit uobis de eo* at the end of the verse in both these citations, although Codex Colbertinus adds *nobis*.[7] The Old Latin form *narrauit* in *Epistula* 147 is probably influenced by the citations of Ambrose earlier in the letter, although this also appears in *Sermo* 73A.1.

JOHN 1:21–2

These verses are only cited verbatim in *Tractatus* 4.7, which has minor variations from the Vulgate. It is likely that Augustine's codex had *dixit* rather than *dicit*, a form unique to the Vulgate in John 1:21. The addition of *tu* after *es* in John 1:22 also has Old Latin parallels, but *non* for *non sum* followed by *et dixerunt ei* in John 1:21 is without precedent, and may be an adaptation.

JOHN 1:23

This is one of two verses in which Augustine reads *eremo* for ἐρήμῳ but all extant Old Latin manuscripts have *deserto*; the other is John 3:14, while in John 6:49 this rendering is found in Codex Usserianus.[8]

[7] Although Augustine only introduces John 1:16 as the words of John the Baptist, it is worth observing that Maximinus describes John 1:18 as spoken by the Baptist at *Collatio cum Maximino* 13. In his reply, at *Contra Maximinum* 2.9.1, Augustine couples John 1:18 with Matthew 18:10 as the words of Jesus, *eiusdem domini uerba*!

[8] *Deserto* occurs in *De consensu* 2.12.25, *Tractatus* 4 and 5, and *Sermones* 288, 293B, 293D, and 308A (as a sequential variant); *eremo* is found in *Sermones* 288, 292, 293, 293A (*Dolbeau* 3), 293C, and 308A (initial citation only). The word is one of the six examples of 'Graecisms' which Milne 1926:xv adduces as evidence that Augustine revised the Gospel based on the Greek, but the parallels elsewhere make this a very unlikely explanation. Burton (2000:145) notes the 'surprising persistence' of the loan-word *eremus* in the Latin Bible, and connects it with early Christian monasticism: this rendering is often peculiar to the African manuscripts (García de la Fuente 1994:142 describes it as an African feature). On Augustine and John the Baptist, see Lienhard 2001:197–213 and Bastiaensen 2003.

Eight of the *Sermones ad populum* have *ego* **sum** *uox*, paralleled by Codices Palatinus and Colbertinus. They also provide seven of the nine citations outside the commentary in *Tractatus* 4.7 which read *parate uiam domino* rather than *dirigite uiam domini* (the other two are both in *Tractatus* 5). *Parate* might be attributed to the Synoptic parallels (Matthew 3:3, Mark 1:3, and Luke 3:15), which affected a number of biblical manuscripts: the other Evangelists follow the Septuagintal text of Isaiah 40:3, *ἑτοιμάσατε τὴν ὁδὸν κυρίου*, whereas John has *εὐθύνατε*. However, the only example of the dative *domino* is in some manuscripts of Jerome's version of Isaiah from Hebrew, and given that Augustine used this translation from early in his career, it seems most likely that this influenced his text.[9] He leaves the genitive unchanged in *Tractatus* 4. The Synoptics also include the second half of the Isaiah citation, *rectas facite semitas eius*, which appears in John 1:23 in Codex Palatinus and *Sermo* 308A.2.

JOHN 1:25–6

The initial citation of John 1:25 in *Tractatus* 4.8 has *et dixerunt*, a reading peculiar to the Vulgate and Codex Brixianus, although it omits the preceding *eum*. This work agrees with the same witnesses for John's words in the next verse, omitting *quidem* and *uos* and reading *stetit*, although it has *nescitis* for *non scitis*. Augustine is often loose when citing the introductions to direct speech, but it is possible that *et dixit* was in his codex in place of *dicens*, as it comes in the middle of a longer text beginning with the previous verse. *Sermones* 292.8 and 379.7 have the standard Old Latin additions in the phrase *ego quidem baptizo uos*. This verse is used to illustrate the use of *in medio* in Psalm 81:1 (*Enarratio* 81.2), which suggests that Augustine

[9] See p. 12 and compare also John 6:45 below. It is also possible that Augustine knew *domino* from an Old Latin witness which has not been preserved, or even a liturgical text: for the influence of liturgy on biblical citations, see Fischer 1972:37 and Frede 1972:469. La Bonnardière 1965:81 shows how Augustine was influenced by a verse of an Ambrosian hymn based on Psalm 18:6.

was familiar with the reading *in medio* in Codices Monacensis and Palatinus.[10] This citation provides his only example of the Old Latin *stat.*

JOHN 1:27

Given the overlap between this verse and the Synoptic tradition, it is not surprising that there is some conflation in citations made from memory, even though Augustine comments on the differences between *corrigiam calciamenti (eius) soluere* (his mental text of John 1:27, cf. Mark 1:7) and *calciamenta portare* (Matthew 3:11 and some manuscripts of Luke 3:16).[11] Like John 1:15, none of his citations have the Vulgate form *uenturus est*: even *Tractatus* 4 reads *uenit*, and features the word order *corrigiam calciamenti eius* at the end of the verse. *Qui fortior me est* (ὁ ἰσχυρότερός μου) only appears in the Synoptics, suggesting that *Tractatus* 35.2 is not a citation of John. Conversely, *qui ante me factus est* (ὅς ἔμπροσθέν μου γέγονεν) is unique to this evangelist, although Nestle–Aland indicates John 1:30 as its original position: Augustine cites this phrase in John 1:27 on five occasions as *qui maior me est* (*Enarratio* 35.9, *Sermones* 290.1.1, 292.8, 293D.3, and 379.7; cf. *Sermo* 293E.1 with *Iohanne maior est*): this could be a loose version of the Greek, but is more likely to be a reminiscence of the comparative in the Synoptics, the phrase *quia prior me erat* in John 1:30, or even Matthew 11:11 (*non surrexit inter natos mulierum maior Iohanne Baptista*). *Sermones* 292.8 and 379.7 both add *autem* to the opening phrase in citations which continue from the previous verse: this is probably added by Augustine.

JOHN 1:29

Augustine's customary repetition of *ecce* in *ecce qui tollit* and the plural *peccata* are paralleled by several Old Latin witnesses.

[10] See p. 65 above.

[11] *De consensu euangelistarum* 2.12.29, quoted on p. 55 above.

JOHN 1:33

The introduction of the dove descending from heaven at John 1:32 into the next verse has no parallel in surviving Latin manuscripts, but is an easy error of memory. Augustine's citations are notable, however, for the range of renderings of ὡς: *sicut*, *tamquam*, and *quasi*, as found in manuscripts at John 1:32, are supplemented by *uelut* (*Tractatus* 7.3; cf. *De baptismo* 5.13.15 and *De trinitate* 15.26.46). The double appearance of *ipse* in most of Augustine's references (*ipse mihi dixit* and *ipse est qui baptizat*) is a feature of Codices Palatinus, Veronensis, and Usserianus. The latter phrase is a key text in Augustine's identification of Christ as the true minister of baptism, against the Donatists (see Berrouard 1969:869–70). Six citations also feature the only examples of *non noueram* in this verse as a rendering of οὐκ ᾔδειν (*De consensu* 2.15.32, *Tractatus* 4.15, 4.16, 5.2, 5.8, and *Sermo* 308A.4), which seems to be part of his mental text. The majority of Augustine's references have the word order *me misit*: this occurs throughout *Tractatus* 4, but *Tractatus* 5 varies and *De consensu* 2 matches the Vulgate. Only *Sermo* 293B.2 adds *et igni* at the end of the verse (cf. Matthew 3:11). La Bonnardière observes that, despite the frequency of these verses in his early anti-Donatist works, Augustine barely cites John 1:32–33 after 410.[12]

JOHN 1:34

Sermo 308A.4, Augustine's one citation outside the *Tractatus*, has *electus dei* rather than *filius dei*: the former appears in four Old Latin witnesses and other versional evidence, but in the Greek tradition ἐκλεκτός is only present in the first hand of Codex Sinaiticus. The

[12] See La Bonnardière 1965:29–33 where she lists some 55 citations of John 1:33 in chronological order, but does not include the allusions at *Tractatus* 94.4 and *De trinitate* 15.26.46 which occur after 410. The figure of the dove links a group of citations on which Augustine relies for his exegesis: he uses its return to the Ark as a figure of the unity of the Church (see La Bonnardière 1965:29–30 and Comeau 1930:156–9).

other variants in this citation (*ego quod uidi, perhibeo, ipse est*) are paralleled in Old Latin manuscripts, but the preceding form of John 1:33 suggests that Augustine has drawn the text from memory for this early sermon.

JOHN 1:38–47

There are several minor variants in the initial citations of *Tractatus* 7, most corresponding to Vulgate or Old Latin manuscripts (*sequentes se* in John 1:38, *et* before *uenerunt* in John 1:39, omission of *autem* from John 1:40, *duxit* and *Iohannis* in John 1:42, omission of *Iesus* from John 1:43, *de ciuitate* in John 1:44, *dixit* for *dicit* in John 1:45). A few omissions are unique to Augustine (*ei* from John 1:38, *primum* from John 1:41, *Philippus a Bethsaida* from John 1:44), which are consistent with slips or abbreviations when preaching before a congregation. He also includes *et* at the beginning of John 1:43, 45, and 47; this may sometimes be part of the introduction to the citation, but in John 1:45 it is present in some Old Latin witnesses. The two other works which cite John 1:41, *Contra Faustum* 12.44 and *Enarratio* 65.4, have the present *interpretatur.* They also read *uerus* rather than *uere* in John 1:47 (*Contra Faustum* 13.16 and 16.19, *Enarrationes* 65.4, 75.2, 121.8). Both of these variants are only paralleled in Codex Monacensis. Although Augustine acknowledges that Nathanael's words in John 1:46 can be taken as a question or a statement (*Tractatus* 7.15, *De doctrina christiana* 3.3.6), he prefers the latter (*Enarratio* 65.4).

JOHN 1:48, 1:50

The rendering of ἡ συκῆ in these two verses divides Vulgate texts with *ficus* from Old Latin sources with *arbor ficulnea* and *arbor fici.* Augustine's initial citation of John 1:48 at *Tractatus* 7.20 has *ficu,* but he replaces this immediately with *id est, sub arbore fici,* which is the only form found thereafter, including the commentary on John

1:50 later.[13] *Sermo* 122 also has *ficu* in the initial citation but *arbore fici* in a sequential variant, while every other work reads *arbore fici.* The present of *antequam* in a sequential variant at *Tractatus* 7.20 offers a further parallel between Augustine's mental text and Codices Monacensis and Usserianus. Augustine treats the fig as a symbol of sinfulness, based on Genesis 3:7 (cf. *Sermones* 69.3.4 and 122.1). The variation between *maiora horum* and *maius his* in John 1:50 is also indicative of text type: *maius his* is a distinctive Vulgate reading, which appears throughout *Tractatus* 7 and in *Sermones* 122 and 123, although *Sermo* 122 is inconsistent; *Enarratio* 44.20 and *Sermo* 89 also read *maiora horum.*[14] Two sermons have an extra word in this verse:

quia dixi cum esses sub arbore fici ***ideo*** *credis.* (*Sermo* 89.5)
quia dixi tibi uidi te cum esses sub arbore fici ***inde*** *miraris.* (*Sermo* 122.2.2)

In contrast to John 4:24, where a similar explanatory particle is unique to Augustine, there are some parallels for this: Codices Aureus, Corbeiensis, and Rehdigeranus all read *propterea* before the final verb, while Tertullian has *ideo* itself.[15] There are no examples of *miraris* elsewhere, although it also appears later in this sermon (cf. *Sermo* 122.5.5).

JOHN 1:51

Berrouard (1962:489–93) observes that Augustine's change from *ad* (found in Codices Palatinus, Veronensis, Rehdigeranus, Monacensis, and two citations of Ambrose) to *super* in this verse is significant for his exegesis. The citation which seems to be earliest, *Sermo* 265B.3 (probably 396–7, but see John 3:13), along with *Sermo* 89.5 from 405, reads *ad filium hominis.* This also appears throughout *Sermo* 123 and in a non-sequential citation at *Tractatus* 57.2, which implies that

[13] On these glosses, see pp. 88–9 and John 1:11 and 21:11.

[14] See p. 124. The literal rendering of the Greek genitive of comparison does not seem to have concerned Augustine; on potential Latin hypercorrection in these verses, see Coleman 1987:40–1.

[15] For other examples of *ideo* as an alternative to *propterea*, see John 9:23, John 12:39, and John 16:15; Tertullian reads *quia dixi uidi te sub ficu ideo credis* at *Aduersus Praxean* 21: it is worth observing that this is evidence for an Old Latin rendering *ficu* not supported by surviving manuscripts.

it is Augustine's mental text. (The plural *caelos apertos* in *Tractatus* 57 is similar to Codex Palatinus.) Based on this reading, Augustine uses the preposition to demonstrate the presence of Christ in both heaven and earth. According to the alternative version (also derived from the Greek ἐπί) which appears in the Vulgate and the other Old Latin witnesses as *supra filium hominis*, Augustine sees preachers as the angels who ascend and descend, without ruling out the ascent and descent of Christ himself (e.g. *Tractatus* 7.23). This is first attested in *Contra Faustum* 12.26 (400/2), and soon after in *Enarratio* 44.20 and *De unitate ecclesiae* 6.14 from 403, giving a fairly precise indication of when Augustine encountered the reading: it is possible that it is connected with his introduction to Jerome's revision. The undated *Sermo* 122 has *super* in its initial text, but *ad* in the two citations when Augustine discusses this verse and provides his earlier explanation: the later exegesis accompanies *super* in *Tractatus* 7.22, and the Vulgate form is also found at *De ciuitate dei* 16.38.2.

JOHN 2:1–2

De consensu 2.17.38 has the Vulgate text of both these verses apart from the omission of *ibi* in John 2:2. *Tractatus* 8.6 presents the following form as a verbatim citation:

altera die nuptiae factae sunt in Cana Galilaeae, et erat ibi mater Iesu. uenerat autem illuc inuitatus ad nuptias cum discipulis suis.

It seems unlikely that this was the reading of Augustine's codex: although *inuitatus* (cf. *De bono coniugali* 3.3) and *cum discipulis suis* are paralleled in Codices Veronensis and Usserianus, *altera* and *uenerat autem* are unique to this citation.

JOHN 2:4

The form in *De uera religione* 16.31, *recede a me mulier; mihi et tibi quid est? nondum uenit hora mea*, is unique, possibly inspired by confusion with a similar passage such as John 20:17. Neither of the Synoptic parallels with *quid mihi et tibi est* are combined with the word *recede* (Mark 5:7, Luke 8:28), and there is no verbal correspondence with the command to Peter *uade retro me* (Matthew 16:23, Mark 8:33). Bresolin 1962 discusses Augustine's influential exegesis of this verse, linking *hora mea* with the Passion narrative.[16] The two tractates which expound John 2:1–11 (*Tractatus* 8 and 9) have remarkably few verbatim citations from the Gospel.

JOHN 2:12

Tractatus 10.2 reads *in Capharnaum*; *De consensu* 2.17.39 just has *Capharnaum.*

JOHN 2:15–16

Augustine only has Old Latin renderings of *σχοινίων*, even at *Tractatus* 10.4: on most occasions he reads *resticulis* with Codex Palatinus (Codex Monacensis has *resticula*), while *Contra Adimantum* 10 has *restibus*, as found in Codices Vercellensis, Veronensis, and Sarzanensis. Augustine uses *resticulis* in John 2:15 to gloss *restes* in Psalm 139 in *Enarratio* 139.9, treating the two words as synonymous: after referring to *resticulae* in *Enarratio* 130.2, he notes *restis enim peccata significat.* The transposition of *boues quoque et oues* in the only verbatim citation of this verse (*Tractatus* 10.4) is probably under the influence of this order in the preceding verse. Augustine interprets *boues et oues* as the writers of Scripture and their audience; *columbas* in John 2:14 is identified with the Holy Spirit (*Tractatus*

[16] More generally, Augustine famously observes that the transformation of water into wine is an annual event in vineyards (*Tractatus* 9.1) and connects the six water jars in John 2:6 with six periods of history (*Tractatus* 9.6; cf. John 4:6). For more on his treatment of the whole pericope, see Comeau 1930:145–6 and Berrouard 1969:896 and 901–3.

10.6–8).[17] In John 2:16, *Tractatus* 10.4 has the Old Latin addition of *et* before *nolite.* Synoptic parallels have affected Augustine's references to both these verses: compare *Quaestiones euangeliorum* 2.48B, quoted on p. 71.

JOHN 2:19

Jesus' words in John 2:19 indicate for Augustine that the agent of the resurrection was not just the Father but the Son as well.[18] His mental text reads *soluite templum hoc et in triduo suscitabo illud*: every word is paralleled in Old Latin manuscripts but none has exactly this reading, which occurs in two of Ambrose's citations (*Explanatio Psalmi* 40.18 and 40.20). The majority of Ambrose's references, however, feature *resuscitabo*, like Tertullian: this is found in Codices Vercellensis and Usserianus, and Augustine reads *resuscitabo* in six verbatim citations. Most references with the Vulgate *excitabo* also have *in tribus diebus* (*De consensu* 4.10.12, *Tractatus* 10.10, and *Enarratio* 65.7). The exceptions are *Tractatus* 12.8 (*in tribus diebus suscitabo*), *Enarratio* 126.2 (*in triduo excitabo*), and *Contra Iulianum* 6.14.42 (*in tribus diebus exsuscitabo*): this last, unique, form appears to be a combination of *suscitabo* and *excitabo.*[19] *Sermo* 315.1.2 alone has *post triduum* (cf. manuscripts of *Sermo* 37.2), while *destruite* for *soluite* in *Enarratio* 85.22 agrees with Codex Brixianus.

JOHN 2:20

The switch to direct speech in the initial citation at *Tractatus* 10.10 is remarkable: *tu* ***dicis*** *in tribus diebus* ***excitabo*** *illud* is not found anywhere else. Although *excitabo* appears in four manuscripts in Fischer's

[17] Elsewhere, Augustine takes *boues et oues* to refer to angels, based on Psalm 8:8; see Knauer 1955:163.

[18] e.g. *Tractatus* 47.7; see the references at Berrouard 1989:141 and Berrouard 2003:156.

[19] See p. 173 above.

collation, it has been corrected to *excitabis* in every instance and none has *dicis.* Eight lines later, however, Augustine reverts to his mental text (*et triduo suscitabis illud*).[20] Augustine has several explanations of the significance of the number forty-six: see Berrouard 1969:916–17.

JOHN 2:21

The reading *hoc autem dicebat* in eight of Augustine's ten citations is not paralleled by any biblical manuscripts: all Latin witnesses listed by Fischer have *ille,* and ἐκεῖνος appears to be invariant in Greek. It may be that Augustine has been influenced by verses such as John 6:6, John 7:39, or John 12:33, where the neuter is almost formulaic. The exceptions, *Tractatus* 10.10 and *De trinitate* 4.5.9 also do not correspond to surviving codices, with *dicebat autem* and *dicebat enim hoc* respectively.

JOHN 2:25

Although the Latin tradition has numerous different renderings of οὐ χρείαν εἶχεν, such as *non necesse habebat* or the Vulgate *opus ei non erat,* which seems to underlie five of Augustine's references to this verse, there is only one surviving parallel for *non opus habebat* in the remaining four citations (*Tractatus* 12.3, *Contra aduersarium legis* 1.20.41, *Enarratio* 63.6, and *Sermo* 100.1; see also John 13:10).[21] *Quisquam* rather than *quis* in the seven citations outside *De consensu* 4.4.5 and *Tractatus* 11.2 is unique to Augustine.

[20] There are, however, comparable changes in person in biblical manuscripts at John 4:17 (*habeo/habes* within the reported speech) and John 10:36 (*blasphemas/blasphemat* introducing the speech). This may reflect a perceived difficulty with the preservation of the Greek tense of original words following a ὅτι *recitatiuum*: on this construction in Latin, see further Burton 2000:189.

[21] Fischer's **Jc** (Paris BN lat 10439) with the word order *opus non habebat*; this is identified as Old Latin in John 1–6 and given the number 33 in Gryson 1999:57.

JOHN 3:3

Both Augustine's citations which read *non uidebit regnum dei* rather than *non potest uidere regnum dei* are due to memory: it appears in a sequential variant at *Tractatus* 11.6 and at *De peccatorum meritis* 1.19.25 before the long citation of this passage drawn from a codex at *De peccatorum meritis* 1.30.59 which has the Vulgate text. This is a significant example of a change of verb form due to flattening which is not paralleled in any surviving biblical manuscripts: variations involving *potest* also occur in Augustine's citations of John 3:5, 5:19, 5:47, 6:44, 6:65, 7:45, 10:29, 14:6, 15:13, and 16:7, which shows that this auxiliary was particularly unstable. The shift appears to be from the potential to the future in order to make the saying more direct.[22]

JOHN 3:4

Augustine's text of the Vulgate, as cited in *Tractatus* 11.6 and *De peccatorum meritis* 1.30.59, appears to have had *iterum* rather than *iterato*, although the latter appears at *De natura et origine animae* 3.11.17. Both are found in Vulgate manuscripts. Similarly, while *De peccatorum meritis* 1.30.59 and *Sermo* 294.8.9 feature *utero* rather than *uentrem*, the other two works have the standard Vulgate form. The variations due to memory in the sequential variants in *Tractatus* 11 and 12 are less well attested elsewhere: *denuo* and the repetition of *homo* have Old Latin parallels, but *intrare* or *redire* for *introire* and *uiscera* for *uentrem* do not occur in surviving manuscripts and are likely to be mistakes by Augustine.

JOHN 3:5

As in John 3:3, the replacement of *potest introire* by *intrabit* in twenty-eight citations (as well as *introibit* in *Contra Iulianum* 2.6.18

22 Coleman (1971:220) notes that *posse* is very rare as a future auxiliary in Latin, so this is unlikely to be an internal Latin variation for the future tense.

and *intrat* in *Epistula* 194.7.31) is not found in any Old Latin manuscript.[23] The majority of Augustine's citations also have *in regnum caelorum* rather than *in regnum dei*, a reading he criticizes at *De natura et origine animae* 3.11.17, which is likely to have been influenced by a Synoptic parallel such as Matthew 5:20. While both these features and *si quis non* (or *qui non*) for *nisi quis* are typical of flattening, *in regnum caelorum* is found in a few gospel manuscripts (e.g. Codex Palatinus). The two citations from memory which read *uidebit* rather than *intrabit* (*Tractatus* 11.1 and 12.8) have been influenced by *uidere* in John 3:3; this is a common mistake, made also by Faustus (*Contra Faustum* 24.1) and in Codex Aureus. The addition of the adjective in *spiritu sancto* features in a number of biblical manuscripts as well: it seems likely to be secondary, inspired by John 1:33 or similar verses. Finally, *Ad Simplicianum* 1.2.2, which may be Augustine's earliest citation of this verse, reads:

nisi quis natus fuerit ex aqua et spiritu sancto non intrabit in regnum caelorum.

Although the other variants have already been discussed, this is the only instance in which Augustine has *natus* rather than *renatus*: the reading is paralleled by Faustus (*Contra Faustum* 24.1) and Codices Brixianus and Usserianus.

JOHN 3:6

Several Old Latin manuscripts have interpolations in this verse characteristic of the so-called 'Western' text of the Gospel.[24] The longest form, found in Codex Vercellensis, is as follows:

quod natum est de carne caro est, *quia de carne natum est*; et quod natum est de spiritu, spiritus est **quia deus spiritus est** *et ex deo natus est.*

Augustine does not provide any evidence for the phrases in italics, but he does have some instances of the words in bold.[25] The clearest

[23] Tischendorf notes some instances of the future in Greek Fathers, and there are parallels in the *Vetus Latina Database.*

[24] See p. 94.

[25] Unlike Ambrose (*De spiritu sancto* 3.10.59), however, Augustine does not identify this as a controversial text.

example is *De fide et symbolo* 9.19, composed in 393, which reads *quod natum est de carne caro est, et quod natum est de spiritu spiritus est, quoniam deus spiritus est.* At *De baptismo* 6.12.19, Augustine quotes Nemesianus from Cyprian's *Sententiae episcoporum* 5, who includes the phrase *quia deus spiritus est.* Although this addition is similar to the canonical form of John 4:24, *spiritus est deus*, in each case there is no variance in word order in the surviving Old Latin manuscripts. It therefore seems likely that whenever Augustine cites the phrase *deus spiritus est*, especially when preceded by *quoniam* or *quia*, he is drawing on the longer version of John 3:6 (e.g. *Sermo* 30.1, *De trinitate* 5.11.12).[26] Augustine has the Old Latin prepositions *de* rather than *ex* in the commentary at *Tractatus* 12.5, but the interpolations do not seem to have been present in his copies of the Vulgate even though they are found in parts of the Vulgate tradition. As noted on pp. 177–8, *quod nascitur* rather than *quod natum est* appears on the lips of Manichees (e.g. *Contra Iulianum opus imperfectum* 3.172–3, *Contra Faustum* 24.1). It is not found in any surviving biblical manuscripts, but is cited by Augustine in *De peccatorum meritis* 2.9.11 and *Sermo* 294.16.16, and could also underlie the phrase *caro de carne nascitur* at *Contra Maximinum* 2.14.34. Other occurrences in Latin Fathers indicate that this present tense rendering of τὸ γεγεννημένον was widespread in the Old Latin tradition.

JOHN 3:8

The initial citations in *Tractatus* 12.5 have numerous minor variations, all present in surviving Old Latin versions as well as some Vulgate witnesses: *nescis* rather than *non scis*, *aut* for *et*, and the addition of *et* before *omnis.* Sequential variants read *et nescis unde ueniat et quo eat*: *et* is paralleled in Codex Palatinus, which also has *eat* along with Codices Veronensis and Usserianus. The long citation at *De peccatorum meritis* 1.30.59, however, corresponds exactly to Weber–Gryson. Augustine's single instance of *inspirat* (*Sermo* 266.7)

[26] The only clear exception is *Sermo* 21.2, which continues with the rest of John 4:24; it is more difficult to allocate citations which simply quote the three words *deus spiritus est* (e.g. *De ciuitate dei* 13.24.3 and *Enarratio* 50.17).

is likely to be an error of memory, although this form does occur in other patristic material. At *Tractatus* 12.7, Augustine rejects the identification of the *spiritus* with the wind, seeing this text instead as a reference to the Holy Spirit.

JOHN 3:9–11

Although *De peccatorum meritis* 1.30.59 agrees with the Vulgate in John 3:9, the three other citations in this work (all in 1.31.60) read *ista* rather than *haec*. This indicates that Augustine did not refer back to his codex after the initial citation of this passage; *ista* appears in Codex Palatinus. All three citations of John 3:10 read *magister in Israhel*, as do many Vulgate texts. Augustine only quotes John 3:11 in the primary citation at *De peccatorum meritis* 1.30.59: here, there are two non-Vulgate forms, *uidemus* and *testificamur*, which are present in the Old Latin tradition. In contrast to the sequential treatment of John 3:9–16 in *Tractatus* 12, Augustine offers a much more developed exegesis of this passage in *De peccatorum meritis* in response to the Pelagian controversy (see Berrouard 1969:928–30).

JOHN 3:12

De peccatorum meritis 1.30.59 has *credidistis* where *Tractatus* 12.7 reads *creditis*. The sequential variants in the commentary reflect Augustine's mental text, as does *Enarratio* 77.17: *terrestria* instead of *terrena* and the word order *si caelestia dixero credetis* are both found in Old Latin witnesses.

JOHN 3:13

Twenty-two of Augustine's citations have the Old Latin word order *de caelo descendit*. Only the Vulgate and Codex Colbertinus have *descendit de caelo* in this verse, although elsewhere in the Vulgate these words normally follow the former pattern (cf. John 6:33, 6:41, 6:51, 6:58). The appearance of the latter order is therefore quite unusual: it occurs in the initial citation at *Tractatus* 12.8, and, presumably from memory, in three later sermons (*Tractatus* 31.9, 111.2, and *Sermo* 144.4.5). Most intriguing is *Sermo* 265B.2, a sermon on the Ascension which the majority of commentators date to 396–7, but has been placed as late as 412. The initial citation of this verse has *descendit de caelo*, but three sentences further on, Augustine reverts to *de caelo descendit*. While this might suggest a liturgical lection corresponding to the Vulgate, *ad* in John 1:51 provides strong evidence for an Old Latin form and early date.

JOHN 3:14

Like John 1:23, in this verse Augustine reads *eremo* for ἐρήμῳ in eleven of his thirteen verbatim citations, including *Tractatus* 12: the exceptions are *De peccatorum meritis* 1.30.59 (from a codex) and 1.32.61 (perhaps influenced by the earlier citation). Again, *eremo* is not present in any Old Latin witnesses, although it does feature in Cyprian and two later manuscripts.[27] Augustine's mental text also includes *sic oportet exaltari*, the reading of Codex Vercellensis, and the word order *exaltauit Moyses*. The additional *super terram* at the end of the verse is unique to *Expositio epistolae ad Galatas* 22.12, and may be intended to reinforce the prophetic parallelism (cf. John 4:7, 8:6, 8:8). In his explanations of this verse, Augustine takes *exaltari* as a reference to the cross, with the serpent as a figure of the death it brings (e.g. *Tractatus* 12.11, *De trinitate* 3.9.20, *De peccatorum meritis* 1.32.61, *Expositio epistolae ad Galatas* 22).

[27] Cyprian *Ad Quirinum* 2.20 (Fahey 1971:376) and Fischer's manuscripts **Eh** (Cambridge UL Kk.I.24) and **Gk** (Kilian-Evangeliar, Würzburg). Tertullian reads *deserto* in his verbatim citations of this verse, but his allusion at *De Idololatria* 2 has *eremo* (Roensch 1871:256).

JOHN 3:15

All thirteen citations have the Old Latin *eum* rather than *ipso*, even *De peccatorum meritis* 1.30.59, and *Tractatus* 12. *Perdat* in the *Corpus Christianorum* edition of *Tractatus* 12.11 is a typographical error for *pereat* (Verheijen 1976:4).

JOHN 3:16

The rendering *unicus* rather than *unigenitus* for μονογενής is attested in six surviving Old Latin manuscripts in John 3:16, more than for John 1:14 or 1:18, as well as Ambrose and Tertullian. Two of Augustine's works read *ut unicum filium suum mitteret* (*De catechizandis rudibus* 17.28 (cf. 4.7 and 22.39) and *Enarratio* 149.4).[28] *Mitteret* in place of *daret* appears to be an anticipation of the next verse (*non enim misit deus filium suum*) although it is found in three Old Latin manuscripts. The strange version of John 3:16 in *Sermo* 265B.4, *sic autem dilexit deus humanum genus ut filium suum unigenitum daret pro saeculi uita*, appears to be a rhetorical expansion drawing on John 6:51 in the form found in Codices Palatinus and Monacensis (*dare... pro saeculi uita*).

JOHN 3:17

Eleven of Augustine's citations either read or support *non uenit filius hominis* in place of *non enim misit deus filium suum in mundum*: the exceptions are *Tractatus* 12.12 and *De peccatorum meritis* 1.30.59, both drawn from a codex (*De trinitate* 15.28.51, with *misit deus filium suum*, may also be an allusion to the canonical text of this verse). As with *non ueni facere* in John 6:38, this has no support in

[28] Hombert's revised dating of *Enarratio* 149 to 404 would match the composition of *De catechizandis rudibus* in 403.

manuscripts of John, but is a paraphrase based on the Synoptic Gospels (e.g. Luke 19:10, Matthew 18:11, etc.) with no support in biblical manuscripts of John. An interesting parallel is provided by Augustine's use of *uenit* before a citation of this verse in the minutes of the Conference of Carthage (*Conf. Carth.* 3.272). In the early *Expositio epistolae ad Romanos inchoata* 23.3, he reads:

non enim iam uenerat filius hominis ut iudicaret saeculum sed ut saluaret mundum.

The combination of the initial paraphrase with the adapted tense of the verbs and the inconsistency of *saeculum* and *mundum* for κόσμος indicates that this is due to memory.

JOHN 3:18–19

Non ueniet in iudicium rather than *non iudicatur* is peculiar to *De agone christiano* 27.29, and is probably a paraphrase. Flattening results in the omission of *autem* from a number of citations. In the lectionary *Sermo* 294.13.14 the presence of the future perfect *crediderit* is important evidence for this form in a biblical manuscript alongside Codex Palatinus and the reconstructed text of Codex Sarzanensis (cf. *Sermo* 215.7). In John 3:19, Augustine's mental text has the word order *tenebras magis quam lucem*, while *mala opera eorum* throughout *Tractatus* 12 is only paralleled in Codex Rehdigeranus; *De peccatorum meritis* 1.30.59 follows the Vulgate.

JOHN 3:20–2

Augustine only cites John 3:20 in the primary citation at *De peccatorum meritis* 1.30.59. This follows the Vulgate. with the exception of *male* for *mala*. Julian of Eclanum's Old Latin text of this verse has been quoted above, as has John 3:21 in *Adnotationes in Iob* 36.[29] As

[29] For Julian, see p. 178; for the *Adnotationes*, see p. 152.

Sermo 128 did not feature John 3:21 in its lection, the reading *qui ergo quaerit ueritatem* rather than *qui autem facit ueritatem* is likely to be an error of memory. *Epistula* 265.5 has the Old Latin readings *exiit* and *morabatur* in John 3:22.

JOHN 3:23–4

Tractatus 13.6 varies from the standard Vulgate text of John 3:23 found in *De consensu* 2.18.42 by reading *ibi* for *illic* and *ueniebant* rather than *adueniebant.* These are paralleled in Old Latin manuscripts. In the next verse, both works have *missus erat*: although this is not listed in the critical apparatus of Weber–Gryson, it probably featured in Augustine's version of the Vulgate.

JOHN 3:26

Tractatus 13 ends the verse *ad illum,* as does Codex Vercellensis. *Sermo* 293.6, Augustine's only other citation, omits *tu* and *hic* but does read *ad eum.*

JOHN 3:27

There are numerous permutations of the words *datum fuerit ei* (or *illi*) in the Old Latin witnesses, and Augustine's citations include no fewer than five of these (cf. John 6:65). No parallels exist for the word order *quidquam accipere,* however, which seems to have been the reading of Augustine's codex at *Tractatus* 13.9. The reduction of *non potest homo* to *nemo potest* is a typical example of flattening applied independently by multiple authors: this appears in *Sermo* 265D.6 and the citation of Julian of Telepte at *De baptismo* 7.21.40. Augustine emphasizes the phrase *de caelo* against the Donatists at *Contra epistulam Parmeniani* 2.15.33 in order to demonstrate the divine origin of baptism, regardless of its human minister. The verse also features in Augustine's anti-Pelagian polemic, demonstrating that even martyrdom is a gift from God (*Sermones* 265D.6, 284.3, and 332.3; see Hombert 2000:219).

JOHN 3:29

Augustine's mental text of the middle sentence of this verse reads:

amicus autem sponsi stat et audit eum, et gaudio gaudet propter uocem sponsi.

Although there is some variety in Latin Bibles, only one offers an exact parallel for this version.[30] Augustine's form is probably due to flattening: his only examples of the Vulgate text are the initial citation of *Tractatus* 13.10 and *Enarratio* 35.9. He cites the final phrase twice: *Tractatus* 14.3 agrees with the Vulgate, while *Sermo* 293.3 has the reading *completum*, as found in Codices Veronensis and Usserianus. As the lection for this sermon on John the Baptist covered his birth, Augustine is likely to have quoted this verse from memory; there is no textual variation in his citations of John 3:30, which was a key verse in his interpretation of the relationship of the Baptist and Jesus.[31]

JOHN 3:31

In all four of his citations (*Tractatus* 14, *Sermones* 192.3.3, 292.4.8, and 293.6), Augustine has the repetition of the phrase *super/supra omnes est* at the end of the verse which is present in four Old Latin manuscripts and the Vulgate, but missing from the earliest Greek witnesses.

[30] Fischer's manuscript **Ot** (Codex Martinianus, Tours); *qui* is also missing from **Ji** and **Gi***, while a total of fourteen manuscripts add *et* (see Fischer 1991:139–40).

[31] For Augustine's various explanations of John 3:30, see Berrouard 1969:940–2; Dulaey 2006a:120–30 considers this verse in *De diuersis quaestionibus* 58, while Augustine's treatment of John the Baptist is further explored by Lienhard 2001:197–213.

JOHN 3:32–4

John 3:32–3 are only cited in *Tractatus* 14. Augustine's Vulgate exemplar included both the initial *et* and *hoc* after *audiuit*, as well as the addition of *deus* in John 3:34, absent from several Old Latin and Greek manuscripts. However, the initial citation of John 3:32 has *testificatur*, replaced by *loquitur* in the next sentence: the Vulgate form *testatur* only appears in the next paragraph.[32] All the references to John 3:33 have *testimonium eius*, which is likely to have been the word order of Augustine's codex.

JOHN 3:36

Prior to the Pelagian controversy, Augustine treated this verse as a warning against refusing to believe the Christian Gospel (*Tractatus* 14.13, *Enarrationes* 57.20, 101.s1.11). From around 412, however, he only cites it in conjunction with justifying the baptism of infants (see Berrouard 1969:945–7, Hombert 2000:534). The reading *incredulus est*, peculiar to the Vulgate and Codex Colbertinus, is found in the majority of his citations: as well as *Tractatus* 14, it features in the lectionary passage of *Sermo* 294 (dated to 413), *Sermo* 130A.7 (from 415), *De peccatorum meritis* 1.20.28, *Epistula* 193, and *Contra aduersarium legis* 1.20.41.[33] Examples of the Old Latin *non credit* appear, surprisingly, in later works: *De peccatorum meritis* 3.2.3, *Enchiridion* 10.33, *Contra Iulianum* 6.24.79, and *Contra Iulianum opus imperfectum* 4.128. All these also have *habet* or *habebit* rather than *uidebit*, as do *Sermones* 130A.7 and 294 and the first citation in *De peccatorum meritis* 1.20.28. Although this is clearly influenced by the first half of the verse, it even appears in Codices Palatinus and

[32] Other examples of variant initial citations in the *Tractatus* which are followed by sequential variants corresponding to the Vulgate can be seen at John 4:25, 6:33, 6:50, 8:30, 10:31, and 19:11.

[33] What appears to be a doublet form at *Sermo* 294.13.14 is probably a paraphrase combining the negation of the first clause (*qui credit in filium*) with the rendering *incredulus* which appears in all the other citations in this sermon.

Aureus, and it is probable that it featured in Augustine's manuscript for *Sermo* 294. Augustine does not know the poorly attested addition at the end of this verse, *et post haec traditus est Iohannis*, for which Codex Palatinus is the only Latin witness.

JOHN 4:1–2

Most of Augustine's ten references to John 4:1 are paraphrases, and it seems probable that the imperfect *baptizabat* in some citations is an adaptation, even though it is paralleled in Codex Corbeiensis. *Epistula* 265.5 reads *quod Iesus plures discipulos* ***haberet*** *et baptizaret*: although *haberet* in place of *faceret* would be an easy mistake to make, it is also found in Codex Vercellensis and Codex Sarzanensis. The presence of *baptizabat* in John 4:2 is better attested in Augustine, and appears in Codices Vercellensis, Bezae, Palatinus, and Monacensis. All biblical manuscripts render καίτοιγε by *quamquam* (apart from Codex Bezae with *et tamen*) but four of Augustine's ten citations have *quamuis*.[34] Augustine is also unique in having *ipse* without *Iesus* in seven citations. This may be flattening, as five of these follow the previous verse in which *Iesus* is named. On the other hand, the two which are not preceded by John 4:1 (*Contra litteras Petiliani* 3.55.67 and *Tractatus* 5.18) and the discussion in *De diuersis quaestionibus* 62 suggest that *Iesus* may have been missing from a codex used by Augustine. *Tractatus* 15.2 and *De consensu* 2.18.42 have the Vulgate text, as expected, which omits the Old Latin *ipse*.

JOHN 4:3

The word *terram* (γῆν) is missing from the Vulgate and the oldest Greek manuscripts: it does not feature in *De consensu* 2.18.42 (or

[34] This is the only instance of καίτοιγε in the New Testament; the reading *cum* in *Epistula* 44.10 is probably a paraphrase, as *cum* is unlikely to render such a weighty particle. *Quamuis* is found at *De unitate ecclesiae* 21.58, *Tractatus* 5.18, *De diuersis quaestionibus* 62.3, and *Retractationes* 1.26 (citing the previous work).

2.45.94), but is present in *Tractatus* 15.2 and *Epistula* 265.5 in keeping with the majority of Old Latin witnesses.

JOHN 4:6

Old Latin manuscripts are inconsistent in rendering πηγή in this verse: Codices Sarzanensis, Rehdigeranus, and Usserianus have *puteus* twice, but on the latter occasion they are joined by Codices Aureus, Brixianus, and Corbeiensis. This term is found in all Augustine's citations except *Tractatus* 15, where *fons* appears both times: the Vulgate reserves *puteus* to render τὸ φρέαρ in John 4:11, while all surviving Old Latin manuscripts have *fons* for πηγή in John 4:14, for obvious contextual reasons. La Bonnardière 1965:57–62 compares Augustine's exegesis of John 4:6–38 in *De diuersis quaestionibus* 64 and *Tractatus* 15 as an indication of chronology. For the connection between the sixth hour and six periods of biblical history, see also *Tractatus* 9.6 on John 2:6.

JOHN 4:7

This appears to be another occasion on which Augustine has altered direct speech to make it more vivid (cf. John 2:4). His earliest citation, *De diuersis quaestionibus* 64.4, adds *mulier* before *da mihi bibere.* Around fifteen years later, in *Enarratio* 68.s1.14 and *Sermo* 99.3.3, he adds *sitio* in the same position, while in *Enarratio* 61.9 these additions are combined: *sitio, mulier, da mihi bibere.* Perhaps Augustine added *mulier* by analogy with John 4:21 or even John 8:10, although its appearance in the commentary at *De diuersis quaestionibus* has the status of a primary citation. *Sitio* seems less likely to be a manuscript reading, however, but by introducing it here Augustine can draw parallels with John 19:28, a connection made explicitly in all four *Enarrationes* (34.s2.4, 61.9, 68.s1.14, 108.19). La Bonnardière 1965:58 points out Augustine's connection of the thirst motif with the food mentioned in John 4:34; he treats the Samaritan woman more generally as a figure of the faith of the nations.

JOHN 4:8–9

As noted above, there are a number of Old Latin readings in this passage at *De diuersis quaestionibus* 64. In John 4:8, *perrexerant* may be a paraphrase or an alternative not attested elsewhere for *ubierant*. The word order and form of John 4:9, *tu cum sis Iudaeus quomodo a me bibere petis cum sim mulier Samaritana?*, which occurs twice in this work, is paralleled in several Old Latin manuscripts. All three writings which cite this verse include the explanatory clause *non enim coutuntur Iudaei Samaritanis*, missing from five of the oldest Latin witnesses as well as Codex Sinaiticus (*Tractatus* 15.11, *De diuersis quaestionibus* 64, and *De trinitate* 15.19.33).

JOHN 4:10

De trinitate 15.19.33 and the commentary in *Tractatus* 15 agree with Weber–Gryson, but five other citations feature variants in this verse. Augustine's mental text appears to have *daret* rather than *dedisset*, as shown by the sequential variant in *Tractatus* 15.12, two citations in *Tractatus* 25, and *Enarratio* 1.3, but this is not present in any Latin Bible. This sequential variant also has *peteres*, found in Codices Vercellensis and Bezae; *Tractatus* 25.10 reads *postulasses* but reverts to *petisses* three lines later. In place of *qui dicit tibi da mihi bibere*, *Enarratio* 1.3 has *qui a te aquam petit*, a very early example of a paraphrase which is repeated in both citations in *Tractatus* 25. *De diuersis quaestionibus* 64.4 alone has the Old Latin *magis* rather than *forsitan*.

JOHN 4:11–12

All Latin versions render τὸ φρέαρ in John 4:11 by *puteus* (cf. John 4:6). Six Old Latin witnesses have *hauritorium* for ἄντλημα, which is found in *De diuersis quaestionibus* 64.5 and 64.8; it also occurs in the non-sequential reference to this passage at *Tractatus* 25.10. The

Vulgate paraphrase *in quo haurias* is read at *Tractatus* 15.13 and *De trinitate* 15.19.33. The citation at *De diuersis quaestionibus* 64.5 reads *unde* **mihi** *habes* **dare** *aquam uiuam?* These additional words are not found in the Greek tradition, although *dare mihi* appears after *aquam uiuam* in Codices Rehdigeranus and Sarzanensis: the parallels between these witnesses and Augustine's text in this work indicate that this may have been the reading of his codex.[35] In John 4:12, *bibet* in the *Corpus Christianorum* edition of *Tractatus* 15.14 is a typographical error for *bibit* (Verheijen 1976:4). Augustine's only other citation of this verse, *De diuersis quaestionibus* 64.5, features the Old Latin *hunc puteum.*

JOHN 4:13–14

The division of these verses in the Vulgate is slightly different to the Greek and Old Latin tradition. Augustine reads *biberit* twice in John 4:13 (*Tractatus* 15.14 and 25.10, *De diuersis quaestionibus* 64.5, and *De trinitate* 15.19.33) despite the Vulgate *bibit... biberit.* He provides examples of all three renderings of *εἰς τὸν αἰῶνα* attested in the surviving Old Latin manuscripts: most citations have *in aeternum*, but *Tractatus* 25.13 and *Enarratio* 67.35 have *umquam* (Codex Sarzanensis), and *De diuersis quaestionibus* 64.5 reads *in sempiternum* (Codices Veronensis and Usserianus). The latter also has *de aqua ista*, and *dedero* rather than *dabo* on both occasions, like Codex Monacensis.

JOHN 4:15

Although *da mihi, domine, de hac aqua*, at *Tractatus* 25.13 looks like a paraphrase, Codex Monacensis also has a prepositional phrase, *de aqua hac.*

[35] Compare also Ambrose's citations at *De Abraham* 1.9.88 and *De uirginitate* 123, which are almost identical to this text. García de la Fuente 1994:276 treats *habeo* with the infinitive in this verse as equivalent to a future tense, but there seems to be an element of ability comparable to the Greek *ἔχειν*. See also Coleman 1971 and John 16:12.

JOHN 4:17

At *De diuersis quaestionibus* 64.5, Jesus' quotation of the Samaritan woman is presented as an accusative and infinitive: *bene dixisti non habere te uirum.* This is unique to Augustine, and the presence of unparalleled examples of this construction elsewhere (e.g. John 19:21 and 21:5) suggests that he may have introduced this. All surviving manuscripts have a clause of the type *bene dixisti quia non habeo uirum*, although some read *habes* (cf. John 2:20).

JOHN 4:18

Most manuscripts and citations of John 4:18 read *nunc quem habes*, but the first and last of the three citations in *Tractatus* 15 alone have *iste quem habes.* This cannot be derived from the Greek (νῦν ὃν ἔχεις), but must be an internal Latin variation based on a misreading of *nunc* as *hunc*: the latter is preserved in Codex Palatinus. Augustine may be responsible for *iste* here, as he is fond of using it elsewhere in place of *hic* in direct speech (cf. John 6:52, 7:27, 7:49, 9:16–17, 9:29, 9:34, 10:21, 11:48, 17:6, 17:24, and 21:21). The reversion to *nunc* at *Tractatus* 15.21 is difficult to explain, however, and *nunc* is found throughout *De diuersis quaestionibus* 64. Augustine rejects the identification of the five husbands with the Pentateuch, and instead connects them with the five senses of the body (*De diuersis quaestionibus* 64.7, *Tractatus* 15.21).

JOHN 4:21–2

The addition of *et nunc est* after *uenit hora* in *Sermo* 198.11 is probably an anticipation of John 4:23. Although Augustine is careful to note the difference between the presence and absence of this phrase in John 5:25 and 5:29 respectively, he has not done so here.

His mental text of John 4:22 has *quoniam* rather than *quia* (*Tractatus* 15.26, *Epistula* 23.4, *Sermo* 199.1.1).

JOHN 4:24

For the interpolation of the words *deus spiritus est* (in that order) earlier in the Gospel, see John 3:6. In three of Augustine's seven citations of the entire verse, we find an additional *ideo*:

spiritus est deus, et **ideo** *qui adorant deum in spiritu et ueritate oportet adorare.* (*Epistula* 92.5; see also *Epistula* 238.2.14 and *Sermo* 21.2)

This is absent from surviving manuscripts: the only parallel is the appearance of *ergo* in Codex Sarzanensis. While *ideo* might be an explanatory addition by Augustine, his consistency suggests that it was found in the tradition already (cf. John 1:50). The two letters and *Sermo* 53.7.7 also feature *deum* rather than *eum*, expanding the pronoun. *Sermo* 16A.9 uniquely reads *debere* rather than *oportet*, as part of an adaptation of the verse.

JOHN 4:25

The three works which cite this verse provide three different words corresponding to ἀναγγελεῖ. *De diuersis quaestionibus* 64.8 has *adnuntiabit* which, along with *nuntiabit*, is the only rendering in the Old Latin manuscripts. The initial citation at *Tractatus* 15.27 reads *omnia nobis demonstrabit*. This seems to be an error of memory, as Augustine immediately reverts to *nobis annuntiabit omnia* in his next citation, which includes the following verse (this is not unprecedented in the *Tractatus*; cf. John 3:32 etc.). The sole instance of *demonstrare* in the Vulgate text of John is at 5:20, which could be reflected here. In *Sermo* 101.2.2, Augustine reads *et omnia nos docebit*, apparently influenced by the description of the Paraclete in John 14:26 and John 16:13. All of Augustine's citations have the future tense *ueniet*, paralleled by Codex Palatinus.

JOHN 4:27

Augustine's version of this text in *Sermo* 101.2.2, an early sermon preached in Carthage, is a paraphrase which ends *non sunt tamen ausi dicere ei quid uel quare cum illa loqueris*. This is a good example of how he might reshape direct speech, as gospel codices all have a form similar to *nemo tamen dixit quid quaeris, aut quid loqueris cum ea* (see also John 4:35).

JOHN 4:28–9

Each of Augustine's citations includes an element of speed in John 4:28, where biblical manuscripts simply read *abiit* (ἀπῆλθεν; cf. John 12:19 and 12:35). *Tractatus* 15.30 has *cucurrit*, *De diuersis quaestionibus* 64.8 has *abiit... festinans*, and *Sermo* 101.2.2 combines both, with *festinanter cucurrit*. The absence of parallels suggests that this has been added by Augustine. Some scholars believe that references to 'running' in this verse may be a characteristic of the Diatessaron, but this is quite poorly attested and unlikely to be Augustine's source.[36] The adaptation in *Sermo* 101.2.2 reads *hydriam dimisit*, similar to Codex Bezae. *Tractatus* 15, the only work which cites John 4:29, has *uenite et uidete* throughout, a variant found in some Vulgate manuscripts.

JOHN 4:32–3

The citation at *De diuersis quaestionibus* 64.4 has Old Latin readings: *escam* rather than *cibum* in John 4:32 and *ad alterutrum* in John 4:33.

[36] For the Diatessaronic evidence, see Petersen 1994:368; Boismard 1987:124–6 tendentiously claims that Augustine has preserved an original reading from the canonical Gospel. Bastiaensen 2003:23–6 identifies the phrase *currere ad ecclesiam* as characteristic of Augustine.

Both occur in Codices Rehdigeranus, Veronensis, and Usserianus, and the latter two also supply a parallel for *dicunt* rather than *dicebant* and Augustine's word order in John 4:33. *Tractatus* 15.31 has *non scitis* in place of *nescitis* in John 4:32, like several Vulgate manuscripts.

JOHN 4:34

Although most verbatim citations have *uoluntatem eius qui me misit*, at *De sermone domini* 1.2.6 Augustine reads *uoluntatem patris mei*, which is also found in the manuscript tradition of *De diuersis quaestionibus* 64.4 and *De sancta uirginitate* 28.28. Despite the presence of *patris* here in Codex Rehdigeranus (and in other Old Latin witnesses at John 5:30 and John 6:38), this is probably a conflation: the citation at *De sermone domini* 2.6.21 has the regular form of text.

JOHN 4:35

The two works apart from *Tractatus* 15 which cite this verse both give paraphrases: *Sermo* 101.2.2 reads *quia adhuc longe est aestas* rather than *quod adhuc quattuor menses sunt et messis uenit* (cf. John 4:27), while *Enarratio* 64.17 has *quia longe est messis* for this phrase and continues with *respicite* instead of *leuate oculos uestros*.

JOHN 4:36–7

Augustine's reversal of the order of these two verses in *Tractatus* 15 is without parallel: the abbreviation suggests that he may not have referred closely to a codex or it may have been damaged in some way.

JOHN 4:38

The sequential variant in *Tractatus* 15.32 has already been cited on p. 114 as an example of memory lapse in this verse, reading *seminastis* in place of *laborastis*. This citation and the two works mentioned in John 4:35 all have the plural *labores*, as do a number of biblical manuscripts, but only Codex Veronensis provides a parallel for *intrastis* rather than *introistis* in *Sermo* 101.2.2 and *Enarratio* 64.17. On Augustine's use of this verse against the Donatists, see La Bonnardière 1965:61.

JOHN 4:39–40

The commentary text of *Tractatus* 15 is Augustine's only citation of these verses, with several variants from the Vulgate. *Multi... Samaritani* rather than *multi... Samaritanorum* is unparalleled, and no manuscript reads *autem* for *ergo* in John 4:40 although this is a known alternative for οὖν elsewhere.[37] *Apud eos* (also found in Codices Veronensis, Bezae, Palatinus, and Usserianus) is a more literal translation of the Greek παρ' αὐτοῖς than *ibi* and contrasts with the use of *ibi* for ἐκεῖ later in the verse.

JOHN 4:42–3

The initial citation in *Tractatus* 15.33 adds *nos* before *audiuimus*, as does Codex Rehdigeranus. A sequential variant later in the same paragraph is clearly secondary, with *uerbum tuam* for *loquellam tuam* and *cognouimus* in place of *nos audiuimus*: neither has any Old Latin parallels. The use of *biduum* in John 4:43 does, however, recall the earlier Latin tradition.

[37] See Parker 1985.

JOHN 4:45

Berrouard 1969:818–19 draws attention to the surprising observation in Augustine's commentary that the Galilaeans did not believe in Jesus (*Tractatus* 16.3), which contradicts the text of John 4:45, *exceperunt eum Galilaei.* This is one of several verses from this passage which are not cited in any of Augustine's surviving works (namely John 4:45, 49, 51–2, and 54): the limited reference to the Gospel in *Tractatus* 16 is unusual, although there is no indication that the circumstances of its delivery were out of the ordinary.

JOHN 4:46–50

Tractatus 16.3, the only citation of these verses, has several non-Vulgate readings which may be paraphrases. The phrase *et ecce quidam regulus* in John 4:46 is intriguing: the Vulgate reads *erat* for *ecce*, which does not appear in any surviving manuscript here (unlike John 1:29). This may have been a blemish in Augustine's codex or a misreading, but it is possible that he added it for the sake of vividness. In John 4:47, Augustine reads *uenit ad eum et rogare coepit*, instead of the Vulgate *abiit ad eum et rogabat eum.* The alteration improves both the sense and the Latin, but there is no evidence that it was introduced by Augustine: *uenit* appears in a number of Old Latin manuscripts and the inchoative rendering is found in other verses (e.g. John 8:8). A sequential variant at *Tractatus* 16.5 has *puer* rather than *filius* in John 4:50: *puer* is found in Old Latin witnesses at John 4:49.

JOHN 5:2–4

The absence of parts of John 5:3b–4 from Latin and Greek manuscripts has led scholars to consider them as three interpolations (see Burkitt 1896:46–53). Although Augustine's many allusions indicate that he was familiar with the content of these verses, his treatment of their text is odd. His surviving works have no verbatim citation of any part of John 5:2 and he neither locates the pool in Bethsaida nor includes the term *probatica*: the sole exception, the title of *Sermo* 124, is likely to be due to later editors. Wright (1979:54) observes that this is unexpected because Augustine normally comments on the Hebrew names in the Bible. In the same article, he shows how Augustine refers to the pool as the *piscina Salomonis*, transferring the *porticus Salomonis* of John 10:23 to the *quinque porticus* of John 5:2, hence the reference to *quinque porticus Salomonis* at *Sermo* 272B.4.[38] Berrouard (1977:717) claims that if, like Ambrose, Augustine knew this text, he did not recognize it as Scripture.[39] Nonetheless, there is sufficient detail in Augustine's allusions to indicate his familiarity with John 5:4 in its customary form even though it is missing from four Old Latin witnesses and some Vulgate manuscripts. Indeed, Dulaey (2006b:313) considers it beyond doubt that Augustine knew the whole passage and treated it as authentic. The only verbatim citation of John 5:3 is in the commentary at *Tractatus* 17.1, which does not include the minor interpolations *paralyticorum* and *expectantium aquae motum*. As for John 5:4, although Augustine refers to the healing of one person following the movement of the water in no fewer than seven works, his three references to the presence of an angel seem to betray a lack of ease with the supernatural agency: *benedictione dei turbabatur aqua* ***tamquam*** *angelo descendente* (*Enarratio* 83.10), ***credas*** *hoc angelica uirtute fieri solere* (*Tractatus* 17.3), and *homines aquam uidebant sed ex motu aquae turbatae* ***intelligebant*** *praesentiam angeli* (*Sermo* 125.3). As Augustine refers frequently to angels elsewhere (including his references to John 1:51, 12:29, and 20:12), this reticence is mysterious: Dulaey (2006b:313) suggests that his intention is to discourage popular superstition attached to

[38] This identification is also made in a number of lists of *capitula* or pericope titles in the Vulgate and Old Latin tradition, the exact origin of which remains unclear (Wright 1979:55). Instances in other Church Fathers are listed at Dulaey 2006b:308 and 319.

[39] He concludes that Augustine was familiar with the first half of the verse, perhaps as a marginal gloss, but not the final phrase; he suggests that its absence from Greek manuscripts might be the reason for Augustine's hesitancy (Berrouard 1977:719), but Augustine makes no observation to this effect as he does for the *Pericope Adulterae*.

particular pools. She goes on to discuss Augustine's exegesis, which treats the descent of the angel and the stirring of the waters as a figure of the Incarnation and Passion: although the identification of the five porches with the Jewish Pentateuch is found in earlier authors, there is much about Augustine's explanation which appears to be original and proved influential in later treatments.[40]

JOHN 5:5

Although all Augustine's citations are abbreviated, none has the pronominal adjective *sua* at the end of the verse, not even *Tractatus* 17 or *De consensu* 2.45.94: this is missing from some Old Latin and Greek witnesses, but is usually present in the Vulgate.

JOHN 5:7

Both verbatim citations (*Enarratio* 132.6 and *Sermo* 125.3), supported by the adaptation at *De consensu* 2.45.94, make it clear that Augustine read *deponat* for *βάλῃ* rather than *mittat*, even though *deponat* is not attested in any surviving manuscript. Only the reported speech at *Tractatus* 17.7 features *mittere*. These two citations also have *mota*, with several Old Latin witnesses, rather than *turbata* as found in Vulgate-related manuscripts and Codex Palatinus. *Sermo* 125 is a lectionary sermon, drawn from a codex, although its form of the final clause at *Sermo* 125.3, *cum enim uenio descendit alius*, is without parallel in the Old Latin tradition for the reading *cum* and omission of *ante me*. Nonetheless, Augustine's immediate comment, *ergo tu non potes postea descendere, si alter* **ante te** *descendat?* supplies the missing words, as well as hinting at the reading *alter* preserved in Codices Vercellensis and Veronensis.

[40] Dulaey 2006b:314–20. The exegesis of this passage is also considered at Comeau 1930:148–50 and Berrouard 1977:77–8.

JOHN 5:8

Outside the primary citations (*Tractatus* 17, *Sermo* 125A), Augustine conflates John 5:8 with Mark 2:11, reading *tolle grabatum tuum et uade in domum tuam* (*Tractatus* 20.2 (twice) and 21.6, *Sermo* 125.10). This text is identical to Mark 2:11, but Augustine shows by the context that he is referring to this passage of John.[41]

JOHN 5:10–11

These verses are only cited in *Tractatus* 17. The insertion of *facere quod facis* after *non licet tibi* has no parallel outside Augustine, and may be an explanatory gloss. The pronoun *ipse* in place of *ille* in John 5:11 is an Old Latin reading in an otherwise Vulgate text.

JOHN 5:13–16

See the analysis of the text of these verses in *Tractatus* 17 on pp. 117–18. The only verse which appears in other works is John 5:14, in which Augustine has the Old Latin form *ne quid tibi deterius contingat* in all five citations, including *Tractatus* 17.11.

JOHN 5:17–18

Half of Augustine's twenty-six citations of John 5:17 read *usque nunc* instead of *usque modo*: this is an Old Latin reading preserved only in Codex Vercellensis, but cited by Augustine as late as *De ciuitate dei*

[41] Dulaey 2006b:327 notes the appearance of the synoptic formula in several other Church Fathers, but does not include Augustine.

22.24.2. *Usque modo* is the only form found in works for which Augustine used a biblical codex: *Tractatus* 17 (and 20), *De consensu* 4.10.13 (twice) and the lectionary *Sermo* 125A. Both forms appear in *Sermo* 125, which also has a paraphrased version of John 5:18, although *uolebant* rather than *quaerebant* is present in Tertullian (*Aduersus Praxean* 21) and Ambrose (*De fide* 2.8.67) (cf. John 7:30, 8:40). *Tractatus* 18 and 20 have the Old Latin *sed etiam* in John 5:18, in contrast to *sed et* in *Tractatus* 17 and *De consensu* 4.10.13. The different exegesis of John 5:17 offered in *Tractatus* 20 supports the observation of Wright (1964:328) that it was not part of the original sequence.

JOHN 5:19

Almost all Augustine's citations of this verse follow his mental text:

quaecumque pater facit, haec eadem et filius facit similiter.

The omission of *enim* and the replacement of *ille* by the noun *pater* are typical of flattening, although the latter also appears in Codices Palatinus and Sarzanensis. The initial *facit* and word order *facit similiter* are paralleled in Old Latin manuscripts as well. Augustine is unique, however, in reading *haec eadem* where biblical witnesses have either one or the other to render ταῦτα (*eadem* derives from reading this as ταὔτα). This seems likely to be a combination of both forms, perhaps for emphasis: the initial citation of the lectionary *Sermo* 126 has *eadem* by itself, while *Tractatus* 19 and the late works *Contra Maximinum* 2 and *Sermo de symbolo* 2.5 just have *haec*. Augustine reverts to *eadem* for a single reference at *Tractatus* 18.8, after reading *haec* in the initial citation. Even so, the two later commentaries on this verse, *Tractatus* 20 and 21, have *haec eadem*, possibly from memory. A secondary citation at *Sermo* 135.2.3 replaces *quaecumque* by *omnia quae* (cf. John 15:15 and 16:15). Both Berrouard and La Bonnardière have extended commentaries on Augustine's exegesis of John 5:19 and the following verses. Berrouard shows that in the earlier sermons, Augustine highlights the final words, *nisi quod uiderit*, while in later writings he emphasizes the verb *poterit.*[42] La Bonnardière (1965:104–18) suggests that the use of John 5:19 to demonstrate the inseparability of the Trinity is a late development in Augustine's thought.

JOHN 5:21–2

The omission of the connective *enim* in many citations of both these verses is due to flattening, which has also led to the recasting of John 5:22 as *pater non iudicat* rather than *neque enim pater iudicat.* Although the word order *omne iudicium* in Augustine's mental text is not paralleled in any surviving Old Latin manuscript, it is shared by Ambrose and Tertullian. *Neminem* (for *non quemquam*) in this verse is peculiar to Augustine's Arian opponents (*Contra sermonem Arrianorum* 11.9 and *Collatio cum Maximino* 18).[43] For a discussion of Augustine's christological use of John 5:21 in conjunction with Philippians 2:6, see La Bonnardière 1965:136. He reconciles the apparent contradiction between John 5:22 and John 8:50 by referring to different senses of the word *iudicium* (*Tractatus* 43.4–9; Berrouard 1988:522–3).

JOHN 5:24

Despite the rendering of μεταβέβηκεν in John 5:24 by a form of *transire* in all biblical manuscripts, Augustine has *transitum facere* in ten citations. The preference for a synthetic form with a general-purpose verb is typical of developments in later Latin. *Sermo*

[42] Berrouard 1971:148 ff.; compare also his notes on this verse at Berrouard 1977:729–31, 738–41, 751–3, and 761–71. He suggests that Augustine may owe the unusual combination of John 5:19 and Matthew 14:25 to Ambrose, although the sense is sometimes different (1971:138). The change in exegesis also justifies the separation of *Tractatus* 20–2 from the rest of the sequence; see further Wright 1964 and 1972:80 ff.

[43] See pp. 169 and 176; the sole other example of *neminem* in the *Vetus Latina Database* occurs in the pseudo-Ambrosian *De Paenitentia* by Victor of Cartenna.

362.22.25, in which Augustine explicitly read from a codex, confirms that *transitum fecit* appeared in a version with a Vulgate text-type in the rest of the passage; Augustine reverts to *transiit* in two sequential variants. Although the Greek perfect appears to be invariant, Latin manuscripts variously have this verb in the future, present, and perfect tenses. The last is most common in Augustine, but he has the present in *Tractatus* 22 (sequential variants with *transitum facit* and *transit*), *Enarratio* 114.7, *Epistula* 55.2, and *Sermones* 127.4.4 and 155.5.5, and even reads *transiet* at *De trinitate* 1.13.30, also found in certain manuscripts of *Epistula* 55 and *De ciuitate dei* 20.5–6.[44] At the end of the verse, the future *ueniet* is also part of Augustine's mental text. Six sequential variants in *Tractatus* 22 have the plural *uerba mea*: this does not feature in biblical manuscripts and is probably a reminiscence of John 12:47.[45] For a summary of Augustine's teaching on the two resurrections based on this and the following verse, see Berrouard 1977:742–5.

JOHN 5:25

Codices Vercellensis and Bezae have *cum* rather than *quando* which occurs in three citations: *De trinitate* 1.13.30 and *Contra Faustum* 17.4 are both early, while the non-sequential citation at *De ciuitate dei* 20.9.4 is much later. Augustine has the Vulgate form throughout *De ciuitate dei* 20.6, as well as John 5:25–7 at *Contra Faustum* 5.4 (discussed on p. 150). As in John 5:28, his citations are split between *uenit hora*, the reading of his codex for *Tractatus* 19, 23 and *Sermo* 362, and *ueniet hora*, which was in his exemplar for *Sermo* 127 and *De trinitate* 1.

[44] *Transitum faciet* is used by Fortunatus the Manichee at *Contra Fortunatum* 3.

[45] Both Tertullian's citations of John 5:24 have a plural, *sermones meos* (*Aduersus Praxean* 21, *De resurrectione mortuorum* 37; see Roensch 1871:262), while Ambrose alone has a singular in John 12:47, *si quis audierit sermonem meum* (*De paenitentia* 1.12.54).

JOHN 5:26

Augustine's mental text of this verse begins with the word order *sicut habet pater*, unparalleled in biblical manuscripts, and usually omits *et* from the phrase *sic dedit filio habere uitam*. The sequential treatment of this verse at *De trinitate* 1.12.26 and 1.13.30 has *ita* in place of *sic*: this rendering of οὕτως is not found here in surviving manuscripts (cf. John 12:50), but is paralleled by Tertullian (*Aduersus Praxean* 21) and Ambrose (*De fide* 5.36). At *De trinitate* 1.11.22 and 2.1.3, however, Augustine reads *sic*.

JOHN 5:27

The gerund *iudicium faciendi* is only attested in Codices Brixianus and Monacensis, but appears in four sequential variants in *Tractatus* 22, as well as *Enarrationes* 48.s1.5 and 74.5. Sixteen of Augustine's citations have *quoniam*, as opposed to fourteen with *quia*: the former occurs in four Old Latin manuscripts (Codices Veronensis, Bezae, Brixianus, and Usserianus), and is the only form found in the lectionary *Sermo* 127.[46]

JOHN 5:28

As in John 5:25, Augustine corresponds to a handful of Old Latin manuscripts with *ueniet hora*. In contrast, the reading *quando* in thirteen citations of John 5:28 has no support from Latin Bibles: all prefer *in qua*, parallel to the Greek ἐν ᾗ. It is probable that this was transferred into Augustine's mental text from John 5:25, where *quando* renders the Greek ὅτε. On the other hand, the lectionary

[46] Berrouard 1977:205 provides more examples and parallels for Augustine's text in this verse, and discusses his exegesis at 1977:746 ff.

Sermo 127 twice has *quando* (with a sequential variant of *ut*), which suggests that it may have appeared in a version now lost. The singular *in monumento* in the citation from a codex at *Sermo* 362.22.25 matches Codex Monacensis.

JOHN 5:29

Although a number of his later citations follow the Vulgate, *qui bona fecerunt... qui mala egerunt*, Augustine's mental text of this verse has two adverbs, *bene* and *male*. The latter is attested in five Old Latin witnesses, but the former is unique to Augustine. The parallelism already present in the verse is enhanced by Latin translations which repeat the same verb despite the variation in the Greek (*ποιήσαντες . . . πράξαντες*). This is also a feature of Augustine's citations: *fecerunt* appears twice in *De consensu* 2.30.71, *Tractatus* 22.13, and *Sermones* 154.11.16 and 223C.1, while he reads *egerunt* at *De fide et operibus* 23.43 and *Sermones* 127.11.15 and 306.5.5. The value of *De trinitate* 1 as a source of Old Latin readings is demonstrated by a form of text unique among Augustine's citations:

et ***prodient*** *qui bona* ***gesserunt*** *in resurrectionem uitae, qui mala* ***gesserunt*** *in resurrectionem iudicii.* (*De trinitate* 1.13.30)

These three verbs are found only in Codices Monacensis, Rehdigeranus, and Usserianus. Eleven citations, including the lectionary *Sermo* 127.11.15 and the late *Contra Iulianum opus imperfectum* 6.36, mark the contrast between the phrases with *autem*; this is paralleled by a number of Old Latin manuscripts. The Vulgate and related manuscripts have *uero*, as do seven of Augustine's citations (four of which come from the codex in *Sermo* 362). The majority of his citations, however, including all three commentary sermons in the *Tractatus in Iohannem* and *De consensu* 2.30.71, have no particle here, so it may have been missing from one of his Vulgate exemplars: it is also absent from the Greek Codex Vaticanus and erased by a corrector of P^{66}.

JOHN 5:30

The two sequential variants in *Tractatus* 22 which add *ita* are paralleled by Codices Veronensis and Usserianus with *sicut audio ita et iudico.* The rendering of δικαία by *uerum* rather than *iustum* is only present in the *Sermo Arrianorum*, which is quoted at *Contra sermonem Arrianorum* 11.9. This may anticipate *uerum* in the next two verses (compare also Augustine's citations of John 7:24 and 8:16). The Arian use of this verse to demonstrate the subordination of the Son led Augustine to a revised interpretation of this text in later works.

JOHN 5:33

The reading *uenistis* in place of *misistis* in *Sermo* 128.1.2 appears to be an error, despite forming part of the lectionary passage for this sermon.

JOHN 5:35

Every Old Latin manuscript translates ὑμεῖς δέ by *uos autem* (except Codex Veronensis, with *uos uero*; cf. John 5:29). Seven of Augustine's nine citations have *et uos*, including the lectionary *Sermo* 128.1.2 and *Sermones* 293D and 341 which may also have followed this passage: this is strong evidence for its featuring in a version now lost, corroborated by Jerome, Rufinus, and Hilary of Poitiers. Augustine's two exceptions are *Sermo* 342.1, with *et* but not *uos*, and *Enarratio* 118.s23.1, which reads *nos autem uoluistis exsultare ad hora in luce eius.*[47] The only other citation with *luce* is *Sermo* 341.18; his other references all have the Old Latin *lumine.*

[47] *Nos* seems to be a typographical error for *uos*, although it is grammatically possible.

JOHN 5:36–8

Sermo 308A.1 alone has the Old Latin *maius quam Iohannem* in John 5:36, although in its final paragraph it also has *maius Iohanne.* The abbreviated citation of the next verse in *Tractatus* 23.2 has the present tense *perhibet* rather than the Vulgate perfect. The only citations of the second half of John 5:37 are both in *Contra Adimantum* 9, and are similar in form:

nec uocem illius aliquando audistis, nec faciem eius uidistis.
nec uocem aliquando eius audistis . . . nec faciem eius uidistis.

No surviving Old Latin manuscript has *nec, aliquando,* or *faciem,* preferring *neque, umquam,* and *figuram* or *speciem.* Nonetheless, as these are possible renderings of the Greek οὔτε, πώποτε, and εἶδος, it seems likely that Augustine is citing a lost version, perhaps influenced by the form used by Adimantus (see pp. 144–5). This citation also has a unique text of John 5:38 with similar characteristics: *nec uerbum eius habetis in uobis manens, quia ei quem ille misit non credidistis.*

JOHN 5:39

All Augustine's citations have a relative clause, reading *scrutamini scripturas in quibus putatis uos* on eight occasions. The commentary text of *Tractatus* 23.2 has *scrutamini scripturam in qua uos putatis,* even though there is no instance of the singular here in Latin Bibles. Likewise, every citation of the following clause has *ipsae* (*ipsa* in *Tractatus* 23) rather than the Vulgate *illae.* Codex Aureus is the only manuscript with both a relative clause and *ipsae,* and it also parallels the word order *putatis uos.* There is a sequential variant in *Sermo* 129, which reads *uos speratis*: this is likely to be an anticipation of John 5:45, also part of the lectionary passage, although it is cited in this verse by Tertullian (*De praescriptione haereticorum* 8).

JOHN 5:43

Augustine's mental text of John 5:43 reads:

ego ueni in nomine patris mei et non suscepistis me. alius ueniet in nomine suo: hunc suscipietis.

This form (or similar) appears in four of Augustine's six citations of the verse (*Tractatus* 29.8 and 51.3, *Enarratio* 105.37, and *Sermo* 129.6.7), and includes several unique readings: no surviving manuscript has *suscepistis* ... *suscipietis* for λαμβάνετε ... λήμψεσθε or *alius ueniet* in place of *si alius uenerit*, while *hunc* is paralleled in Codex Palatinus. *Enarratio* 117.21 and the initial citation in the lectionary *Sermo* 129.1.1, which are probably Augustine's earliest citations (see La Bonnardière 1965:149), both have the reading of the majority of Old Latin codices, including *accepistis* ... *accipietis*. The consistent variant readings in his customary form were possibly also present in a manuscript known to Augustine.

JOHN 5:44

Only the Vulgate-influenced *Speculum* 28 has *qui* ... *accipitis* and *quaeritis* for λαμβάνοντες and ζητεῖτε in this verse. All five of Augustine's other citations have a double participle:

gloriam ab inuicem ***expectantes*** *et gloriam quae a deo solo est non* ***quaerentes***.

Codices Rehdigeranus and Palatinus have *quaerentes* at the end of the verse, but *expectantes* is unparalleled.[48] As it occurs three times in the lectionary *Sermo* 129, including a slip when Augustine says *quaerentes* but immediately corrects himself to *expectantes* (*Sermo* 129.2.2, quoted on pp. 37–8), it seems highly likely that this appeared in his exemplar. This sermon also twice reads *quomodo potestis* **mihi** *credere*

[48] The first hand of Codex Sinaiticus as well as several minuscules and Greek Fathers wrote the participle ζητοῦντες, which corresponds to *quaerentes*.

rather than *quomodo potestis* **uos** *credere*: again, given these are primary citations, *mihi* may derive from a manuscript although it could anticipate John 5:46.

JOHN 5:45

The lectionary *Sermo* 129 has yet another unusual form of text:

non ego uos accuso apud patrem: est qui uos accusat, Moyses, in quem uos speratis.

This is Augustine's only citation of this verse, and although the opening appears to be a paraphrase of *nolite putare quia ego accusaturus sim uos apud patrem*, the present tense *accuso* is found in three Old Latin manuscripts. In the second half, *accusat* appears in some Vulgate witnesses, and *in quem* is the regular Old Latin reading.

JOHN 5:46

Augustine's mental text of John 5:46 typically omits the first *enim*, reading *si crederitis Moysi, crederitis et mihi* on twenty-five occasions. The Vulgate and majority of Old Latin manuscripts have *forsitan* before *et mihi*, although it is absent from Codices Palatinus, Vercellensis, and Monacensis. It only features twice in Augustine: the initial citation in *Sermo* 129.1.1, and the early *De diuersis quaestionibus* 64.6 (cf. John 8:19, where *forsitan* is missing from later citations in *Tractatus* 37). Codex Bezae has *utique* in this position, which is found in a non-sequential citation at *Tractatus* 30.6. Five early citations have the word order *ille enim de me scripsit* at the end of the verse (*Contra Faustum* 16.22 (twice), *De diuersis quaestionibus* 64.6, *Quaestiones euangeliorum* 2.38.4, and *Sermo* 1.2). This is not paralleled in surviving manuscripts.

JOHN 5:47

As with John 5:45, the only citation of this verse appears in *Sermo* 129.1.1:

cum autem uerbis illius non creditis quomodo potestis mihi credere.

This has elements of paraphrase, such as *mihi* for *meis uerbis* and *potestis credere* for *credetis* (cf. John 3:3), which may cast doubt on Augustine's accuracy: there are similarities with the form of John 5:44 in this sermon.

JOHN 6:1–5

These verses are not expounded in the *Tractatus.* Augustine makes two verbatim citations of John 6:5. *De consensu* 2.46.95 is basically Vulgate, with the distinctive reading *subleuasset* and the ending:

dicit ad Philippum 'unde ememus panes ut manducent hi?'

Sermo 2.2 precedes an accurate citation of John 6:6 with:

ait inquit *Philippo 'habetis panes, date illis manducare.'*

There is no support for this text in any manuscript of John. Instead it appears to be a clear example of conflation, as all three Synoptic accounts of the Feeding of the Five Thousand include the response *date illis manducare* (Matthew 14:16, Mark 6:37, Luke 9:13).[49]

JOHN 6:6

Augustine twice replaces the connective *enim*: Codices Bezae and Corbeiensis have *autem*, like *Sermo* 71.10.15, but there is no parallel for *nam* at *De sermone domini* 2.9.31.

[49] *Sermo* 2 is dated to 404/5 in Gryson 2007. In Frede 1995, however, it was assigned to 391 which would make it one of Augustine's earliest preserved sermons, and perhaps indicative of his lack of familiarity with the Bible in this period (cf. *Epistula* 21.3).

JOHN 6:9–11

These three verses are only cited verbatim in *De consensu* 2.46.95, where they are identical to the Vulgate, and in *Tractatus* 24.4: the readings in the latter, which seem to betray alterations internal to the Latin text, are discussed on p. 119. As noted there, the omission of *hordeacei* from the initial citation in *Tractatus* 24 appears to be an oversight, as it appears in the commentary: Augustine applies this word to the Old Testament, in opposition to *triticei*, perhaps mindful of the use of *hordeaceus* at 2 Kings (IV Regum) 4:42 or the Old Latin version of Judges 5:8 (cited at *Quaestiones de Iudicibus* 29). While he takes the five loaves and the five thousand as indicative of the Law of Moses and the Jewish people in keeping with his usual exegesis of this number, he offers several different interpretations of the two fish in *Sermo* 130.1.

JOHN 6:15–24

John 6:15–18 are cited at *De consensu* 2.47.100 in a form identical to Weber–Gryson, but *Tractatus* 25 again features a number of variants, some similar to the previous group of verses. Although the purpose clause *ut raperent* in John 6:15 is characteristic of the Vulgate and related manuscripts, no version reads *uenerant*: the pluperfect does not correspond to the Greek μέλλουσιν ἔρχεσθαι and is likely to be an internal alteration (cf. John 15:15 in *Tractatus* 17). It is impossible to say whether the omission of *alia* is deliberate or not: it is technically redundant, but is found in all gospel codices in John 6:22. Other forms are paralleled in Old Latin witnesses: *nauiculam* in John 6:17, *eum accipere*, *in nauim* and *in quam* in John 6:21, the omission of *Iesus* from John 6:22, and the plural *uidissent turbae* and *in nauiculas* in John 6:24. As Berrouard (1977:437) notes, *tunc ad eos uenit Iesus* at the end of John 6:19 in *Tractatus* 25.6 is a borrowing inspired by Matthew 14:25 or Mark 6:48.

JOHN 6:26

Tractatus 25.10 uniquely has the reading *manducastis ex panibus meis.* Although *meis* is not present in any biblical witness, it also features in one manuscript of *De consensu* 4.10.15. It is possible that this is a reminiscence of *panem meum* at John 13:18 in Codex Monacensis, or Psalm 40:10 which Augustine cites with *panes meos* at *De ciuitate dei* 17.18.1. *De consensu* 4.10.15 has several non-Vulgate readings, which suggest that Augustine may have been quoting from memory: the word order *signa uidistis* is only found in Codex Palatinus, one of two Old Latin witnesses with *satiati* for *saturati*, while no surviving manuscript has *edistis de panibus* in place of *manducastis ex panibus.*

JOHN 6:27

Augustine's mental text of this verse begins *operamini escam quae non corrumpitur*, as found in seven citations including three early works: *De Genesi contra Manichaeos* 2.9.12, *De sermone domini* 2.7.26–7, and *Enarratio* 5.15. The Vulgate version appears at *De consensu* 4.10.15 and the initial citation of *Tractatus* 25; seven subsequent sequential variants have the word order *cibum non qui perit*, while one reverts to *escam.* The lectionary *Sermo* 130A (*Dolbeau* 19) reads *operamini escam quae non perit*, comparable to most Old Latin witnesses apart from the position of *non* which is unique to Augustine. No surviving manuscript has *corrumpitur*, even though the passive is a more literal rendering of τὴν ἀπολλυμένην. It seems likely that this was present in a version no longer preserved. Augustine only cites the final part of the verse (*hunc enim pater signauit deus*) in his commentary, where he explains *signauit* as a reference to anointing and illustrates it with Psalm 44:8 (*Tractatus* 25.11).

JOHN 6:28–9

Both Augustine's citations of John 6:28 outside *Tractatus* 25, *Sermo* 130A.2 (*Dolbeau* 19) and *De praedestinatione sanctorum* 7.12, have the singular, *opus dei.* This may simply be an anticipation of the next verse. The initial citation of John 6:29 in *Sermo* 130A ends *ut credatis in illum quem ille misit.* Augustine later reverts to *eum,* although *ille misit* is clearly his mental text in other works. His exploration based on this verse of the differences between *credere deo, credere deum,* and *credere in deo* was widely adopted in later exegesis.[50] Augustine resolves the difficult question of the relationship between faith and works by emphasizing the complement in *opus dei* in order to describe faith as a divine work which crowns human endeavour (references at Berrouard 1977:791–3).

JOHN 6:31

The phrase *dedit illis manna manducare* rather than *panem de caelo dedit eis manducare* in Augustine's only citation, *Tractatus* 25.12, seems to be a paraphrase: Augustine includes the words *panem de caelo* in his subsequent comment, so they probably appeared in the manuscript in front of him.

JOHN 6:32–3

At *Tractatus* 25.13, Augustine has an unusual division of these two verses, reading:

. . . sed pater meus dedit uobis panem de caelo. uerus enim panis est qui de caelo descendit.

[50] See Hombert 2000:527–40. The discussion at Berrouard 1977:842–5 precedes the discovery of *Sermo* 130A.

Most Latin Gospels have the accusative, *uerum*, describing *panem*, and begin the next verse with *panis enim*, like the Greek. Codex Aureus has a partial parallel, reading *uerus panis enim dei*, but Augustine's form with *enim* in second position is more natural. The phrase following the citation, *uerus ergo ille panis est qui dat uitam mundo*, reflects the form of text just given. However, seven lines later Augustine reverts to a text much closer to the Vulgate:

pater meus dat uobis panem uerum. panis enim dei est qui descendit de caelo.

Although the appearance of a Vulgate form after the initial citation is not unparalleled (e.g. John 3:32 etc.), the origin of the earlier version is a mystery, particularly as it appears in the context of a four-line citation which Augustine might be expected to have drawn from his codex.

JOHN 6:35–7

The variants *uenit* for *ueniet* in John 6:35 and *credidistis* for *creditis* in John 6:36 are both paralleled in Vulgate as well as Old Latin witnesses, and so may derive from the manuscript used for *Tractatus* 25. In John 6:37, *qui uenerit* in the initial citation is matched by Codex Palatinus, although in all sequential variants Augustine has *ueniet* as found in some Vulgate witnesses.

JOHN 6:38

Augustine uses this and the preceding verse to develop his doctrine of Christ's humility (see Comeau 1930:323 and *Tractatus* 25.15 ff.). His customary form, *non ueni facere*, is a paraphrase of the words *descendi de caelo non ut faciam*: this reading can be seen as early as *Enarratio* 9.3 and *Expositio epistolae ad Galatas* 3.5, and it appears throughout his commentary apart from the initial citation at *Tractatus* 25.15. Nonetheless, this is also found in numerous other Fathers, including Tertullian (*De resurrectione mortuorum* 34) and Hilary of

Poitiers (*Explanationes Psalmorum* 68.9, 91.6, 139.2 and *De trinitate* 3.9). This exemplifies how the same processes of flattening may be applied by different authors; for a similar paraphrase in Augustine, see John 3:17. All verbatim citations outside the *Tractatus* have the Old Latin word order *me misit*.

JOHN 6:39

Tractatus 25 reads *resuscitabo* instead of *resuscitem* throughout: although matched by Codex Vercellensis, the future tense in Augustine may be an anticipation of the next verse. The latter is true of the pronoun *eum* in a sequential variant: *illud* in the initial citation is present in some Vulgate manuscripts. The form *pereant* rather than *perdam* in *Sermo* 170.10.10 is part of a paraphrase.

JOHN 6:40

Sermo 14A (*Dolbeau* 20) has the future perfects *uiderit* and *crediderit*, paralleled only in Codex Palatinus, as well as the unique *suscitabo* rather than *resuscitabo* and the omission of *omnis*: the consistent text of this lectionary sermon is likely to reflect Augustine's exemplar. In *Sermo* 170, the plurals *habeant* and *eos* are an adaptation.

JOHN 6:42–3

The changes of word order (*hic dicit, descendi de caelo*) in *Tractatus* 26 are paralleled elsewhere, but Augustine alone has *dixerunt* at the beginning of John 6:42. His three citations of the next verse are all different. The initial citation at *Tractatus* 26.2 has *nolite murmurare ad inuicem*, the same as the first hand of Codex Aureus. Later this appears as *quid murmuratis in inuicem?* (*Tractatus* 26.11), an invention of Augustine. At *De praedestinatione sanctorum* 8.13, he reads *nolite murmurare inuicem* as found in three Old Latin and some Vulgate witnesses.

JOHN 6:44

Augustine's mental text of this verse shows numerous indications of flattening. The potential *potest uenire* has become a simple present (cf. John 3:5, 6:65), the original relative clause is omitted, and the focus is kept on the initial *nemo*:

nemo uenit ad me nisi quem pater adtraxerit.

The compound verb *adtraxerit* occurs in the majority of Old Latin witnesses. Evodius (*Epistula* 160.4 in Augustine's corpus) and Petilianus (*Contra litteras Petiliani* 2.84.185) cite the verse in an identical form, while two of Ambrose's citations also begin *nemo uenit ad me* (*De fide* 5.149, *Expositio euangelii secundum Lucam* 8.9). It is likely that these are further examples of similar alterations made independently (cf. John 6:38). Augustine expounds this verse referring to Vergil's *trahit sua quemquam uoluptas* (*Eclogae* 2.65) at *Tractatus* 26.4. In later treatments, such as *Sermo* 131.2.2, he gives greater emphasis to the verb *adtraxerit* as an indication of God's initiative (Berrouard 1977:806–9).

JOHN 6:45

Nine of Augustine's sixteen citations have the ablative *deo*, including the early *De sermone domini* 2.6.20 and 2.10.37 and later works such as *Enarratio* 118.s32.3. All Old Latin witnesses read *docibiles dei*, a Graecism corresponding to διδακτοὶ θεοῦ (cf. John 1:50 and 14:12). Jerome's version of Isaiah 54:13 has an ablative, *doctos a domino*, but this is sufficiently far from the gospel text to be unlikely to have influenced Augustine. It is more probable that the ablative *deo* was present in a Latin version no longer extant. *Epistula* 193.4.13 (quoted at *De quaestionibus Dulcitii* 3.6) reads *dociles*, also unique to Augustine. He uses the choice of *uenit* rather than *potest uenire* in this verse as an argument against Pelagianism (*De gratia Christi* 1.14.15; see Berrouard 1977:501).

JOHN 6:46

The form *sed qui est a deo*, appearing from memory in a sequential variant at *Tractatus* 26.9 and two citations in *Contra Maximinum* 1.3, is a flattened version of the biblical *nisi is qui est a deo*, with no parallels elsewhere.

JOHN 6:49

This is the first occurrence of *eremo* in Augustine which finds a parallel in an Old Latin manuscript, Codex Usserianus (cf. John 1:23, 3:14). It only features in one sermon, *Sermo* 352.3 (delivered outside Hippo in 404), whose word order, *manducauerunt manna in eremo*, is closer to Codex Monacensis. *Epistula* 186.8.28 and *Contra aduersarium legis* 2.5.18 follow the same sequence (with *deserto*). The reading *parentes* rather than *patres* in Augustine's citation of his opponent at *Contra aduersarium legis* 2.5.17 is not present in any Latin Bible, and Augustine subsequently reverts to the usual term.

JOHN 6:50

The participle *descendens*, peculiar to the Vulgate and Codex Colbertinus, corresponds to the Greek. Augustine usually has the Old Latin relative clause, *qui de caelo descendit*, which appears in the initial citation at *Tractatus* 26.12, but reads *descendens* later in this paragraph, implying that his initial citation was from memory (cf. John 3:32 etc.). The word order *manducauerit ex ipso*, however, occurs throughout Augustine's commentary. The only other citation with *descendens* is *Epistula* 186.8.28, composed a few years later.

JOHN 6:51 (6:51–2 IN THE VULGATE)

The Vulgate numeration splits John 6:51 into two verses, resulting in a discrepancy with the standard Greek and Old Latin editions which are followed in this study. In the first half of the verse, Augustine agrees with the majority of Latin Gospels, reading *ego sum panis uiuus*. The sole exception, *ego sum panis uitae* at *De sermone domini* 2.7.25, corresponds to Codex Vercellensis. In the second part, beginning *si quis manducauerit* (John 6:52 in the Vulgate), Augustine has two Old Latin readings in comparatively late works. *De ciuitate dei* 17.5.5, *De peccatorum meritis* 1.20.27 and 1.24.34, and *Sermo* 228B.3 all read *saeculi* for *mundi* (found in Codices Palatinus and Monacensis) and *dedero* for *dabo*, in which they are joined by *Contra Maximinum* 2.17.2 and Codices Palatinus, Veronensis, and Usserianus.

JOHN 6:52 (6:53 IN THE VULGATE)

Although the gerund characteristic of the Vulgate, *dare ad manducandum*, appears in *Tractatus* 26, the Old Latin reading *dare manducare* features in *Enarrationes* 33.s1 and 33.s2. The latter also uniquely reads *iste poterit* rather than *potest hic*, which is perhaps another example of Augustine's preference for this pronoun (cf. John 4:18 etc.).

JOHN 6:53 (6:54 IN THE VULGATE)

Augustine's mental text of this verse has been subject to flattening, including conflation with John 6:51, 54, 56, and similar verses: in place of *nisi manducaueritis* he reads *nisi quis manducauerit*, while *carnem filii hominis* has become *carnem meam*. The latter is also found in Evodius *De fide contra Manichaeos* 37 (probably borrowed from *Contra Faustum* 12.8; cf. John 19:34) and Ambrose (*De paradiso* 9.42, *Explanatio Psalmi* 43.37.2), who in addition reads *nisi qui manducauerit* in *De sacramentis* 6.2. All Augustine's citations, including the commentary at *Tractatus* 26.15, prefer the Old Latin future *habebitis* (or *habebit*) to *habetis*, unique to the Vulgate.

JOHN 6:55 (6:56 IN THE VULGATE)

The lectionary *Sermo* 132, both in the title and body of the sermon, reads:

caro mea uere esca est et sanguis meus uere potus est.

Despite the late date assigned to this sermon (*c.*420) there are clear parallels with the Old Latin tradition, especially Codex Vercellensis, which alone has the word order *esca est* and *potus est*. *Enarratio* 33.s1.8 is identical to this manuscript, while *Enarratio* 135.9 and *Sermo* 131.1.1 also have *esca*, and *Contra aduersarium legis* 1.24.52 shares this word order: only *Tractatus* 26 corresponds to the Vulgate.

JOHN 6:56 (6:57 IN THE VULGATE)

Augustine does not provide any evidence for the interpolated form of this verse referring to the body of Christ, found in Codices Vercellensis, Bezae, and Corbeiensis (cf. p. 94). If it had been present in his codex for *Sermo* 132, it seems likely that he would have mentioned it in this sermon to catechumens on how to receive communion. The Old Latin word order *carnem meam... sanguinem meum* is found in five of Augustine's six citations: *Tractatus* 26 has *carnem meam* but *meum sanguinem*.

JOHN 6:59–60 (6:60–1 IN THE VULGATE)

Sabbato is missing from the citation of John 6:59 at *De correptione et gratia* 22 and this verse is not cited in the commentary at *Tractatus* 27: its inclusion in the title of this sermon is likely to be the work of a later editor using a version of the Vulgate.[51] In the next verse, *Tractatus* 27.2 uniquely has *itaque* in place of *ergo*, which may have appeared in Augustine's codex. Four citations, including two from the lectionary *Sermo* 131, have the word order *eum potest*, not attested in surviving biblical manuscripts. In *Enarratio* 98.9, *intellegere* seems to be an error of memory for *audire*.

JOHN 6:61–2 (6:62–3 IN THE VULGATE)

The commentary text in *Tractatus* 27.3 has *de eo* (cf. *de illo* in Codex Bezae). Both other citations of the whole verse read *de hoc*, but *De correptione et gratia* 22 has the present tense *murmurant*, as in Codices Bezae and Colbertinus. In the next verse, two sequential variants in *Tractatus* 27 have *cum uideritis* rather than *si ergo uideritis*: although Codex Aureus also has *cum*, the context shows that this is probably due to flattening.

JOHN 6:63 (6:64 IN THE VULGATE)

Apart from the initial citation at *Tractatus* 27.4, all ten of Augustine's citations insert *autem* after *caro*, which reinforces the antithesis. This appears in Codex Sarzanensis, despite the lack of correspondence with Greek manuscripts. In three citations, Augustine reads *nihil prodest* rather than the Vulgate *non prodest quicquam* (*Enarratio* 98 (twice), *Tractatus* 11.5; cf. *De consensu* 4.10.15).[52] The anacoluthon

[51] See p. 95; Tischendorf only lists *Tractatus* 27.

[52] The form *prode est* at *De consensu* 4.10.15 is also found in Codices Veronensis, Bezae, Palatinus, and Rehdigeranus. Löfstedt 1911:184–8 describes it as a late Latin development.

resulting from a literal translation of the Greek idiom, *uerba quae ego locutus sum uobis spiritus est et uita*, appears in the initial citation at *Tractatus* 27.6, as well as *Tractatus* 11.5, *Enarratio* 98.9, and several Old Latin witnesses. The Vulgate, however, has the plural *sunt*, which features later in *Tractatus* 27.6 as well as seven other citations (cf. John 6:32–3 and 6:50).

JOHN 6:64 (6:65 IN THE VULGATE)

Quidam in uobis rather than *quidam ex uobis* is peculiar to *Tractatus* 27: it occurs in no other citations or surviving biblical manuscripts.

JOHN 6:65 (6:66 IN THE VULGATE)

The reading *uenit* for *potest uenire* is an indication of flattening (cf. John 3:3, 6:44, etc.). This appears in twelve citations, including the lectionary *Sermo* 131, although Augustine has *potest uenire* an equal number of times. *Sermo* 131 and *De praedestinatione sanctorum* 20.40 read *nisi cui datum fuerit*: there is no support for this in biblical manuscripts and it seems to be an adaptation, as other citations in the same works have the regular form (cf. John 3:27).

JOHN 6:66–7 (6:67–8 IN THE VULGATE)

The commentary text in *Tractatus* 27 has an Old Latin reading in each of these verses. The perfect *ambulauerunt* in John 6:66, which also features at *Enarratio* 98.9, is only preserved in Codex Vercellensis. (Both *Enarratio* 98 and *Epistula* 173.10 show that Augustine's mental text reads *recesserunt* rather than *abierunt retrorsum*; cf. John 18:6.) In John 6:67 *Tractatus* 27 includes *ire* rather than *abire*, in common with all Augustine's other citations except two references in

Tractatus 11.5. This latter sermon has some additional material in these verses:

sic euangelista loquitur: *et dominus ipse remansit cum duodecim; et illi ad eum: 'domine, ecce illi dimiserunt te'; et ille: 'numquid et uos uultis abire?'.*

(*Tractatus* 11.5)

Despite the formulaic introduction, this appears to be a paraphrase and finds no support in Latin Gospels.

JOHN 6:68 (6:69 IN THE VULGATE)

In epistolam Iohannis 1.12 and *Enarratio* 54.23 and 54.24, the three citations outside the *Tractatus*, all have the singular, *uerbum uitae aeternae*, even though every biblical manuscript has the plural, *uerba* (ῥήματα). Both works also delay the phrase *ad quem ibimus* (*Enarratio* 54) or *quo ibimus* (*In epistolam Iohannis 1*) to the end of the verse. Cyprian (*Epistula* 59.7) also has *uerbum*, while Tertullian (*Aduersus Praxean* 21) reads *quo ibimus*, but it is not clear whether these were present in Old Latin codices.

JOHN 6:70 (6:71 IN THE VULGATE)

The word order *unus ex uobis*, in nine of ten citations, is the majority Old Latin reading. These include *Tractatus* 27.10: the sole exception is *De Genesi ad litteram* 11.24.

JOHN 7:1

The sequential variant at *Tractatus* 28.2 condenses *non enim uolebat* to *nolebat*; it also has *occidere* in place of *interficere*, only attested here in Codices Vercellensis and Bezae (cf. John 7:20, 8:40).

JOHN 7:3–4

Both *Tractatus* 28 and the lectionary *Sermo* 133 have *opera* **tua**, peculiar to the Vulgate and Codex Brixianus. *Tractatus* 28 uniquely adds *tu* before *facis*. In John 7:4 these two works have *enim* rather than the Vulgate *quippe*, although they do omit *huic* before *mundo*. Despite their similarity of text, Hombert 2000:343 observes that they display very few points of contact in the exegesis of this passage.

JOHN 7:6

The commentary text in *Tractatus* 28, in common with four Old Latin manuscripts, has *uenit* in place of *aduenit*. The latter is found in both Augustine's other citations, *Sermo* 133.1 and *De consensu* 4.10.16.

JOHN 7:8

Tractatus 28 reads *diem festum hunc* twice. The initial citation of *Sermo* 133 has *hunc* with *istum* in later citations, but corresponds to Old Latin manuscripts with *ascendite* **in** and *tempus meum*.

JOHN 7:10

Augustine gives several slightly different versions of John 7:10. The initial citation of *Tractatus* 28 conforms exactly to the Vulgate:

et ipse adscendit ad diem festum non manifeste sed quasi in occulto.

Later in this sermon, however, four sequential variants end with *quasi latenter*, while a fifth reads *tamquam in occulto*. At *Tractatus* 31.1, a reminiscence has *uelut occulte*. There is no parallel in Latin manuscripts for *uelut* or *tamquam* here (cf. John 1:32–3). In *Sermo* 133, the initial citation is identical to the Vulgate but for the form *quasi occulte*. This corresponds to Codex Monacensis; *latenter*, which also appears in *Epistula* 82.18 and *Contra Faustum* 22.36, is only preserved in Codex Palatinus (without *quasi*). Earlier in the verse, where all biblical manuscripts have *manifeste* or some form of *palam* for φανερῶς, three citations read *euidenter*: *Epistula* 82.18, *Contra Faustum* 22.36, and the final citation at *Sermo* 133.7. It could be argued that this form originated as a parallel to *latenter*, but in *Sermo* 133.7 *euidenter* is found in opposition to *quasi occulte*. This suggests that it may, in fact, have appeared in a version known to Augustine.[53]

JOHN 7:12

The reading *quia propheta est* rather than *quia bonus est* in two early citations of John 7:12 (*Adnotationes in Iob* 5, *De sermone domini* 1.5.14) is probably inspired by John 7:40 where the words of another crowd are reported, *hic est uere propheta*. (No variant to ἀγαθός is recorded in Greek.) Both these citations, as well as *Enarratio* 28.7, have the Old Latin reading *populum* rather than *turbas*.[54] In three secondary citations, Augustine has *alii . . . alii* rather than *quidam . . . alii*, the only form found in the biblical manuscripts: there is no strong evidence that he knew this from a codex.

JOHN 7:16

On all occasions except *Tractatus* 29 and the first citation in *Tractatus* 54.2, Augustine has the Old Latin word order *me misit*; only the

[53] This type of adverb may be characteristic of an African translation: compare *audenter* in John 7:13 and *personaliter* in John 7:24 in Codex Palatinus.

[54] At *Locutiones in Heptateuchum* 1.203, Augustine sets out the following pairs of renderings: *turba* and ὄχλος, *populus* and δῆμος, *plebs* and λαός. This suggests that he had not consulted the Greek text for this verse. Another possible source of *propheta* is the confession of the man born blind at John 9:17, *ille autem dixit quia propheta est*; Milne 1926:xxiii proposes Matthew 16:14.

Vulgate and Codex Aureus read *misit me* (cf. John 7:33, 8:16). In *Collatio cum Maximino* 5, his opponent adds *patris* to this phrase, as found in Codex Rehdigeranus. La Bonnardière (1965:99–100) shows how Augustine initially takes this verse as an example of Christ's humanity (e.g. *De trinitate* 1.11.22) but later interprets it in terms of his identity with the divine (e.g. *Tractatus* 29.5); in contrast, Berrouard (1977:839–41) claims that Augustine is always aware of the verse's ambiguity. All the citations are listed at Hombert 2000:535.

JOHN 7:19–24

The text of Augustine's commentary, *Tractatus* 30, which comprises his only verbatim citations of John 7:19–23, has already been discussed above.[55] All six works which cite John 7:24 have *personaliter*, the translation of κατ' ὄψιν in Codices Palatinus and Monacensis. A sequential variant in the lectionary *Sermo* 178 substitutes *secundum personam*, as found in Codices Vercellensis, Bezae, and Usserianus. Four works read *rectum iudicium* for τὴν δικαίαν κρίσιν (*Tractatus* 30, *Enarrationes* 71.4 and 118.s26.1, *De baptismo* 2.7.10). This is not found in the Old Latin manuscripts, which all have *iustum iudicium*. It is tempting to suggest that Augustine's mental text was influenced by the phrase *recta iudicate* in a similar context at Psalm 57:2, but although this verse is cited before John 7:24 at *De agone christiano* 27.29, this and *Sermo* 178 both have the regular form *iustum*.

JOHN 7:25–8

The principal citations of these verses are in *Tractatus* 31, which has a few variations from the Vulgate. The reading *quaerebant* for *quaerunt* in John 7:25 is paralleled by Codex Usserianus, which also agrees with *illi* rather than *ei* in the next verse. In John 7:27, *Tractatus* 31.2 reads *istum nouimus* in place of *hunc scimus*. Although *nouimus* is

[55] See pp. 116–17; four sermons allude to *daemonium habes* in John 7:20.

present in three Old Latin witnesses, there is no other example of *istum*: this has been noted elsewhere in Augustine's citations which feature direct speech (cf. John 4:18, 9:16, 9:24, and 9:29). The addition of *ecce* also seems to be characteristic of Augustine (cf. John 1:29, 4:46, 14:30), and this is seen in a loose reference to John 7:25 in *Sermo* 133.7, which reads *ecce hic est, ecce docet. De consensu* 4.10.16 and *Tractatus* 31 indicate that Augustine's copy of the Vulgate had *nescitis* rather than *non scitis* in John 7:28 (cf. John 3:8, but also John 4:33). The initial citation in *Tractatus* 31 also has the word order *me misit.* The Old Latin *nostis* for *scitis* appears in a sequential variant, as well as twice in *Tractatus* 37.10 (cf. John 8:19).

JOHN 7:30

Sermo 133.7 has a paraphrase which includes *apprehendere eum uolebant.* The correspondence between *uolebant* and ἐζήτουν is worth noting: it is not found here in any Latin Gospels but occurs in Augustine's citations of John 5:18 and 8:40.

JOHN 7:31–2

In John 7:31 *facturus est* for *faciet* in the commentary text of *Tractatus* 31 is preserved in Codices Vercellensis and Monacensis, although no surviving manuscript puts *numquid* at the beginning of the direct speech. The omission of *principes et pharisaei* in the next verse is probably an adaptation, given the mention of *principes* at the beginning of the sentence. Nonetheless, these words are also absent from Codices Veronensis and Palatinus.

JOHN 7:33

The addition of *tunc* before *uado* in Augustine's only citation of this verse, *Tractatus* 31.8, is not matched by any codex but is also a feature of his citations of John 8:36. The word order *me misit* is found in most Old Latin witnesses (cf. John 7:16); *dicit*, however, is not paralleled in biblical manuscripts and may be an adaptation.

JOHN 7:36

Despite reading *quaeretis* in John 7:34, *Tractatus* 31 has *quaeritis* two verses later, as well as the word order *ubi ego sum* and the addition of *uos* before *non potestis*. *Sermo* 129.3, Augustine's only other citation, does read *quaeretis*.

JOHN 7:37–8

Flattening is probably the reason that *si quis sitit* is sometimes reduced to *qui sitit*, and that *ad me* is missing from thirteen citations of John 7:37; even so, both are paralleled in a few gospel manuscripts. Augustine normally follows this shorter form with a version of John 7:38 featuring the word order *flumina aquae uiuae fluent de uentre eius* and the omission of *sicut dixit scriptura*, which suggest that he is citing from memory. The frequent absence of the latter phrase indicates that, unlike Cyprian and Ambrose, Augustine did not understand this verse as a prophecy about Christ, even though he identifies the 'living waters' with the Holy Spirit (e.g. *In epistolam Iohannis* 6.11, *Enarratio* 97.8, *Sermo* 160.2). This is also shown by his division of John 7:37 and 7:38 in *Enarratio* 103.s1.10: the addition of *dicat adhuc* between the verses implies that he was not aware of the earlier tradition of punctuating before *sicut* in John 7:38.[56] The six citations which do include the reference to Scripture in John 7:38 all have the present tense, *dicit* (*De unitate ecclesiae* 23.65, *Quaestiones de Iudicibus* 36, *Tractatus* 32.2, *Enarratio* 92.7, *De diuersis quaestionibus* 64.4, and *De trinitate* 15.19.33). This is only preserved in certain

[56] See Turner 1923:67–70 and Fahey 1971:386. Patristic parallels are supplied by Berrouard 1977:852–4.

Vulgate manuscripts and Codex Aureus, but the early date of *De diuersis quaestionibus* 64 suggests that this reading may have been more widespread.

JOHN 7:39

Like the previous two verses, most citations of John 7:39 display indications of flattening, omitting one or more phrases as well as the connective *enim*. The difference between *dicebat*, in seventeen citations, and *dixit* (only in the initial citation of *Tractatus* 32, *Contra Maximinum* 2.22.3 and *De trinitate* 15.19.33) reflects a Greek variant. Augustine always has the rendering *qui accepturi erant* for ἔμελλον λαμβάνειν, and this may have inspired the replacement of *credentes* by *qui credituri erant* in ten citations. However, the future participle is also present in Codex Usserianus and four of Ambrose's citations.[57] Augustine reads *nondum erat spiritus datus* in almost all his citations (including the commentary in *Tractatus* 32): the text *non erat spiritus* is unique to the Vulgate. His only examples of *non* are *Contra Cresconium* 2.14.17, *De perfectione iustitiae hominis* 15, *Tractatus* 63.2 and two sequential variants in *Tractatus* 32.6, but all of these include *datus*. Conversely, Augustine does not have any examples of the Old Latin additions of *sanctus* (Codices Palatinus, Veronensis, Bezae, Brixianus, and Monacensis), or *in eos* (Codices Bezae and Brixianus). Eleven citations, including the early works *De diuersis quaestionibus* 64 and *Enarratio* 7.6, have *autem* where the Vulgate reads *enim*. *Autem* appears in five Old Latin manuscripts, among them Codices Monacensis and Palatinus. Fourteen citations end with *clarificatus*, seven of which read *erat clarificatus*, like Codex Palatinus. Seven other works, including the commentary in *Tractatus* 32, have *erat glorificatus*. Augustine rejects the narrow interpretation of this verse which suggests that the Holy

[57] *Exameron* 3.1.6, *Explanatio Psalmorum* 1.35 and 36.61, *De spiritu sancto* 1.156. This suggests that, alongside πιστεύσαντες and πιστεύοντες, the Greek tradition may also have had a future participle πιστεύσοντες. Codex Usserianus is the only manuscript in Fischer's collation with *credituri* (Fischer 1991:197).

Spirit was only given after Jesus' resurrection: rather, he claims that it refers to the visible manifestation of the Spirit at Pentecost (see Berrouard 1977:854–6).

JOHN 7:45–9

The text of these verses in *Enarratio* 58.s1.7 is as follows:

quare ergo, inquiunt, *non eum potuistis adprehendere? et responderunt: nemo umquam hominum sic locutus est, sicut ille.* et illi fortes: *numquid aliquis pharisaeorum in illum credidit, aut aliquis scribarum, nisi populus iste nesciens legem?*

This is likely to be a paraphrase produced from memory, which would explain Old Latin parallels, such as *nemo umquam* (Codex Palatinus), alongside phrases not found elsewhere (e.g. *aut aliquis scribarum*) and the omission of John 7:47. Features typical of Augustine's mental text are also evident, such as *posse* with the infinitive (cf. John 3:3 etc.), *iste* (cf. John 4:18, 6:52 etc.), and *nescire* (cf. John 7:28). The text of this passage in *Tractatus* 33.1 is identical to the Vulgate, with the exceptions of *de* rather than *ex* in John 7:48 and *non enim quisquam sic loquitur homo* in John 7:46. Although *quisquam* appears in four Old Latin manuscripts, *loquitur* is only included in a longer form alongside *locutus est* (Codices Aureus, Colbertinus, and Bezae), which suggests that Augustine may have adapted the direct speech here too.

JOHN 7:50–2

Augustine's only reference to John 7:50 is a paraphrase at *Tractatus* 33.2, which includes the Old Latin pluperfect, *uenerat* (Codices Palatinus, Usserianus, and Colbertinus). The same sermon adds *scripturas* in John 7:52, as found in several Vulgate as well as Old Latin witnesses, possibly by analogy with John 5:39.

JOHN 7:53–8:11

Augustine is one of the earliest Church Fathers not to question the authenticity of the *Pericope Adulterae* and to cite it in full, although he is aware that it is missing from some manuscripts (*De adulterinis coniugiis* 2.7.6, quoted on p. 80). His text in *Tractatus* 33 corresponds to the Vulgate for the most part, but in John 8:6–11 he only gives a few phrases verbatim. In the lectionary *Sermo* 16A, too, he seems to paraphrase the reading. Substantial citations also occur in *Enarratio* 50 and *Sermo* 13. There is comparatively little overlap between the text of these different accounts: Berrouard (1977:859–60) suggests that this is an indication of the textual fluidity of the passage, but as the three sermons were preached in different churches Augustine is likely to have used a separate exemplar on each occasion. Surviving Old Latin Gospels which include these verses also display considerable variation.[58]

JOHN 7:53–8:1

Tractatus 33.2 omits the initial *et* from John 7:53, possibly due to adaptation. This may also be responsible for the form *inde Iesus perrexit* in John 8:1 in the next paragraph: neither is paralleled in biblical manuscripts.

JOHN 8:3

Although *Tractatus* 33.4 has the present tense *adducunt*, found in most Latin witnesses (cf. *adducentes* in *Enarratio* 102.11), Augustine's

[58] The principal work on the text of the *Pericope Adulterae* remains Becker 1963, although its history is also discussed at length in Petersen 1997:192–9 and Parker 1997:95–102. Knust 2006 shows how the exegesis of the pericope developed through the variant readings, although neither she nor Becker includes the citations from Augustine's *Sermones* 13, 16A, 272B, and 302 or *Enarrationes* 30.2.s1 and 102.

other citations support the perfect *adduxerunt*, as in Codices Colbertinus and Palatinus (*Epistula* 153.4.9, *Enarratio* 50.8, *Sermones* 13.4 and 16A.4). This variant is also present in Greek. *Enarratio* 50 may reflect the additional *ad eum* in Codices Corbeiensis and Colbertinus (cf. *Sermo* 13 with *adduxerunt ante eum*); *illi* after *autem* only appears in *Tractatus* 33, supported again by *Enarratio* 102.

JOHN 8:4–5

Comprehensa, in *Sermo* 16A.4, is paralleled by Codex Bezae alone: *Tractatus* 33.4, *Enarratio* 50.8 and the other biblical manuscripts have *deprehensa*. In John 8:5, *Sermo* 16A.4 has a full clause, *ut quaecumque fuerit in adulterio comprehensa*, in place of the words *τὰς τοιαύτας*. This is similar to Codices Colbertinus and Corbeiensis, which add *ut qui in adulterio deprehenditur*. These two manuscripts also add *de ea* at the end of the verse: this is not found in *Sermo* 16A, but *Enarratio* 50.8 has *tu* ***de illa*** *quid censes?* which may reflect a similar text.

JOHN 8:6–8

Although the Greek of both John 8:6 and John 8:8 has only (*κάτω*) *κύψας*, several Latin witnesses read *inclinato capite*, introducing a verbal reference to John 19:30.[59] This parallel would have exegetical appeal for Augustine (cf. John 4:7). Both his citations which include this part of John 8:6 have *inclinato capite* rather than *inclinans* (*Contra Faustum* 22.25 and *Enarratio* 30.2.s1.7), while of his five references to John 8:8, *Enarratio* 102.11 reads *inclinato capite* and *Sermo* 272B.5 has *inclinauit caput*. (In *Sermo* 16A.5 *conuersus* appears

[59] The Greek of John 19:30 is *κλίνας τὴν κεφαλήν*: Codex Palatinus has *inclinato capite* in both John 8:6 and 8:8 (and also adds *caput* in John 8:7 and 8:10), while Codices Colbertinus and Corbeiensis and two other manuscripts (Be and Bt in Fischer 1991) have this reading in John 8:6 alone.

in place of this participle, but this may be a paraphrase.) All biblical manuscripts have *scribebat* in both John 8:6 and 8:8, but for the latter *Sermones* 13.5 and 272B.5 have an inchoative form, *coepit scribere* (cf. John 4:47). Codices Bezae and Corbeiensis also add *digito* to this verse (from John 8:6), which appears in *Tractatus* 33.5 and *Sermo* 272B.5. Two of Augustine's citations preserve the only evidence for *rursum* rather than *iterum* in John 8:8 (*Tractatus* 33.5 and *Enarratio* 102.11; cf. John 4:46 and 13:12). In John 8:7, he reads *prior* fourteen times, along with Codices Bezae, Corbeiensis, and Palatinus; only *Enarratio* 50.8 has the majority form *primus*. Latin Gospels are also divided between *mittat*, *iaciat*, and *iactet* in this verse, all three of which are found in Augustine. Both *mittat* and *iaciat* appear in *De adulterinis coniugiis* 2.6.7 and *Epistula* 153.4, while the sermons just read *mittat*; his only citation with *iactet* is *Enarratio* 102.11. At the beginning of the direct speech in John 8:7, most biblical manuscripts have *qui sine peccato est uestrum*. Although over half Augustine's citations have *uestrum*, the word is absent from *De adulterinis coniugiis* 2.14.14, *Contra aduersarium legis* 1.20.44, and *Sermones* 13.4 (both times) and 302.15.14; this is only paralleled in patristic sources (e.g. Ambrose *Epistulae* 50.5 and 68.2) and may be flattening. Elsewhere Augustine reads *qui in uobis sine peccato est* (*Enarratio* 102.11), *si quis est in uobis sine peccato* (*Sermo* 272B.5), *qui se scit sine peccato esse* (*Enarratio* 50.8), *qui se scit uestrum sine peccato esse* (*Sermo* 16A.4), and *qui sciret se esse sine peccato* (*Epistula* 153.4.11). Both *in uobis* and *se scit* are unique to Augustine, but may reflect versions known to him.[60]

JOHN 8:9

Enarratio 50.8 begins this verse with an ablative absolute, *illi hoc audito*, which may be a paraphrase, even though this is Augustine's only citation with *remansit*. The Latin versions which include εἶς καθ' εἶς normally translate it as *unus post unum*, but three of his

[60] Hombert 2000:504–5 gives a list of Augustine's citations of John 8:7 with their *orchestration scripturaire*.

citations uniquely have *unus post alterum* (*Contra aduersarium legis* 1.20.44, *Enarratio* 50.8, and *Sermo* 13.5). Two other works add the detail *omnes* (*Tractatus* 33.5 and *Sermo* 16A.4), also found in Codices Bezae, Colbertinus, and Corbeiensis. Augustine never has the verb *exiebant*, reading *discesserunt* in *Enarratio* 50.8 and *Sermones* 13.5 and 272B.5, *regressi sunt* in *Sermo* 16A.4, and *recesserunt* in *Tractatus* 33.5 and *Contra aduersarium legis* 1.20.44. Codices Colbertinus and Corbeiensis have *recesserunt*, albeit later in the verse, while *discesserunt* only appears in one Latin manuscript from the first millennium. Similarly, there are only two surviving codices with a phrase corresponding to ἕως τῶν ἐσχάτων, attested in several Greek majuscules and Family 13: one reads *usque ad iuniorem* while the other has *usque in ultimis*.[61] This occurs twice in Augustine, in two further forms: *usque ad minores* (*minorem* in one manuscript, which omits *omnem*) at *Sermo* 16A.4 and *usque ad minorem* at *Sermo* 272B.5, the sole instances of this phrase in the *Vetus Latina Database*. He therefore provides not only unique patristic testimony but also the earliest evidence for these words in the Latin tradition. Furthermore, what appears to be the introduction to this verse in *Sermo* 272B.5, *illi autem considerantes conscientias suas*, corresponds exactly to a phrase which occurs in some later Greek manuscripts, καὶ ὑπὸ τῆς συνειδησέως ἐλεγχόμενοι, supported by Bohairic versions but absent from all Latin Bibles.[62] This seems to underlie the phrase *unusquisque iam interrogans conscientiam suam* as well at *Enarratio* 102.11 (with *unusquisque* corresponding to ἕκαστος in some Greek witnesses), while a further reference to conscience is present in the allusion at *Sermo* 302.15.14, *uerbo graui et acuto compunctis cordibus, conscientias suas agnouerunt*.[63] *Sermo* 272B.5 completes its remarkable text of this verse with a unique form of the final clause, *et relicta est illa mulier sola*: several Old Latin witnesses have *relictus est Iesus solus*, but there is no parallel for the

[61] **Bw** (Würzburg Univ. M.p.th.f. 67) and **Sx** (Complutensis 1, Madrid) respectively in Fischer 1991; **Jy** (Split, Cathedral) is the sole witness with *omnes discesserunt*.

[62] Codex K (017), one of the Greek majuscules with this phrase, also supplies the Greek behind one of Augustine's forms of John 14:30.

[63] Becker 1963:63–4 describes both additional phrases in this verse as clearly secondary. The line *cecidit saeuitia, tremente conscientia* also appears in the context of this verse at *Epistula* 153.4.11 (see further the allusions listed at Knust 2006:527).

woman by herself (cf. *solam mulierem miseram relinquerunt* at *Sermo* 302.15.14). Even though it is not clear whether this passage was the liturgical reading preceding *Sermo* 272B, Augustine's citation of five verses in sequence suggests that it reflects a written source.

JOHN 8:10–11

As with its rendering of κατακύψας in John 8:6 and 8:8, Codex Palatinus adds *caput* when translating ἀνακύψας in John 8:7 and 8:10. There is no trace of this in Augustine's citations of the former verse, but his only full citation of John 8:10 reads:

leuauit autem dominus caput et ait ei: quid est, mulier? nemo te damnauit? (*Sermo* 272B.5)

The replacement of the question *ubi sunt qui te accusabant?* by *quid est?* is without parallel in biblical codices and yet Augustine shows no knowledge of the alternative form. He is also unique in reading *damnauit* (*Sermones* 13.5 and 272B.5) in this verse, although Codex Corbeiensis has *damnabo* for the same verb in John 8:11, along with eleven of Augustine's fourteen citations.[64] As for ἀπὸ τοῦ νῦν, which the Old Latin witnesses render by either *ex hoc (iam)* or *amplius (iam)*, on ten occasions out of eleven Augustine has *deinceps (iam)*, a rendering peculiar to him. The exception is *Speculum* 28 which, as usual, reproduces the Vulgate. Augustine's earliest citation of John 8:11, *De sermone domini* 1.16.43, appears to have a rather loose text, *uade uide deinceps ne pecces*, but this is surprisingly close to Ambrose's *uade et amodo uide ne pecces* (*De Abraham* 1.4.23, *Epistulae* 50.17, 64.6, 68.17). When referring to this citation at *Retractationes* 1.19.6, however, Augustine reverts to his customary form.

[64] Ambrose also cites John 8:11 with *damnabo*. Tischendorf cites a number of manuscripts with uncompounded forms of κρίνειν (rather than κατακρίνειν) which would correspond to *damnabo* (see also Petersen 1997:191). The reading *damnauit... damnabo* in *Sermo* 272B.5 is less certain following the discovery of a new manuscript which, like one of the two other witnesses, has *condemnauit... condemnabo* (Dolbeau 1998:199).

JOHN 8:12

Only the adaptation of this verse at *De consensu* 4.10.17 has *lux* for both instances of τὸ φῶς in John 8:12, as in the Vulgate. In *Tractatus* 34 and 35 Augustine consistently reads *lumen uitae* at the end of the verse, and begins with *ego sum lumen mundi* at *Tractatus* 34.9 and *Enarratio* 118.s23.1. There is an equivalent distribution among the Old Latin witnesses, where only Codices Palatinus, Sarzanensis, and Usserianus have *lumen mundi*, but seven manuscripts have *lumen uitae*. Augustine's word order in his mental text, *qui me sequitur*, is paralleled by Codices Vercellensis, Veronensis, and Bezae: on two occasions, he lapses into *qui credit in me* (*Enarratio* 42.4 and *Sermo* 140.1).

JOHN 8:13–14

In John 8:13 Augustine does not have the Vulgate and majority Old Latin form *testimonium perhibes* in any citation, nor the characteristic Vulgate addition of *ipso. Tractatus* 35 and 36 both read *testimonium dicis*, as found in Codices Bezae, Palatinus, and Sarzanensis. In *Contra Faustum* 16.13, Augustine follows the lead of Faustus at 12.1 and 16.2, reading *testificaris*, which corresponds to Codex Vercellensis. On the other hand, for John 8:14 at *Tractatus* 35.4 he does have *testimonium perhibeo*, even though all Latin Gospels follow the same rendering as the previous verse (cf. John 8:18).

JOHN 8:16–18

Tractatus 36 and 37 have the word order *misit me* in both John 8:16 (where it is only found in a few Vulgate manuscripts) and John 8:18. Three other citations of John 8:18 have *me misit*: among these *Contra Faustum* 13.5 and 16.13 repeat Faustus' text from earlier, and in the latter the unusual *nempe* at the beginning of John 8:17 also comes from Augustine's opponent. The initial citations of John 8:17 are inconsistent: *Tractatus* 36 has the regular *quia*, but *Tractatus* 37 has the only surviving example of *quod*. In John 8:18 both commentaries have *testimonium perhibere*, while *testificari* at *Contra Faustum* 16.13 derives from Faustus (cf. John 8:13–14).

JOHN 8:19–20

Contra aduersarium legis 2.5.19, Augustine's only citation outside *Tractatus* 37, has the Old Latin *nostis* for *scitis*, like one sequential variant in the commentary (cf. John 7:28). In the next verse, the addition of *Iesus* in *Tractatus* 37 corresponds to some Old Latin and Vulgate manuscripts, although there is no parallel for *dominus*, the reading of *Tractatus* 38. *Nondum* rather than *necdum* in both these citations is the standard Old Latin text.

JOHN 8:22–3

The past tense *dixit* in *Tractatus* 38 is only paralleled in Codex Palatinus. Augustine's verbatim citation of John 8:23 at *De patientia* 19.16 reads *uos de deorsum estis, ego de sursum sum*. This is a comparatively late example of an Old Latin reading: Codices Palatinus and Usserianus alone have *susum* (sic) rather than *superioribus* or *supernis*. Augustine's exploration of *deorsum* and both *sursum* and *susum* at *In epistolam Iohannis* 8.2 may therefore be a reminiscence of this verse, which he only cites in three works.

JOHN 8:24

Like the Greek tradition, most Old Latin manuscripts have a plural, *peccatis uestris*, on both occasions. This is Augustine's text throughout *Tractatus* 38 and 39, even though the Vulgate has the singular, *peccato uestro*, at the end of the verse. In these, his sole citations of these verses, Augustine explains the absence of copula for *ego sum* by reference to Exodus 3:14 (cf. John 8:28, 8:58, 13:19).

JOHN 8:25

The Old Latin reading *principium* **quod** *et loquor uobis* is attested in five citations (*Epistula* 149.2.25, *De consensu* 4.10.17, *De Genesi ad litteram imperfectum liber* 3, *De Genesi contra Manichaeos* 1.2.3, *De trinitate* 1.12.24); eight other references read *quia*, like the Vulgate and Codex Veronensis. Although the latter could derive from interpreting the Greek as ὅτι rather than ὅ τι, it might also be an internal Latin development: *quia* and *quod* are interchangeable, and both introduce speech (cf. John 8:17) or serve as causal conjunctions. As *quia* occurs in a reminiscence in *Confessiones* 12.28.39, it is possible that Augustine was familiar with this in an Old Latin text.[65]

JOHN 8:26–7

As in John 8:16, *me misit* also appears in the Vulgate tradition and is Augustine's sole reading in *Tractatus* 39 and 40. *Tractatus* 40.2, his only citation of John 8:27, reads:

non intellexerunt Iudaei quod de patre illis diceret.

There is barely any verbal similiarity between this and the Vulgate, *et non cognouerunt quia patrem eis dicebat*, but it does have several points of contact with Codex Veronensis, which reads *et non intellexerunt quoniam de deo patre diceret eis.* Even if Augustine is paraphrasing, his text may still reflect an Old Latin source.

[65] *Sermo* 1.2 also reads *quia*, dated to 393/5 in Frede 1995 but revised to 410/11 in Gryson 2007. Berrouard 1988:270–1 gives references to supplement and correct Comeau 1930:53, although it should be noted that Weber's subsequent edition of *De Genesi contra Manichaeos* prefers *principium quod.*

JOHN 8:28–30

Augustine's citation at *Contra Faustum* 6.9, *ego fallere non didici: quod sentio loquor*, which he attributes to Christ, has been connected with John 8:28 on the basis of *docere* and *loquor*, but is too loose to be a genuine correspondence.[66] *Tractatus* 40.3 refers back to Augustine's treatment of *ego sum* in *Tractatus* 38.8, alluding to Exodus 3:14 (see also John 8:58). One sequential variant has the Old Latin *scietis*, while *Tractatus* 54.1 uniquely reads *agnoscetis*. In John 8:29 and 8:30, Old Latin witnesses provide parallels for the word order *me relinquit* and *eo* rather than *illo* in *Tractatus* 40. In the latter verse, even though *eo* appears at *Tractatus* 40.2 when Augustine summarizes the lection, by the time he comments on the verse at *Tractatus* 40.7, he reverts to the Vulgate *illo* (cf. John 3:32 etc.). The replacement of *ei* by *patri* in John 8:29 at *Contra Maximinum* 2.14.8 is typical of flattening, and Augustine has taken it over from Maximinus (*Collatio* 10 and 22).

JOHN 8:31

The commentary text in *Tractatus* 40 differs from that in *Tractatus* 41:

dicebat ergo dominus ad eos qui crediderant in eum Iudaeos: si uos manseritis in uerbo meo, uere discipuli mei eritis. (*Tractatus* 40.8)

dicebat ergo Iesus ad eos qui crediderant ei Iudaeos: si manseritis in uerbo meo, uere discipuli mei eritis. (*Tractatus* 41.1)

The non-Vulgate readings *crediderant* and *uerbo* have Old Latin support. In fact, *sermone* is peculiar to the Vulgate, and only appears in *De consensu* 2.70.138 and *Speculum* 28. Augustine's mental text omits *uos* before *manseritis* in twenty-two citations, although this has no parallel in biblical manuscripts, and in eleven citations he prefers *estis* to *eritis* at the end of the verse: both of these readings occur in

[66] See the discussion of *agrapha* on p. 76.

the lectionary *Sermo* 134, preached in Carthage from an Old Latin codex. In addition to *Tractatus* 40, two other works support *crediderant in eum*: *Sermo* 346.2 has it twice, alongside the rare Old Latin *autem* for *ergo*, while *In epistolam Iohannis* 4.2 also has *permanseritis*, which features in *Sermo* 193.2 and the same Old Latin witnesses as *crediderant*. The extent of the citations in *Sermo* 346 suggests that Augustine may have referred to a codex.

JOHN 8:32

Although the reading *liberauit* for *liberabit* is a common error in Latin manuscripts because of the similarity in sound, Augustine normally reads the future here in keeping with *cognoscetis* earlier in the verse: this is shown by his gloss *id est liberos faciet* in *Epistula* 149.2.27. Migne, however, reads *liberauit* in *In epistolam Iohannis* 4.2: there is nothing in the context to justify Augustine's use of the past tense, and his following comments about hope and expectation rather than present reality suggest that this too should have the future. By reading this verse in conjunction with John 8:36, Augustine is able to identify *ueritas* and *filius* (e.g. *Tractatus* 108.2; cf. John 14:6 and 17:17).

JOHN 8:33

Two citations have *filii Abrahae* (*Enarrationes* 46.11 and 148.17), where all manuscripts read *semen Abraham*, following the Greek σπέρμα. This seems to be a reminiscence of John 8:39, where all manuscripts have *filii* (τέκνα), or John 8:37, in which both readings are found. *Sermo* 342.4 has a citation *nos de seruitute non sumus nati, patrem habemus Abraham*, which has been identified with this verse: despite the reference to slavery, it seems more likely to be a loose conflation of *patrem habemus Abraham* in Matthew 3:9 (parallel Luke 3:8) and *nos ex fornicatione non sumus nati* (John 8:41).

JOHN 8:35

De consensu 2.70.138 and *Tractatus* 41.8 read *autem* twice in this verse, after *seruus* and *filius*: this is paralleled in the Vulgate tradition as well as Codices Vercellensis, Bezae, and Usserianus, and probably featured in Augustine's copy of Jerome's version. Four other citations, which may represent his mental text, omit the first instance of *autem*: there is no support for this in Latin Gospels.

JOHN 8:36

Augustine's customary form, appearing in twenty-eight citations, is *si uos filius liberauerit, tunc uere liberi eritis.* His only example of the Vulgate text is *De consensu* 2.70.138. The omission of *ergo* after *si* and fronting of *uos* is typical of flattening, and occurs in three further citations without *tunc* (*Epistula* 190.6, *Contra epistulas Pelagianorum* 2.2.2, and *Sermo* 342.4). There is no parallel for *tunc* in biblical manuscripts, but Augustine is so consistent that it may have originated in a Latin version which has since been lost: it appears throughout his commentary in *Tractatus* 41 and is found in numerous other Latin Fathers, although some of these may have been influenced by Augustine (see also John 7:33).

JOHN 8:38–9

Augustine reads *patrem meum* in *Tractatus* 42, the only work which cites John 8:38: this occurs in both Old Latin and Vulgate sources as well as certain Greek manuscripts. His mental text of John 8:39 has *facta Abrahae*, shown by eleven citations. *Tractatus* 42 alone reads *opera* with the majority of Latin Gospels, but *facta* matches Codex Palatinus.[67] Seven of the references with *facta* also read *facite*,

[67] The rendering *facta* is also seen in Petilianus' citation of John 10:37 at *Contra litteras Petiliani* 2.12.27. In this case, it is not preserved in any Old Latin witness, but as it also appears in Cyprian (*Ad Quirinum* 2.6) it is likely that it was found in African Bibles.

peculiar to the Vulgate and Codex Corbeiensis. *Sermones* 121.3 and 342.4 have the Old Latin *faceretis* (*facerent* in the adaptation at *Contra Faustum* 33.5), while *Enarratio* 148.17 provides a rare example of the pluperfect *fecissetis*: this is only paralleled in psalm commentaries by Hilary of Poitiers and Cassiodorus.

JOHN 8:40

Augustine prefers *occidere* to *interficere* in the sequential variants in *Tractatus* 42 in John 8:37 and this verse. He also switches from *locutus sum* to *dico*, for which there is no support in biblical manuscripts. Both these variants appear in Augustine's single other citation of John 8:40, *Sermo* 121.3, which additionally has *uultis* rather than *quaeretis*. This rendering of ζητεῖτε is also used by Tertullian (*Aduersus Praxean* 22, *De carne Christi* 15; cf. John 5:18 and 7:30).

JOHN 8:44

Augustine reads ***a** patre* throughout *Tractatus* 42 and in *Enarrationes* 26.s2.18 and 44.12, *Contra Iulianum opus imperfectum* 4.129, and *Sermones* 294.15, 352.3, and 360A.1; his other citations have *ex patre*. The Vulgate *ex propriis* only occurs in the initial citation of *Tractatus* 42. Twenty citations read *qui loquitur mendacium de suo loquitur*. Out of context, this appears to be flattened: it is broader in scope than the original reference to the devil and Augustine employs it in a very general way. On the other hand, his text is almost identical to Codex Palatinus (apart from *mendacium* for *mendum*): *qui* (instead of *cum*) appears in two more Old Latin manuscripts, as does *de suo* in place of *ex suis propriis*. As noted on pp. 151–2, even though Augustine criticizes Petilianus at *Contra litteras Petiliani* 2.13.30 for reading *accusator* rather than *homicida*, this may have been the text of the Donatist's African version.

JOHN 8:47

Augustine's three citations of John 8:47 outside *Tractatus* 42 occur in two early works, *Ad Simplicianum* 1.2.18 and *De duabus animabus* 9 (twice), which both read *uos propterea non auditis quia non estis ex deo*. All surviving manuscripts have *propterea uos*, but Codex Corbeiensis has the word order *non estis ex deo*. This verse and John 8:44 were used by the Manichees to claim that man was not made in the image of God.

JOHN 8:48

The seven citations of John 8:48 apart from *Tractatus* 43 read *nonne uerum dicimus*, and six of these also omit the pronouns *nos* and *tu* (the exception is *Enarratio* 125.15). The rendering of καλῶς by *uerum* is not paralleled here in Old Latin manuscripts, which have *bene* or *recte* (cf. John 13:13 in *Enarratio* 92.3). It is possible that this rendering may have appeared in a version now lost, perhaps as a deliberate change in order to remove the juxtaposition of *bene* and *dicere*, which had developed a specialized Christian meaning.[68] As Augustine does not alter his commentary text, however, it is unlikely that he introduced *uerum*: he is more interested in Jesus' refusal in the next verse to deny the charge of being a Samaritan, which he explains etymologically as *custos* (*Tractatus* 43.2, *Enarrationes* 125.15 and 136.7). He also supplies the information that the congregation beat their breasts during the liturgical reading of the calumny *daemonium habes* in John 8:48 (*Enarratio* 48.s2.4).

JOHN 8:50

All references, including *Tractatus* 43, have *est qui quaerat et iudicet*, which is found in certain Vulgate witnesses as well as the majority of

[68] See, for example, Mohrmann 1961:40, where she observes that in this 'Christian' usage, it takes an accusative rather than a dative direct object.

Old Latin manuscripts. Augustine's resolution of the apparent contradiction between this verse and John 5:22 has already been noted above (p. 229); similarly, he relies on two senses of *gloria* in *Tractatus* 43.9 to remove any conflict between this verse and John 17:5.

JOHN 8:52

Tractatus 43 has the word order *mortem non gustabit*, matching the previous verse. The sequential variant in *Tractatus* 43.13 is the only surviving example of *modo* for *nunc* in this verse.

JOHN 8:54

In *Tractatus* 43.14, Augustine reports an Arian exegesis of John 8:54 which claims that the Father who glorifies is greater than the Son. Berrouard (1971:145) notes that this is similar to the Arian explanation of John 17:1 found in Ambrose (*De fide* 4.10.136).

JOHN 8:55

The Vulgate is inconsistent in its rendering of the three instances of *οἶδα* in this verse, with *noui* followed by *scio* twice: Augustine's only citation, *Tractatus* 43.15 has *noui* twice but reverts to *scio* in the final phrase. This implies that Augustine did not revise his copy of the Vulgate on the basis of a Greek text.[69]

JOHN 8:56

Augustine's mental text for this verse is *Abraham concupiuit uidere diem meum, et uidit et gauisus est*, supported by eleven of thirteen

[69] See further pp. 97–8.

citations. The exceptions are *Tractatus* 43.16 and Augustine's citation of Maximinus at *Contra Maximinum* 2.26.8 (but not his own citations later in the same paragraph). The Old Latin witnesses have *exultauit* (or *laetabatur*) *ut uideret*, corresponding to ἠγαλλιάσατο ἵνα ἴδῃ, but Augustine's consistency suggests that *concupiuit uidere* may have featured in a version now lost; it is widespread in the Latin patristic tradition and there are at least three Greek Fathers with ἐπεθύμησεν rather than ἠγαλλιάσατο (cf. John 14:2).[70] Augustine's exegesis of this verse is set out at Berrouard 1988:526–9.

JOHN 8:58–9

Nine citations of John 8:58 have the majority Old Latin reading, *ante Abraham ego sum*. Only the Vulgate and Codex Brixianus read *antequam Abraham fieret ego sum*, found in *Tractatus* 43.17, *Enarratio* 104.10 and *Sermo* 225.1.1, all of which were delivered after 414.[71] Unlike his treatment of the absolute use of *ego sum* in John 8:24 and 8:28 with reference to the Old Testament, in this verse Augustine takes the present tense verb as an indication of Jesus' divine preexistence (*Tractatus* 43.17, *In epistolam Iohannis* 2.5, *Sermo* 225.1.1). The reversion to *mitterent* rather than *iacerent* in the sequential variant to John 8:59 at *Tractatus* 43.18 corresponds to several Old Latin witnesses (cf. John 8:7).

JOHN 9:1–2

John 9 is treated by Augustine in *Tractatus* 44 and five lectionary sermons, *Sermones* 135, 136, 136A, 136B, and 136C.[72] Unlike Origen,

[70] See the *Vetus Latina Database*. On the Greek side, Tischendorf cites Epiphanius, to which may be added Didymus the Blind and Ephraem Graecus. There is no similar variation for ἀγαλλιαθῆναι in John 5:35.

[71] Frede 1995 dates *Sermo* 225 to 400/5, but this has been revised in Gryson 2007 to 428/9.

[72] Lawless 1996 and 1997 discuss the rhetorical features of Augustine's exposition of John 9 in *Tractatus* 44.

he takes the blind man as representative of the human race (Comeau 1930:152), and reads the story of progressive illumination as an allegory of Christian initiation (Berrouard 1989:401–7). One of the characteristics of his biblical citations in this passage appears to be a preference for *iste* rather than *hic* in direct speech, as seen in John 9:2 at *Sermo* 136.1: it is paralleled here by Codices Colbertinus and Palatinus (cf. John 4:18 etc.). The initial citation at *Tractatus* 44.3 has *hic an*: the latter word is also in Codex Colbertinus in place of *aut* in all other witnesses. This is one of a number of non-Vulgate readings which indicate that for this sermon Augustine was relying on a manuscript which was less similar to Weber–Gryson than the rest of the commentary. The end of John 9:2 in *Sermo* 136.1, *quoniam caecus natus est*, corresponds to Codices Veronensis and Usserianus, confirming this sermon as a source of Old Latin readings despite its late date of 416/18.[73] Augustine's reference to John 9:1 at *Tractatus* 44.3 suggests that his codex may have had *exiens* rather than *praeteriens*, even though this is not present in surviving manuscripts.

JOHN 9:3

None of Augustine's citations has a singular verb with *opera*, although this anacoluthon arising from direct translation of the Greek is preserved in the majority of Latin Gospels. Some Vulgate witnesses have *manifestentur*, as in *Tractatus* 44.3. Elsewhere Augustine reads *manifestarentur*, which appears alongside *ostendantur* in *Sermo* 136.1: neither is found here in surviving biblical witnesses, but the rendering *ostendere* is paralleled in other verses (e.g. John 7:4, 21:1, and 21:14). This sermon also uniquely reads *ipso* rather than *illo*.

JOHN 9:4

The text *ego ueni ut faciam opera eius* instead of *me oportet operari opera eius* appears to be a paraphrase like those of John 3:17 and John

[73] See p. 128.

6:38, with no support in biblical manuscripts despite citations with *facere* in other Church Fathers (e.g. Tertullian *Aduersus Praxean* 22). Even so, this form appears in all four citations of this verse and the title in the lectionary *Sermo* 135. Similar paraphrases in other verses indicate that Augustine does not follow the text of the Gospel closely in this sermon but quotes from memory.

JOHN 9:5–7

In *Tractatus* 44, *hoc* before *mundo* in John 9:5 is an Old Latin feature. This sermon has *liniuit* in John 9:6, one of two renderings only present in Vulgate witnesses. Augustine's eight other references to this verse have *inunxit*, which is closer to the Old Latin tradition, although as the five gospel manuscripts with this verb read *superunxit* it is possible that he has preserved a rendering of ἐπέχρισεν from a version now lost.[74] Similarly, all his citations of John 9:7 outside *Tractatus* 44 (including *Sermones* 136A, 136B, and 136C) have *piscina*, found in Codex Palatinus alone, rather than *natatoria*. Dulaey 2003:45–53 considers the exegesis of these verses in detail: both of Augustine's explanations of the mixture of dust and saliva, symbolizing either the Old Testament or the Incarnation, are unparalleled in earlier Latin tradition. As the identification with the Incarnation is restricted to later works, she suggests a date of 406–8 for *Sermones* 136A and 136C.

JOHN 9:9–12

These verses are only cited in *Tractatus* 44, with a handful of minor variants. Although Augustine has the distinctive Vulgate *nequaquam* for οὐχί, he omits the preceding *autem* from John 9:9. The

[74] The only other examples of *inungere* in the *Vetus Latina Database* are both present participles, in Quodvultdeus *Contra Iudaeos* 17.5 and the eighth-century *Sententiae sanctorum patrum* 66.

commentary also features the Old Latin *oculi tui* in John 9:10, but the ethic dative reappears in an addition to John 9:12 at *Tractatus* 44.8, *ille qui tibi aperuit oculos*: this expansion seems to be due to Augustine and is probably an anticipation of certain Old Latin versions of John 9:17.

JOHN 9:16–17

Tractatus 44.9 includes a form of John 9:16 which occurs in certain Vulgate manuscripts:

non est hic homo a deo qui sabbatum non custodit.

His other five verbatim citations (*Quaestiones de Iudicibus* 49, *Sermones* 122.2.2, 136.3, 136.4, and 258.1) follow the pattern:

non est iste (homo) a deo qui (sic) soluit sabbatum.[75]

Soluit sabbatum seems too loose a version of τὸ σάββατον οὐ τηρεῖ to reflect a biblical manuscript: it is more likely that Augustine is remembering John 5:18, ἔλυεν τὸ σάββατον. However, Codices Vercellensis and Veronensis also contain *sic* in John 9:16, like *Sermo* 136 and *Quaestiones de Iudicibus* 49. All Old Latin witnesses read *hic*, so the rendering *iste* in all five citations is unique to Augustine. The same is true of *Sermo* 136C.3 in John 9:17, which alone has *homine isto* rather than *illo* or *eo* (cf. John 4:18 etc.).

JOHN 9:18

The subjunctive *uocarent* in Augustine's sole citation, *Tractatus* 44.10, is paralleled by Codex Palatinus.

[75] The initial *nos scimus* in *Sermo* 136 is borrowed from John 9:20.

JOHN 9:22–4

Sermo 136A.4 presents what seems to be a paraphrase of John 9:22–3 as a verbatim citation:

> *timebant enim*, inquit, *parentes eius ne confiterentur Christum et tollerentur de synagoga*. et ideo dixerunt: *aetatem habet, ipsum interrogate.*

No biblical manuscript has the parents as the subject of the clauses with the subjunctive. Codex Vercellensis, however, does read *et ideo* rather than *propterea* at the beginning of the next verse (cf. John 12:39 and 16:15). John 9:24 provides two more examples of *iste*, in *Enarratio* 73.21 and *Sermo* 112A.12. Unlike John 9:16 and 17, here the pronoun is matched by Codices Palatinus and Usserianus.

JOHN 9:27–8

Although Augustine's citations of these two verses at *Enarrationes* 39.26 and 40.9 do not appear in the context of a gospel lection, they are remarkably close to Old Latin forms, reading *esse* rather than *fieri* in John 9:27 and *dicentes* for *et dixerunt* in the next verse. The latter reveals the influence of biblical style on the Latin translators because, unusually, the Greek tradition has two co-ordinated finite verbs. At the beginning of John 9:28 *Enarrationes* 39 and 40 add *et illi*, corresponding to certain Greek manuscripts with οἱ δέ and similar to *ad illi* in Codices Vercellensis, Bezae, and Brixianus. All five citations of this verse read *tu sis discipulus eius* (*tu discipulus eius sis* in *Tractatus* 44.12): the subjunctive is well attested in both Old Latin and Vulgate traditions.

JOHN 9:29–30

Every Latin Gospel has *hunc* in John 9:29, but the commentary at *Tractatus* 44.12 reads *istum*. The paraphrase at *Enarratio* 73.21 alone has *nouimus* for *scimus* on both occasions (cf. John 7:27 and 8:55). In John 9:30, *Tractatus* 44.13 does not include *enim*, found only in the Vulgate and Codices Brixianus and Aureus, nor the distinctive Vulgate word order *meos oculos.*

JOHN 9:31

Augustine does not appear to notice that some biblical manuscripts distinguish between *audit* and *exaudit* when rendering the two instances of ἀκούει in this verse.[76] *Tractatus* 44, following the Vulgate, has the pattern *audit... exaudit*; this is similar to *audit... exaudiet* at *Contra epistulam Parmeniani* 2.8.17, which is taken from the Old Latin source used by Augustine's opponent. At *Contra Faustum* 12.9 Augustine reads *exaudit* twice, in keeping with the majority of Old Latin witnesses. His mental text is *scimus quia peccatores deus non exaudit* which occurs in all five of the lectionary sermons: the only other exception to this is *De baptismo* 5.20.28, which, like *Contra epistulam Parmeniani*, has *deus peccatorem non audit.* The singular *peccatorem* is not preserved in Latin Bibles: in both cases, Augustine is likely to be citing another source (cf. Cyprian *Sententiae episcoporum* quoted at *De baptismo* 7.26.50). The form *si quis dominum coluerit* used by the Donatist Parmenianus and repeated by Augustine is comparable to Codex Palatinus.

JOHN 9:34

The text *proiectus est iste de synagoga* occurs in *Sermo* 135.5.6 and *Sermo* 136A.4 (without *iste*). Despite the similarity of these two lectionary sermons, this seems to be a paraphrase: no Latin manuscript has *proiecerunt* even though Codex Rehdigeranus adds *extra synagogam.* Similarly, *miserunt* in place of *eiecerunt* in *Sermones* 136.3 and 136C.5 is not paralleled by biblical codices (cf. John 8:7, 8:59).

[76] On the theological nuance of these verbs, see Burton 2000:93.

JOHN 9:36–8

Tractatus 44 uniquely has *ait* for *dixit* in John 9:36; the introduction to the direct speech is not cited in any of the other sermons. In the next verse, *Sermo* 135.5.6 reads *uides* rather than *uidisti*: it omits the profession of faith, *credo domine*, from John 9:38, but, like the verbatim citation at *Sermo* 136C.5, has *prostratus* rather than the biblical manuscripts' *procidens*. This agreement suggests that this rendering of *προσεκύνησεν* appeared here in a version which is no longer extant; elsewhere in the Gospel (John 4, John 12:20) it is always translated by *adorare*.

JOHN 9:39

The majority of Augustine's citations correspond to surviving manuscripts, although several omit *ego* or *in hunc mundum* through flattening. A non-sequential citation at *Tractatus* 33.1 reads *ego ueni ut non uidentes uideant et uidentes caeci fiant*. All surviving Old Latin manuscripts have two relative clauses, *qui non uident* and *qui uident*, as does every other reference Augustine makes to this verse, but Greek witnesses read *οἱ μὴ βλέποντες . . . οἱ βλέποντες*. This correspondence may simply be coincidental, as he is likely to have been citing from memory (cf. John 11:52). At *Contra aduersarium legis* 2.11.37, Augustine is probably responsible for introducing *non solum . . . sed etiam*, not paralleled in any biblical manuscript (cf. John 1:16). Hardy (1974:107–8) notes that the need for a mediator is the focus of Augustine's exposition of this verse.

JOHN 9:40–1

The addition of *quidam* before *ex Pharisaeis* in both *Tractatus* 44.17 and 45.1 seems to be part of Augustine's introduction rather than a biblical variant. In John 9:41, *nunc autem* in *Tractatus* 45, *Enarratio*

105.5 and *Sermo* 136B.2 rather than *nunc uero* (*Tractatus* 44 and Vulgate) is supported by six Old Latin witnesses. Both verses occur in *Enarratio* 65.5, which followed a lection from John 10. The form *num sumus caeci?* in John 9:40 appears to be a paraphrase, but there is greater verbal correspondence in the next verse:

ait illis dominus: si caeci essetis, peccatum non haberetis. modo autem quia dicitis uidemus, peccatum uestrum in uobis manet.

While the word order and readings such as *dominus* and *modo* are not paralleled in the Old Latin tradition, the inclusion of *in uobis* is significant, as it is only attested in Codices Vercellensis and Veronensis and not found in Greek.

JOHN 10:1–2

The three works which cite John 10:1 verbatim all give different renderings of the Greek *ἀλλαχόθεν*. The initial citation of *Tractatus* 45.2 reads *aliunde*, like the Vulgate and the majority of Old Latin manuscripts. *Enarratio* 95.3 and an allusion at *Tractatus* 45.3 both have *per aliam partem*, found in Codices Rehdigeranus, Sarzanensis, and Usserianus. As this also appears twice in the lectionary *Sermo* 137.5.5, it seems likely that it was Augustine's mental text. By contrast, the initial citation at *Sermo* 137.4.4 has *ex alia parte* (cf. Codices Colbertinus and Bezae), while later in the same paragraph and at *Sermo* 137.10.12 Augustine reads *per alteram partem* (as in Codex Palatinus). Three of the variant citations of John 10:1 in *Sermo* 137 as well as *Enarratio* 95.3 follow John 10:2, which indicates that they are drawn from memory. All six references to John 10:2 outside *Tractatus* 45, whether before or after John 10:1, have the Old Latin *ianuam* rather than *ostium*. This is also the case in his citations of John 10:7 and John 10:9.[77]

[77] For Augustine's exegesis of the door and the shepherd, see Comeau 1930:165–9; the role played by Augustine's theory of predestination and the contemporary sectarian situation in his explanation of this passage is treated by Berrouard 1989:423–30.

JOHN 10:5

The future *fugient* is only found in the Vulgate and Codex Bezae: *Tractatus* 45 reads *fugiunt* with all other Old Latin witnesses, despite the future in Greek.

JOHN 10:8

Augustine's criticism of his opponent's text at *Contra aduersarium legis* 2.4.16 has already been mentioned on pp. 172–3. The addition of *ante me*, paralleled in Codex Bezae, also appears in Faustus' reference to this verse at *Contra Faustum* 16.2, which Augustine repeats without comment at *Contra Faustum* 16.12. Nonetheless, his three other citations of this verse, namely *Tractatus* 45.8, the correction at *Contra aduersarium* 2.4.16, and a brief quotation at *Enarratio* 90.s1.1 omit these two words. Augustine is cited in the critical apparatus of Nestle–Aland for this omission: although in the first two cases he is a Vulgate witness, *Enarratio* 90.s1 was delivered in 412, possibly in Carthage, and followed the liturgical reading of this verse, so may have been based on an Old Latin text.[78] This is supported by the reading *qui* rather than *quotquot*, only attested in Codex Sarzanensis. This also features in *Contra Faustum* both times and as a sequential variant at *Tractatus* 45.11. In commenting on this verse at *Tractatus* 45.12, Augustine adduces 2 Timothy 2:19 to support his theory of predestination.

JOHN 10:10–11

Contra Gaudentium 1.16.17, Augustine's only citation of John 10:10 outside *Tractatus* 45, reads *ut occidat et perdat* in place of *ut furetur*

[78] Tischendorf gives the text of the other two references, but does not mention *Enarratio* 90.s1. He cites *Tractatus* 45, noting that, although *ante me* is missing from the citation, in his commentary Augustine supplies the words *praeter me* at this point (*Tractatus* 45.8, 45.11).

et mactet et perdat. This is probably due to memory: *occidat* is the majority Old Latin reading, but no manuscript omits *furetur.* Augustine's commentary is preceded by a similar text in an allusion at *Tractatus* 45.3, *perdere uolebant, mactare et occidere,* which combines the distinctive Vulgate reading *mactare* with the Old Latin *occidere*: the initial citation at *Tractatus* 45.15 is identical to Jerome's version. His mental text of the second half of John 10:11 is *pastor bonus animam suam ponit pro ouibus.* This comprises several Old Latin features including *ponit* rather than *dat.* It is found throughout the lectionary *Sermo* 138, and is supported by all citations except *Tractatus* 46, which has *dat*: Greek manuscripts are divided between δίδωμι and τίθημι in this verse and John 10:15 (cf. John 10:17). A number of citations with *ponit* also have the Old Latin *ouibus suis.*

JOHN 10:12–13

The omission of words and reordering show that most of Augustine's references to John 10:12 are paraphrases. *Enarratio* 141.11 and *Sermo* 138.1, however, include the Old Latin *autem* as the second word, missing from the Vulgate, Codex Aureus, and *Tractatus* 46. There is no manuscript support for *cum uiderit* in place of *uidet,* although it appears in *Enarratio* 141 and a sequential variant at *Tractatus* 46.7. The absence of *mercennarius autem fugit* from the beginning of John 10:13 in *Enarratio* 141 and *Sermones* 137.10.12 and 138.1.1 is more likely to be the omission of repetitive material (it appears at *Sermo* 137.5.5) even though it does not feature in Codices Palatinus and Bezae. All nine citations of this verse, including *Tractatus* 46 and the lectionary sermons, support *non est ei* (or *illi*) *cura.* This distinctive rendering matches Codices Bezae, Brixianus, Rehdigeranus, and Usserianus; other Latin versions have *non pertinet ad eum.*

JOHN 10:16

The text and exegesis of this verse is considered in detail in Berrouard 1990.[79] He gives the following form as representative of Augustine's mental text of this verse, although there are frequently minor variations (e.g. *ex* for *de*, and *eas*, *has* or *illas* for *ipsas*):

habeo alias oues quae non sunt de hoc ouili. oportet me et ipsas adducere ut sit unus grex et unus pastor.

The omission of the initial *et* and the phrase *et uocem meam audiunt* is an indication that this citation has undergone flattening. The only citation which differs substantially is the reading *uado adducam eas* in place of *oportet me et ipsas adducere* in the early *Sermo* 4.18 (dated 403): this seems to be an error of memory. Most Old Latin witnesses read *et fiet unus grex*, but Codex Colbertinus has *et erit unus grex*, which appears in six citations from both early and late works (e.g. *Expositio epistolae ad Romanos* 57.3 and *Tractatus* 117.5). Augustine reads *ut sit unus grex* on twenty-one occasions, including *De consensu* 3.4.14. Only *Tractatus* 47 and 49 have *unum ouile*, unique to the Vulgate (the Old Latin witnesses which have *ouili* for αὐλῆς earlier in the verse read *grex* for ποίμνη). Even these feature *ut sit* and *ut esset* respectively, and while Augustine introduces purpose clauses into other citations (e.g. John 1:14), the weight of attestation suggests that *ut sit* appeared in a codex known to him. Berrouard, who describes this as 'presque certain' (1990:293), divides Augustine's use of this verse into two categories according to whether the emphasis is on the initial or final phrase: the latter may be subdivided into those which focus on the unity of the flock or the uniqueness of the shepherd. Nonetheless, apart from the exposition in *Tractatus* 47, Augustine simply adduces the verse as a proof text, for example, citing it alongside Matthew 15:24 on the subject of welcoming Gentiles into the Church.[80]

[79] The thirty-two references he gives should be supplemented by *Epistula* 93, *De consensu* 3.4.14, *Expositio epistolae ad Galatas* 31.8, *Tractatus* 49.27, *Enarrationes* 105.36–7, 113.s1.2, 113.s2.10, and *Sermones* 265.9.11, 285.5, and 295.5.5.

[80] La Bonnardière 1986:131; see also Berrouard 1989:442–5.

JOHN 10:18

The majority of Augustine's seventy citations of John 10:18 also display a flattened form:

potestatem habeo ponendi animam meam et potestatem habeo iterum sumendi eam. nemo tollit eam a me sed ego eam pono a me.[81]

Seventeen citations add *et iterum sumo eam* or *ut iterum sumam eam* after this text, which is a conflation with John 10:17. The reading *ponendi animam meam* also appears in Codex Aureus (first hand, later corrected to *ponendi eam*) and Ambrose (*De fide* 2.2.25 and *De bono mortis* 10.43). Four citations have *recipiendi* for λαβεῖν (*Epistulae* 55.16 and 140.14.36, *Enarratio* 39.24, *Sermo* 111.2; cf. *Enarratio* 63.3 with *recipere*): this rendering only occurs on one other occasion in the *Vetus Latina Database*, a sermon attributed to Chrysostom. The presence of *accipiendi* in manuscripts of *De diuersis quaestionibus* 80.3 has been discussed on p. 141, while *Sermo* 122.3.3 has *assumendi* like a number of other Latin Fathers. The final part of the verse, *hoc mandatum accepi a patre meo*, is only cited in *Tractatus* 47 and *Contra Maximinum* 2.14.9: the latter has the Old Latin rendering *praeceptum*, following the text of Augustine's opponent in the *Collatio*.

JOHN 10:21

The two citations outside *Tractatus* 47, *Enarratio* 48.s2.4 and 53, both have *ista uerba*: the replacement of *haec* by *ista* matches Augustine's preference for this pronominal form elsewhere (cf. John 4:18, 9:2, 9:16 etc.) and so may not derive from a manuscript.

[81] This is analysed on p. 69.

JOHN 10:24

Most Old Latin versions render ἕως πότε by *usque quo*, while *quousque* occurs in the Vulgate and three other witnesses: the latter is found, as expected, in *De consensu* 4.10.18 and *Tractatus* 48. Augustine reads *quamdiu* in *Contra Faustum* 12.44 and *Sermo* 293D.4 (alongside *quousque*). There is a parallel for this rendering in Codices Colbertinus and Corbeiensis at Matthew 17:17, so it is possible that Augustine knew it in a manuscript of John. However, there is no support for the plural *animas nostras*, which appears in both citations of *Sermo* 293D.4.

JOHN 10:27

Augustine's only instance of *oues meae* by itself, a reading characteristic of the Vulgate and related manuscripts, is *Tractatus* 48.5. In eight other citations, three of which are in *Sermo* 46, he reads *quae sunt oues meas*, comparable to *oues quae sunt meae* in Codex Bezae: this appears to be his mental text, as these references omit the phrase *et ego cognosco eas*. *De peccatorum meritis* 1.27.40 has:

qui de ouibus meis sunt, uocem meam audiunt; et ego noui illas et secuntur me.

The opening phrase is identical to Codex Corbeiensis and similar to Codex Palatinus, while the only example of *noui* rather than *cognosco* appears in Codex Usserianus. As suggested on p. 167, this unexpected Old Latin reading in a work which uses the Vulgate elsewhere may indicate that Augustine was relying on another source.

JOHN 10:28–9

The sequential variants in *Tractatus* 48 seem to be errors of memory: the future tense *dabo* in John 10:28 is influenced by *peribunt* and *rapiet*, while *nemo rapit oues meas* probably combines the replacement of the pronoun *eas* with an anticipation of *nemo* in the next verse, although there are three Old Latin witnesses that read *nemo rapit* here. Augustine's only other citation of this verse, *De peccatorum meritis* 1.27.40, has the Old Latin *illis* rather than *eis*. In John 10:29, the reduction of *potest rapere* to *rapit* is comparable to his treatment of *potest* elsewhere (cf. John 3:3 etc.). The only non-Vulgate reading which features in his initial citation is the word order *maius est omnibus*, as found in Codices Vercellensis and Usserianus: despite the variation in Greek, most Latin versions have the neuter here.

JOHN 10:30–2

Augustine frequently uses John 10:30 to counter sectarian doctrines, pointing out the plural of the verb *sumus*, but the singular *unum* (e.g. *Tractatus* 36.9 and 37.6, *De trinitate* 5.9.10 and 7.6.12).[82] His only citations of John 10:31 appear in *Tractatus* 48. The first reference to this verse has the Old Latin *tulerunt* rather than *sustulerunt* and omits *Iudaei*. Two lines later Augustine cites John 10:31–3 with the Vulgate form of text (except that *illum* is replaced by *eum*). (For similar variations in the *Tractatus*, cf. John 3:32 etc.) This citation also has the word order *bona opera* in John 10:32, paralleled in Codex Bezae. The only other instance of John 10:32, *Enarratio* 63.3, is clearly a paraphrase, taking the word *occidere* from its context: *tanta opera bona, inquit, ostendi uobis: propter quod horum me uultis occidere?*

[82] See further Berrouard 1988:471–2 and Comeau 1930:284. John 14:10 is similarly employed at *Tractatus* 71.2.

JOHN 10:36

De trinitate 2.5.9 has three Old Latin readings in this verse, all of which appear in Codices Veronensis and Usserianus: *hunc* before *mundum*, *quoniam* in place of the second *quia*, and *blasphemat* rather than *blasphemas* (for other changes of person, see John 2:20, 4:17, and 6:53).

JOHN 10:37–8

Tractatus 48, Augustine's only citation of John 10:37, has the word order *mihi credere*. In the next verse, it uniquely has *in illo* for *in patre* (cf. John 10:31). Although *creditis* rather than *uultis credere* at *Contra Faustum* 13.5 has been adopted from Faustus' text at *Contra Faustum* 12.1, this corresponds to the predominant Greek form which is found in other Latin Fathers but no gospel manuscripts.

JOHN 10:39–40

In John 10:39 *adprehendere* rather than *prendere* throughout *Tractatus* 48 is the reading of all Old Latin manuscripts as well as certain Vulgate witnesses. Augustine continues with *ibi* for *illic* at the end of the next verse, paralleled in five Old Latin codices. The omission of *erat* at *Tractatus* 48.12 is a typographical error in the *Corpus Christianorum* edition (Verheijen 1976:5).

JOHN 11:1

The raising of Lazarus is the chief of the three resurrection stories used by Augustine to explain the sacrament of reconciliation: for a full account of his exegesis, see La Bonnardière 1968:188–97. The whole pericope is expounded in *Tractatus* 49, which features most of the distinctive Vulgate readings despite numerous minor variations from this text-type. In John 11:1 it includes the plural *sororum*, found in a couple of Old Latin and Vulgate manuscripts; *De consensu* 2.79.154 has the singular.

JOHN 11:3–4

The initial citation in *Tractatus* 49.5 adds *eius* after *sorores*, as do most Old Latin witnesses. In John 11:4 *ut glorificaretur deus in filio suo* at *Ad Simplicianum* 2.5 is an error of memory. Nonetheless, it is noteworthy that in this early work Augustine has the rendering *glorificare*, found in Codex Bezae as well as the Vulgate and related witnesses.

JOHN 11:7

The move of *iterum* from the end of the verse to after *dicit* at *Tractatus* 49.7 is not paralleled in biblical manuscripts.

JOHN 11:10–16

Most of the initial citations in *Tractatus* 49 feature a single non-Vulgate reading which corresponds to Old Latin witnesses: *in nocte* in John 11:10, *excitem* in John 11:11, the omission of *eius* from John 11:12, *quod* for *quia* in John 11:13, *quia* for *quoniam* in John 11:15, and *et moriamur cum illo* at the end of John 11:16. Augustine summarizes John 11:11–12 and 14 from memory in *Sermo* 98.4.4: *est* rather than *erit* in John 11:12 is without parallel, as is the addition of *dico uobis* in John 11:14, although Codex Bezae repeats *amicus noster* in John 11:14 from three verses previously.[83]

[83] Matzkow–Jülicher–Aland cite the Fragmentum Sangallense as a witness to *amicus noster* in John 11:14, but this is misleading as this lectionary manuscript

JOHN 11:25–6

Tractatus 49 begins John 11:25 with the present tense *dicit*, in keeping with some Vulgate manuscripts. Although *De consensu* 4.10.18 and *Tractatus* 49.15 have *etiamsi mortuus fuerit* for κἂν ἀποθάνῃ, Augustine's seven other citations read *licet moriatur*, including the lectionary *Sermo* 173. Only this sermon and *Enarratio* 56.14 have *uiuit* rather than *uiuet*, like Codices Veronensis and Corbeiensis. In John 11:26 *Sermo* 173 omits *omnis* with the Fragmentum Sangallense but includes *in aeternum*.

JOHN 11:31–2

Tractatus 49.17 has *illa* rather than *ea* in John 11:31, as do Codex Vercellensis and some Vulgate witnesses. Four Old Latin witnesses read *Maria autem* in the next verse, like *Tractatus* 49.18, while the word order *frater meus non esset mortuus* is present in the Fragmentum Sangallense.

JOHN 11:33, 35

In place of *qui uenerant cum ea plorantes*, *Tractatus* 49.18 uniquely reads *qui cum illa erant plorantes*: perhaps *erant* was a copying error in Augustine's codex (*plorantes* is unique to the Vulgate). All three citations of John 11:33 have *semetipsum* for *seipsum*: both occur in the Latin tradition, as does *infremuit* in his two other references to this verse (*De sermone domini* 1.12.35 and *Sermo* 98.6.6). In contrast, almost all Augustine's allusions to John 11:35 have *flere*, including the translation of Chrysostom which he quotes in *Contra Iulianum*

summarizes the preceding verses before beginning its verbatim citation at John 11:15. The evidence of Codex Bezae weakens claims that *amicus noster* in John 11:14 is a Diatessaronic reading (Petersen 1994:143).

1.6.24. Latin Gospels universally read *lacrimatus est.*[84] Augustine insists that the active verb *turbauit* in John 11:33 demonstrates Jesus' control of his own emotions (*Tractatus* 49.18; see also *Tractatus* 60.5 and his interpretation of John 12:27).

JOHN 11:37–9

Augustine's only citation of John 11:37, *Tractatus* 49, has the same word order as Codex Aureus, *ex ipsis dixerunt.* Both *Tractatus* 49 and *De sermone domini* 1.12.35 have *rursus* rather than *rursum* in the next verse. In John 11:39, all surviving Old Latin manuscripts render ἄρατε τὸν λίθον by *tollite lapidem*, but this is not found in any of Augustine's citations. Throughout *Tractatus* 49 he reads *lapidem remouete*, supported by *De trinitate* 8.5.7 and possibly also *Sermo* 139A.2: the latter also has *auferte lapidem*, which appears in *De diuersis quaestionibus* 65. Augustine's use of *remouete* is paralleled in three other patristic citations, while *auferre* renders αἴρειν elsewhere.[85] In all eight of his verbatim citations outside *Tractatus* 49, Augustine reads *putet*, as in Codex Bezae and the Fragmentum Sangallense. These include *De diuersis quaestionibus* 65:

dicit illi Martha: domine, iam quarta dies est et putet.

This early work reproduces a number of Old Latin readings, even though the word order is peculiar to Augustine: several biblical manuscripts omit *soror eius qui mortuus fuerat*, a distinctive Vulgate reading, and Codex Palatinus reads *quarta diei.*

[84] This is the only instance of ἐδάκρυσεν in the Greek New Testament and *lacrimari* in the Vulgate (apart from Tobit and Sirach): *flere* translates λυπεῖν in John 16:20 and κλαίειν in John 20:11. Tertullian has *lacrimatur super Lazarum* (*De carne Christi* 9) and *flens Lazarum* (*Aduersus Praxean* 27).

[85] The *Vetus Latina Database* lists *remouere* in Ambrose (*De paenitentia* 2.56), the *Expositio Iohannis iuxta Hieronymum* (based on Augustine), and Paulinus of Aquileia (*Carmen* 4). Cyprian has examples of *auferre* for αἴρειν not preserved in Old Latin manuscripts at John 1:29 and John 10:18 in *Ad Quirinum* 2.15 and 2.24.

JOHN 11:41–2

At *Contra Maximinum* 2.14.8, Augustine has *quia* rather than the Vulgate *quoniam* in John 11:41, which differs from Maximinus in *Collatio cum Maximino* 14. The text of the following verse, however, with *et ego sciebam* and *propter eos qui circumstant*, is identical to the form cited by his opponent. Latin Gospels all have a singular noun (*turbam* or *populum*), but the version in these citations does away with the anacoluthon of the singular *circumstat* followed by the plural *credant* (cf. Tertullian *Aduersus Praxean* 23).

JOHN 11:43–4

Most of Augustine's sermons, including the initial citation of *Tractatus* 49, have the word order *magna uoce* in John 11:43. Four sermons read *prodi foras* (*Sermones* 67.1.2, 128.12.14, 295.3.2, 352.3.8), which appears in three Old Latin witnesses: Codices Veronensis and Usserianus, and the Fragmentum Sangallense. All other manuscripts have *ueni foras*, although there is no verb in Greek. In the next verse, only the Vulgate and Codex Aureus read *statim prodiit* rather than *exiit* (*exiuit*). Augustine has *statim prodiit* in *Tractatus* 49 and *prodiit* alone at *Sermo* 295.3.2; *exiit* occurs later in *Sermo* 295 as well as *De diuersis quaestionibus* 65, while his other allusions hint at *processit* (*Enarrationes* 70.s2.3 and 101.s2.3, *Sermo* 98.6.6; cf. the Vulgate at John 8:42 and 18:4). The word order *manus et pedes* seems to be unique to Augustine (*Tractatus* 49.24, *De diuersis quaestionibus* 65, *Sermo* 295.3.2). Matthew 18:18 (*quae solueritis in terra soluta erunt et in caelo*) is frequently used by Augustine to illustrate *soluite* in John 11:44 in keeping with the theme of penitence (see further La Bonnardière 1968:196 and Berrouard 1989:469–73). Five citations, including *Tractatus* 49, have *illum* rather than *eum*, as do four Old Latin codices.

JOHN 11:45–7

The initial citations in *Tractatus* 49 add *Iesus* after *fecit* in John 11:45 and omit *ergo* in John 11:47, while a sequential variant for John 11:46 reads *quidam uero ex eis*: all these are paralleled in the Old Latin tradition.

JOHN 11:48

Among Augustine's fourteen citations of this verse, only *Tractatus* 49.26 and *Enarratio* 105.37 follow the Vulgate rendering of ἐὰν ἀφῶμεν αὐτὸν οὕτως as *si dimittimus eum sic*. On other occasions he uniquely has *si dimiserimus eum uiuere* (*Tractatus* 93.3, *Enarrationes* 40.1 and 55.17) or *si illum dimiserimus uiuum* (*Enarratio* 62.18), while in five citations the complement of *eum* is omitted altogether. *Dimiserimus* is present in Codices Vercellensis and Bezae, while *si relinquamus eum sic* in *Enarratio* 13.6 is identical to Codex Veronensis. *Enarratio* 68.s2.10 has *istum* for *eum* (cf. John 4:18 etc.). Like most Old Latin witnesses, Augustine prefers *tollent nobis*, a dative of disadvantage: given the equivalence of *tollere* and *auferre* noted in John 11:39, *auferent* in *Enarratio* 55.17 may preserve another Old Latin reading in this verse. However, with the exception of *Tractatus* 49.26 and *Sermo* 10.8, Augustine's eleven citations of the end of the verse feature the double *et* preserved only in the Vulgate, *et locum et gentem*.[86] As this corresponds exactly to Greek manuscripts, it is likely that it was found in an Old Latin version. The two sermons which read *regnum* rather than *gentem* (*Enarrationes* 52.9 and 68.s2.10) may both have been preached in Thagaste (see p. 136), so this could be a peculiarity of biblical codices in Augustine's birthplace.[87] The extra material in three *Enarrationes* (*omne saeculum*

[86] *Sermo* 10.8 is the only example of the reversal of these terms, *gentem et locum*, which Birdsall (1957:62) notes in Chrysostom and Augustine. He also supplies a number of patristic parallels for the omission of *sic* (οὕτως) in this verse, including Photius and Cyril of Alexandria.

[87] A number of other Church Fathers have *regnum*, including Quodvultdeus, which suggests that this might be an African reading.

post illum ibit in 17.44, *saeculum post illum abiit* in 40.1, and *omnes ibunt post illum* in 64.1), is a conflation with Old Latin forms of John 12:19, although it may show that Augustine was conscious of a phrase between *dimittimus* and *uenient*; his omission of the canonical text, *omnes credent in eum et*, from all citations except *Tractatus* 49 and *Enarrationes* 13 and 105 is simply an abbreviation (Metzger 1971:392, *contra* Boismard).

JOHN 11:50

Several of Augustine's citations of this verse appear to be flattened, with the omission of *nobis*, *pro populo*, and sometimes even *homo*: the full form is only found in three citations (*Epistula* 187.12.37, *Tractatus* 49.27, *Enarratio* 105.37). Again, this shorter version is found in other Latin and Greek Fathers.

JOHN 11:51

While four of Augustine's citations have *Iesus moriturus erat*, three read *oportebat Iesum mori* (*Contra Faustum* 16.23, *Enarratio* 40.1, *Sermo* 315.1.2 with *Christum*; cf. *Quaestiones de Iudicibus* 49). This is unique to Augustine: *oportebat* may be a reminiscence of or replacement for *incipiebat*, used to render ἔμελλεν in seven Old Latin manuscripts.[88]

JOHN 11:52–4

One of Augustine's four citations of John 11:52, *De correptione et gratia* 20, features non-Vulgate readings paralleled in Old Latin

[88] John 4:47 is also rendered as *incipiebat mori* in some manuscripts, which works better in the context of the sick boy: similar forms are found in John 7:35 and 14:22, but no surviving manuscript reads *incipere* for ἤμελλεν ἀποθνήσκειν in John 18:32.

manuscripts, *sed etiam* (Codex Usserianus), and *dispersos* rather than *qui erant dispersi* (Codices Vercellensis and Palatinus). These are identical to the type of variants noted in John 9:39, namely the introduction of antithesis and a literal rendering of a Greek participle, and while no surviving Old Latin correspondences exist for that verse, they are present on this occasion. In both instances, however, it seems likely that Augustine was citing from memory. The initial citation of *Tractatus* 49 and *Enarratio* 105.37 have *sed ut*, omitting *et* which is a reading distinctive of the Vulgate. Both variants for John 11:54 at *Tractatus* 49.28, *palam* for *in palam* and the addition of *suis* after *discipulis*, occur in Old Latin witnesses.

JOHN 11:55–7

Tractatus 50, which supplies Augustine's only full citations of these verses, features several distinctive Vulgate readings alongside Old Latin forms. After *proximum* (peculiar to the Vulgate and Codex Veronensis), *ergo* in place of *autem* is without parallel, although *ascenderunt ergo* rather than *et ascenderunt* later in the verse is matched by three witnesses. In John 11:56 *inter se* rather than *ad inuicem* appears in Codices Palatinus and Vercellensis, but all manuscripts have *conloquebantur* or *dicebant*: the uncompounded form *loquebantur* is unique. While Augustine has the Old Latin *uenit* for the uniquely Vulgate *ueniat* in this verse, in John 11:57 he includes the characteristic Vulgate form *pontifices.*

JOHN 12:1–2

Both citations of John 12:1 at *De consensu* 2.78.152–3 have the Old Latin *in* before *Bethaniam*, although it is missing from the Vulgate

See further Löfstedt 1911:210. On *oportere* as a possible future periphrasis, see García de la Fuente 1994:56 and the overlapping domains described by Coleman (1971:217–21).

and *Tractatus* 50. Conversely, in the next verse *Tractatus* 50 has the word order *ibi cenam* and omits *erat* after *unus*.

JOHN 12:3

The rendering of *οὖν* by *uero* is rare in the Old Latin tradition (see Parker 1985:258–9). Its appearance in the initial citation of *Tractatus* 50.6 could represent a lost version, although it is more likely that *uero* has been repeated from the previous verse. (In Augustine's other citations, *uero* appears as an alternative to *autem* for δέ, e.g. John 9:41, 11:46, 16:10.) On Augustine's symbolic exegesis of this passage in *Tractatus* 50, see Comeau 1930:152–3.

JOHN 12:6

The four verbatim citations outside *Tractatus* 50 have the Old Latin reading *auferebat*, attested in Codices Vercellensis, Palatinus, and Colbertinus. On the other hand, *omnia quae mittebantur de dominicis loculis auferebat* in *Epistula* 108.3.8 seems to be a paraphrase. *Tractatus* 50 has the Vulgate *pertinebat* and *portabat*, although it also reads *ad illum* and *et* after *habere*. Augustine often uses this verse to show that the presence of a betrayer was tolerated among the disciples (e.g. *De opere monachorum* 5.6, *Epistula* 43.23).

JOHN 12:7–9

These verses are only cited in *Tractatus* 50. In keeping with certain Vulgate manuscripts, it reads *in diem* in John 12:7 and has the future *habebitis* on both occasions in John 12:8. It also adds *Iesus* after *suscitauit* in the next verse, a gloss which seems to have featured in Augustine's codex and is present in Codex Bezae.

JOHN 12:12–18

Tractatus 51 is the only source for Augustine's text of these verses: the accusative *Hierosolymam* in John 12:12 is well attested in Vulgate codices. His citations otherwise correspond to the Vulgate, except for the transposition *scripta erant* in John 12:16 (cf. John 20:31).

JOHN 12:19

Tractatus 93.3 and *Enarratio* 67.6 both read *totus mundus*, reversing the order of these words in biblical manuscripts. *Enarratio* 40.13 is clearly a paraphrase, reading *occidamus eum ne saeculum post illum pergat.* However, the choice of *pergit* rather than the biblical *abiit* or *uadit* may be an example of a 'faster' verb to dramatize the action (cf. John 4:28).

JOHN 12:22–3

Tractatus 51 has *dicunt* for *dixerunt* in John 12:22, in keeping with some Latin manuscripts and the Greek present tense. *Glorificetur* rather than *clarificetur* in the next verse, found in both *Tractatus* 51 and 52, is the last example in John of *glorificare* rendering δοξάζειν in numerous Vulgate witnesses. Although Weber–Gryson adopts *clarificare* in John 12:23, like Codex Brixianus, most manuscripts and editions (as well as the *Tractatus in Iohannem*) do not switch until John 12:28.[89]

[89] For a table of these renderings in different manuscripts, see Burton 2000:68, although this misrepresents the Vulgate in John 12:23 and 12:28. The edition of Wordsworth–White prefers *glorificetur* in John 12:23, also found in over fifty manuscripts in Fischer's collation.

JOHN 12:24

Only *Enarratio* 140.2 and the partial citation at *Tractatus* 51.9 have a text identical to the Vulgate; *Tractatus* 52 omits *ipsum*, but is the sole other example of *frumenti*, while the lectionary *Sermo* 329 corresponds to the Vulgate apart from *tritici*. The rest of Augustine's references to this verse are paraphrases produced from memory and usually abbreviated. They either have the Old Latin *tritici* or omit this altogether, and many feature the words *mortificatum* and *multipliciter*. The last-mentioned (*Enarrationes* 73.13 and 79.2; *Sermones* 218.15.15, 305.1, and 305.2) seems too loose to represent *multum fructum affert*: it is possible that Augustine was inspired by a parallel such as *Didache* 9.4 or the Parable of the Sower (Matthew 13:3 etc.).[90] In addition to the Old Latin *tritici*, *Sermo* 335E.2 has *nisi cadat*, like Codex Palatinus, and *remanet*, like Codex Brixianus. *Remanet* is supported by three other works, while *Sermo* 361.10 has *manebit*. *Nisi ceciderit* appears in *Sermo* 111.2 and *Enarratio* 68.s1.10 (as well as an adaptation in *Enarratio* 140.25). The reading *reddit* for *adfert* in *Enarratio* 68.s1 is probably an error of memory.

JOHN 12:25

Augustine's mental text incorporates conflations with the Synoptic Gospels (Matthew 10:39 etc.). The form in *Sermo* 313D.1 is typical of the resultant text:

qui amat animam suam perdet eam, et qui perdiderit eam propter me inueniet eam.

There are also examples of *illam* for either or both instances of *eam*, matching Codices Vercellensis and Palatinus. *Sermo* 305.2 includes the phrase *in hoc saeculo*, and *Epistula* 243.5 and *Sermo* 313C read *in isto saeculo*: it is probable that *saeculo* appeared here once in a biblical codex (cf. John 12:31, 12:46 etc.), especially as it features in Cyprian

[90] On Augustine's use of the *Didache*, see Albaric 1986:94 and Altaner 1952:208.

(*Ad Quirinum* 3.16).[91] The Vulgate *odit* is only found in *Tractatus* 51 and 52, although *Epistula* 243.5 twice has *oderit*; *Tractatus* 51 has the Old Latin *custodiet eam*, while *Tractatus* 52 is identical to Weber–Gryson. At both *Tractatus* 51.10 and *Sermo* 331.1.1 Augustine observes that this verse can be interpreted either as a statement or an exhortation.

JOHN 12:26

Augustine's explicit comment at *Sermo* 319.3.3 is the only remaining evidence for the manuscript reading *ubi sum ego illic et diaconus meus*. This represents a borrowing of the Greek term, *διάκονος*, used specifically of a Christian minister: here Augustine applies it to the protomartyr Stephen, who was also one of the first deacons.[92] The omission of *erit* at the end of the sentence in this sermon is a feature of several Old Latin manuscripts. Codices Palatinus, Vercellensis, and Usserianus provide a parallel for *ibi* in place of *illic*, as found in a sequential variant at *Tractatus* 51.12 and the initial citation of *Tractatus* 52 (cf. John 3:23, 10:40).

JOHN 12:27

Saluifica in this verse is unique to Codex Veronensis and the Vulgate. It appears in *Tractatus* 52, but the non-sequential citation at *Tractatus* 60.1 has *salua*, and *Epistula* 140.11.29 supports *libera*, both of which are attested in Old Latin witnesses (cf. John 12:47). The change

[91] *Sermo* 368 in the Augustinian corpus, which is now attributed to Caesarius of Arles but may be based on a lost sermon of Augustine, has the following text for its lection: *qui amat animam suam perdet illam . . . qui autem odit animam suam in hoc saeculo in uitam aeternam inueniet eam*. The use of *saeculo* and *inueniet* may therefore be traces of Augustine's text.

[92] On the technical Christian term *diaconus*, see Mohrmann 1949:79–80, where her contention that Augustine was unaware of *minister* in this specialized sense is based on this citation: Augustine's argument, however, concerns the interchangeability of the two words, which does not support her claim.

in word order to *hac hora* and *hanc horam* in the initial citation of *Tractatus* 52 is shared by some biblical manuscripts, although *Tractatus* 60 has the Vulgate sequence; *Epistula* 140 uniquely reads *illa hora* and *illam horam*. As with John 11:33, Augustine interprets the verb *turbare* as a deliberate display of emotion by Jesus in order to reassure later followers (*Tractatus* 60.5, *Sermo* 305.4).

JOHN 12:28

Several Greek witnesses have υἱόν rather than ὄνομα, which suggests that Augustine's reading *filium tuum* in two early works, *Sermo* 12.5 and *De trinitate* 2.10.18, may derive from a scriptural codex: all surviving Old Latin versions read *nomen tuum*, but a dozen Vulgate manuscripts have *filium tuum* (see Fischer 1991:344). Alternatively, the parallel with John 17:1 may have led both Augustine and biblical copyists astray: as Tischendorf observes, *Contra Adimantum* 9 conflates John 17:5 and 12:28. This is one of three citations which are preceded by *sonuit uox* (see also *De trinitate* 1.4.7 and 2.10.18 and an allusion at *Tractatus* 54.7), although there does not seem to be a parallel for this in any manuscript.

JOHN 12:29–30

Tractatus 52 has two minor variations, both attested in other Vulgate witnesses: *dicebat* for *dicebant* in John 12:29, and *haec uox* rather than *uox haec* in the next verse.

JOHN 12:31

Thirteen of Augustine's citations have *missus est* where Greek manuscripts read ἐκβληθήσεται: most Old Latin codices have a future verb, in keeping with the Greek tradition, but five read *mittitur*. There is no support for the past tense in any Latin or Greek manuscripts, although Augustine's consistency suggests that it may have been known to him from an exemplar.[93] The future tense only appears at *Tractatus* 52 and *Contra Iulianum* 6.2.4, in the distinctive Vulgate form *eicietur.* Three works all dated to 394/5, *Enarratio* 9.8, *Sermo* 12, and *De sermone domini* 1.2.9, all read *huius saeculi*: this probably represents a rendering of *κόσμου* in a version no longer preserved (cf. John 12:25, 12:46, and 14:27). Augustine's two interpretations of the designation *princeps huius mundi*, based on this verse and 1 Corinthians 2:6 respectively, are both set out at *Sermo* 12.2; he considers that the expulsion from the heart of the believer takes place at baptism, while affirming the continued presence of the devil in unbelievers (e.g. *Tractatus* 52.7–8; see further Berrouard 1989:330–1).

JOHN 12:32

The reading *omnia traham post me* in the initial citation *Tractatus* 52.11 is only paralleled in one manuscript in Fischer's collation: all others read *ad* instead of *post.*[94] It may have appeared in Augustine's codex, but an error of memory is plausible as *trahere* is often followed by *post* (compare the allusion at *Enarratio* 59.9). His other citations, *Adnotationes in Iob* 39, *Enarratio* 140.25, and a sequential variant at *Tractatus* 52.12 have the Old Latin reading *cum (ego) exaltatus fuero.* Despite *πάντας* in the majority of Greek manuscripts, Augustine only ever reads *omnia* in this verse, in keeping with the entire Latin tradition: in fact he notes explicitly:

non autem dixit: omnes, sed *omnia.* (*Tractatus* 52.11)

[93] Even though the solecism *eiecitur* is found in a handful of Vulgate witnesses, this seems to be a misspelling for the present tense (Fischer 1991:354). In John 15:6, however, both *mittetur* and *missus est* are found in Old Latin manuscripts, corresponding to *βάλλουσιν*.

[94] **Gk** (Kilian-Evangeliar, Würzburg); cf. John 3:14.

This enables him to read his own doctrine of predestination into the verse, understanding *omnia* as the entirety of each believer rather than all humanity (see Comeau 1930:67–8).

JOHN 12:35

Two citations have *diem* rather than *lucem*: *Enarratio* 138.22 and *De uera religione* 42.79. Although Augustine uses this to gloss *dies* in Psalm 138, it seems most likely that this is an error of memory, introducing *diem* in opposition to *tenebrae* later in the verse.[95] The unique reading *currite* for *ambulate* (*Tractatus* 12.14) may be a 'speeding up' of the action inspired by the urgency of this verse (cf. John 4:28 and 12:19). This presumably also underlies the double *ambulent* at *Confessiones* 10.23.33; this adaptation lacks the Old Latin *tempus* after *modicum*, a reading peculiar to the Vulgate and Codex Aureus which is unexpected in an early work. Augustine's commentary text at *Tractatus* 52.13 appears to read *ergo ambulate*, although *ergo* may simply introduce the citation; Codex Bezae has *ambulate ergo*, and *ergo* is included in one manuscript of *De uera religione* 42.

JOHN 12:37–40

The citation of these verses in *De dono perseuerantiae*, dated to 429, has been quoted in full on p. 178: the Old Latin readings, unexpected in such a late work, include *crediderunt* in John 12:37 and two paralleled only by a single manuscript in Fischer's collation: *ideo* rather than *propterea* in John 12:39 (cf. John 9:23, 13:11 etc.) and *cor illorum* in John 12:40.[96] In John 12:40 the word order *cor eorum* in *Tractatus* 53 and *Quaestiones euangeliorum* appendix 13 is also found in some Vulgate sources. *Contra Iulianum opus imperfectum* 6.10 has

[95] See p. 143.
[96] **Bw** (Würzburg Univ. M.p.th.f. 67); see also John 8:9.

the Vulgate *eorum cor* and *sanem eos*, but like the contemporary *De dono perseuerantiae* reads *nec intellegant*, not found in any Latin Gospel. Augustine's charitable exposition of these verses, allowing for the possibility that the Jews might convert after Jesus' death, is exemplified at *Tractatus* 53.11 (cf. John 15:26 and the discussions at Comeau 1930:216–17 and Berrouard 1989:481–4).

JOHN 12:42

Tractatus 53 conforms to the Vulgate text, unlike Augustine's three other references to this verse (*Tractatus* 93.2, *Enarratio* 115.1, and *Sermo* 286.1.1). First, they all qualify *principes* with *Iudaeorum*, probably influenced by John 3:1 or John 19:21. Similarly, *propter metum Iudaeorum* in *Tractatus* 93 rather than *propter Pharisaeos* introduces a typical Johannine motif (cf. John 7:13, 19:38, 20:19). Codex Monacensis provides a parallel for *propter Iudaeos* in *Sermo* 286 and reads *ne de synagoga expellerentur*, comparable to *ne expellerentur de synagogis* in *Enarratio* 115 and *Tractatus* 93 (with *pellerentur*). The plural *synagogis* here is unique to Augustine, although it occurs in the Vulgate at John 16:2 for the same underlying Greek word (cf. also John 18:20). He also seems to have introduced *audebant confiteri* in place of *confitebantur* (*Tractatus* 93, *Sermo* 286; cf. John 7:45).

JOHN 12:43

In common with five Old Latin manuscripts, *Sermo* 286.1.1 (delivered after 425) and both citations in *Enarratio* 115 (around 403) read *amauerunt* rather than *dilexerunt*. Unlike *De baptismo* 2.11.16, biblical codices have no example of the present tense *diligunt*. Seven of Augustine's ten citations (*Tractatus* 53 and 54 and *Speculum* 28 follow the Vulgate) omit the second *gloriam*: this is also missing from Codex Corbeiensis, although in these references it may be the result of flattening.

JOHN 12:44

The omission of *autem* from *Tractatus* 54 is probably an adaptation: the commentary otherwise matches the Vulgate. The lectionary *Sermo* 140 and *De trinitate* 1.12.27 have the Old Latin word order *qui me misit* (cf. John 7:16, 7:33, 8:16 etc.). *De trinitate* 1 also reads *non in me credit* throughout, as found in Codices Colbertinus and Monacensis. Augustine cites both John 7:16 and John 14:1 at *De trinitate* 1.12.27 to address the contradictions apparent in this verse and John 12:47–8.

JOHN 12:46

Both of Augustine's citations of John 12:46 outside *Tractatus* 54 are in *De peccatorum meritis* 1: *ego lux in saeculum ueni, ut omnis qui crediderit in me non maneat in tenebris* (1.24.35; 1.25.38 has *credit*). The second clause is identical to Codex Palatinus, while *saeculum* is likely to have appeared in a version now lost (cf. John 12:25, 12:31, and 14:27).

JOHN 12:47

De trinitate 1.12.26 reads *si quis non audit uerba mea, ego non iudicabo illum*. The negative *non* and absence of *et non custodierit* are paralleled by Codex Palatinus, although these could be due to flattening. The future *iudicabo*, found throughout *De trinitate* 1, matches Greek witnesses accented κρινῶ rather than κρίνω and probably appeared in an Old Latin version: it is present in seven manuscripts in Fischer's collation. As in John 12:27, several of Augustine's citations provide alternatives to the Vulgate *saluificem*: *saluum faciam* occurs in *Tractatus* 36.4 and *De trinitate* 1, while *saluem* is supported by a looser allusion at *Tractatus* 39.6.

JOHN 12:48–50

The Old Latin readings in *De trinitate* 1 continue with the following text of John 12:48–9:

qui me spernit et non accipit uerba mea habet qui se iudicet... uerbum quod locutus sum ipsum iudicabit illum in nouissima die.... quia ego, inquit, *non ex me locutus sum, sed ille qui me misit pater, ille mandatum mihi dedit quid dicam et quid loquar.* (*De trinitate* 1.12.26)

Most of the non-Vulgate readings are present in the Old Latin tradition apart from *se iudicet* and *ille mandatum mihi.* The plural form of John 12:48 in *Enarratio* 32.2.s2.2 is an adaptation. *Sermo* 140.3 consistently reads *qui me misit, ipse mihi mandatum dedit*: all surviving Old Latin codices have *ipse*, but none omits *pater.* Both Augustine's citations of the second half of John 12:50, *Tractatus* 54.8 and *De trinitate* 1.12.26, omit *ergo* before *ego*: this is also missing from several Old Latin witnesses, although it may be due to parablepsis. *De trinitate* 1.12.26 continues with *ita ut dixit mihi pater sic loquor.* Codices Vercellensis and Palatinus have *ita* for the penultimate word (οὕτως), but no Latin Bible has *ita ut* rather than *sicut* for the earlier καθώς: this rendering seems to be characteristic of the text-type used for *De trinitate* 1 (cf. John 5:26).

JOHN 13:1

Only *Tractatus* 55.1 and *De trinitate* 2.17.29 of Augustine's eleven citations broadly correspond to the Vulgate text of this verse (the former has *hora eius*, while the latter reads *de* for *ex*). His mental text of the second phrase is *cum autem uenisset hora ut transiret Iesus de hoc mundo.* This is supported by eight sermons (*Enarrationes* 68.s1.2, 120.6, 138.8, 140.25, and *Sermones* 103.5.6, 104.6, 155.5.5, 179.6.6). No biblical manuscript has *cum uenisset hora* here, although this phrase is common elsewhere (e.g. John 19) and *cum* with the pluperfect subjunctive appears later in the sentence and twice in the next three verses. Despite the pluperfect in the majority of Greek manuscripts, it seems likely that Augustine is reproducing this feature of biblical style from memory; the addition of *Iesus* later in the verse is a further indication of flattening. *Epistula* 55.2, which has the Old Latin *transiret de*, reads *cum* ***uidisset*** *Iesus quia uenit hora.* This is probably an error, although there is some support for ἰδών rather than εἰδώς.

JOHN 13:2

The compound verb *inmisisset* is found in some Vulgate traditions as well as Codices Bezae and Aureus, so it is probable that its occurrence in *De consensu* 3.1.4 reflects Augustine's codex, even though it does not feature at *Tractatus* 55.3. All four citations (including the paraphrases at *Sermones* 67.2.4 and 301.6.4) have *in cor* rather than *in corde*, which is widely attested in biblical manuscripts. *Sermo* 67 also supports the Old Latin reflexive, with *immisit se diabolus.*

JOHN 13:6–8

The omission of *ergo* from the initial citation of John 13:6 in *Tractatus* 56 is an adaptation, as it is present twelve lines later. Augustine's other citation, in *Enarratio* 92.3, anticipates John 13:8 with *non lauabis mihi pedes* in this verse. This suggests that he was citing from memory, despite the length of this citation. In John 13:7 *Tractatus* 56 has *dixit* for *dicit*, and all three citations of John 13:8 have *habebis*: both occur in Vulgate manuscripts.

JOHN 13:9

Augustine only cites John 13:9 on three occasions. *Tractatus* 56.2 corresponds to the Vulgate. *Epistula* 265.5 reads *uerum etiam* rather than *sed et*: all Old Latin manuscripts have *sed*, but four combine this with *etiam*. It is possible that Augustine has emphasized the contrast (cf. John 9:39 and 11:52). *Enarratio* 92.3 has *non pedes tantum, sed et caput et totum.* This citation is likely to be from memory (see John 13:6), hence the omission of *manus*, but the final words, *et totum*, are of interest. Petersen (1994:380–4) believes this to be a Diatessaronic reading, reflecting the Tatianic practice of baptism by total immersion. It seems unlikely, however, that Augustine would have been influenced by the Diatessaron in a sermon preached in Hippo in 412, and more probable that he was familiar with the text-type of Codex Vercellensis which also has this phrase.[97]

JOHN 13:10

The Vulgate text, *non indiget ut lauet*, is only found in *De natura et origine animae* 3.9.12. Two citations read *non indiget nisi ut pedes lauet* (*Epistula* 265.5 and *Tractatus* 80.3), but the two commentary sermons have *non habet opus nisi pedes lauare* (*Tractatus* 56.3, supported by an allusion in *Tractatus* 57.1) and *non habet necessitatem nisi pedes lauare* (*Tractatus* 58.1). The latter rendering of ἔχει χρείαν is the most common in Augustine: *non habet necessitatem iterum lauandi* appears at *De baptismo* 2.14.19, *De unitate ecclesiae* 22.63 and *Enarratio* 92.3, similar to Codices Vercellensis and Monacensis although these omit *iterum*. *Non opus habet iterum lauari* is the text of *Contra Cresconium* 1.31.37: while *opus habere* is not attested in surviving Old Latin manuscripts, its appearance in Augustine's commentary and similarity to the Greek strongly suggest that it derives from a version which has not been preserved (cf. John 2:25).[98] The unique reading *non eum oportet iterum lauari* in *Epistula* 44.10 is less compelling in itself, but *lauari* does correspond to νίψασθαι. The

[97] See p. 97.

[98] The only other example of *habet opus* in the *Vetus Latina Database* is Quodvultdeus *Liber promissionum* 4.23. De Bruyne (1931:541) identifies the rendering of χρείαν ἔχειν by *opus habere* as a characteristic of Augustine's text of the Epistles. His analysis of John 13:10 (1931:596), however, which suggests that Augustine deliberately avoided the Vulgate reading in *Tractatus* 56 and made his own translation in *Epistula* 44, is overly complicated and inconsistent with the preference already claimed for *opus habere*.

three citations attributed to Augustine by Petilianus (*Contra litteras Petiliani* 2.22.49 (twice) and 2.24.56) all read *non habet causam nisi pedes lauandi*, almost identical to Codex Palatinus. The addition of *nisi pedes* is supported by a number of Old Latin, Vulgate, and Greek manuscripts. The rendering *qui lotus est semel* for the Greek participle ὁ λελουμένος occurs in *Contra Cresconium*, *De unitate ecclesiae*, *Epistula* 44, *Tractatus* 58, and *Enarratio* 92 (cf. *Contra litteras Petiliani* 2 and some manuscripts of *Epistula* 265). Many of these inveigh against the Donatists, and the adverb *semel* suits Augustine's polemic, arguing against the rebaptism practised by the sect. However, the appearance of *semel* in Codex Colbertinus and the Fragmentum Mediolanense, as well as Tertullian and Optatus, implies that Augustine was not responsible for its introduction: furthermore, *Epistula* 44 predates his engagement with the Donatist controversy. The inclusion of *iterum* in the five works listed above is absent from all surviving biblical codices but paralleled by earlier Latin Fathers.[99] Several precedents have been suggested for Augustine's connection of the foot-washing in this verse with Song of Songs 5:3 (*Tractatus* 56 and 57).[100]

JOHN 13:13–14

The citation in *Enarratio* 92.3 continues to show variants typical of memory: while the initial *dicitis* rather than *uocatis* in John 13:13 corresponds to Codices Vercellensis and Palatinus, the omission of *et domine* and the reading *uerum dicitis* can both be attributed to flattening. The presence of *uerum* in his mental text appears to be

[99] Tertullian *De baptismo* 12.3 reads *qui semel lauit non habet necesse rursum*, Optatus 4.4 and 5.3 have *qui semel lotus est non habet necessitatem iterum lauandi* and Jerome *Aduersus Iouinianum* 2.3 reads *qui lotus est non necesse habet uti iterum lauet.* The Latin patristic evidence for this verse is discussed at Berrouard 1993:404. There is one example of ἅπαξ in Epiphanius (*Panarion* 30.21.4).

[100] La Bonnardière 1965:83–4 proposes Ambrose's *De spiritu sancto*, while Comeau 1930:39 and Altaner 1952 both point to Origen. Berrouard 1993:82–3 notes that there is a difference between Origen's and Augustine's application of the image, and suggests that the connection was made independently; he treats Augustine's exegesis of *Song of Songs* 5:2–3 at Berrouard 1993:407–11.

confirmed by the gloss on this verse at *Tractatus* 58.3, *bene dicitis quia uerum dicitis* (cf. John 8:48). *Enarratio* 92.3 paraphrases John 13:14 as:

si ergo ego, magister et dominus uester, laui uobis pedes, quomodo oportet uobis inuicem faciatis.[101]

Although the final phrase appears to anticipate John 13:15 (where Codex Palatinus has *quomodo* and *faciatis*), there is support for the sequence *magister et dominus* and *inuicem* in Old Latin witnesses, some of which also have *quanto magis* for Augustine's *quomodo.* Throughout *Tractatus* 58, Augustine has the word order *debetis et uos,* even though this is not paralleled in surviving manuscripts. *Enim* for *etenim* at *Speculum* 28 is, by contrast, well attested in Vulgate tradition.

JOHN 13:16

Augustine's three citations of this verse agree with the Vulgate and most Old Latin witnesses. The five occasions on which he cites Cyprian *Epistula* 54.3, however, consistently read *esse non potest maior domino suo seruus.*

JOHN 13:18

None of the three works which cite the second half of this verse include the distinctive Vulgate reading *contra me. Tractatus* 59 and 60 have *leuabit super me,* with the majority of Old Latin manuscripts, while in *De ciuitate dei* 17.18.1, John 13:18 follows a citation of Psalm 40:10 itself and it seems that Augustine has repeated the same text rather than switch to the version given by the evangelist.

[101] Despite the expectation of an infinitive after *oportet,* both Migne and the *Corpus Christianorum* edition have *faciatis.*

JOHN 13:19–20

The word order *ut cum factum fuerit credatis* in *Tractatus* 59, the only work to cite these verses, is also found in the Vulgate tradition. Unlike his treatment of the absolute use of *ego sum* in John 8:24, 8:28, and 8:58, Augustine supplies a predicate in his commentary on John 13:19, *ego sum de quo illa scriptura praecessit* (*Tractatus* 59.1). For his transmission of an Arian interpretation of John 13:20 in this sermon, see La Bonnardière 1965:81–3.

JOHN 13:23–5

The addition of *praecipue* or *amplius* before *diligebat* in *Sermones* 120.1 and 135.7.8 respectively in John 13:23 is not paralleled in biblical manuscripts, although Codices Corbeiensis and Usserianus add *ualde* at the end of the verse. The phrase *prae ceteris diligebat* is also found in the context of John 13:25 in *De continentia* 11.25 and *Sermones* 20A.8 and 114.4. Augustine's motivation appears to have been to avoid a reading which suggested that Jesus did not love his other disciples (see further Dideberg 1986:192). In both verses, Augustine's citations are divided between *recumbere* and *discumbere*: he shows a preference for the latter, even though this rendering is only preserved in Codex Usserianus (lacunose in John 13:25). La Bonnardière 1965:79–80 draws attention to the similar exegesis of *innuit* in John 13:24 with reference to the book of Wisdom in both *Tractatus* 61.6 and *De trinitate* 15.10.19; the omission of *huic* from *Tractatus* 61 appears to be an oversight. All three citations of this verse otherwise follow the Vulgate, which does not include *interroga*.[102]

[102] On Augustine's treatment of John 13:25 (and parallels in earlier authors) see Berrouard 1969:57–63 and 1977:116–17.

JOHN 13:26

Although no surviving Old Latin or Vulgate witness has the uncompounded forms *tinctum* and *tinxisset* in this verse, Augustine's consistency in *Tractatus* 61 and 62 suggests that these renderings were present in his codex. These are his only verbatim citations of this verse apart from the Vulgate text at *De consensu* 3.1.3. The division of Greek witnesses between *βάψας* and *ἐμβάψας* offers an interesting parallel.[103]

JOHN 13:27

The rendering *buccellam* is only found in the Vulgate and Codices Aureus and Corbeiensis: it appears in *De consensu* 3.1.3–4, but *Tractatus* 61 and 62 revert to the Old Latin *panem*. Berrouard 1993:152 gives a list of passages in which Augustine illustrates this word with 1 Corinthians 11:27 or 29. Augustine's citations have no fewer than four different words corresponding to *τάχιον*. Both commentaries read *citius*, but the others are unique to Augustine: *cito* in *Enarratio* 3.1, *uelociter* at *Enarratio* 103.s3.12, and *celeriter* at *Tractatus* 51.12. As the comparatives *uelocius* and *celerius* also appear in Old Latin witnesses, Augustine may have been familiar with these renderings but read them as positives, in keeping with linguistic developments in Latin.[104] This verse is sometimes conflated with John 13:2, giving rise to *intrauit in cor eius* (*Enarratio* 3.1, *Sermo* 313E.4; cf. *De Genesi contra Manichaeos* 2.14.20, *Enarratio* 136.9); three other citations, among them *De consensu* 3.1.4 have the Old Latin *in eum*.

[103] As in John 13:10, the only other example of Augustine's text in the *Vetus Latina Database* is Quodvultdeus *Liber promissionum* 3.19.

[104] On the comparative as positive, see Plater and White 1926:67; Burton 2000:177 considers these particular adverbs.

JOHN 13:31–3

In *Tractatus* 62, *ait* rather than *dicit* in John 13:31 has no Vulgate parallels, but is present in Codex Palatinus. The phrase *si deus clarificatus est in eo* at the beginning of the next verse is absent from several Old Latin and Vulgate witnesses, possibly through haplography: it is not included in the editorial text of *De consensu euangelistarum* 3.1.4, although it is found within the manuscript tradition. There is no doubt that Augustine read it in his two other citations of John 13:32, *Tractatus* 63 and 64. All three citations of John 13:33 (*De consensu* 3.2.5 and 3.2.6, *Tractatus* 64) have *quaeritis* rather than *quaeretis*, and *De consensu* consistently omits *uos*, which seems to be without precedent.

JOHN 13:34–5

Augustine often cites these verses in an abbreviated form from memory, possibly also influenced by the similarities with John 15:12 and 15:17. Thirty references to John 13:34 read:

mandatum nouum do uobis ut uos inuicem diligatis.

The majority of other citations correspond to the Vulgate, including *Tractatus* 64 and 65, but *De consensu* 3.2.5–6 omits *ut* from the final clause.[105] His mental text of John 13:35 has *scient*, like Codices Vercellensis, Bezae, Monacensis, and Usserianus, rather than *cognoscent*, although two early citations have a passive unattested in biblical manuscripts, *cognoscitur* at *Ad Simplicianum* 2.1.9 and *cognoscetur* at *De diuersis quaestionibus* 71.1 (cf. John 14:6 and 16:23). Both of these read *si uos inuicem diligatis* for *si dilectionem habueritis ad inuicem*. The same conflation with the previous verse is also found in *Contra Faustum* 17.6, while *si uos inuicem dilexeritis* appears at *De baptismo*

[105] Augustine's explanation of John 13:34 is considered at Berrouard 1993:428–9, who notes that he frequently couples this text with Matthew 22:39, Galatians 5:4, or Romans 13:10.

3.19.26 and *Sermo* 350.1. Only *Epistula* 108.6.17 features the form *si ueram dilectionem habueritis in uobis*: the adjective is absent from the Greek tradition, but is present in Codices Vercellensis and Colbertinus. However, there is no surviving Old Latin parallel for *in uobis*. Even though the citations of John 13:35 in *De consensu* match the Vulgate, *Tractatus* 65 and *Enarratio* 118.s12 read *in inuicem*.

JOHN 13:36–7

Augustine's mental text of John 13:36 has the word order *me sequi modo*, also present in Codex Bezae (and the majority of Old Latin manuscripts in John 13:37). *Enarrationes* 103.s3.9 and 140.24 both read *sequeris me postea*, which may be an error of memory although *me* appears in Codices Veronensis and Bezae. In the next verse, the commentary in *Tractatus* 66 has *quare te non possum sequi modo*.

JOHN 13:38

Augustine's citations in *Sermones* 147, 286, 295, 299, and 340A conflate this verse with Matthew 26:34, reading *priusquam* (or *antequam*) *gallus cantet, ter me negabis*.[106] Of his other references, *De consensu* 3.2.5 and 3.2.7 correspond exactly to Weber–Gryson, while *Tractatus* 66 has the future *pones* and, like *Tractatus* 67, prefers the word order *ter me neges*: both are found in Vulgate manuscripts.

JOHN 14:1

The construal of the Greek πιστεύετε . . . πιστεύετε as *creditis* . . . *credite* is only found in the Vulgate and Codex Brixianus. Augustine prefers the double imperative from the Old Latin tradition in nine of

[106] See p. 72.

his ten citations, including *Tractatus* 67; the exception is *De consensu* 3.3.9.

JOHN 14:2–3

La Bonnardière (1965:67) notes that Augustine does not use John 14:2 with reference to infant baptism outside *De natura et origine animae* 3.11.15 and *Tractatus* 67 (see also Berrouard 1993:436–40). In the first of these citations Augustine criticizes his opponent's reading *apud patrem meum* despite his own use of this paraphrase for *in domo patris mei* in three earlier works (*Enarratio* 60.6, *Sermo* 239.2.2, and *De sancta uirginitate* 26.26). Indeed, *apud patrem meum* and its Greek counterpart παρὰ τῷ πατρί are so widespread in patristic citations that it has been suggested that this reading should be included in a critical apparatus.[107] *Sermo* 239.2.2 has several Old Latin features in these two verses, such as *alioquin* for *si quo minus*, the uncompounded forms *iero et parauero*, and *assumam* for *accipiam*, but as it also has the paraphrase *in domo patris mei*, unique variants such as *ibo* for *uado* in John 14:2 and *ueniens* in John 14:3 should probably be ascribed to memory. *Contra Faustum* 16.19 also has *iero*, with Codex Monacensis, and ends John 14:3 with *ueniam et adsumam uos ad me*, as found in Codex Vercellensis. The lection of John 14:2 prompts Augustine to defend his doctrine of predestination in *Tractatus* 68 (cf. John 15:16 and 17:5). Four commentary sermons consider John 14:3; *Tractatus* 67 has the Vulgate word order, but *Tractatus* 68, 69, and 70 all read *ubi ego sum*.

[107] Elliott 1986:136. Fee seems undecided, first stating that 'one rightly suspects that here something has been lost in the MS which is available only in patristic evidence', but going on to say 'I would hazard a guess that the short form *never* existed in any MS, but rather became the popular form of citation in a kind of oral tradition.' (Fee 1971:172–3); the latter position is also adopted by Metzger (1971:391). Augustine's text of John 8:56 is also restricted to patristic sources.

JOHN 14:6

This verse provides three titles of Christ which Augustine frequently uses as a key to interpret other verses (e.g. John 8:32, 17:17).[108] All biblical manuscripts read *uia et ueritas et uita*; the omission of the first *et* in seventeen citations is peculiar to Augustine. The appearance of *ianua* in *Sermo* 12.1 and *Sermo* 142.5.5 is a conflation with John 10:9, also made by Fortunatus (*Contra Fortunatum* 3). In addition, *Sermo* 12.1 and Fortunatus have *potest uenire*, a characteristic of Augustine's other citations from memory (e.g. John 3:3 etc.). The text *per me itur ad patrem* in a very early sermon, *Enarratio* 5.3, seems to relate to this verse. It is similar to the gloss on John 14:6 at *De doctrina christiana* 1.34.38: *hoc est per me uenitur, ad me peruenitur, in me permanetur.* The use of the passive has been noted in some of his citations of John 13:35 and may be a stylistic feature of Augustine's early works.

JOHN 14:7

This verse is only cited in *Tractatus* 70, where its text is unclear. For the distinctive Vulgate readings *cognouissetis . . . cognouissetis . . . cognoscitis*, the initial citation in the *Corpus Christianorum* edition has *cognouistis . . . cognouistis . . . cognoscitis* (although it notes that some manuscripts have *cognouissetis* for the first two instances, and even *cognoscetis* for the second, which is preferred by Berrouard). Migne reads *cognouistis . . . cognouistis . . . cognoscetis*, and the three subsequent citations in both editions have *cognoscetis* for the final verb. Alexanderson 1999, however, claims on internal evidence that two of these should read *cognoscitis*. A new edition may clarify the situation.

[108] See further Berrouard 1993:443–6, who identifies eighty-two instances of *ego sum uia* alone.

JOHN 14:9

Although *non nostis me* is found in some Old Latin witnesses, *patrem non nostis* (*Enarrationes* 58.s1.10 and 102.10), *patrem nescitis* (*Sermo* 264.2), and *me nescitis* (*Tractatus* 37.5) are peculiar to Augustine. *Patrem* has been introduced from the previous verse or next clause, while *nescitis* is an adaptation. All surviving Old Latin Gospels have a past tense, *uidit ... uidit*, but some Vulgate manuscripts have *uidet ... uidet*. The present tense is comparatively widespread in Augustine and appears in fourteen works, including *Tractatus* 70 and *Sermo* 142 (which probably included these verses in its lection), as well as the manuscript traditions of several more. It is possible that it was present in an Old Latin version no longer preserved: *uidet* occurs in *Sermo* 359B (*Dolbeau* 2) from 404 and a number of manuscripts of *De trinitate* 1.8.17. Nonetheless, more than half Augustine's citations have the past tense. He also prefers a chiastic word order which juxtaposes the two verbs, *qui me uidit uidit et patrem*, as found in Codices Vercellensis, Brixianus, Monacensis, and Usserianus. Augustine uses this verse to illustrate Christ's eventual appearance as equal to the Father, alongside more customary interpretations (Berrouard 1977:221; 1993:447–50). He cites this verse from Ambrose's commentary on Luke three times in *Epistula* 147, always in the form *et adhuc me non cognouistis*.

JOHN 14:10

None of Augustine's citations supports the additional phrases found in some Old Latin manuscripts. Seven out of eleven works, however, include *sua* at the end of the verse: the possessive adjective in Latin is only found in Codex Bezae (corresponding to αὐτοῦ on the Greek side). Other Greek witnesses have αὐτός, which underlies *ipse* in the Old Latin tradition. Three citations have both, reading *ipse facit opera sua* (*Tractatus* 20.6, *Enarratio* 67.23, and *Quaestiones euangeliorum* 2.33.3): this seems to be a conflation due to memory (cf. *sua propria* in John 1:11). Augustine uses this verse, like John 5:19, in conjunction with Jesus' walking on the water at Matthew 14:25 to show the inseparability of the Trinity (e.g. *Tractatus* 20.6 and *Contra sermonem Arrianorum* 15.9; see further Berrouard 1977:242). He also treats it in the same way as John 10:30, to refute both Arians and Sabellians simultaneously (e.g. *Tractatus* 71.2).

JOHN 14:13–14

Augustine has *quaecumque... haec* in both *Tractatus* 71 and 72, although *Tractatus* 72 later reverts to *quodcumque... hoc*, which is the sole form in *Tractatus* 73 and all biblical manuscripts. The appearance of the plural in the initial citations of two sermons suggests that it may have come from his codex. In John 14:14 neither *Tractatus* 71 nor 73 has *me*, in common with most Old Latin witnesses. These are Augustine's only citations of these verses. He punctuates after *faciam* in John 14:13, as shown at *Tractatus* 73.4, where *ut glorificetur pater in filio* is read as part of John 14:14.

JOHN 14:16–17

Augustine's sole citation of John 14:16 with *ut maneat uobiscum*, peculiar to the Vulgate, is in *Tractatus* 74. The text of both these verses in *De trinitate* 1 has already been quoted above.[109] It includes Old Latin forms such as *aduocatum* (for *paracletum*) and *ut uobiscum sit*, which otherwise only appear in Augustine's quotations of other sources: *aduocatum* at *Contra sermonem Arrianorum* 19.9, *ut uobiscum sit* at *Contra Maximinum* 2.26.14 and *qui uobiscum sit* in a citation of Ambrose at *Epistula* 148.2.6. The future tense *cognoscetis* in John 14:17 in *Tractatus* 74, 76, and 77 is paralleled in Vulgate manuscripts (cf. John 14:7); *Epistula* 148.2.6 and *Tractatus* 75 both have *cognoscit* in place of the distinctive Vulgate reading *scit*. Unlike

[109] Pp. 153 and 155. The citations in *De trinitate* 1 are very similar to Maximinus at *Collatio cum Maximino* 12.

Augustine's commentary with *autem*, this verse in *De trinitate* 1 may derive from Greek manuscripts without the particle δέ, although it omits the previous phrase.

JOHN 14:19

Tractatus 75 and 76, the only works in which Augustine cites this verse, have the Old Latin *uidebitis* rather than *uidetis*.

JOHN 14:21

Augustine understands this verse as a promise to Jesus' disciples that they will see his future glory (see Berrouard 1977:306–7 with references). He quotes it from memory dozens of times (e.g. *Epistula* 147.11.27, *Tractatus* 40.9) in the form:

qui diligit me mandata mea custodit, et qui diligit me diligetur a patre meo, et ego diligam eum et ostendam meipsum illi.

This is similar to Codices Vercellensis and Monacensis, the only Old Latin manuscripts with *custodit*, which read *ostendam illi meipsum* like Codices Bezae and Palatinus. Five works read *qui habet mandata mea et seruat ea*, like the Vulgate (*Tractatus* 21 and 75, *De trinitate* 4.19.26, *Enarratio* 85.21, and *Speculum* 28). Four of these have *manifestabo* rather than *ostendam*, joined by *Sermo* 277.17.16, *Tractatus* 101.5, and *Contra epistulas Pelagianorum* 3.7.19 (the exception is *Tractatus* 21). The only deviation from the Vulgate in the commentary in *Tractatus* 75 is *et qui* rather than *qui autem*; the latter appears in *Enarratio* 85 and *Speculum* 28 (and *De trinitate* 1.9), but *et qui* may be a rendering of ὁ δέ in a manuscript no longer preserved. Finally, the version of this verse in *Enarratio* 139.18, with *qui audit praecepta*, is distinct from all Augustine's other citations, and it was suggested above that it reflects the codex he used that day in Thagaste (cf. John 11:48).[110]

[110] See pp. 137–8; *Enarratio* 139 also reads *et qui*.

JOHN 14:22

De trinitate 1.9.18, Augustine's only citation of this verse outside *Tractatus* 76, reads *domine, quid factum est quia ostensurus es te nobis et non huic mundo?* This Old Latin form agrees with readings uniquely preserved in Codex Monacensis (*ostensurus es*) and Codex Usserianus (*te* for *te ipsum*).

JOHN 14:23–4

All Augustine's citations of John 14:23, including *Tractatus* 76 and *Speculum* 28, have *mansionem.* This is found in a number of Vulgate witnesses, even though Weber–Gryson and Codex Aureus read *mansiones.* Variations such as *intramus* for *ueniemus* (*Sermo* 198.11) and *habitamus* for *mansiones apud eum faciemus* (*De trinitate* 7.6.12) are errors of memory. In John 14:24 most Latin Gospels have *sermonem,* which has been attracted into the case of the relative. The nominative is clear in Greek (ὁ λόγος) but is surprisingly poorly attested in Latin: *sermo* only appears in Codex Vercellensis, which omits the relative clause. Augustine's only citations of this verse, both in *Tractatus* 76.5, have *sermo,* which could be either his own correction or an early Vulgate reading not preserved elsewhere. For Augustine's attempt to resolve the riddle of this verse by attention to the use of singular and plural, see *Tractatus* 76.5, quoted on p. 54.

JOHN 14:25–6

All biblical codices have *apud uos manens* in John 14:25, so it is likely that *cum adessem uobiscum* in *Sermo* 265A.1 is a paraphrase. This citation also has *commonebit uos* in the next verse, another unique reading although it is similar to *commouebit uos* in Codex Bezae. The commentary in *Tractatus* 77 reads *commemorabit uos,* as do Codices Vercellensis and Usserianus, but in *Tractatus* 104.1 Augustine has the

Vulgate *suggeret uobis*.[111] *De trinitate* 1.12.25 (cited on p. 153) has further Old Latin readings: it was noted that these include *declarabit* instead of *docebit*, not paralleled elsewhere. This seems an unlikely rendering of διδάξει, and may therefore be an error of memory.

JOHN 14:27

Augustine's mental text, appearing in nine citations, reads:

pacem meam do uobis, pacem meam relinquo uobis.

This order of the clauses is paralleled in Codices Veronensis and Monacensis and other Church Fathers including Ambrose and Optatus. Only *Enarratio* 71.1 and *Tractatus* 77 have the Vulgate sequence; they also omit *meam* before *relinquo*, as does *De diuersis quaestionibus* 75.1. Augustine explains the absence of *meam* in his commentary in terms of present and future possession, while suggesting that it could be understood in both phrases (see Berrouard 1993:461–3). *Dimitto* rather than *relinquo* in *De utilitate ieiunii* 11.13 and Petilianus' citation at *Contra litteras Petiliani* 2.22.49 is found in Codex Bezae and Cyprian (*De catholicae ecclesiae unitate* 24). Nonetheless, there is no extant manuscript with *saeculum* for ὁ κόσμος (*Contra Gaudentium* 2.12.13, perhaps relying on Gaudentius from *Contra Gaudentium* 1.23.26): this African rendering probably appeared in a version known to the Donatist (cf. John 12:25, 12:31, 12:46).

JOHN 14:28

Only the initial citation of *Tractatus* 78 has *ego* before *uado*, which is absent from both later citations and *Tractatus* 79. Three works have

[111] Berrouard 2003:45 suggests that *Tractatus* 104.1 was corrected in order to conform with the Vulgate, as it is the only example of the Vulgate form in Augustine's citations. If this were the case, however, we would expect the commentary at *Tractatus* 77 to have been altered: as Augustine's mental text after 420 often features Vulgate readings, this could explain the form of the later citation, probably made from memory.

eo rather than *uado*, a rendering only supported by a correction of *ego* in Codex Vercellensis: it seems to have featured in the codex used by Augustine at *De trinitate* 1.9.18, although *Sermones* 229G.4 and 264 also have citations with *uado*. *Quoniam pater maior me est*, as found in Codices Veronensis and Bezae, appears in seventeen citations, although it is sometimes difficult to determine whether *quoniam* is part of the citation or its introduction. Other manuscripts have *quoniam* for *quia* earlier in the verse, which Augustine reads at *De trinitate* 1.9.18 (and one citation in *Sermo* 264.4; cf. Maximinus in *Collatio cum Maximino* 13). Augustine frequently counters the Arian use of this verse by claiming that the Son is only inferior to the Father in respect of his humanity (cf. Berrouard 1993:463–6).

JOHN 14:30

A number of secondary citations include *huius* before or after *mundi*, but the basic form of Augustine's mental text omits it through flattening:

ecce, uenit princeps mundi et in me nihil inueniet.

Even though *ecce* is not supported by any gospel codices and may well be added by Augustine, it is present in thirty-two citations (cf. John 4:46, 7:25). *Inueniet* corresponds to εὑρήσει, which is poorly attested in Greek: in Latin it only occurs in Codex Brixianus. Twenty-eight of Augustine's citations have *nihil inueniet* (*inueniet nihil* in *Contra Iulianum opus imperfectum* 4.78), which is highly likely to derive from a lost version translating the same Greek text as Codex Brixianus.[112] Augustine has a present tense, *nihil inuenit*, on ten occasions, including a quotation of Jerome *Aduersus Iouinianum* 2 at *De peccatorum meritis* 3.7.13. This also occurs in three of Ambrose's citations, and this broad attestation suggests that *nihil inuenit*

[112] This text, εὑρήσει οὐδέν, is found in a handful of Greek manuscripts including Codex K (017) (cf. John 8:9). Codex Bezae reads οὐκ ἔχει οὐδὲν εὗρειν, underlying the Latin Codices Bezae and Vercellensis.

appeared in an Old Latin manuscript too.[113] It is worth observing that whenever Augustine reads *non . . . quidquam* rather than *nihil*, he feels the need to gloss it with a phrase such as *morte dignum* (*Confessiones* 7.21.27 and *Quaestiones de Deuteronomio* 55; cf. *Tractatus* 79.2 and *Epistula* 164.2.5; there may be influence from Luke 23:15). La Bonnardière (1986:224) considers all Augustine's references to *praepositus mortis* as allusions to John 14:30, but there is no mention of death here in any biblical witness. On the other hand, the phrase *praepositus magistratus huius saeculi* at *De sermone domini* 2.14.47 may well allude to an Old Latin form of this verse (cf. Codex Palatinus in Luke 24:20); *magistratus* is also used at *Expositio epistolae ad Galatas* 32.9 and *Sermo* 12.2 (sometimes identified as John 16:11).

JOHN 14:31

Fourteen of Augustine's sixteen citations of John 14:31 read:

sed ut sciant omnes quia uoluntatem patris mei facio, surgite, eamus hinc.

This is typical of Augustine's mental text, combining omission, paraphrase, and an Old Latin form (*scire* rather than *cognoscere*). John 15:15 in *De trinitate* 1 offers a parallel for *uoluntatem*. The exceptions, *Quaestiones de Deuteronomio* 55 and *Tractatus* 79, both correspond to the Vulgate.

JOHN 15:1–5

In this pericope Augustine generally uses *sarmentum* (found in six Old Latin manuscripts) in works dated before 412, and *palmes* in later writings, including his commentary in *Tractatus* 80, *Contra*

[113] Caragliano (1946:219) believes that Ambrose used two exemplars, one with *inuenit* and one with *inueniet*. Some Greek Fathers have εὑρίσκει οὐδέν: Tischendorf lists Origen and Epiphanius, which may be supplemented by Athanasius and Chrysostom.

Iulianum opus imperfectum and *Speculum*. The only definite instance of *sarmentum* after 412 is at *Contra Gaudentium* 2.8.9; *Enarratio* 30.2.s1 is on the borderline, while *Sermo* 113 has not been assigned a date. Augustine frequently cites from memory: conflated forms of John 15:1 and 15:5 such as *ego sum uitis uera, uos estis sarmenta, pater meus agricola* (*Sermo* 213.9.9) are common (cf. Berrouard 1998:80 and p. 70 above). Apart from *Tractatus* 80, his citations of John 15:2 are also paraphrased: most omit the initial *omnem* and prefer *quod non dat fructum* to *non ferentem fructum*. Four add *pater meus* from the previous verse. Six out of eight works have *maiorem fructum*, like Codex Monacensis; *Sermo* 162A.7 has *maius fructum*, while *Tractatus* 80 reads *fructum plus* (these may stem from Greek variants). *Praecidet* and *excidet* in place of *tollet* (*Sermones* 162A and 313E.6 respectively) are probably anticipations of John 15:6 in an Old Latin version. Augustine cites the whole of John 15:3 in *Contra Cresconium* 2.12.15 and *Tractatus* 80: with the exception of the initial citation in the latter, he has *uerbum quod* in keeping with Codices Vercellensis, Monacensis, and Usserianus.[114] Augustine relies on John 15:5 for his definition of a sacrament: *accedit uerbum ad elementum et fit sacramentum* (*Tractatus* 80.3).[115] This verse is most commonly cited in anti-Pelagian works, although Augustine uses it of the apostles in *Sermo* 101 (see Hombert 2000:238–9).

JOHN 15:6

Tractatus 81 has four variants from Weber–Gryson which occur elsewhere in the Vulgate tradition: *arescet*, *eum*, *mittent*, and *ardet*. All of these are attested in certain manuscripts of *Speculum* 28.

[114] Berrouard 1998:75 suggests that the initial citation derives from memory, and that *uerbum* is the text of his codex for the *Tractatus*. Although this is possible, the pattern demonstrated on pp. 113–14 suggests that the opposite is more likely.

[115] He applies the same principle to the Eucharist at *Sermo* 229.3. Berrouard 1998:438–42 and Comeau 1930:169–72 discuss his exegesis of this passage, and further bibliography on Augustine's understanding of sacraments is listed at Berrouard 1969:640.

JOHN 15:10

The allusion in *Epistula* 140.28 seems to reflect the Old Latin *caritate* for *dilectione*. Apart from the word order *dilectione eius* in *Speculum* 28, both Augustine's other citations correspond to the Vulgate.

JOHN 15:12

Speculum 28, the initial citation of *Tractatus* 83, and *Sermo* 332 all have the Vulgate *praeceptum*.[116] Augustine reverts to his preferred form *mandatum* in both sequential variants and throughout *Tractatus* 84 (cf. John 14:21). His one other citation, *De mendacio* 6.9, which is also the earliest, is identical to Codex Vercellensis, reading both *mandatum* and *sicut et ego dilexi uos*.

JOHN 15:13

Augustine's mental text, in the majority of his citations, reads:

maiorem hac caritatem nemo habet quam ut animam suam ponat pro amicis suis.

Five works begin the verse *maiorem dilectionem nemo habet* (*De diuersis quaestionibus* 80.3, *De mendacio* 6.9, *In epistolam Iohannis* 7.7, *Enarratio* 90.s2.13, and *De trinitate* 4.13.17). A few other citations also omit *hac*, but the most characteristic feature of Augustine's text is the addition of *quam*, which occurs in twenty-five citations. Although this is not preserved in any manuscript, its appearance in Cyprian (*Ad Quirinum* 3.3) strengthens the case for its presence in a version no longer extant. It does not appear in the commentaries in *Tractatus* 84 and 85, which correspond to the Vulgate apart from the word order

[116] *Sermo* 332 on martyrdom, preached around 418, may have followed the liturgical reading of this passage but this is not explicit.

ponat quis; *Speculum* 28 alone has the regular *quis ponat.* The alternative *potest habere* for *habet* in *In epistolam Iohannis* 7.2 and 7.7 is typical of Augustine's citations from memory (cf. John 3:3 etc.).

JOHN 15:15

Augustine tends to omit the second phrase, reading instead *iam non dicam uos seruos sed amicos* as early as *Expositio epistolae ad Romanos* 54.20 and *Enarratio* 5.9.[117] *Dicam*, which occurs in ten citations, is only found in Codex Monacensis. The explanatory clause appears in four works: *Enarratio* 7.1 reads *quia seruus nescit quid facit dominus eius*, while *De Genesi contra Manichaeos* 1.7.11 and *Tractatus* 85 have the subjunctive *faciat*, found in a number of Vulgate and Old Latin manuscripts. *De trinitate* 1.12.23, with *seruus enim nescit uoluntatem domini sui*, is a paraphrase (cf. John 14:31). In the second half of the verse, Augustine has the Old Latin form *omnia quae* in all citations apart from *Tractatus* 85 and 86: most of these also have the word order *uobis feci*, paralleled by Codices Vercellensis and Monacensis. This verse provides an illustration of a scriptural practice frequently invoked by Augustine, the use of the perfect in place of the future: comparison with John 16:12 indicates that the process *omnia... nota feci uobis* is not yet complete at the time of speaking (e.g. *Sermo* 27.5 and *Tractatus* 86.1). Augustine also sees this phenomenon in the Septuagintal form of Isaiah 45:11, *qui fecit quae futura sunt*, which he cites in conjunction with John 15:15 at *Tractatus* 105.4 (see also John 17:4, 17:14, 17:22, and 20:29, and Berrouard 1998:452–3).

JOHN 15:16

The Old Latin word order *ego uos elegi* features in six works, although four of these also have the more common *ego elegi uos* (*Tractatus*

[117] This example of flattening is also found in Cyprian (*Epistula* 63.15 and *De catholicae ecclesiae unitate* 2).

86 and 87, *De praedestinatione sanctorum* 17.34, *De gratia et libero arbitrio* 18.38). Augustine's use of this verse to support his theory of predestination is exemplified by *Tractatus* 86.2 and *De praedestinatione* 17.34 (cf. John 14:2 and 17:5).

JOHN 15:18

The initial citation of *Tractatus* 87 reads *quoniam* for *quia*; while the latter occurs in *Tractatus* 88, this has the word order *si odit uos mundus* and only *Tractatus* 89 is identical to the Vulgate. *Sermones* 96.7.8 and 313G.1 have *prius* rather than *priorem*, the reading of Codices Vercellensis and Monacensis, although these citations do not agree with these manuscripts in the rest of the verse. *Saeculum* for *mundus* in *Contra Gaudentium* 1.26.29 is also a feature of Gaudentius' text cited earlier in the paragraph (cf. John 14:27 and 16:2).

JOHN 15:19

All six of Augustine's citations, including *Tractatus* 87, 88, and 95, read *essetis*, an Old Latin alternative for *fuissetis*. *De patientia* 19.16 additionally has *hoc mundo* and *quod suum est*: the latter, also in *Sermo* 313G.1, is only paralleled by Codex Brixianus. Augustine's customary word order *ego uos de mundo elegi* does not appear here in biblical codices and may be influenced by John 15:16.

JOHN 15:22

The phrase *et locutus fuissem eis* is missing from seven citations through flattening. Both commentaries and six other references have the word order of the majority of Old Latin manuscripts, *et locutus eis fuissem*: the only exceptions are *Epistula* 194.6.26 and the initial citation of *Sermo* 71. Berrouard 1998:457 notes that Augustine always understands the *peccatum* of this verse as the failure of the Jews to believe, apart from *De gratia et libero arbitrio* 2.2 when he states that it is the crucifixion of Jesus.

JOHN 15:25–7

In John 15:25 *Tractatus* 91 and 92 both have *adimpleatur* rather than *impleatur*, which suggests that Augustine read this in his codex even though it no longer survives in a biblical manuscript (cf. John 13:26; this time there is no corresponding Greek alternative). A sequential variant in *Tractatus* 92.1 does have *impleatur*. The only other citation of John 15:25 is *De trinitate* 15.17.30: *oderunt* rather than *odio habuerunt* is also found in some Old Latin and Vulgate witnesses. The majority of Augustine's references to John 15:26 have *de patre procedit*, although *a patre* occurs frequently, and even *ex patre* at *De trinitate* 4.20.29. Hombert 2000:74–5 notes that Augustine appears only to use *procedere* of the Holy Spirit in works written after 413.[118] The only three citations of John 15:27, *Tractatus* 92, 93, and 109, have a future tense, *perhibebitis*, which is widespread in the Vulgate tradition and probably based on the previous verse. Augustine introduces one of his favourite topics, the conversion of the Jews after the death of Jesus, on the basis of the future *perhibebit* in John 15:26 (*Tractatus* 92.1; cf. John 12:38–40 above).

JOHN 16:2

Extra synagogas throughout *Tractatus* 93 is unique to Augustine, although Codices Vercellensis, Colbertinus, and Corbeiensis contain *extra synagogam*. Otherwise, this is Augustine's only citation to correspond to the Vulgate. In *Sermo* 313G.4, he reads:

[118] For more on Augustine's use of this verse in his description of the Trinity, see Berrouard 1998:476–9.

ueniet hora ut qui uos occiderit putet se obsequium praestare deo.

With the exception of *Tractatus* 93, all Augustine's references support *ueniet, putet* (paralleled by Codices Bezae and Palatinus, which also read *occiderit*), and the omission of *omnis. Contra litteras Petiliani* 2.92.206 twice has *tempus* for *hora*, following Petilianus' earlier text. The last three words, rendering λατρείαν προσφέρειν τῷ Θεῷ, are of greatest interest. At *Contra Gaudentium* 1.23.26. Augustine corrects his opponent's text *uictimam dare deo*, which may be an African version not preserved elsewhere, to *officium deo facere*, the form of his other three references (*Epistula* 185.5.20, *Contra Faustum* 22.70, and *Contra litteras Petiliani*, where it is also read by Petilianus). This too is not found in surviving manuscripts, but there is little doubt that it was once part of the Old Latin tradition as it features three times in Cyprian (*Epistula* 58.2, *Ad Fortunatum* 11, *Ad Quirinum* 3.16).

JOHN 16:3

Both Augustine's citations, *Contra Gaudentium* 1.23.26 and *Tractatus* 93.3, have *haec facient uobis* and *cognouerunt*. The addition of *uobis* occurs in Vulgate as well as Old Latin traditions, while *cognouerunt* in place of *nouerunt* is paralleled by Codices Bezae, Palatinus, Brixianus, and Monacensis. The initial *sed* in *Contra Gaudentium* is an Old Latin form.

JOHN 16:4–5

Tractatus 94 begins John 16:4 with *haec ergo*, despite *sed haec* in *Tractatus* 93: this is probably an adaptation. In the next verse it has the majority Old Latin reading *nunc autem* for *at nunc*. Note that the Vulgate and Greek traditions differ in their division of these verses.

JOHN 16:7

Instead of *uadam* five Old Latin manuscripts have *eam*, Augustine's reading in *Contra Maximinum* 2.26.14, *Sermo* 270.2, and *De trinitate* 1.8.18. He has various forms of *si enim non abiero*, which only appears as such in *Tractatus* 94 and the lectionary *Sermo* 143. The most common is *nisi ego abiero*, as found in Codex Palatinus, while *De trinitate* 1 has *nam si non abiero*. Later in the verse, *De trinitate* 1.12.25 and *Contra sermo Arrianorum* 4.4 (cf. 19.9) read *cum ego iero mittam illum ad uos* and also refer to *aduocatus* rather than *paracletus*, showing parallels with Codices Palatinus and Monacensis. Five citations have *non potest ille* (or *ipse*) *uenire* in place of *non ueniet ad uos*. This alteration is characteristic of Augustine (cf. John 3:3 etc.).

JOHN 16:8–11

Among the Old Latin manuscripts, only Codex Vercellensis has *ipse* to render ἐκεῖνος in John 16:8. Nonetheless, its presence in four works, including *Sermo* 144 on this lection, confirms that Augustine was familiar with this reading. All citations except one have *crediderunt* in the next verse: these include *Sermones* 143 and 144, and *Tractatus* 95, but not *Tractatus* 94. Flattening results in the omission of *uero* from several references to John 16:10.[119] *Sermo* 144 begins with the Old Latin alternative *autem*, then omits the connective, and later has *uero*. It also provides Augustine's only example of *uero* rather than *autem* in John 16:11, paralleled by Codex Usserianus. All four works to cite this verse, *Tractatus* 94 and 95 and *Sermones* 143 and 144, have the majority Old Latin word order *huius mundi* (cf. John 12:31 and 14:30).

[119] On Augustine's understanding of the significance of *iustitia* in John 16:10, see Berrouard 1998:463–5.

JOHN 16:12

Twenty-one of Augustine's citations read *non potestis illa portare*, as do the majority of Old Latin manuscripts. In addition, *Enarratio* 5.7 has *portare illa*, while *illa audire* in *Sermo* 179.5.5 is a simple error. The pronoun *illa* is only missing from *Tractatus* 96, 97, 98, *Enarratio* 118.s6.1, and *De Genesi contra Manichaeos* 1.7.11, although some manuscripts of this early work read *ea portare* as in Codex Veronensis. Variants in two other early citations, *sed nunc non potestis illa portare* (*De diuersis quaestionibus* 53.4) and *sed adhuc non potestis illa portare* (*De sermone domini* 2.20.67; also certain manuscripts of *De diuersis quaestionibus* 53) could reflect Old Latin readings now lost: *nunc*, *modo*, and *adhuc* are interchangeable elsewhere (e.g. John 5:17, John 16:24), but *adhuc* may have been repeated from earlier in this verse. In *Tractatus* 97 Augustine seeks to counter the heretical use of this verse to justify additional 'secret' teachings (cf. Berrouard 1998:470–4).

JOHN 16:13

While all Greek manuscripts in Nestle–Aland and Tischendorf read ὁδηγήσει, the Vulgate and Codices Aureus, Colbertinus, and Rehdigeranus have *docebit*. This would normally render διδάξει (cf. John 14:26): the patristic reading διηγήσεται, found in Cyril of Jerusalem and Eusebius, corresponds elsewhere to *enarrabit*.[120] Most of Augustine's works have *docebit uos omnem ueritatem* (*De consensu* 4.10.20, *Tractatus* 46, 96, and 100, *De trinitate* 1 and 2, and *De ciuitate dei* 11.31). Many Vulgate witnesses also omit *in*, but the two citations in *De trinitate* 1.8.18 imply that Augustine knew this in an Old Latin exemplar. At *Tractatus* 96.4 and 100.1.3, he refers explicitly to a variant found in some manuscripts, *deducet uos in omni ueritate.*

120 In the Gospels, διηγεῖσθαι only appears at Mark 5:16, Mark 9:9, Luke 8:39, and Luke 9:10, none of which has *docere*. For Cyril and Eusebius, see Mullen 1997:166 and Muncey 1959:xlvi.

An identical text is preserved in Codex Corbeiensis. Berrouard 1998:466–7 suggests that Augustine shows some hesitation with this reading due to the ablative, but his citation of the same construction in Psalm 85:11 (*Tractatus* 96.4) tells against this. However, this version only occurs in *Tractatus* 96 and 100; Augustine's principal alternative is based on *ipse uos inducet in omnem ueritatem*, which appears in five early works (*Contra Faustum* 32, *Contra Felicem* 1.10, *De diuersis quaestionibus* 38 (with a different word order), *De fide et symbolo* 9.19, *Soliloquia* 1.3 (adaptation)). The verb *inducet* is only preserved in Codex Palatinus, but was probably more widespread, as it is also cited by Augustine's Manichaean opponents Faustus and Felix. Augustine reads *ipse* before *docebit* in *Tractatus* 46.4 (cf. *De trinitate* 1.8.18), although *ille* is the only form found in Latin Gospels. Later in the verse, *Contra sermonem Arrianorum* 23.20 has the Old Latin readings *se* for *semetipso* and *audierit*.

JOHN 16:14–15

As noted on p. 170, *honorificabit* in John 16:14 at *Contra sermonem Arrianorum* 23.19 reproduces the rendering of the Arian sermon (cf. John 17:4). In *Tractatus* 99, 100, and *De trinitate* 2 Augustine reads *clarificabit.* He describes the Arian use of this text to establish a hierarchy within the Trinity at *Tractatus* 100.4, where he admonishes his congregation to hear this verse 'with Catholic ears' (*catholicis audite auribus, catholicis percipite mentibus*; compare the *regula sana catholica* at *Tractatus* 18.2). As in John 15:15, his preferred text of John 16:15 is *omnia quae* (only preserved here in Codices Bezae and Palatinus), but Augustine allows *omnia quaecumque* to stand in *Tractatus* 99 and 100 and the first two citations in *De trinitate* 2.[121] All his citations of this verse have *de meo accipiet*, as found in several Vulgate manuscripts and all Old Latin witnesses except Codex Palatinus: three of these, however, omit the preceding *quia* (*Contra*

[121] Note that La Bonnardière 1965:74–5 dates the citations of John 16:14–15 in *De trinitate* 2.3 to the revision of the book after 420.

sermonem Arrianorum 23.19 and 20, *Contra epistulam Parmeniani* 2.15.34). *Contra epistulam Parmeniani* also has *ideo* for *propterea*, like Codex Vercellensis.

JOHN 16:18

Apart from *Tractatus* 101, Augustine's sole reference to this verse is a conflation with John 6:61 at *Enarratio* 68.s1.7. The final words, *non scimus quid dicat*, shows the influence on Augustine of versions similar to Codices Palatinus and Usserianus.

JOHN 16:19–22

John 16:19–21 are only cited in *Tractatus* 101, with a Vulgate text, and *Sermo* 210. The readings of the latter have been quoted on p. 131 above: these feature Old Latin forms which are paralleled in manuscripts and other Fathers alongside paraphrases and abbreviations. The most unusual verse is John 16:21, with the phrases *tristitia est illi* and *sed cum peperit fit gaudium magnum*. Like *Sermo* 210, the majority of Old Latin versions are based on a Greek text with ἡμέρα rather than ὥρα. In John 16:22 the future *tollet* in *Tractatus* 101.3 agrees with one branch of the Vulgate, while *Sermo* 210.5.7, *Enarratio* 33.s2.9, and *De trinitate* 1.10.20 all have *auferet*, with some Old Latin witnesses.

JOHN 16:23

De opere monachorum 27.35, dated around 405, has an abbreviated form: *si quid petieritis in nomine meo dabitur uobis*. The passive is also found in Codex Palatinus, but all Latin Gospels include *patrem* or *a patre*, which indicates that this may be a flattened form cited from memory (cf. the passives in John 13:35 and 14:6).

JOHN 16:24

Augustine observes that this verse can be interpreted in two ways, depending on whether the emphasis is placed on *quidquam* or *in nomine meo* (e.g. *Tractatus* 102.2). The text and date of the lectionary *Sermo* 145 have been considered above; its title and initial citation is identical to Codex Monacensis, reading *usque nunc nihil petiistis,* although sequential variants have *usque modo* and *adhuc.*[122]

JOHN 16:25

In the four *Tractatus* with this verse (*Tractatus* 102, 103, 106, and 113), Augustine reads *patre meo.* The adjective is not found in any biblical manuscripts, and while this would be a simple addition to make from memory, Augustine's consistent form here (in contrast to John 16:23) suggests that this may have been in his copy of Jerome's version. His only other citations, both in *De trinitate* 1.10.21, exhibit similarities with Codex Vercellensis, the sole witness with *similitudinibus* in place of *prouerbiis,* and Codex Palatinus, which reads *quando* instead of *cum.* No surviving version has *manifeste* here for *palam,* but this rendering of παρρησίᾳ is found in Codices Rehdigeranus and Usserianus at John 10:24, so it is very likely that it featured in Augustine's exemplar. His interpretation of this verse in *De trinitate* 1.10.21, referring to the world to come, stems in part from the future tense *ueniet hora*; at *Tractatus* 102.3, where his text has *uenit hora,* he criticizes the earlier explanation on the grounds that there will be no need in heaven for the requests implied by *petetis.*

JOHN 16:26–8

De trinitate 1.10.21 has the Old Latin readings *illa die* in John 16:26 and *amatis* in John 16:27. Unlike Augustine's commentary, it omits

[122] See pp. 129–30.

the final *de uobis*, a variant paralleled in three Old Latin manuscripts and some Greek sources. Augustine's mental text of John 16:28 reads *ego a patre exii et ueni in hunc mundum.* The addition of *hunc* is found in all references apart from *Tractatus* 102 and 103, which correspond to the text distinctive of Codex Aureus and the Vulgate.[123]

JOHN 16:30

Tractatus 103.1, Augustine's sole citation, has *nosti* rather than *scis.* This is found in Codices Usserianus, Palatinus, Colbertinus, and Corbeiensis.

JOHN 16:32

The Vulgate text *uenit hora et iam uenit ut dispergamini unusquisque in propria* appears in *Tractatus* 103 and 106. Augustine's other forms of this phrase are paraphrases, but may reflect Old Latin versions: *Tractatus* 21.17 reads *ueniet hora ut unusquisque discedat ad sua*, *Enarratio* 109.13 has *ecce itis quisque ad sua*, and *Enarratio* 138.22 reverses the order of the clauses and reads *ueniet hora ut . . . eat unusquisque in uiam suam.* An allusion at *Enarratio* 140.24 reads *quando dimiserunt te omnes solum et ierunt unusquisque in sua.* The rendering *in sua* occurs in three Old Latin witnesses, while four have *in sua regione/suam regionem*; *ueniet* is also paralleled in Old Latin manuscripts, and *dismittatis* in Codex Bezae may be reflected in *Enarratio* 140. In the second half of the verse, *Contra sermonem Arrianorum* 3.4 and *Contra Maximinum* 2.18.6 both have *qūoniam* for *quia*, as do Codices Veronensis, Bezae, and Usserianus. For Augustine's use of this verse against the Arians in *Tractatus* 21 and 42 and *Contra sermonem Arrianorum*, see La Bonnardière 1965:116.

[123] The text of this verse quoted by Faustus at *Contra Faustum* 12.1, *a patre meo processi*, is not preserved in any biblical manuscripts, but this rendering of ἐξῆλθον occurs in the majority of Old Latin witnesses at John 8:42 (cf. John 11:44 and 18:4).

JOHN 16:33

The addition following the text of John 16:33 in *Enarratio* 33.s3, *pacem in terra uobis non promitto*, perhaps based on Luke 12:51, has already been discussed.[124] *Enarratio* 92, which cites this verse four times, is one of three works which reads *in mundo autem pressuram* rather than *in mundo pressuram habetis*. It also has *dico* for *locutus sum*, while another of these works, *Exposito epistolae ad Romanos inchoata* 10.12, has *dixi*. Most Old Latin witnesses include *autem*, but the other two variants are not present in gospel manuscripts (cf. John 18:23). *Tractatus* 103 and *Sermo* 276 have *habeatis* rather than *habetis*, in keeping with some Vulgate codices. These two sermons have the only examples of the distinctive Vulgate reading *confidite, ego uici mundum* (cf. *Tractatus* 104.2). Augustine's mental text, corresponding to Old Latin manuscripts, is *gaudete quia ego uici saeculum* (*mundum* in *Sermones* 51.1.2 and 97.4.4). Two citations have *quoniam* (*Enarratio* 23.7 and *Sermo* 329.2), but *scitote* in *De agone christiano* 1.1 is an error of memory.

JOHN 17:1

The initial citation in *Tractatus* 104.2 reads *ut et filius tuus clarificet te*. The additional *et* is present in Codex Monacensis and some Vulgate manuscripts, matching a Greek alternative. This is the single occasion on which it occurs in Augustine: *Tractatus* 104.3 and *Tractatus* 105 and 106 have the regular text.

JOHN 17:3

Augustine's shorter references to this verse are of limited textual value and may have been influenced by credal statements. Nonethe-

[124] See p. 76.

less, it is clear that he knew it in at least two forms: *unum uerum deum*, preserved only in Codex Vercellensis, is found in longer citations in at least eleven works, including *De trinitate* 1, *De consensu* 3.25.86, and *Tractatus* 3, 19, 21, and 101. A similar number of writings have the reading of most other gospel manuscripts, *solum uerum deum*, including not only the commentaries at *Tractatus* 105 and 106, but also *De diuersis quaestionibus* 35.2. Another early work, *De duabus animabus* 10, has the form *solum et uerum deum*, matching Codices Veronensis, Palatinus, and Monacensis, while Augustine's first two citations omit the first word completely.[125] The unusual doublet form *unus et solus (et uerus) deus* in allusions in the later parts of *De trinitate* 1 and 2 has also been considered above.[126] A few citations omit *autem* (e.g. *De moribus* 1.25.47, *Sermones* 217.1, 362.29.30); although this is likely to be flattening, it does correspond to a Greek variant. *Enim* in *Enarratio* 85.21 is unique. In his exegesis, Augustine is more concerned with punctuating or re-ordering the verse to establish the divinity of Christ than the rendering of *μόνον* (cf. *Contra Maximinum* 2.15.4 responding to Maximinus at *Collatio cum Maximino* 15, *Epistula* 238.4.22, *Sermo* 217.1, *Tractatus* 105.3, *De spiritu et littera* 22.37).

JOHN 17:4–5

All three renderings of *δοξάζειν*, *clarificare*, *honorificare*, and *glorificare* are normally preserved in the Old Latin tradition (e.g. John 17:5, John 17:10), but only the first two are found at John 17:4. There is no obvious reason why *glorificare* is missing, and while Augustine reads *honorificaui* in these verses at *Contra sermonem Arrianorum* 23.19 and *clarificaui* in *Tractatus* 105 and 106, *ego te glorificaui* at *Contra sermonem Arrianorum* 31.29 and *De trinitate* 2.4.6 supplies the missing term in John 17:4 (cf. John 21:19).[127] *Tractatus* 43.9 also has

125 *De libero arbitrio* 2.2.6 and *De moribus* 1.25.47; see p. 139.

126 Page 154.

127 On the distribution and origin of the renderings of *δοξάζειν*, see Burton 2000:68 and 134. Jerome states in *Epistula* 106.30 that his retention of *clarificare* in John 17 for the Vulgate was deliberate (Sparks 1970:523).

glorificare in John 17:5, reading *glorifica me ea gloria quam habui apud te antequam mundus esset.* This fronting of *apud te* is supported by three Old Latin manuscripts, some Greek witnesses, and other Church Fathers: Augustine has *apud te priusquam mundus fieret* at *Contra Adimantum* 9, *Enarratio* 15.5, and *De trinitate* 1.13.31. The substitution of *esse* for *habere* in John 17:5 is another reading preserved only in patristic sources, including *claritas qua eram* at *Enarratio* 15.5 and *claritate qua fui* at *Contra Adimantum* 9. The commentaries at *Tractatus* 105 and 106 have the ablative *claritate,* which co-exists with *claritatem* in the Vulgate tradition. Augustine takes the past tenses *clarificaui* and *habui* in these verses in support of his doctrine of predestination (*Tractatus* 105.5; cf. John 14:2 and 15:16). On the use of the past tense *consummaui* in anticipation of a future event, see the comments on biblical style at *Tractatus* 105.4 and 106.1 (cf. John 15:15, 17:14, and 17:22).

JOHN 17:6

In a sequential variant at *Tractatus* 106.4, Augustine adds the word *istis* after *hominibus* (cf. John 4:18 etc.). For his commentary on this verse, see Berrouard 2003:470–1.

JOHN 17:10–11

The same word order as Codex Bezae, *omnia mea tua sunt,* is found in the five citations of John 17:10 outside the *Tractatus* (*De trinitate* 1.11.23 reverses the clauses). The reading *tua mea* for *mea tua sunt* on both occasions in *Tractatus* 107 could be an oversight, but the verb is missing from most Old Latin and Greek manuscripts as well as *Enarratio* 67.15 and *De trinitate* 1. (It is present in *Tractatus* 100.4 and *Sermo* 135.2.3.) At the end of John 17:11 *Collatio cum Maximino* 14 and *Contra Maximinum* 1.12 both have a repetitive *unum sumus.* Despite variation in gospel manuscripts, this is probably a conflation with John 17:22.

JOHN 17:14–17

Some Vulgate witnesses also have the word order *eos odio habuit* like Augustine's sole citation of John 17:14, *Tractatus* 108.1. Augustine understands this as another instance of the biblical use of the perfect in place of the future (*Tractatus* 108.1; cf. John 15:15, 17:4, and 17:22). While both *Tractatus* 108 and 115 have the regular Vulgate text of John 17:15, *Adnotationes in Iob* 38 combines Old Latin readings with errors of memory.[128] Augustine's observation at *Tractatus* 108.3 on the equality of *uerbum* and *sermo* in John 1:1 and 17:17 has been quoted on p. 79: *uerbum tuum* occurs in five Old Latin manuscripts. He also uses this verse to support the identification of Christ as truth (cf. John 8:32, 14:6).

JOHN 17:19–20

The two references to John 17:19 outside *Tractatus* 108 both omit *ego* before *sanctifico*, as do some Latin and Greek manuscripts. While most of Augustine's citations of the next verse have *pro his . . . pro eis*, *Tractatus* 106.2 (which precedes the commentary sermons on this verse) and *Enarratio* 47.14 have *pro his* twice, and *Contra Maximinum* 1.12 *pro eis* on both occasions. *Enarratio* 47 reads *uerbum illorum* and *Contra Maximinum* 2.22.1 *uerbum ipsorum*; all of these variants are found in Latin Bibles. *Tractatus* 109 is devoted to an explanation of this verse: Berrouard 2003:472–3 has a summary of Augustine's exegesis.

JOHN 17:21–3

Five sequential variants in *Tractatus* 110 have the word order *ut credat mundus*, implying that this was Augustine's mental text of

[128] See p. 152.

John 17:21. This matches some Vulgate sources, but Augustine may have been influenced by the similar sequence in John 17:23, where his reading *ut cognoscat mundus* (*Tractatus* 110 and *Contra Maximinum* 2.22.1) is well attested in Old Latin manuscripts. The addition of *et* after *sicut* in John 17:22 is found throughout the Latin tradition, probably by analogy with John 17:11. It appears in ten of Augustine's thirteen citations, including both *De consensu* 1.4.7 and *Tractatus* 110.3. Four out of five works, including *Tractatus* 110, read *dedi illis*: only *Epistula* 238.4.28 has *dedi eis*. Augustine treats this verse as another example of the biblical use of the perfect tense for a future event (*Tractatus* 110.3; cf. John 15:15 etc.). Hombert 2000:73 notes that citations of John 17:21 and 23 are restricted to later works and are only found in conjunction with 1 Timothy 2:5 at *De trinitate* 4.8.12 and in *Enarratio* 67.23 (from 415).

JOHN 17:24

All Old Latin manuscripts render *κἀκεῖνοι* by *et illi*, apart from Codex Palatinus with *et hi*. Augustine only reads *et illi* on three occasions (*Tractatus* 111, *Sermones* 135.4.5 and 319.3.3), but has *et ipsi* sixteen times and four examples of *et isti*. His mental text was clearly *et ipsi*, appearing in five sequential variants in *Tractatus* 111. As this occurs throughout the lectionary *Sermo* 217 as well as Cyprian (*Ad Quirinum* 3.58), it seems likely that *et ipsi* was present in a manuscript (cf. John 16:8 in Codex Vercellensis).[129] The case is less clear for *isti*, which usually translates *οὗτος*, but as Ambrose uses *isti* five times it too may derive from a version no longer preserved.

[129] The initial citation at *Sermo* 217.2 actually has a paraphrase, *ibi sint isti*, which Augustine immediately corrects to *et ipsi sint mecum*, although the title in Migne has taken the first version. *Sermo* 359.9 has a similar paraphrase: *uolo ut ubi ego sum ibi sint et isti mecum.*

JOHN 17:25–6

Three minor variations in these verses demonstrate the inconsistency between the gospel text of *De consensu* and the *Tractatus*. *Tractatus* 111 omits *et* before *mundus* in John 17:25 and has *quam* rather than *qua* in John 17:26; both are paralleled in Latin biblical manuscripts. In fact, Augustine comments on the unusual construction:

> non est usitata locutio: *dilectio quam dilexisti me, in ipsis sit, et ego in ipsis;* usitate quippe diceretur, dilectio qua dilexisti me. de graeco quidem ista translata est; sed sunt similes et latinae. (*Tractatus* 111.6)

De consensu 3.3.9, despite agreeing with the Vulgate in the preceding cases, reads *eis feci* for *feci eis* in John 17:26.

JOHN 18:1–3

The oldest known manuscript of *Tractatus* 112–13, Monte Cassino 523, has the Old Latin *Cedri* rather than *Cedron* (in the text of the *Corpus Christianorum* edition). *Tractatus* 112 provides the only citations of John 18:2–3. In the former it omits *ipsum* in keeping with many Vulgate and Greek witnesses, while in John 18:3, Augustine has *principibus* alone for τῶν ἀρχιερέων. This corresponds to the Vulgate Codex Mediolanensis, and may have appeared in Augustine's exemplar, although for the same term at John 18:10 he has *principis sacerdotum* with the majority of Old Latin versions.[130]

JOHN 18:4–7

The past tense *dixit* in John 18:4 at *Tractatus* 112 is also found in some biblical manuscripts. *De consensu* 3.5.15 has *quid quaeritis?* in

[130] On the Latin renderings of ἀρχιερεύς, see Burkitt 1908 (cf. John 19:41). It should be noted that at least one early manuscript of *Tractatus* 112.2, Paris BN lat

this verse, but *quem quaeritis?* in John 18:7. This is paralleled by Codex Palatinus and part of the Vulgate tradition, even though the Greek appears to be invariant. Similarly, the editorial text of *De consensu* chooses *nazorenum* in John 18:5 but *nazoreum* in John 18:7, where there is considerable variation in the textual tradition. No Old Latin witness has *nazorenum* on the first occasion, yet it features in Codex Palatinus in John 18:7. The *Tractatus* have *nazarenum* throughout, like the Vulgate. Augustine's seven citations of John 18:6 outside *De consensu* 3.5.15 and *Tractatus* 112 all support *redierunt retro* rather than *abierunt retrorsum*. Although three Old Latin manuscripts have *retro*, none has *redierunt* for ἀπῆλθον. This may have occurred in a version no longer extant, but as none of these citations is longer than five words Augustine's text is probably due to memory: two citations (*Tractatus* 31.6, *Enarratio* 34.s2.3) also add *omnes*, which has no parallels (but cf. John 8:9).

JOHN 18:9–12

Four of Augustine's five citations of John 18:9 have *eis* for *ipsis*; *eis* is also present in certain manuscripts of *De consensu* 3.5.15. Despite the reference to John 17:12 in this verse, the likelihood of influence is comparatively small as the text is not given verbatim. In John 18:10 the variant *seruum principis sacerdotum* in *Tractatus* 112, Augustine's only citation, has been mentioned at John 18:2.[131] Certain manuscripts of *De consensu* 3.5.16 have the Old Latin reading *non uis (ut) bibam* at John 18:11, found in some Vulgate witnesses. Finally, Codex Aureus provides the only parallel for *autem* in place of *ergo* in the commentary on John 18:12 in *Tractatus* 112 (cf. John 19:13 and 19:29).

1959, reads *principibus sacerdotum*; see also the note on John 18:10 below. Monte Cassino 523 twice has the word order *sciebat autem et locum Iudas qui tradebat eum* in John 18:2, but does not include John 18:3.

[131] On the other hand, two early manuscripts of *Tractatus* 112.5 read *principis seruum* here (Paris BN lat 1959 and Rome Vallicelliana A14) for which there is no parallel in biblical manuscripts, even though it agrees with the editorial text of John 18:2 at *Tractatus* 112.2.

JOHN 18:13–20

Tractatus 113 has several minor variants in these verses: the omission of *et* at the beginning of 18:13, *dedit* rather than *dederat* in John 18:14, the word order *alius discipulus* in John 18:16 and *eius* for *suis* in John 18:19. Of these, only *dedit* and *eius* correspond to surviving gospel codices, being in each case the majority Old Latin reading. In John 18:15, *De consensu* 3.6.19 omits *Iesum* and repeats *alius* (after *ille*), while two verses later *De consensu* 3.6.23 includes *ergo* after *numquid* and reads *de* for *ex*. There are various Vulgate forms of John 18:18. *Tractatus* 113 agrees with witnesses reading *calefaciebant se*, which is also present in certain manuscripts of *De consensu* 3.6.23, as is *calefaciebant* by itself, but the editorial text has *calefiebant* followed by *calefaciens se*. The *Corpus Christianorum* edition of *Tractatus* 113 and almost all Latin Gospels read *in synagoga* in John 18:20, but Berrouard 2003:226 prefers *in synagogis*, present in all manuscripts used by the Maurists and paralleled by Codex Usserianus.

JOHN 18:23

Three of Augustine's five citations have *exprobra* for μαρτύρησον (*Epistula* 138.2.13, *De mendacio* 15.27, and *De sermone domini* 1.19.58; *De consensu* 3.6.24 and *Tractatus* 113 read *testimonium perhibe*). The consistency of this unusual rendering suggests that it featured in a version now lost, especially as it occurs several times in Cyprian (*Epistulae* 3.2, 59.4, 66.3). Augustine reads *dixi* rather than *locutus sum* in *Epistula* 138 and *De mendacio*, which is not preserved in biblical witnesses (cf. John 16:33), while *De sermone domini* 1.19.58 omits *autem* before *bene*.

JOHN 18:24–7

These verses are only cited in *De consensu* 3 and the *Tractatus*. The oldest manuscript of *Tractatus* 113, Monte Cassino 523, has one variant from the *Corpus Christianorum* editorial text in each verse (cf. John 18:2). The most interesting of these is *continuo* rather than *statim* in John 18:27, which is only preserved in Codex Palatinus.

JOHN 18:28

Both *Tractatus* 114 and *De consensu* 3.7.28 read *ad Caipham* (*Caifan* in the latter), as do most Latin Gospels, despite *ἀπὸ τοῦ Καιάφα* in Greek; as noted above, this suggests that Augustine had not compared his text with a Greek exemplar.[132] *Tractatus* 114 repeats *ut* before *manducarent*, like the majority of Old Latin manuscripts.

JOHN 18:31–2

Augustine's mental text of John 18:31 features the Old Latin *occidere* for *interficere*, as shown in *Tractatus* 115.1 and *Enarratio* 63.4 (cf. John 7:1, 8:40, 16:2 etc.). The commentary text of *Tractatus* 114 in the next verse corresponds to Vulgate witnesses with the word order *morte esset moriturus*, unlike *De consensu* 3.8.35.

JOHN 18:33–4

The omission of *ergo* from John 18:33 in *Tractatus* 115 is probably an adaptation. While this sermon includes *et* at the beginning of John 18:34, it is missing from *De consensu* 3.8.35, several Old Latin manuscripts and the Greek tradition.

[132] Pp. 97–8; see also John 21:12 below.

JOHN 18:36–9

All Augustine's citations of John 18:36 except *De consensu* 3.8.35 have the word order *non est de hoc mundo.* In addition, *Tractatus* 115 reads *regnum meum* on all three occasions and *uocem meam* in John 18:37. In John 18:36, it includes the Old Latin *utique* after *ministri mei*, which appears in some manuscripts of *De consensu* 3.8.35. Berrouard 2003:260 notes that, unlike Ambrose, Augustine correctly takes both instances of *hoc* in John 18:37 as accusative. In John 18:38 *Tractatus* 115 has *dixit* for *dicit* both times: the second instance is attested in Codices Colbertinus and Palatinus, but there is no parallel for the first. *De consensu* 3.8.35 repeats *ut* before the second *dimittam* in John 18:39, an explanatory addition absent from biblical witnesses.

JOHN 19:1

The omission of *ergo* from *Tractatus* 116 is probably an adaptation, because this is the first verse cited in the sermon.

JOHN 19:3–6

The alternative *palmas* is found for *alapas* in certain manuscripts of *De consensu* 3.8.35 and 3.9.36. This is the majority Old Latin reading at John 19:3 and also appears in a number of Vulgate witnesses. Nonetheless, the editorial text of *De consensu* reads *alapas* here and *alapam* (with no variation noted) in John 18:22 (*De consensu* 3.6.24; cf. *Tractatus* 113.4 and 116.1). The same manuscripts of *De consensu* 3.8.35 also have the Old Latin *foras habens* at John 19:5, but the Vulgate *portans* appears at *De consensu* 3.13.46 without exception. Both citations of John 19:4 in *De consensu* feature the word order *eum uobis*, while *uobis* is missing from *Tractatus* 116.2. In John 19:6 *Tractatus* 116.3 is the only one of Augustine's citations to read *crucifige crucifige eum*, in common with some Vulgate sources. The expansion of Pilate's words in *Enarratio* 68.s1.6, *non inuenio causam ullam in hoc homine quare occidendus sit*, is a gloss based on Luke 23:14.

JOHN 19:8

Tractatus 116.4 has *hoc uerbum*, like four Old Latin witnesses, rather than *hunc sermonem* as in the two citations in *De consensu* (cf. John 8:31, John 15:3).

JOHN 19:10

No biblical codex supports *respondes* for *loqueris* (*Enarratio* 73.8 and *Sermo* 299E.2). The five citations outside *De consensu* and *Tractatus* 116, all in sermons, display Augustine's mental text with *occidendi* and *dimittendi* (*Enarrationes* 29.s2.7, 73.8, 103.s3.22; *Sermones* 299E.2, 313D.4). Although gerunds appear in the Old Latin tradition, *occidere* in place of *crucifigere* is unique to Augustine: substitution with a less specific term is characteristic of flattening (cf. John 10:32, 19:10). The order of these two verbs is reversed in *Enarratio* 29.s2.7, *Sermo* 313D.4, Codex Palatinus, and several Greek witnesses.

JOHN 19:11

Augustine's mental text is based on the following:

non haberes in me potestatem nisi data tibi esset desuper.

This is the form of some of his early citations, *De diuersis quaestionibus* 69.9 and 79.5, and *Ad Simplicianum* 2.1.4: *in* for *aduersum* is paralleled by Codices Vercellensis, Brixianus, and Monacensis, while Codex Palatinus omits *ullam*. Only *De consensu* 3 and *Tractatus* 116 have *aduersum* and *ullam*; there are three changes of word order in the initial citation at *Tractatus* 116.5, but a few lines later Augustine follows the Vulgate sequence for everything apart from *aduersum me potestatem* (cf. John 3:32 etc.). *Enarratio* 9.6, his first reference to this verse, reads *tibi datum fuisset*: the Old Latin pluperfect is also cited in *De consensu* 3.13.46, *Enarratio* 49.5, and the first occasion in *Enarratio* 32.2.s2.12, while *datum* occurs in *Sermo* 299E.2 and *De trinitate* 3.7.12. as well.

JOHN 19:12–14

Tractatus 116 includes *enim* after *omnis* in John 19:12, present in certain Vulgate and Old Latin manuscripts. Like Codex Brixianus, it has *autem* for *ergo* in the next verse: this is also found in certain manuscripts of *De consensu* 3.8.35, but not *De consensu* 3.13.46 (cf. John 18:12 and John 19:29). *Pascha* in John 19:14 is indeclinable throughout *De consensu* 3, while *Tractatus* 116 and 117 have *paschae*. *De consensu* 3.13.50 is a loose allusion which omits *pascha* and substitutes *fere* for *quasi* (cf. John 6:10). For Augustine's comparison of John 19:14 and Mark 15:25, see *De consensu* 3.13 and *Tractatus* 117.

JOHN 19:15

De consensu 3.8.35 and 3.13.46 have *tolle* only once, in contrast to *tolle, tolle* at *De consensu* 3.13.40. *De consensu* 3.13.46 also features the Old Latin *clamauerunt* for *clamabant*. The addition of *enim* after *responderunt* is peculiar to *Tractatus* 116 and may be an adaptation. Four of Augustine's five citations outside *De consensu* and *Tractatus* 116 read *nos non habemus regem*, as do Codices Vercellensis, Palatinus, and Usserianus; *Enarrationes* 55.2 and 63.8 add *solum* before *Caesarem*: this is almost without parallel, and Augustine may be responsible (cf. John 9:39).[133]

[133] The only other examples of *solum* in the *Vetus Latina Database* are one pseudo-Augustinian sermon and Quodvultdeus, although Sedulius Scottus adds *tantummodo*.

JOHN 19:17–18

The allusions with *portare* at *Tractatus* 9.12, *Sermo* 218.2.2, and *Enarratio* 30.2.s2.9 show that Augustine was familiar with the rendering of Codices Brixianus, Monacensi, and Usserianus, despite reading *baiulare* in his verbatim citations in *De consensu* and *Tractatus* 117. The first two citations of John 19:18 in *Tractatus* 117 have the word order *crucifixerunt eum*, although a later sequential variant and *De consensu* 3.10.37 read *eum crucifixerunt.*

JOHN 19:20–2

The addition of *rex Iudaeorum* to John 19:20 in both Augustine's verbatim citations, *Tractatus* 117.4 and *Enarratio* 55.2, appears to be a repetition from the previous verse. All five citations of John 19:21 outside *Tractatus* 117 include reported speech, as in *Enarratio* 58.s1.1:

noli scribere 'rex Iudaeorum', sed scribe quia ipse dixit se regem esse Iudaeorum.

This is one of three citations to include an imperative in the second clause not attested in biblical witnesses: *Enarratio* 56.3 also has *scribe* (and adds *sic* after *scribere*), while *Enarratio* 80.11 reads *noli facere... sed fac quod.* These variations suggest that Augustine was quoting from memory (cf. John 4:17 and John 21:5). Although *Tractatus* 117 reads *pontifices Iudaeorum*, the adaptation in *Sermo* 218.7.7 supports the Old Latin *principes Iudaeorum* (cf. John 18:2 and 10). Only *Enarratio* 56 features *respondit eis* in John 19:22, again from memory despite the parallel with Codex Brixianus.

JOHN 19:23

Augustine's mental text reads *erat ibi tunica desuper texta*, supported by all references except the expected Vulgate form in *De consensu* and *Tractatus* 118, and *Sermo* 159B.18 (*Dolbeau* 21) which adds *quaedam* before *tunica.* Following Cyprian (*De catholicae ecclesiae unitate* 7), Augustine interpreted the tunic without seam as an image of the Church, and often used this verse against the Donatists who threatened Christian unity (e.g. *Tractatus* 13.13; see Aubineau 1971:41–3 and Berrouard 1969:937–8). The division of the clothes into four parts is taken to represent the whole world, supported by the phrase *per totum* (*Tractatus* 118.4).

JOHN 19:24

Inter se commonly renders πρὸς ἀλλήλους in the Old Latin tradition (e.g. John 4:33, 6:52, 11:56, 16:17), so *Tractatus* 13.13 and *Sermo* 159B.18 may reflect a version no longer preserved. However, both these citations continue with *non diuidamus eam sed sortem super eam mittamus,* which clearly derives from memory: Augustine has taken the Psalm citation from the second half of the verse and recast the earlier phrase to conform to this text. In John's version of Psalm 21:19, *partiti sunt* is unique to the Vulgate: the Old Latin rendering *diuiserunt* appears in the four citations outside *Tractatus* 118 and 119 and *De consensu* 3.12.39, although the allusion at *Sermo* 218.9.9 reads *sortiti sunt potius quam partiti.*

JOHN 19:25

De consensu 3.21.58 has the singular, *stabat,* found in some Vulgate and Old Latin manuscripts. Despite the variety of alternatives for *iuxta* in Old Latin witnesses, none has *circa,* which occurs in an allusion at *Tractatus* 8.9.

JOHN 19:28

Augustine's two verbatim citations, *Tractatus* 119 and *De consensu* 3.17.54, both omit *iam*, as do several Latin Gospels. *De consensu* 3.17.54 also corresponds to codices with *dixit* rather than *dicit*. The connection Augustine makes between *sitio* in this verse and John 4:7 has been mentioned on p. 216.

JOHN 19:29

For the second word, *Tractatus* 119 reads *ergo*; *autem* in *De consensu* 3.17.54 is not preserved here in biblical manuscripts. This may be an alternative translation of *οὖν*, as in the Old Latin tradition at John 19:26, but it could also derive from the Greek variant *δέ*.[134] Augustine shows no awareness of the reading *perticae* rather than *hyssopo*: his four allusions with *harundine* probably relate to Matthew 27:48 (*Sermo* 300.4.4, *Tractatus* 31.6, 37.9, and 47.11).

JOHN 19:30

Augustine's mental text of Jesus' final words is *perfectum est*, found in Codex Palatinus and eight of his thirteen citations. The others, including *Tractatus* 119, have *consummatum est*, which at *De Genesi ad litteram* 4.11 is used as a gloss on *consummauit*. Codex Palatinus is also one of two witnesses for *reddidit spiritum*, which appears in *Tractatus* 31.6 and *Sermones* 37.2 and 218.12.12. *Sermo* 5.3, quoted above, is identical to this manuscript apart from reading *dimisit spiritum*.[135] *Emisit spiritum*, widely attested in Latin Fathers, occurs

[134] Parker 1985:265 connects *autem* with *δέ* in this verse.
[135] See p. 122; *dimisit* also appears in Tertullian (*Apologeticum* 21).

in *Enarrationes* 33.s2.7 and 86.5. Augustine's linking of this verse with the *Pericope Adulterae* is discussed as part of the treatment of *inclinato capite* in John 8:6 and 8:8.

JOHN 19:34

The majority of Augustine's allusions to this verse have the verbs *percussit* (for *aperuit*) and *profluxit* (for *exiuit*). There is some support for the former in Old Latin witnesses, based on the itacistic Greek alternatives ἔνυξεν and ἤνοιξεν. In his only verbatim citation, *Tractatus* 120.2, Augustine draws attention to the use of the word *aperuit* rather than *percussit* or *uulnerauit*, and connects the 'opening' of Jesus' side with both the creation of Eve from Adam and the door into Noah's Ark.[136] No biblical codex, however, reads *profluxit*, which seems to be a contextual alternative suggested by memory: other forms such as *profudit* (*De Genesi contra Manichaeos* 2.24.37) and *manauit* (*Sermo* 218.14.14 etc.) are equally unlikely renderings of ἐξῆλθεν. Given Augustine's connection of the blood and water with the sacraments of the Church, it is possible that he was inspired by a liturgical text (cf. John 1:23).

JOHN 19:35–6

Tractatus 120 has the word order *testimonium eius* in John 19:35, and *impleretur* for *impleatur* in John 19:36. Both are paralleled in the Vulgate tradition. Augustine's other citation of John 19:36, *os eius non comminuetis* in *Contra Faustum* 12.30, combines Old Latin features with a verb only preserved in the Vulgate.

[136] *Vigilanti uerbo euangelista usus esset, ut non diceret: latus eius percussit, aut uulnerauit, aut quid aliud, sed: aperuit.* For further references, see Berrouard 1969:904–6 and 2003:484–6. Evodius *De fide* 32 also alludes to this verse with *percussum* and *profluxit* (Féliers 1966:64).

JOHN 19:37

It is sometimes difficult to decide whether Augustine is citing Zechariah 12:10 or John 19:37. Ten gospel citations, including three in *De trinitate* 1, have *uidebunt in quem pupugerunt*: Codex Palatinus is the sole witness with *pupugerunt* (cf. John 19:30). In the commentary at *Tractatus* 120.3, and in *In epistolam Iohannis* 4.5 and *Contra sermonem Arrianorum* 11.9, Augustine reads *uidebunt in quem confixerunt.* This is not found in Old Latin or Vulgate manuscripts, but *confixerunt* is the term used in Jerome's translation of Zechariah 12:10 from Hebrew, *aspicient ad me quem confixerunt.* Augustine considers this and the Septuagint version (with *insultauerunt*) at *De ciuitate dei* 20.30.3, but it is unlikely that this influenced his gospel text: the treatment of John 13:18 in *De ciuitate dei* 17.18.1 shows that Augustine did not usually compare citations in the Gospels with the prophetic books. It is more probable that *confixerunt* in John 19:37 comes from a version no longer preserved, a hypothesis supported by its appearance in Tertullian (*De carne Christi* 24 and *De resurrectione mortuorum* 26).[137]

JOHN 19:39–41

Tractatus 120 omits *et* before *Nicodemus* in John 19:39, as do some Old Latin manuscripts. In John 19:40, for which this sermon again provides the only citation, Augustine has *illud* rather than *eum* and the word order *mos est Iudaeis.* Both are paralleled in Vulgate

[137] This verse is discussed at La Bonnardière 1986:311 although she does not include the citation from *In epistolam Iohannis* or the evidence from Tertullian which argue in favour of an early date for *confixerunt.* The textual tradition of Augustine's works adds further forms: the majority Old Latin reading *compunxerunt* is found in two manuscripts at *Contra sermonem Arrianorum* 11.9, and in at least one witness (Paris BN lat 1959) for both citations of John 19:37 in *Tractatus* 120. A further early manuscript of *Tractatus* 120, however, Berlin Phillipps 1676, has the Vulgate *transfixerunt.*

witnesses: *illud*, although dependent upon *corpus*, is closer to the Greek *αὐτό*. Like the evangelist, Augustine connects this mention of Nicodemus with John 3, but he also links the new tomb in John 19:41 with the virgin birth (*De fide et symbolo* 5.11; cf. John 3:4).

JOHN 20:1–4

All Latin Gospels have *cum adhuc tenebrae essent* in John 20:1; while *cum adhuc obscurum esset* at *Quaestiones de Iudicibus* 46 may be a paraphrase, this is also found in Ambrose (*Explanatio Psalmi* 43.14). In John 20:2 the presence in some citations of *dominum meum* (*Contra Iulianum opus imperfectum* 2.61, *Sermones* 229K.2 and 245.1.1) and the singular *nescio* (*Sermones* 229L.1, 246.2) betrays the influence of John 20:13, which has also affected biblical manuscripts.[138] *De consensu* 3.24.68 has the present tense *currit* in John 20:2 and *praecurrit* in John 20:4, paralleled by some Vulgate witnesses.

JOHN 20:5–8

Augustine reads *introiit* in the treatment of this passage at *De consensu* 3.24.68 but in the next paragraph reverts to the Old Latin *intrauit* for all three verses, joined by *Sermo* 246.2 at John 20:6 and *Sermo* 229L.1 at 20:8. *Tractatus* 120 has *introiuit* in John 20:5 and 20:6, and *introiit* in 20:8. The commentary also reads *uidit* rather than *uidet* in John 20:5 and 20:6, along with *Sermones* 245.1.1 and 246.2 respectively. There are no extended citations of these verses in the lectionary sermons.

[138] Note also Augustine's comment on the addition of *meum* in *Tractatus* 120.6, quoted on p. 26.

JOHN 20:9

Tractatus 120 and *De consensu* 3.24.68 correspond exactly to Weber–Gryson, but are followed by minor sequential variants (*sciebat* in *De consensu* 3.24.69, *oporteret* at *Tractatus* 120.9). The four other sermons on this lection all read *scripturas* rather than *scripturam*, and *oportebat* for *oportet*. For *sciebant*, *Sermo* 244 uniquely has *nouerant*, while *sciebat* occurs in *Sermo* 245 and *nouerat* at *Sermones* 229L and 246 (all three times). *Sermo* 229L also substitutes *Iesum* for *eum*, like some manuscripts of *Sermo* 246 and Codex Brixianus.

JOHN 20:11

The editions of *Tractatus* 121 read *cum*, the text of the majority of Old Latin versions, but at least two early manuscripts of this work have *dum* (cf. John 18:10 and 19:37).

JOHN 20:13–16

In John 20:13 there is a sequential variant *sustulerunt* in *Tractatus* 121.2, matching Codices Monacensis and Usserianus. All three citations of the next verse (*De consensu* 3.24.68–9 and *Tractatus* 121.2) have *uidit* for *uidet*, attested in part of the Vulgate tradition (cf. John 20:6). Both references to John 20:15 in *De consensu* have *est*, whereas *esset* appears in *Tractatus* 121. *Sermo* 229L reads:

si tu tulisti eum, dic mihi ubi posuisti eum et ego tollam eum.

As all the non-Vulgate readings are paralleled in Old Latin witnesses, this lectionary sermon seems to have been based on an Old Latin text (thus also *quod interpretatur domine* in the next verse). *Sermones* 246.3 and 375C.1 have *abstulisti* in John 20:15, not preserved in any manuscript. Augustine may have been paraphrasing in the former, as he reads *ostende* for *dic* and *est* rather than *dicitur* in John 20:16.

Sermo 375C is closer to Old Latin versions: it omits *mihi*, but has *dic* for *dicito*, and *illum tollam*.

JOHN 20:17

Augustine interprets the command *noli me tangere* as a mystical indication of Christ's divinity which can only be touched by faith (e.g. *Tractatus* 26.3, *Sermo* 245.2.2; see further Berrouard 2003: 86–7). All five of his citations outside *Tractatus* 121 and *De consensu* which include the middle phrase have an abbreviated form: *uade et dic fratribus meis* occurs in *Epistula* 140.17.43, *Enarrationes* 7.1 and 48.s1.8, and *Sermo* 265F.2, while *Sermo* 229L.2 reads *uade et dic discipulis meis.* Neither is found in Latin Bibles, and it is possible that Augustine was influenced by the parallel at Matthew 28:10, *ite nuntiate fratribus meis.* The three citations with *uado* instead of *ascendo* have simply swapped the two verbs in the sentence, again without precedent (*Quaestiones de Genesi* 59, *Tractatus* 21.3, *De fide et symbolo* 9.18). There is also no manuscript evidence for *ascendam* rather than *ascendo*: given that this follows the paraphrase in *Sermones* 229L.2 and 265F.2, it is likely to be due to memory. The same is true of the reversal of *deum* and *patrem* at *Tractatus* 21.3 and *Sermo* 229L.2. Some Old Latin witnesses repeat *ad* before these nouns, as in *Sermo* 229L: *De consensu* 3.24.68 has *ad deum* twice (with *ad patrem* twice in one manuscript), but in the next paragraph the editorial text follows the Vulgate (although *ad* continues in part of the textual tradition).

JOHN 20:18–21

In *De consensu* 3.24.69, his second citation of John 20:18 in this work, Augustine reads *uenit ergo.* A handful of biblical manuscripts add *ergo* (*οὖν* in Greek), and in one edition it also appears at *De consensu* 3.24.68. The allusions to John 20:19 in *Epistulae* 95.7 and 137.2.8, and *Sermones* 191.1.2, 277.12.12, and 376.1.1 all have *ostia.* A longer paraphrase of the day's lection is given in *Sermo* 247.1, with *cum sero factum esset*, *ostia*, and *timorem*, readings all paralleled in Codex Vercellensis. The unique Vulgate reading *fores* at *De consensu* 3.25.74–5, followed by the Old Latin *ostia*, has already been discussed.[139] This citation also has *dixit* where *Tractatus* 121 reads *dicit* with the Vulgate. The commentary includes *congregati* after *discipuli*, as do some Vulgate witnesses, the allusion at *De consensu* 3.23.85, and certain manuscripts of *De consensu* 3.25.74. *Tractatus* 121 also has the feminine *die illa*, characteristic of Old Latin manuscripts, and the word order *cum hoc dixisset* in John 20:20. While several Latin Gospels have *pax uobiscum*, its appearance in a few references in John 20:19 and 20:21 may betray the influence of the liturgy (cf. John 1:23). As with John 19:41, Augustine links the entry behind closed doors to the virgin birth (*Epistula* 137.2.8).

JOHN 20:22

Most citations have *insufflauit*, but one has *sufflauit* (*Epistula* 265.2; cf. Codex Monacensis), and one *inspirauit* (*De baptismo* 3.18.23; cf. Cyprian *Epistula* 73.7). On five occasions Augustine adds the detail *in faciem eorum* (*Epistula* 265.2, *Tractatus* 32.6, *Sermo* 265.7.8) or *in faciem discipulorum* (*Contra epistulam fundamenti* 10, *Contra litteras Petiliani* 2.32.76; also certain manuscripts of *De trinitate* 4.20.29). This is not found in any Old Latin witness (Codex Bezae adds *in eos*), although it occurs in one later gospel manuscript and a number of Latin Fathers.[140] A possible origin for this reading is presented by *De ciuitate dei* 13.24.1, where Augustine juxtaposes the Vulgate form of John 20:22 and an Old Latin version of Genesis 2:7 which reads

[139] See pp. 160–1.

[140] The sole manuscript with *insuflauit in faciem eorum* in Fischer 1991:521 is **Ce** (Essen, Münsterschatz); **Kc*** (Colmar, Bibl. Muncipale 38) and **Ia** (Milano, Bib. Capitolare II.D.3–1) read *insuflauit in eis*. The *Vetus Latina Database* lists Gregory the Great, Jerome's translation of Didymus, Maximinus, Nicetas, Quodvultdeus, and the anonymous *Contra Varimadum* among others which include *in faciem*. Tischendorf notes various versions and a couple of Church Fathers in support of the dative, but only the Sahidic for *in eorum faciem*.

insufflauit in faciem eius. The verbal and exegetical links between the two passages make it likely that the wording of one has affected the other (cf. John 4:7, 8:6, and 8:8). Nonetheless, Durand (who does not remark on the textual variation) maintains that Augustine wishes to make a distinction between John 20:22 and Genesis 2:7, because he does not identify the breath with the Spirit, but treats it as a sign (e.g. *De trinitate* 4.20.29 and *De ciuitate dei* 13.24.1).[141] Both *dicit* and *dixit* are found in Vulgate manuscripts (Augustine has *dixit* at *De consensu* 3.25.74 and *Tractatus* 121), while five Old Latin witnesses read *ait* (cited at *De baptismo* 3.18.23, *Contra epistulam Parmeniani* 2.11.24 (twice), and *De trinitate* 15.26.45). No biblical manuscript, however, has the participle *dicens*: this appears in six of Augustine's citations, including *De consensu* 3.1.4, *De ciuitate dei* 13.24.1, and the two citations with *in faciem discipulorum*.

JOHN 20:23

Augustine's mental text is a flattened version in which the parallelism has been reinforced:[142]

si cui dimiseritis peccata dimittentur ei, si cui tenueritis tenebuntur.

This includes several Old Latin features: *dimiseritis* and *dimittentur* are in Codex Bezae, and *tenueritis* and *tenebuntur* in Codices Vercellensis and Monacensis, while *si cui* at the beginning of the verse matches Codices Brixianus and Palatinus. Three sermons read *dimittuntur*, which is not preserved in the Old Latin tradition (*Sermones* 71.13.23, 99.9.9, 295.2.2). Of Augustine's primary citations, *Tractatus* 121 and 122 have *quorum remiseritis peccata remittuntur eis, et quorum retinueritis retenta sunt*, while *De consensu* 3.25.74 ends *et quorum detinueritis detenta sunt*. The former appears in the Vulgate tradition, while three Old Latin manuscripts have *detinueritis*. Augustine cites this verse almost exclusively against the Donatists,

[141] Durand 1978:101–7, 124; see also Comeau 1930:273, Berrouard 1998:475–6, and Hombert 2000:75.

[142] On the development of this verse in *De baptismo*, see p. 164.

referring to baptismal forgiveness rather than other penitential rites; he draws particular attention to the fact that verse 22 is immediately followed by verse 23, connecting the gift of the Holy Spirit with the remission of sins.[143]

JOHN 20:25

The opening clause of Thomas' speech is only found in *Tractatus* 121.5, with the Vulgate alternative *fixuram*. The rest of this citation is identical to Weber–Gryson, but elsewhere Augustine abbreviates this verse: *et mittam digitum meum . . . et mittam manum meam* is replaced by *nisi misero manum meam* (*Enarratio* 63.17 and *Sermo* 145A.1), *nisi misero digitos meos* (*Enarratio* 21.s2.17 and *Sermo* 159B.12, cf. *In epistolam Iohannis* 1.3), *nisi misero manus meas* (*Sermo* 375C.1), and *nisi digitum misero* (*Sermo* 258, twice). *Sermo* 112.4.4 has the longest form:

nisi misero digitos meos in clauorum et uulnerum loca, et nisi manum meam in latus eius misero, non credam.

Despite the Old Latin parallels for *misero*, this is a paraphrase like the others. *Enarratio* 21.s2 and *Sermo* 88.2.2 also have *uulnerum*, while eleven of Augustine's seventeen references include the verb *tangere*, normally in the form *tetigero*, and seven feature the word *cicatrices*. These are all unique to Augustine, and it is clear that even in *Sermones* 258 and 375C, preceded by this lection, he is relying on memory.

JOHN 20:27

Augustine paraphrases Jesus' reply to Thomas in a similar manner to John 20:25. At least twelve allusions mention *cicatrices*, while the

[143] See La Bonnardière 1967:38 and 250 (the latter has a list of the eighteen times this verse is cited, repeated at La Bonnardière 1968:200) and Berrouard 2003:362.

command takes a series of forms, including *ueni mitte manum tuam, incredule* (*Enarratio* 21.s2.17), *ecce, digitos tuos mitte per latus meum* (*Sermo* 112.5.5), *mitte digitos et palpa cicatrices* (*In epistolam Iohannis* 3.2), and *ueni tange mitte manus tuas in latus meum* (*Sermo* 375C.2). As before, there are few points of contact with biblical wording. Augustine normally has no hesitation in affirming that Thomas actually touched Jesus, although at *Tractatus* 121.5 he admits that this is not explicitly stated in the narrative (see Berrouard 2003:364).

JOHN 20:29

Thirteen of Augustine's twenty citations of the first clause, including *De consensu* 3.25.75, read *quia uidisti credidisti*, omitting *me*. The pronoun is also absent from Codices Vercellensis, Palatinus, and Usserianus. Only *Sermo* 361.13.13 has an additional *et* before *credidisti*. Augustine has two forms of the second half of this verse. The first, found in almost all Latin Gospels, is *beati qui non uiderunt et crediderunt*: this appears on eight occasions.[144] His preferred text, however, *beati qui non uident et credunt*, occurs twice as often and is unique to him, not even appearing in another Latin Father. (The closest are Tertullian *De resurrectione mortuorum* 34 and the Latin Chrysostom with *uident et credent*, while Cyprian *Ad Quirinum* 2.6 reads *uiderunt et credunt*.) This might be an alternative rendering of the Greek aorist participles from a version no longer preserved: it is introduced in *Sermo* 259.1 (dated to 393/400) as the text of the liturgical reading, although the other lectionary sermon, *Sermo* 375C, has paraphrases in John 20:25 and 27 which cast doubt on its accuracy. On the other hand, the present tense could be the result of flattening, in order to increase the potential application of the saying. Augustine's first citation of this verse, *Enarratio* 8.6, has a one-off reading, *beati qui non uiderunt et credituri sunt*. At *Tractatus* 121.5 Augustine treats the form with the perfect tense as a further example of the biblical use of the perfect for the future, but this is

144 *De consensu* 3.25.75, *Tractatus* 121.5, *Epistula* 147.3.8, *Enarrationes* 63.17 and 76.4, *Sermones* 143.3.3, 158.5.5, 158.8.8.

unlikely in itself to have affected his text (cf. John 15:15, 17:4, 17:14, 17:22).[145]

JOHN 21:1

Sermo 248 paraphrases this verse with *ostendisse*, which suggests that, like Codex Vercellensis, Augustine's manuscript for the lection had *ostendit* rather than *manifestauit*.

JOHN 21:3

The allusions in *Sermones* 248.1.1 and 252.1.1 have the Old Latin reading *ceperunt* (cf. *Sermo* 249.1), but the reference to *tota nox* in both sermons may betray the influence of Luke 5:5. Augustine's only other citation, *Tractatus* 122.5, reads *apprehenderunt* in place of the Vulgate *prendiderunt*. This is found in only two of the four hundred manuscripts in Fischer's collation, although *prehenderunt* in Codex Monacensis suggests that the reading may have been present in an Old Latin version (cf. John 21:10).[146]

JOHN 21:6

Augustine's mental text, occurring in over twenty citations, is *mittite retia in dexteram partem*. The only exception is *Tractatus* 122, which has two distinctive Vulgate forms also in Codex Aureus, *mittite in dexteram nauigii rete*. The rest of the verse in *Sermo* 249.1 is a

[145] The interpretation of the present tense in this verse, placing contemporary Christians on the same level as the Apostles, is in keeping with earlier Latin tradition, but differs from Origen: see Comeau 1930:200.

[146] Fischer 1991:567 lists two witnesses with *adpraehenderunt*: **Hd** (Book of Armagh; Trinity College Dublin 52) and **St** (Liber Toletanus; Madrid Bibl. Nacional Vitr. 1–13).

paraphrase, as shown by *fecerunt* in place of *miserunt* (cf. John 19:10) and the repetition of *retia*, but *poterant* for *ualebant* does have some Old Latin support. Augustine links the significance of the right-hand side with the sheep and the goats in Matthew 25:34 (e.g. *Sermo* 252A.4).

JOHN 21:8–10

Augustine's only citations of these verses are in *Tractatus* 122 and 123. In John 21:8 he follows manuscripts which lack *a* before *cubitis*, while in John 21:10 both sermons read *apprehendistis* (cf. John 21:3). Such consistency implies that this was the text of his exemplar.

JOHN 21:11

Augustine paraphrases this verse in *Sermo* 251.3.3, using *adduxerunt* and *attraxerunt* in place of *traxit*. His mental text for the second half of this verse is exemplified by *Sermo* 252.2.2:

et cum tam magni essent, retia non sunt disrupta.

Four Old Latin manuscripts have *retia* for *rete*, but while Codex Veronensis reads *ruptum*, all others have *scissum* or *scissa*. Nine of Augustine's works feature *disrupta* (including the lectionary *Sermones* 229M and 252), alongside *rupta* in *Epistula* 55.31, and *scissum* in *Tractatus* 122 and the lectionary *Sermones* 249, 250, 251, and 252A. Although *disrupta* could be a rendering of ἐσχίσθη not preserved elsewhere, it is possible that Augustine has been influenced by the parallel in Luke 5:6 with *rumpere*: he frequently compares these two catches of fish, but maintains that they refer to two different occasions (e.g. *De consensu euangelistarum* 4.9.10). The most significant reading is *tam magni*. All surviving Old Latin witnesses read *et cum tanti essent*, with the exception of *et cum multi essent* in Codex Palatinus. Only three citations have *tanti*: Augustine's commentary at *Tractatus* 122.5 and *Sermones* 251.3.3 and 252.1.1. In these two lectionary sermons, he glosses *tanti* with *id est, tam magni*, his customary means of replacing an unexpected reading with one which is more familiar (cf. John 1:11, 1:48 and pp. 88–9). His mental text, *cum tam magni essent*, appears in eleven other citations, while *Tractatus* 123.1 has *cum magni essent*. There is no example of τοσοῦτος being rendered by *tam magnus* in gospel manuscripts.[147] Instead, this unique reading seems to derive from the emphasis Augustine places on the size of the fish, apparent in both his earliest references to the verse:

ceperunt pisces qui omnes magni erant, id est iustos significabant.

(*De agone christiano* 26.28)

et ideo magnos, id est perfectos et regno caelorum aptos habet.

(*De diuersis quaestionibus* 57.2)

This is also seen in *Epistula* 55.31, from 400. In his commentary on John 21:11 at *Tractatus* 122.9, Augustine makes a lengthy cross-reference to Matthew 5:19, *magnus uocabitur in regno caelorum*, citing also the parable of the fisherman from Matthew 13:48, where the good fish are selected for the kingdom of heaven.[148] This, together with his use of Matthew 25:34 to illuminate John 21:6, shows the close textual links which may even have affected his text of the present verse. The significance of the number one hundred and fifty-three is one of Augustine's favourite topics, to which he devotes *De diuersis quaestionibus* 57. Pontet (1946:300–1 and 512) notes that although Augustine explains this as fifty times three plus three in works written before 400, from *Epistula* 55 onwards he starts referring to the triangular number of seventeen.

[147] It occurs on eight other occasions: *tantus* is the only form in Old Latin versions at Matthew 8:10 and 15:33 (twice) and John 12:37 and 14:9, and the majority reading at Luke 7:9 (some witnesses have *talis*) and John 6:9 (Codices Vercellensis and Bezae read *tam multos*); *tot* or *quot* is found at Luke 15:29. Augustine glosses *tantum* with *tam multum* at *Locutiones in Heptateuchum* 7.8 on Judges 2:20. Despite the equivalence of *tantus* and *tam multus* in later Latin, *tam magnus* does not seem to be an alternative: the closest parallel is the use of *multitudo* in place of *magnitudo* (Löfstedt 1911:147–9).

[148] The use of *magnos* rather than *bonos* in this parable in the Venetian gospel harmony and Gospel of Thomas 8 (Quispel 1975:98–103) is most unlikely to have influenced Augustine.

JOHN 21:12

Tractatus 123.1, Augustine's only citation of this verse, has *discumbentium*. This is paralleled in Codices Aureus and Colbertinus and manuscripts of the Vulgate, even though it probably arose from a misreading of *discentium* (which corresponds to τῶν μαθητῶν). The presence of *prandete* earlier in the verse, together with *recumbere* in John 21:20 and *discumbentium* correctly in John 13:28, meant that the error was not obvious to a Latin reader. As noted above, this implies that Augustine had not compared his text of this verse with a Greek version (cf. John 18:28).[149] This citation also has *est* for *esset*, in keeping with all Old Latin and several Vulgate witnesses.

JOHN 21:13–14

Augustine reads *accipit* rather than *accepit* in *Tractatus* 123, both of which occur in the Vulgate tradition of John 21:13. In the next verse, two more variants involve Vulgate alternatives: *resurrexisset* and *discipulis suis*. Both appear in *Tractatus* 123; the editorial text of *De consensu* 3.25.82 too has *resurrexisset*, but *suis* is only present in certain manuscripts of this work.

JOHN 21:15–17

There are several subtle differences in the Greek text of the dialogue between Jesus and Peter which are not usually reproduced in Latin translations. Several manuscripts render ἀγαπᾶν by *diligere* and φιλεῖν by *amare*, but a distinction is never made between βόσκε

[149] See pp. 97–8. There is a comparable misreading of *descendentium* for *discentium* at Luke 19:37 in Codex Aureus and some Vulgate manuscripts; see further Fischer 1972:88.

and *ποίμαινε*, the distribution of *agnos* and *oues* matches *ἀρνία* and *πρόβατα* in Codices Brixianus and Corbeiensis alone, and *scis* and *nosti* rarely correspond to *οἶδας* and *γινώσκεις* in John 21:17.[150] Augustine's ignorance of these is demonstrated by his frequent statements that the three questions and answers are identical (e.g. *Sermo* 340A.3, *De consensu* 3.2.5). He normally paraphrases the exchange, which makes it impossible to assign his citations to individual verses even though many feature *amare* alongside *diligere*, and *agnos* with *oues*. Only at *De ciuitate dei* 14.7.1 does he observe that Jesus switches from *diligis* to *amas* in John 21:17 whereas Peter uses *amo* throughout: even here, however, he plays down the change by emphasizing the similarity of the two terms. Most citations are likely to have been made from memory, given the similarity of Augustine's treatment of the verses and alterations such as *Petre* rather than *Simon Iohannis*.[151] Augustine seems to have been familiar with the addition of *plus his* in John 21:15 in an Old Latin source, even though it is only preserved in the Vulgate and Codex Brixianus: these words feature in four of the lectionary sermons (*Sermones* 147, 229O, 229P, and 299B) which have Old Latin readings elsewhere despite dating from after 412. He twice has the word *ouiculas*, peculiar to John 21:16 in Codex Veronensis (*Sermones* 147.2.2 and 295.5.5). Codex Colbertinus, in the same verse, provides the sole example of *diligo* in any of Peter's responses, which also appears in *Sermones* 229P.2 and 253.1.1. Finally, *Sermones* 138.4.4 and 299A.1 read *scis* followed by *nosti* in John 21:17, as attested in Codices Veronensis and Corbeiensis; Augustine's other citations all have *scis* on both occasions, a reading distinctive of Codex Bezae and the Vulgate. When using this verse against the Donatists, Augustine always emphasizes that the pronoun in *pasce oues meas* asserts Christ's ownership of the flock.[152]

[150] It should be noted that Nestle–Aland treats the reading *oues* in most Old Latin manuscripts in John 21:15 as evidence supporting *πρόβατα*.

[151] The recurrence of particular phrases in Augustine's exegesis of John 21:15–19 is considered, along with some of the readings in his biblical text, in Pellegrino 1967. Pellegrino observes that putting these citations into chronological order reveals little of significance.

[152] See further the collection of passages assembled at Hombert 2000:285–6.

JOHN 21:18

A surprising number of variants peculiar to Augustine occur in his citations of this verse, alongside some Old Latin readings. Several are present in *In epistolam Iohannis* 5.11:

cum iuuenis esses, praecingebas te et ibas quo uolebas. cum autem fueris senior, alius te praecinget et tollet te quo tu non uis.

This is the only citation with both *praecingebas* and *praecinget*, like the majority of Old Latin manuscripts: *Sermo* 297.1.2 also has *praecingebas* and *Enarratio* 68.s1.3 *praecinget*. The form *cum iuuenis esses*, similar to Codex Brixianus, is cited at *Sermo* 340A.3 as well. Five other citations, including the lectionary *Sermo* 147.3.3, have *ibas quo uolebas*, the text of Codex Colbertinus, while *Sermones* 296.2.3, 297.1.2, and 299.7 read *ibas quo uelles*. The latter is unique to Augustine, as are his versions of the beginning of the next sentence: all Latin Gospels render γηράσῃς by *senueris*, but in addition to *fueris senior* above, he has *senior factus fueris* in four sermons, and *senex fueris factus* in the lectionary *Sermo* 299. Although there may have been some influence from the beginning of the verse, it is possible that at least one of these phrases appeared in a translation now lost. Augustine's mental text of the final words is:

alter te cinget et feret quo tu non uis.

Thirteen works have this exact form, including three sermons on this text (*Sermones* 147, 299, and 299B). No fewer than eighteen works feature *alter*, only preserved in Codex Vercellensis. The reading of most Gospels, *alius*, is cited at *In epistolam Iohannis* 5, *Enarratio* 68.s1, and the commentary at *Tractatus* 123: even these include *tu* before *non*, paralleled in both Old Latin and Vulgate witnesses. The most remarkable feature is *feret*, present in sixteen works. (The form *tollet* in *In epistolam Iohannis* 5 is also unique to Augustine, as is the doublet, *et tollet et feret*, in *Sermo* 344.3.) Every Latin version has a reflex of *ducere* here for οἴσει, even though the other nine instances of *ducere* in John translate ἄγειν. The sixteen occurrences of φέρειν (future οἴσειν) elsewhere in the Gospel correspond to *ferre* in the Old Latin manuscripts, although a contextual alternative is sometimes supplied (e.g. *facere* in John 2:8, 15:4, and 15:8). Augustine's citations of this verse, therefore, alone match the practice of the Latin tradition in the rest of John. An explanation for the inconsistency may be provided by Codex Bezae, which reads ἀπάγουσιν and *ducent*: perhaps the Old Latin *ducet* translates an alternative Greek reading (ἀπ)ἄξει which has not been preserved in biblical manuscripts. This hypothesis is lent some support by Chrysostom's use of ἄξουσιν in three citations.[153] Augustine always interprets this verse as a reference to Peter's death (Pellegrino 1967:418–19).

JOHN 21:19

The lectionary *Sermones* 147.3.3 and 299.7, joined by *Sermo* 296.2.3, have *dicebat* rather than *dixit.* This may have been present in a version no longer extant: the imperfect is found in at least one Greek minuscule. The rendering of δοξάσει by *glorificaturus* is paralleled elsewhere, and its absence from surviving Old Latin codices seems accidental (cf. John 17:4–5). Augustine cites it on five occasions: *glorificaturus esset* in *Tractatus* 51.10, and *glorificaturus erat* in four works including the lectionary *Sermo* 299B.2. All Latin Gospels have *esset* in this verse, but *erat* occurs alongside *esset* in a similar construction in John 12:33 and John 18:32. Furthermore, Augustine reads *clarificaturus erat* in the lectionary *Sermo* 299, *In epistolam Iohannis* 5.11 and a sequential variant at *Tractatus* 123.5. On the other hand, the initial citation of *Tractatus* 123 and the third sermon on this passage, *Sermo* 147, both have the regular *clarificaturus esset.*

JOHN 21:20–1

Tractatus 123 reads *tradet* for *tradit* in John 21:20: both occur in Vulgate witnesses. The citation at *Contra Faustum* 17.4 has Old Latin

[153] These are listed in Tischendorf. The addition of οὕτως in John 21:22 offers a parallel for Codex Bezae as the only witness to a Greek text underlying the Latin tradition; similarly, in John 10:18, only Codex Bezae has ἆραι for λαβεῖν, which appears to be the source for *tollendi* in Codex Colbertinus.

features, omitting *illum* and *sequentem* and reading *dixerat* and *tradet*. These, and the similarity of the nearby citations of John 21:24–5 to extant manuscripts, suggest that the unique forms *recumbebat* and *domino* may represent readings from a codex. In John 21:21 *Sermo* 253.3.4 alone has *iste quid* in place of *hic autem quid* (cf. John 4:18 etc.).

JOHN 21:22–3

All citations from the three works in which Augustine cites these verses omit *si* before *sic*, including *Tractatus* 124 and *De consensu* 3.25.78 (which only cites John 21:22). This is widespread in both Old Latin and Vulgate traditions. There are parallels between the lectionary *Sermo* 253 and Codices Monacensis and Vercellensis: *illum* for *eum* (in certain manuscripts) and the omission of *quid ad te*. The reported speech and variants in the version of John 21:23 at *Sermo* 253.3.4 indicate that this is a paraphrase:

secutus adiunxit uerba sua in euangelio et ait natum fuisse famam inter fratres propter hoc uerbum quia discipulus ille non esset moriturus . . . non autem dixit eum non fuisse moriturus, sed tantum dixit sic eum uolo manere donec ueniam; tu me sequere.

Augustine's only other citation of this verse, *Tractatus* 124, also has *inter fratres* in keeping with Codices Monacensis and Usserianus and some Vulgate manuscripts.

JOHN 21:24

De consensu 2.12.25 and *Tractatus* 124 correspond to the Vulgate, apart from *discipulus ille* in the commentary: the influence of the previous verse also affects certain Vulgate manuscripts. *Contra Faustum* 17.4 includes an interesting variant, *qui testificatur de Iesu*. Most manuscripts have *de his*, translating the Greek περὶ τούτων, but it seems that *HIS* was misread at some point in Latin as the *nomen sacrum* for *Iesus*, *IHS*. The accusative, *de Iesum* (*IHM*) is found here in Codices Palatinus and Vercellensis; the latter also has *testificatur* along with Codex Monacensis.

JOHN 21:25

Sermo 98.3.3 is a paraphrase, shown by the omission of *singula* and *qui scribendi sunt*, as well as the addition of *totum* before *mundum*, and *posse* before *capere* (cf. John 3:3 etc.). However, *posse*, which appears in the reported speech at *De consensu* 4.8.9, is attested in Codices Vercellensis and Monacensis and may have been known to Augustine through this text-type. *Tractatus* 124 follows the Vulgate, while the only other verbatim citation (*Contra Faustum* 17.3) is almost identical to Codex Usserianus:

et alia quidem multa fecit Iesus, quae si scriberentur singula nec ipsum existimo capere mundum qui scribuntur libros.

References

Abbreviations used in the references

AGLB	*Aus der Geschichte der lateinischen Bibel.*
ANTF 5	Aland, Kurt, ed. (1972). *Die alten Übersetzungen des Neuen Testaments, die Kirchenväterzitate und Lektionare.* Arbeiten zur neutestamentlichen Textforschung 5. Berlin; Walter de Gruyter.
Augustine through the Ages	Fitzgerald, Allan D. *et al.* (1999). *Augustine through the Ages. An Encyclopaedia.* Grand Rapids MI: Eerdmans.
Augustinus–Lexikon	Mayer, Cornelius P., ed. (1986–). *Augustinus-Lexikon.* Basel: Schwabe and Co.
Augustinus Magister	Cayré, Fulbert, ed. (1954). *Augustinus Magister. Congrès International Augustinien. Paris 21–24 Sept 1954. Vol. 1. Communications; Vol 2. Communications, Vol 3. Actes.* Paris: IEA.
BA	*Bibliothèque Augustinienne.*
Benoît–Prigent	Benoît, André and Prigent, Pierre, ed. (1971). *La Bible et les Pères: Colloque de Strasbourg 1969.* Paris.
Biblia Augustiniana	La Bonnardière, Anne-Marie, ed. (1960–75). *Biblia Augustiniana.* EAA 11, 18, 21, 26, 42, 49, 67. Paris: IEA.
Biblia Patristica	Allenbach, J. *et al.*, eds. (1975–). *Biblia Patristica. Index des Citations et Allusions Bibliques dans la Littérature Patristique.* Paris: CNRS.
BTA 2	Bright, Pamela, ed. (1999). *Augustine and the Bible. The Bible through the Ages* 2. Based on *Bible de tous les temps* 3 (BTT 3). Notre Dame, Indiana.
BTT 2	Fontaine, Jacques and Pietri, Charles, eds. (1985). *Le monde latine antique et la Bible. Bible de tous les temps* 2. Paris: Beauchesne.

BTT 3 — La Bonnardière, Anne-Marie, ed. (1986). *Saint Augustin et la Bible. Bible de tous les temps* 3. Paris: Beauchesne.

CHB 1 — Ackroyd, P. and Evans, C. F., eds. (1970). *The Cambridge History of the Bible. Volume 1. From the Beginnings to Jerome.* Cambridge: Cambridge University Press.

CHB 2 — Lampe, G. W. H., ed. (1969). *The Cambridge History of the Bible. Volume 2. The West from the Fathers to the Reformation.* Cambridge: Cambridge University Press.

Collectanea Augustiniana 1 — Schnaubelt, Joseph C. and Fleteren, Frederick van, eds. (1990). *Augustine: 'Second Founder of the Faith'.* New York: Peter Lang.

Collectanea Augustiniana 2 — Lienhard, Joseph T. *et al.*, eds. (1993). *Augustine: Presbyter Factus Sum.* New York: Peter Lang.

Collectanea Augustiniana 5 — Fleteren, Frederick van and Schnaubelt, Joseph C., eds. (2001). *Augustine: Biblical Exegete.* New York: Peter Lang.

CSEL — *Corpus Scriptorum Ecclesiasticorum Latinorum.*

EAA — Collection des Études Augustiniennes, série antiquité.

Ehrman–Holmes — Ehrman, Bart D. and Holmes, Michael W., eds. (1995). *The Text of the New Testament in Contemporary Research. Essays on the Status Quaestionis.* Studies and Documents 46. Grand Rapids, Michigan: Eerdmans.

IEA — Institut des Études Augustiniennes.

JECS — *Journal of Early Christian Studies.*

JTS — *Journal of Theological Studies.*

Miscellanea Agostiniana — Casamassa, Antonio, ed. (1931). *Miscellanea Agostiniana. Testi e Studi.* Rome: Tipografia Polyglotta Vaticana.

Philologia Sacra — Gryson, Roger (1993). *Philologia Sacra. Biblische und patristische Studien für Hermann J. Frede und Walter Thiele zu ihrem siebzigsten*

	Geburtstag. 1. Altes und Neues Testament. 2. Apokryphen, Kirchenväter, Verschiedenes. AGLB 24. Freiburg: Herder.
REA	*Revue des études augustiniennes* (*Revue des études augustiniennes et patristiques* from 2005).
VC	*Vigiliae Christianae.*

Augustine's writings have normally been consulted and quoted according to the most recent edition listed in Gryson 2007. There are a couple of exceptions: the edition of the *Enarrationes in Psalmos* by Dekkers and Fraipont (*Corpus Christianorum* series latina 38–40) has been used throughout; the text of *Sermones ad populum* 51–396 has been taken from the website www.augustinus.it which reproduces Migne's *Patrologia Latina* along with the supplementary sermons (apart from the *Sermones Dolbeau*).

References

Albaric, Michel (1986). 'Une catéchèse eucharistique. Le Sermon 227.' BTT 3: 87–98.

Albl, Martin C. (1999). *'And Scripture Cannot Be Broken.' The Form and Function of the Early Christian Testimonia Collections.* Leiden: Brill.

Alexanderson, Bengt (1999). 'Adnotationes Criticae in Augustini *In Iohannis Euangelium Tractatus.*' *Electronic Antiquity* 5.1 (February 1999). Published online at http://scholar.lib.vt.edu/ejournals/ElAnt/V5N1/tractatus.html

Altaner, Berthold (1951). 'Augustinus, Gregor von Nazianz und Gregor von Nyssa.' *Revue Bénédictine* 61: 54–62.

—— (1952). 'Augustinus und die griechische Patristik.' *Revue Bénédictine* 62: 201–15.

Anoz, José (2002). 'Cronología de la producción agustiniana.' *Augustinus* 47: 229–312.

Aubineau, Michel (1971). 'Dossier Patristique sur Jean XIX, 23–4: la tunique sans couture du Christ.' Benoît-Prigent: 9–50.

Baarda, Tjitze (1986). '"The Flying Jesus". Luke 4:29–30 in the Syriac Diatessaron.' *VC* 40: 313–41.

—— (1993). 'John 1:5 in the *Oration* and *Diatessaron* of Tatian. Concerning the reading *καταλαμβάνει*.' *VC* 47: 209–25.

Bardy, Gustave (1954). 'Les méthodes de travail de saint Augustin.' *Augustinus Magister* 1: 19–29.

Barrett, C. K. (1970). 'The Interpretation of the Old Testament in the New.' CHB 1: 377–411.

Bastiaensen, Antoon A. R. (2003). ' "He must Grow, I must Diminish." (John 3:30): Augustine of Hippo Preaching on John the Baptist' in *Jerusalem, Alexandria, Rome: Studies in ancient cultural interaction in honour of A. Hilhorst*, ed. Florentino García Martínez and Gerald P. Luttikhuizen. 13–26.

Becker, Ulrich (1963). *Jesus und die Ehebrecherin. Untersuchungen zur Text- und Überlieferung von Joh. 7,53–8,11.* (Beihefte zur Zeitschrift für die neutestamentliche Wissenschaft 28). Berlin: Verlag Alfred Töpelmann.

Berger, Samuel (1893). *Histoire de la Vulgate pendant les premiers siècles du moyen age.* Reprint. New York: Burt Franklin.

Berrouard, Marie-François (1962). 'Saint Augustin et le ministère de la prédication. Le thème des anges qui montent et qui descendent.' *Recherches augustiniennes* 2: 447–501.

—— ed. (1969). *Œuvres de saint Augustin 71. Homélies sur l'Évangile de saint Jean I–XVI.* BA/Desclée de Brouwer.

——(1971). 'La date des Tractatus I–LIV in Iohannis Evangelium de saint Augustin.' *Recherches augustiniennes* 7: 105–68.

—— ed. (1977). *Œuvres de saint Augustin 72. Homélies sur l'Évangile de saint Jean XVII–XXXIII.* BA/Desclée de Brouwer.

—— ed. (1988). *Œuvres de saint Augustin 73A. Homélies sur l'Évangile de saint Jean XXXIV–XLIII.* Paris: IEA.

—— ed. (1989). *Œuvres de saint Augustin 73B. Homélies sur l'Évangile de saint Jean XLIV–LIV.* Paris: IEA.

——(1990). 'Deux peuples, un seul troupeau, un unique Pasteur: Ecclésiologie de saint Augustin et citations de Jean 10:16.' *Collectanea Augustiniana* 1: 275–301.

—— ed. (1993). *Œuvres de saint Augustin 74A. Homélies sur l'Évangile de saint Jean LV–LXXIX.* Paris: IEA.

—— ed. (1998). *Œuvres de saint Augustin 74B. Homélies sur l'Évangile de saint Jean LXXX–CIII.* Turnhout: Brepols.

—— ed. (2003). *Œuvres de saint Augustin 75. Homélies sur l'Évangile de saint Jean CIV–CXXIV.* Paris: IEA.

——(2004). *Introduction aux homélies de Saint Augustin sur l'évangile de Saint Jean.* EAA 170. Paris: IEA.

Birdsall, J. Neville (1957). 'Photius and the Text of the Fourth Gospel.' *New Testament Studies* 4: 61–3.

Bischoff, Bernard (1990). *Latin Palaeography. Antiquity and the Middle Ages.* Translated by Dáibhí Ó Cróinín and David Ganz. Cambridge: Cambridge University Press.

Bochet, Isabelle (1997). *Notes complémentaires à la Doctrine Chrétienne (De doctrina christiana).* BA 11/2, ed. Madeleine Moreau. Paris: IEA.

——(2004). *«Le firmament de l'Écriture». L'herméneutique augustinienne.* EAA 172. Paris: IEA.

Bogaert, Pierre-Maurice (1988). 'La Bible latine des origines au moyen âge. Aperçu historique, état des questions.' *Revue Théologique de Louvain* 19: 137–59, 276–314.

——(1998). 'La Bible d'Augustin. État des questions et application aux sermons Dolbeau.' In *Augustin Prédicateur (395–411) Actes du colloque.* EAA 159: 33–47. Paris: IEA.

——(2006). 'Les bibles d'Augustin.' *Revue Théologique de Louvain* 37: 513–31.

Boismard, Marie-Émile (1987). 'Critique textuelle et problèmes d'histoire des origines chrétiennes' in *Recherches sur l'histoire de la Bible latine* ed. R. Gryson and P.-M. Bogaert (Cahiers de la revue théologique de Louvain 19) 123–36.

Bonner, Gerald (1970). 'Augustine as Biblical Scholar.' CHB 1: 541–63.

——(1986). *St Augustine of Hippo. Life and Controversies.* Revised edition. Norwich: The Canterbury Press.

Bouton-Touboulic, Anne-Isabelle (2006). 'Autorité et Tradition. La traduction latine de la Bible selon Saint Jérôme et Saint Augustin.' *Augustinianum* 45.1: 185–229.

Bresolin, Angelo (1962). 'L'esegesi di Giov. 2,4 nei Padri Latini.' *REA* 8: 243–73.

Brown, Peter (2000). *Augustine of Hippo. A Biography. A New Edition with an Epilogue.* London: Faber and Faber.

Burkitt, F. C. (1896). *The Old Latin and the Itala.* Texts and Studies 4.3. Cambridge: Cambridge University Press.

——(1908). '"Chief Priests" in the Latin Gospels.' *JTS* 9: 290–7.

——(1910). 'Saint Augustine's Bible and the *Itala*.' *JTS* 11: 258–68, 447–58.

——(1920). 'Itala Problems'. In *Miscellanea Amelli. Scritti varii di letteratura ecclesiastica dedicati al Rev.mo Abate Ambrogio Amelli* 25–41. Monte Cassino and Rome: Typographia Pontificia.

——(1927). 'Reviews: A Reconstruction of the Old-Latin Text...of the Gospels used by Saint Augustine, by C.H. Milne MA.' *JTS* 28: 101–5.

Burton, Philip (2000). *The Old Latin Gospels. A Study of their Texts and Language.* Oxford: Oxford University Press.

——(2007). *Language in the* Confessions *of Augustine.* Oxford: Oxford University Press.

Caragliano, Tindaro (1946). 'Restitutio critica textus latini evangelii secundum Iohannem ex scriptis S. Ambrosii.' *Biblica* 27: 30–64, 210–40.

Cipriani, Nello (2006) 'La biblioteca della Chiesa d'Ippona.' *Augustinianum* 45.2: 539–47.

Coleman, Robert (1971). 'The Origin and Development of Latin *Habeo* + Infinitive.' *Classical Quarterly* (new series) 21: 215–32.

——(1987). 'Vulgar Latin and the diversity of Christian Latin.' In *Latin Vulgaire—Latin Tardif* 1, ed. J. Herman 37–52. Tübingen: Max Niemeyer.

Comeau, Marie (1930). *Saint Augustin, exégète du quatrième évangile.* Paris: Beauchesne.

De Bruyne, Donatien (1913). 'L'Itala de saint Augustin.' *Revue Bénédictine* 30: 294–314.

——(1927). 'Encore l'Itala de saint Augustin.' *Revue d'histoire ecclésiastique* 23: 779–85.

——(1931). 'Saint Augustin Reviseur de la Bible.' *Miscellanea Agostiniana* 2: 521–606. Rome.

Decret, François (1970). *Aspects du manichéisme dans l'Afrique romaine. Les controverses de Fortunatus, Faustus et Felix avec saint Augustin.* Paris: IEA.

——(1978). *L'Afrique manichéene (IVe–Ve siècles). Étude historique et doctrinale. Tome I. Texte, Tome II. Notes.* Paris: IEA.

Deferrari, Roy J. (1922). 'St Augustine's Method of Composing and Delivering Sermons.' *American Journal of Philology* 43: 97–123, 193–219.

Dekkers, Eligius (1952). 'Les autographes des Pères Latins.' In *Colligere Fragmenta. Festschrift Alban Dold*, eds. B. Fischer and V. Fiala 127–39. Beuron: Beuroner Kunstverlag.

Deléani, Simone (1992). 'Un emprunt d'Augustin à l'Écriture: «Redite praevaricatores ad cor» (*Isaie* 48, 8b).' *REA* 38.1: 29–49.

Dideberg, Dany (1986). 'Saint Jean, le disciple bien-aimé, révelateur des secrets du Verbe de Dieu.' BTT 3: 189–201.

Dolbeau, François (1993). 'Le sermon 374 de saint Augustin sur L'Épiphanie. Édition du texte original.' *Philologia Sacra* 2: 523–59.

——(1996). *Augustin d'Hippone, Vingt-six sermons au peuple d'Afrique.* EAA 147. Paris: IEA.

——(1998). 'Finale inédite d'un sermon d'Augustin (S. Mai 158), extraite d'un homéliaire d'Olomouc.' *REA* 44.2: 181–203.

Drobner, Hubertus R. (2000). *Augustin von Hippo. Sermones ad populum. Überlieferung und Bestand. Bibliographie—Indices. VC* supplement 49. Leiden: Brill.

——(2004). 'Die Predigkunst Augustins.' *Theologie und Glaube* 94: 22–32.

Dulaey, Martine (2002). 'L'apprentissage de l'exégèse biblique par Augustin. Première partie. Dans les années 386–389.' *REA* 48: 267–95.

——(2003). 'L'apprentissage de l'exégèse biblique par Augustin. (2) Années 390–392.' *REA* 49: 43–84.

——(2005). 'L'apprentissage de l'exégèse biblique par Augustin. (3) Années 393–394.' *REA* 51: 21–65.

——(2006a). 'Recherches sur les *LXXXIII Diverses Questions* d'Augustin. 1) *Questions* 44 et 58–60.' *REA* 52: 113–42.

——(2006b). 'Les paralytiques des Évangiles dans l'interprétation patristique. Du texte à l'image.' *REA* 52: 286–328.

Dulaey, Martine and Klöckener, Martin (2002). 'Evangelium.' *Augustinus-Lexikon* 2: 1144–50.

Durand, M.-G. de (1978). 'Pentecôte johannique et Pentecôte lucanienne chez certains Pères.' *Bulletin de littérature ecclésiastique* 79: 97–126.

Duval, Yves-Marie (1985). 'L'Écriture au service de la catéchèse.' BTT 2: 262–88.

Elliott, J. K. (1986). 'The Purpose and Construction of a Critical Apparatus to a Greek New Testament' in *Studien zum Text und zur Ethik des Neuen Testaments. Festschrift zum 80. Geburtstag von Heinrich Greeven* 125–43 ed. Wolfgang Schrage. Berlin and New York: De Gruyter.

——(1992). 'The Translations of the New Testament into Latin: The Old Latin and the Vulgate.' *Aufstieg und Niedergang der römischen Welt* 2.26.1 (Religion) ed. Wolfgang Haase and Hildegard Temporini, 199–245. Berlin and New York: de Gruyter.

——(1993). 'Non-canonical Sayings of Jesus in Patristic Works and in the New Testament Manuscript Tradition.' *Philologia Sacra* 2: 343–54.

Fahey, Michael Andrew (1971). *Cyprian and the Bible: A Study in Third-Century Exegesis.* Beiträge zur Geschichte der Biblischen Hermeneutik 9. Tübingen: J. C. B. Mohr.

Fee, Gordon D. (1971). 'The Text of John in *The Jerusalem Bible:* A Critique of the Use of Patristic Citations in New Testament Textual Criticism.' *Journal of Biblical Literature* 90: 163–73. Reprinted in Eldon J. Epp and Gordon D. Fee, *Studies in the Theory and Method of New Testament Textual Criticism.* Grand Rapids: Eerdmans. 1993.

——(1995). 'The Use of the Greek Fathers for New Testament Textual Criticism.' Holmes-Ehrman 191–207.

Féliers, Jeanne-Huberte (1966). 'L'utilisation de la Bible dans l'œuvre d'Evodius.' *REA* 12: 41–64.

Fischer, Bonifatius (1972). 'Das Neue Testament in lateinischer Sprache. Der gegenwärtige Stand seiner Erforschung und seine Bedeutung für die griechische Textgeschichte.' ANTF 5: 1–92.

——(1985). *Lateinische Bibelhandschriften im frühen Mittelalter.* AGLB 11. Freiburg: Herder.

——(1986). *Beiträge zur Geschichte der lateinischen Bibeltexte.* AGLB 12. Freiburg: Herder.

Fischer, Bonifatius (1991). *Die lateinischen Evangelien bis zum 10. Jahrhundert. IV. Varianten zu Johannes.* AGLB 18. Freiburg: Herder.

Fleteren, Frederick van (2001). 'Principles of Augustine's Hermeneutic: An Overview.' *Collectanea Augustiniana* 5: 1–32.

Foster, Paul (2006). 'Recent Developments and Future Directions in New Testament Textual Criticism: Report on a Conference at the University of Edinburgh, 27 April 2006.' *Journal for the Study of the New Testament* 29.2: 229–35.

Frede, Hermann Josef (1971). 'Bibelzitate bei Kirchenvätern. Beobachtungen bei der Herausgabe der «Vetus Latina».' Benoît-Prigent: 79–96.

——(1972). 'Die Zitate des Neuen Testaments bei den lateinischen Kirchenväter. Der gegenwärtige Stand ihrer Erforschung und ihre Bedeutung für die griechische Textgeschichte.' ANTF 5: 455–78.

——(1995). *Kirchenschriftsteller. Verzeichnis und Sigel.* Vetus Latina 1/1 (4. Aktualisierte Auflage). Freiburg: Herder.

Fredouille, Jean-Claude (1985). 'Les lettrés chrétiens face à la Bible.' BTT 2: 25–42.

——(1996). '«Latin chrétien» ou «latin tardif»?' *Recherches augustinennes* 29: 5–23.

Frend, W. H. C. (1952). *The Donatist Church. A Movement of Protest in Roman North Africa.* Oxford: Clarendon Press.

Gamble, Harry Y. (1995). *Books and Readers in the Early Church. A History of Early Christian Texts.* New Haven and London: Yale University Press.

García de la Fuente, Olegario (1994). *Latín bíblico y latín cristiano.* Madrid: Editorial CEES.

Gibson, Margaret T. (1993). *The Bible in the Latin West.* The Mediaeval Book 1. Notre Dame, Indiana: University Press.

Grant, R. M. (1970). 'The New Testament Canon.' CHB 1: 284–308.

Green, R. P. H. (1995). *Augustine. De Doctrina Christiana.* Oxford: Clarendon Press.

Green, William M. (1959). 'A Fourth Century Manuscript of Saint Augustine?' *Revue Bénédictine* 69: 191–7.

——(1962). 'Textual Notes on Augustine's *De doctrina christiana.*' *REA* 8: 225–31.

Gribomont, Jean (1985). 'Les plus anciennes traductions latines.' BTT 2: 43–65.

——(1987). 'Aux origines de la Vulgate' in *La Bibbia 'Vulgata' dalle origini ai nostri giorni. Collectanea Biblica Latina* 16 ed. T. Stramare 11–20. Rome: Libreria Vaticana.

Gryson, Roger (1978). 'Les citations scripturaires des œuvres attribuées à l'évêque arien Maximinus.' *Revue Bénédictine* 88: 45–80.

——(1999). *Altlateinische Handschriften/Manuscrits Vieux Latins. Première partie: Mss 1–275.* Vetus Latina 1/2A. Freiburg: Herder.
——(2007). *Répertoire général des auteurs ecclésiastiques latins de l'antiquité et du haut moyen âge.* Vetus Latina 1/1 (fifth edition, replacing Frede 1995). Freiburg: Herder.
Hagendahl, Harald (1947). 'Methods of Citation in Post-Classical Latin Prose.' *Eranos* 45: 114–28.
——(1967). *Augustine and the Latin Classics.* 1. *Testimonia.* 2. *Augustine's Attitude.* Studia Graeca et Latina Gothoburgensia 20: 1–2. Göteborg: Acta Universitatis Gothoburgensis.
——(1983). *Von Tertullian zu Cassiodor. Die profane literarische Tradition in dem lateinischen christlichen Schrifttum.* Studia Graeca et Latina Gothoburgensia 44. Göteborg: Acta Universitatis Gothoburgensis.
Hardy, Richard P. (1974). *Actualité de la Révélation Divine. Une étude des «Tractatus in Iohannis euangelium» de Saint Augustin.* (Théologie Historique 28). Beauchesne: Paris.
Harrison, Carol (2001). ' "Not Words but Things": Harmonious Diversity in the Four Gospels.' *Collectanea Augustiniana* 5: 157–73.
Harrison, Rebecca R. (1986) 'Jerome's Revision of the Gospels'. University of Michigan Ph.D. thesis; available through University Microfilms International.
Hockey, F. (1976). 'St Augustine and John I, 3–4.' *Studia Patristica* 14.3: 443–5.
Hombert, Pierre-Marie (2000). *Nouvelles Recherches de Chronologie Augustinienne.* EAA 163. Paris: IEA.
Houghton, H. A. G. (2008). 'Augustine's adoption of the Vulgate Gospels.' *New Testament Studies* 54.
Knauer, Georg Nicolaus (1955). *Psalmenzitate in Augustins Konfessionen.* Göttingen: Vandenhoek and Ruprecht.
Knust, Jennifer Wright (2006). 'Early Christian Re-Writing and the History of the *Pericope Adulterae.*' *JECS* 14.4: 485–536.
La Bonnardière, Anne-Marie (1963). 'Quelques remarques sur les citations scripturaires du *De gratia et libero arbitrio.*' *REA* 9: 77–85.
——(1965). *Recherches de chronologie augustinienne.* EAA 23. Paris: IEA.
——(1967). 'Pénitence et réconciliation des Pénitents d'après saint Augustin—I, II.' *REA* 13: 31–53, 249–83.
——(1968). 'Pénitence et réconciliation des Pénitents d'après saint Augustin—III.' *REA* 14: 181–204.
——(1975). 'La Bible «liturgique» de saint Augustin.' *Théologie Historique* 35: 147–60.
——(1986). 'L'initiation biblique d'Augustin' (BTT 3: 27–47); 'Augustin, ministre de la parole de Dieu' (BTT 3: 51–7); 'La Chananéenne,

préfiguration de l'Eglise' (BTT 3: 117–43); 'Evodius et Augustin' (BTT 3: 213–27); 'Le canon des divines Ecritures' (BTT 3: 287–301); 'Augustin a-t-il utilisé la «Vulgate» de Jérôme?' (BTT 3: 303–12); 'Le *Speculum quis ignorat*' (BTT 3: 401–9).

Lamb, J. A. (1970). 'The Place of the Bible in the Liturgy.' CHB 1: 563–86.

Lancel, Serge (ed. and trans.) (1972–5). *Actes de la conférence de Carthage en 411.* Sources Chrétiennes 194 (1972), 195 (1972), 224 (1975). Paris: Éditions du Cerf.

——(2002). *Saint Augustine.* Translated by Antonia Neville from *Saint Augustin* (Librairie Fayard, Paris 1999). London: SCM.

Lawless, George (1992). 'Augustine's Use of Rhetoric in His Interpretation of John 21: 19–23.' *Augustinian Studies* 23: 53–67.

——(1996). 'The Man Born Blind: Augustine's Tractate 44 on John 9.' *Augustinian Studies* 27.2: 61–79.

——(1997). 'Listening to Augustine: Tractate 44 on John 9.' *Augustinian Studies* 28.1: 51–66.

Leloir, Louis (1962). *Le Témoignage d'Éphrem sur le Diatessaron.* CSCO Subsidia 19. Louvain: CSCO.

Lienhard, Joseph T. (1996). 'Reading the Bible and Learning to Read: The Influence of Education on St Augustine's Exegesis.' *Augustinian Studies* 27.1: 7–25.

——(2001). 'John the Baptist in Augustine's Exegesis.' *Collectanea Augustiniana* 5: 197–213.

Loewen, Howard J. (1981). 'The Use of Scripture in Augustine's Theology.' *Scottish Journal of Theology* 34.3: 201–24.

Löfstedt, Einar (1911). *Philologischer Kommentar zur Peregrinatio Aetheriae. Untersuchungen zur Geschichte der lateinischen Sprache.* Anastatic reprint of 1936. Uppsala: Almquist and Wiksell.

Lowe, E. A. (1931). 'A List of the Oldest Extant Manuscripts of Saint Augustine with a note on the Codex Bambergensis.' *Miscellanea Agostiniana* 2: 235–51.

McCarthy, Michael C. (2007). '"We Are Your Books": Augustine, the Bible and the Practice of Authority.' *Journal of the American Academy of Religion* 75.2: 324–52.

McGurk, Patrick (1994). 'The Oldest Manuscripts of the Latin Bible.' In *The Early Medieval Bible* ed. Richard Gameson 1–23. Cambridge: Cambridge University Press.

Margerie, Bertrand de (1983). *Introduction à l'histoire de l'exégèse. III. Saint Augustin.* Les Éditions du Cerf: Paris.

Marrou, Henri-Irénée (1938). *Saint Augustin et la fin de la culture antique.* Paris: De Boccard.

——(1949). *Saint Augustin et la fin de la culture antique. 2. Retractatio.* Paris: De Boccard.

Metzger, Bruce M. (1971). 'Patristic Evidence and the Textual Criticism of the Church Fathers.' *New Testament Studies* 18: 379–400. Reprinted in Metzger 1980.

——(1977). *The Early Versions of the New Testament. Their Origins, Transmission and Limitations.* Oxford: Clarendon Press.

——(1979). 'St Jerome's Explicit References to Variant Readings in Manuscripts of the New Testament' in *Text and Interpretation: Studies in the New Testament presented to Matthew Black*, ed. Ernest Best and R. McL. Wilson (Cambridge: University Press 1979) 179–190. Reprinted in Metzger 1980.

——(1980). *New Testament Studies: Philological, Versional and Patristic.* Brill: Leiden.

——(1994). *A Textual Commentary on the Greek New Testament. Second edition.* Stuttgart: Deutsche Bibelgesellschaft.

Milewski, Douglas. (2002). 'Augustine's 124 Tractates on the Gospel of John: the *Status Quaestionis* and the State of Neglect.' *Augustinian Studies* 33.1: 61–77.

Milne, C. H. (1926). *A Reconstruction of the Old-Latin Text or Texts of the Gospels used by Saint Augustine.* Cambridge: Cambridge University Press.

Mizzi, J. (1954). 'The Latin Text of Matt. V-VII in St Augustine's «De Sermone Domini in monte».' *Augustiniana* 4: 234–78.

Mohrmann, Christine (1932). 'Das Wortspiel in den augustinischen Sermones.' *Mnemosyne* 3.3: 33–61; reprinted in Mohrmann 1961.

——(1949). 'Les origines de la latinité chrétienne à Rome.' *VC* 3: 67–106, 163–83.

——(1958). 'Saint Augustin écrivain.' *Recherches Augustinennes* 1: 43–66.

——(1961). *Études sur le latin des chrétiens. Tome I. Le latin des chrétiens. Deuxième édition.* Rome: Edizioni di Storia e Letteratura. Includes 'Quelques traits caractéristiques du latin des chrétiens' (21–50); 'Saint Augustine and the «Eloquentia»' (351–70).

Monceaux, Paul (1923). *Histoire littéraire de l'Afrique chrétienne depuis les origines jusqu'à l'invasion arabe. VII. Saint Augustin et le Donatisme.* Anastatic reprint of 1963. Bruxelles: Culture et Civilisation.

Moreau, Madeleine, ed. (1997). *Sancti Augustini De doctrina christiana libri 4. BA* 11/2. Paris: IEA.

Mullen, Roderic L. (1997). *The New Testament Text of Cyril of Jerusalem.* New Testament in the Greek Fathers 7. Atlanta GA: Scholars Press.

Müller, Gerhard Anselm (2003). *Formen und Funktionen der Vergilzitate bei Augustin von Hippo. Formen und Funktionen der Zitate und Anspielungen.* Studien zur Geschichte und Kultur des Altertums. Neue Folge. Reihe 1 Band 18. Paderborn: Ferdinand.

Muncey, R. W. (1959). *The New Testament Text of St. Ambrose.* Texts and Studies, new series 4. Cambridge: Cambridge University Press.

Munier, Charles (1972). 'La tradition manuscrite de l'Abrégé d'Hippone et le canon des Écritures des églises africaine.' *Sacris Erudiri* 21: 43–55.

——(1974). *Concilia Africae. A.345–A.525. Corpus Christianorum* series latina 149. Turnhout: Brepols.

Mutzenbecher, Almut (1984). 'Die Nachtrag zu den Retraktationen mit Augustins letzten Werken.' *REA* 30: 60–83.

Norris, John M. (1993). 'The Theological Structure of Augustine's Exegesis in the *Tractatus in Iohannis Evangelium*.' *Collectanea Augustiniana* 2: 385–94.

North, J. Lionel (1995). 'The Use of the Latin Fathers for New Testament Textual Criticism.' Ehrman-Holmes: 208–23.

O'Donnell, James J. (1980). 'Augustine's Classical Readings.' *Recherches augustiniennes* 15: 144–75.

——(1992). *Augustine, Confessions.* Oxford: Clarendon Press.

Paoli-Lafaye, Elisabeth (1986). 'Les «lecteurs» des textes liturgiques.' BTT 3: 59–74.

Parker, D. C. (1985). 'The Translation of ΟΥΝ in the Old Latin Gospels.' *New Testament Studies* 31: 252–76.

——(1992). *Codex Bezae. An Early Christian Manuscript and its Text.* Cambridge: Cambridge University Press.

——(1997). *The Living Text of the Gospels.* Cambridge: Cambridge University Press.

Pellegrino, Michele (1967). 'Doppioni e varianti nel commento di S. Agostino a Giov. XXI, 15–19.' In *Studi in onore di Alberto Pincherle* (*Studi e materiali di storia delle religioni* 38: 1–2) 403–19.

Petersen, William L. (1994). *Tatian's Diatessaron. Its Creation, Dissemination, Significance and History in Scholarship. VC* supplement 25. Leiden: Brill.

——(1995). 'The Diatessaron of Tatian.' Ehrman-Holmes: 77–96.

——(1997). 'ΟΥΔΕ ΕΓΩ ΣΕ [ΚΑΤΑ]ΚΡΙΝΩ. John 8:11, the *Protevangelium Iacobi* and the History of the *Pericope adulterae*.' In *Sayings of Jesus: Canonical and Non-Canonical* eds. Petersen, Vos, and de Jonge 191–221. Leiden: Brill.

Petitmengin, Pierre (1985). 'Les plus anciens manuscrits de la Bible latine.' BTT 2: 89–127.

——(1994). 'Codex.' *Augustinus-Lexikon* 1: 1022–37.

——(2003). 'Recherches sur Augustin et le livre antique.' In *La Tradition Vive. Mélanges d'histoire des texts en l'honneur de Louis Holtz.* ed. Pierre Lardet 3–14. Paris-Turnhout: Brepols.

Petzer, Jacobus H. (1995). 'The Latin Version of the New Testament.' Ehrman-Holmes: 113–30.

Plater, W. E. and White, H. J. (1926). *A Grammar of the Vulgate, being An Introduction to the Study of the Latinity of the Vulgate Bible.* Oxford: Clarendon Press.

Plinval, Georges de (1943). *Pélage. Ses écrits, sa vie et sa réforme.* Lausanne: Librairie Payot.

Polman, A. D. R. (1961). *The Word of God According to St Augustine* (trans. A. J. Pomerans). London: Hodder and Stoughton.

Pontet, Maurice (1946). *L'exégèse de saint-Augustin prédicateur.* Thèse pour le Doctorat ès lettres de l'Université de Lyon. Aubier: Éditions Montaigne.

Quentin, H. (1927). 'La prétendue Itala de saint Augustin.' *Revue Biblique* 36: 216–25.

Quispel, Gilles (1975). *Tatian and the Gospel of Thomas. Studies in the History of the Western Diatessaron.* Leiden: Brill.

Rebillard, Éric (2000). 'A New Style of Argument in Christian Polemic: Augustine and the Use of Patristic Citations.' *JECS* 8.4: 559–78.

Roensch, Hermann (1871). *Das Neue Testament Tertullians. Aus den Schriften des Letzteren möglichst vollständig reconstruirt.* Leipzig: Fuess Verlag.

Sawyer, John F. A. (1999). *Sacred Languages and Sacred Texts.* London and New York: Routledge.

Saxer, Victor (1985a). 'Bible et liturgie.' BTT 2: 157–88.

——(1985b). 'La Bible chez les Pères latins du IIIe siècle.' BTT 2: 339–69.

Schildenberger, Johannes (1952). 'Die Itala des hl. Augustinus.' In *Colligere Fragmenta. Festschrift Alban Dold.* eds. B. Fischer and V. Fiala 84–102. Beuron: Beuroner Kunstverlag.

Schmid, Ulrich B. (2003). 'In Search of Tatian's Diatessaron in the West.' *VC* 57.2: 176–99.

——(2005). *Unum ex Quattuor. Eine Geschichte der lateinischen Tatianüberlieferung.* AGLB 37. Freiburg: Herder.

Simonetti, Manlio (1994). *Biblical Interpretation in the Early Church. An Historical Introduction to Patristic Exegesis.* Translated by John A. Hughes from 'Profilo Storico dell' Esesgesi Patristica' (1981). Edinburgh: T. and T. Clark.

Solignac, A. (1987). 'Le texte biblique d'Augustin et les manuscrits de ses oeuvres exégétiques.' In *Texte und Textkritik: eine Aufsatzsammlung* ed. J. Dümmer 549–52. Berlin: Akademie Verlag.

Sparks, H. F. D. (1970). 'Jerome as Biblical Scholar.' CHB 1: 510–41.

Stanley, Christopher D. (1992). *Paul and the Language of Scripture: citation technique in the Pauline Epistles and contemporary literature.* Cambridge: Cambridge University Press.

Steinhauser, Kenneth B. (1995). 'Codex Leningradensis Q.v.I.3.: Some Unresolved Problems.' In *De doctrina christiana. A Classic of Western Culture* 33–43. ed. Duane W. H. Arnold and Pamela Bright. Notre Dame: University of Notre Dame Press.

Stock, Brian (1996). *Augustine the Reader. Meditation, Self-Knowledge and the Ethics of Interpretation.* Cambridge MA: Harvard University Press.

Sutcliffe, E. F. (1948). 'The Name "Vulgate"'. *Biblica* 29: 345–52.

—— (1969). 'Jerome.' CHB 2: 80–101.

Thiele, Walter (1972). 'Probleme der Versio Latina in den Katholischen Briefen.' ANTF 5: 93–119.

Tilley, Maureen A. (1997). *The Bible in Christian North Africa: The Donatist World.* Minneapolis: Fortress Press.

Tkacz, Catherine Brown (1996). '*Labor Tam Utilis*: The Creation of the Vulgate.' *VC* 50: 42–72.

Turner, C. H. (1923). 'On the Punctuation of St John vii 37, 38.' *JTS* 24: 66–70.

Vaccari, A. (1961). 'Les traces de la *Vetus Latina* dans le *Speculum* de Saint Augustin.' *Studia Patristica* 4.2 (TU 79): 228–33.

Van den Hout, M. P. J. (1955). 'A propos de la nouvelle édition des Tractatus in Iohannis Evangelium de saint Augustin dans le Corpus Christianorum.' *Augustiniana* 5: 296–308.

Verbraken, Pierre-Patrick (1976). *Études critiques sur les sermons authentiques de saint Augustin.* Instrumenta Patristica 12. Steenbrugge: Abbatia S. Petri.

Verheijen, Luc (1976). *Catalogus Verborum quae in operibus Sancti Augustini inveniuntur. 1. Tractatus in Evangelium Ioannis. Corpus Christianorum 36.* Thesaurus Linguae Augustinianae. Eindhoven.

Vessey, Mark (1993). 'Conference and confession: literary pragmatics in Augustine's "*Apologia contra Hieronymum*"'. *JECS* 1: 175–213. Reprinted in Vessey 2005.

—— (1996). 'The forging of orthodoxy in Latin Christian Literature: a case study.' *JECS* 4: 495–513. Reprinted in Vessey 2005.

—— (1998). '*Opus imperfectum*: Augustine and his readers, 426–435 AD.' *VC* 52: 264–85. Reprinted in Vessey 2005.

—— (1999). 'The Great Conference: Augustine and his Fellow Readers.' BTA 2: 52–73.

—— (2005). *Latin Christian Writers in Late Antiquity and their Texts.* Variorum: Ashgate.

Westcott, B. F. and Hort, F. J. (1882). *The New Testament in the Original Greek. Introduction—Appendix.* Cambridge and London: Macmillan.

White, Carolinne (1990). *The Correspondence (394–419) between Jerome and Augustine of Hippo.* Studies in Bible and Early Christianity 23. Lampeter: Edwin Mellen Press.

Wiles, M. F. (1970). 'Origen as Biblical Scholar.' CHB 1: 454–89.

Willis, G. G. (1962). *St Augustine's Lectionary.* Alcuin Club 44. London: SPCK.

——(1966). 'Patristic Biblical Citations. The importance of a good critical text, illustrated from St Augustine.' *Studia Patristica* 7.1 (TU 92) 576–9.

Wilmart, A. (1931). 'Operum S. Augustini Elenchus a Possidio eiusdem discipulo Calamensi episcopo digestus. Post Maurinorum labores nouis curis editus critico apparatu numeris tabellis instructus.' *Miscellanea Agostiniana* 2: 149–233.

Wright, David F. (1964). '*Tractatus* 20–22 of St Augustine's *In Iohannem*.' *JTS* new series 15: 317–30.

——(1972). 'The Manuscripts of St Augustine's *Tractatus in Euangelium Iohannis*: A Preliminary Survey and Check-List.' *Recherches augustiniennes* 8: 55–143.

——(1979). '*Piscina Siloa* or *Piscina Salomonis*? (Possidius, *Indiculum* X 6.57).' *REA* 25: 47–60.

——(1981). 'The Manuscripts of the «Tractatus in Iohannem»: A Supplementary List.' *Recherches augustiniennes* 16: 59–100.

Young, Frances M. (1997). *Biblical Exegesis and the Formation of Christian Culture.* Cambridge: Cambridge University Press.

Zarb, Seraphinus M. (1938). *De Canone et Textu Sacrorum Librorum in Operibus S. Augustini.* Rome: V. Ferri.

Ziwsa, Carolus, ed. (1893). *S. Optati Milevitani libri VII. Accedunt decem monumenta vetera ad Donatistarum historiam pertinentia.* CSEL 26. Vienna.

Index of Biblical References

Index of Ancient Authors

CYPRIAN

EVODIUS

HILARY OF POITIERS

JEROME

OPTATUS

POSSIDIUS

Subject Index